PRAISE FOR THE FIRST EDITION

"M. W. Daly has produced a lucid and solidly grounded historical context for the current troubles in Darfur. He introduces the long-standing patterns of political and socioeconomic interaction that have prevailed among the communities comprising the sultanate and exposes the complex web of relations with neighboring lands that developed over the centuries. Important among the latter were ties to successive nineteenth- and twentieth-century regimes centered in the Nile valley, whose policies were rarely helpful to Darfur and occasionally were catastrophic. Many readers will find particular merit in the careful grounding of recent Darfur events in their wider political settings at the national level; this approach clarifies the motives of all the actors in the unfortunate drama. All will appreciate the unflinching but sensitive treatment of atrocity in the discussion of the war itself and the insightful analysis of the fragile but significant Darfur Peace Agreement of May 2006." – Jay Spaulding, Kean University

"Daly provides a much-needed portrait of the history of Darfur. He skillfully places the current crisis in the historic contexts that have shaped peoples and society in Darfur over the centuries. Diplomats and NGO officials should have this volume on their desk as they attempt to understand the historic foundations of society in Darfur and its current catastrophic problems." – John Voll, Georgetown University

"For scholars of Africa, this monograph provides the solid, detailed historical background and the trenchant analysis that we must have in order to live up to our responsibility to explain the Darfur tragedy to all who will listen." – *International Journal of African Historical Studies*

"Few provide the depth of historical analysis presented in this book. M. W. Daly is an expert on the history of the Sudan and Egypt and so is ideally placed to put recent events into a proper perspective. His research is a most important contribution to bettering our understanding of Darfur and it should be read by anyone attempting to comprehend recent events." – *The Historian*

"*Darfur's Sorrow* is deeply engaging, well researched, and highly poignant.... There is little question...that students and scholars alike will find Daly's account of Darfur extremely insightful, especially in light of recent literature on the region that has obscured the social and political complexity of its history." – *International Journal of Middle East Studies*

DARFUR'S SORROW

The Forgotten History of a Humanitarian Disaster

Darfur's Sorrow is the first general history of Darfur to be published in any language. The book surveys events from before the founding of the Fur sultanate in the sixteenth century through the rise and establishment of the Fur state and its incorporation into the Anglo-Egyptian Sudan in 1916. The narrative continues with detailed coverage of the brief but all-important colonial period (1916–56) and Darfur's history as a neglected peripheral region since independence. The political, economic, environmental, and social factors that gave rise to the current humanitarian crisis are discussed in detail, as is the course of Darfur's rebellion, its brutal suppression by the Sudanese government, and the lawless brigands known as *janjawid*. This second edition brings the story up to date and includes an analysis of attempts to save Darfur's embattled people and to bring an end to the fighting.

M. W. Daly has received many honors and awards, including fellowships from the universities of Durham, Khartoum, and Tel Aviv, as well as residencies at Oxford, Durham, the Woodrow Wilson Center (Washington, DC), and elsewhere. He is also the recipient of the John Frederick Lewis Award of the American Philosophical Society. Daly is the author of many books and articles on the history of the modern Middle East and Northeast Africa, including *Imperial Sudan: The Anglo-Egyptian Condominium, 1934–1956* (1991) and, with P. M. Holt, *A History of the Sudan: From the Coming of Islam to the Present Day,* now in its fifth edition. He is the general editor of *The Cambridge History of Egypt* and has contributed more than a hundred articles and reviews to scholarly journals.

DARFUR'S SORROW

The Forgotten History of a Humanitarian Disaster
Second Edition

M. W. DALY

CAMBRIDGE
UNIVERSITY PRESS

CAMBRIDGE UNIVERSITY PRESS
Cambridge, New York, Melbourne, Madrid, Cape Town, Singapore,
São Paulo, Delhi, Dubai, Tokyo

Cambridge University Press
32 Avenue of the Americas, New York, NY 10013-2473, USA

www.cambridge.org
Information on this title: www.cambridge.org/9780521131872

First published 2007
Reprinted 2007 (twice), 2008 (seven times)
Second edition published 2010

Printed in the United States of America

A catalog record for this publication is available from the British Library.

Library of Congress Cataloging in Publication data

Daly, M. W.
Darfur's sorrow : the forgotten history of a humanitarian disaster / M. W. Daly. – 2nd ed.
p.   cm.
Includes bibliographical references and index.
ISBN 978-0-521-19174-6 (hardback)
1. Sudan – History – Darfur Conflict, 2003– 2. Darfur (Sudan) – Ethnic relations.
3. Darfur (Sudan) – History.   4. Genocide – Sudan – Darfur.   I. Title.
DT159.6.D27D35   2010
962.404'3–dc22   2010000564

ISBN   978-0-521-19174-6 Hardback
ISBN   978-0-521-13187-2 Paperback

In memory of Peter and Nancy Holt

CONTENTS

ix

CONTENTS

LIST OF FIGURES

PREFACE TO THE
SECOND EDITION

With the failure of the Abuja Peace Agreement of May 2006 the Darfur conflict entered a new phase. Since then the forces arrayed there against the Sudanese government have fractionalized to a degree no less confusing for having been predictable. The Khartoum government itself, after entering into an uneasy coalition with its longtime enemies the Sudan People's Liberation Movement, has faced new challenges as national elections loom and the all-important Southern referendum of 2011 grows near. These developments, international events, clear but tenuous improvements in the dire situation of Darfur's refugees, and the availability of more reliable sources have all suggested the need to bring the account of *Darfur's Sorrow* up to date. The opportunity has also been taken to correct errors and to update the Chronology and Bibliography. My thanks are owed to those who, in published reviews and private correspondence, have pointed out mistakes and suggested amendments, and in particular to Shari Chappell at Cambridge University Press.

MWD
Waterville, Maine
July 2009

ACKNOWLEDGMENTS

My thanks are due to a number of individuals and institutions, without whose help this book could not have been written. Professor Robert O. Collins and Dr. Endre Stiansen deserve special thanks for their help in the initial stages of the project. A Fellowship of the National Endowment for the Humanities (Washington, DC) and a John Hope Franklin Fellowship of the American Philosophical Society permitted the sustained time and travel I needed to devote to scattered and varied sources. Professor Jay Spaulding gave generously of his time and deep knowledge in commenting on a draft. Ms. Jane Hogan, as always, was of great assistance in helping me to make the best possible use of the University of Durham's superb Sudan Archive. In obtaining otherwise unavailable source materials, I relied on the helpful staff of the Waterville Public Library, and on the library of Bowdoin College, Professor Lidwien Kapteijns, Professor Beniah Yongo-Bure, Mr. Wang Xiao-Yong, and Professor Thomas Coohill. To them all I owe my thanks – and assurance that the mistakes in this volume are my own.

M. W. Daly
Waterville, Maine

CHRONOLOGY OF EVENTS

c. 1650–c. 1680	Reign of Sulayman; establishment of the Fur sultanate.
1752/3–1785/6	Reign of Sultan Muhammad Tayrab.
1785	Annexation of Kordofan.
1787/8–1803	Reign of Sultan Abd al-Rahman.
1803–38	Reign of Sultan Muhammad al-Fadl.
1821	Egyptian conquest of Kordofan.
1838–73	Reign of Sultan Muhammad al-Husayn.
1874	Battle of Manawashi; Egypt annexes Darfur.
1881	Outbreak of the Sudanese Mahdiyya.
1882	British occupation of Egypt.
1884	Darfur falls to the Mahdi.
1885	Death of the Mahdi and accession of the Khalifa Abdallahi.
1888–89	Revolt of "Abu Jummayza."
1898	Anglo-Egyptian conquest of the Sudan; return of Ali Dinar as sultan of Darfur.
1899	"Condominium Agreement" establishes the Anglo-Egyptian Sudan.

1916	Anglo-Egyptian occupation of Darfur.
1921	Revolt of Abdallahi al-Sihayni.
1922	Powers of Nomad Sheikhs Ordinance.
1924	Revolution of 1924; evacuation of Egyptian Army.
1936	Anglo-Egyptian Treaty.
1953	Anglo-Egyptian Agreement on Sudanese Self-Government and Self-Determination.
1955	Mutiny in Southern Sudan.
1956	(1 January) Independence of the Sudan.
1958	Military coup overthrows Sudanese parliamentary regime.
1964	"October Revolution" overthrows military government.
1965	Restoration of parliamentary government.
1969	Military coup establishes "May Regime" of Jaafar Muhammad Nimayri.
1972	Addis Ababa Agreement ends first civil war.
1975	Assassination of President Tombalbaye of Chad; accession of Felix Malloum.
1980	Ahmad Ibrahim Diraige elected governor of Darfur.
1982	Hissene Habre takes power in Chad.
1983	(June) Nimayri "redivides" Southern Sudan into three "regions." (July) Establishment of Sudan People's Liberation Movement/Army (SPLM/SPLA). (September) Nimayri decrees *Shari'a* the law of the land.
1984–85	Drought and famine in Darfur.

1985	(April) Nimayri ousted; Transitional Military Council takes power.
1986	Third parliamentary regime established; al-Sadiq al-Mahdi as prime minister.
1987–89	"War of the Tribes" in Darfur.
1989	Military coup under Omar Hasan al-Bashir overthrows parliamentary regime.
1990	Idris Deby takes power in Chad.
1991	(February) Sudan reorganized into states; Darfur is one. (November) SPLA force invades Darfur, is quickly crushed by January 1992.
1994	Darfur divided into three "states."
1996	Ossama bin Ladin leaves Sudan.
1998	(August) U.S. attack on pharmaceutical factory at Khartoum North.
1999	(January) Fighting breaks out in Northern Darfur.
2000	Publication of the *Black Book*.
2003	Upsurge in *janjawid*/government-rebel fighting; by year's end, 1 million refugees.
2003	(February) Manifesto of SLA published. (March) Justice and Equality Movement announced. (September) Cease-fire negotiations in Chad.
2004	(August) Negotiations begin in Abuja. (September) United States describes events in Darfur as "genocide."
2005	Comprehensive Peace Agreement ends civil war in Southern Sudan. (July) Declaration of Principles signed in Abuja.

2006	(May) Darfur Peace Agreement signed in Abuja; two rebel factions refuse.
	(September) African Union's peacekeeping mandate expires, is renewed; by year's end, 2.5 million refugees, war dead estimated at 400,000.
2007	(8 February) Tripoli Agreement ends border war between the Sudan and Chad; fighting continues thereafter.
	(11 October) SPLM suspends participation in the Sudan's Government of National Unity.
2008	(May) Insurrection of western Sudanese in Khartoum suppressed with heavy casualties.
	(14 July) International Criminal Court indicts President al-Bashir for "crimes against humanity."
2010	(February) Sudanese national elections scheduled.
2011	Referendum on future status of the Southern Sudan due under terms of 2005 Comprehensive Peace Agreement.

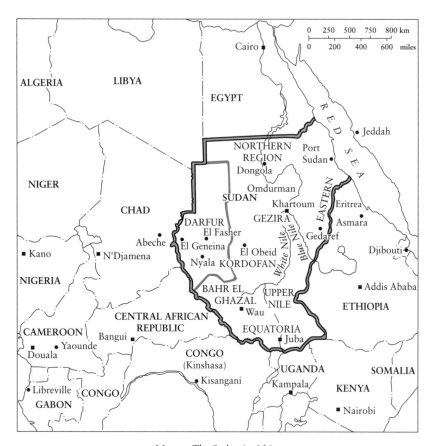

Map 1. The Sudan in Africa

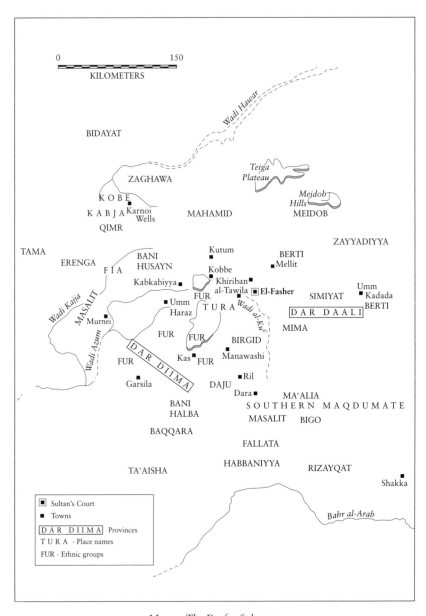

Map 2. The Darfur Sultanate

xxii

THE "ABODE OF THE BLACKS"

DISASTER IN DARFUR

Until the depredations of the fearsome rabble known as *janjawid* began to filter into the international consciousness in 2003, Darfur was one of the least-known places in the world. Poor, remote, landlocked, and sparsely populated, it was obscure even to the rest of the Sudan. Darfur's western borders are as far from the Red Sea as they are from the Atlantic, and the overland journey from Khartoum, the Sudanese capital on the Nile, still takes days across the desert. Darfur has no valuable minerals (although oil drillers live in hope), no famous sons or daughters, no natural wonders or monuments to attract any but the hardiest foreign visitors. When word of the killings began to seep out in 2003, it seemed to a perplexed world to be news from a void.

But Darfur has a history. At a crossroads of Africa and the Muslim Middle East, it has traded for centuries between them, and its peoples reflect in their languages and cultures, and in their blood, a rich heritage. As part of *bilad al-Sudan* – the "land of the Blacks" – the medieval Arab geographers' term for the Sahel, Darfur also straddles the *hajj* routes along which West Africans have for centuries made the pilgrimage to Mecca and left their mark. Arabic and Muslim culture slowly permeated, and coexisted with, indigenous traditions. To the outsider, all the people of Darfur are black, and it is ethnicity rather than "race" that sets them apart.

Until 1916, when it became one of the very last African territories to fall to European imperialism, Darfur was an autonomous sultanate, with a long line of noble rulers governing from El Fasher, whose very name ("the camp") bespoke the martial history of the state. When the

Sudan became independent in 1956, Darfur had therefore experienced European rule, of a kind, for only forty years; the day the Union Jack came down, there must have been many who remembered when the British had arrived and some even the day when the last sultan, Ali Dinar, had himself returned from captivity at Omdurman at the fall of the Mahdi's empire in 1898. A few old men might even have been boys in 1874, when al-Zubayr Pasha, the merchant prince whose personal domain stretched a thousand miles westward from the Upper Nile, had with his slave army defeated and killed the Fur sultan, only to see his conquest annexed by the Khedive of Egypt. In eight decades, remote Darfur had witnessed enormous change.

When in 1916 the British sirdar in Khartoum put aside for a moment the secret schemes that culminated in T. E. Lawrence's sideshow in Arabia, the taunts of the Fur sultan provoked his wrath. But the Anglo-Egyptian annexation of Darfur had no more ambitious motive than pacification – and denying more territory, however poor, to the equally land-grabbing French moving eastward. The colonial regime imposed in Darfur was therefore one that prized law and order, in a suitably rough-and-ready way, over what would come to be called "economic development" or preparation for independence. In the Sudan, investment was largely limited to the vicinity of the capital, the agricultural region to its south, and the towns along the colonial railway that connected these to the Red Sea. Darfur, as indeed much of the rest of the country, was neglected.

The result of neglect was that the colonial inheritance, bequeathed at independence, went to a small group who, by dint of geography, access to educational and commercial opportunities, and luck, had been in the right place at the right time. What followed has been called "internal colonialism," by which the ruling elite, concentrated in Khartoum and a few other areas, controlled politics and the economy. They did a poor job of it and, by the 1980s, after a succession of parliamentary and military regimes, the Sudan was a case study in bad government, the local effects of international agencies' bad policies, and the skewed priorities of the Cold War. Darfur provided votes when elections were held and cheap migratory labor but was still the ignored wild west, an undeveloped corner of one of the world's least-developed countries.

In the 1980s Khartoum, and the wider world, began to pay greater attention to Darfur, with results that would not benefit its people. To the west lay Chad, a former French territory even poorer and more complex than Darfur, and to the north Libya, whose mercurial leader, Colonel Muammar Gaddafi, dreamt of expanding an Islamic empire of his own into the weak postcolonial states of the Sahel. Trilateral local relations of great complexity and constant shifts resulted and were further complicated by the fitful involvement, for their own reasons, of France, the United States, and other powers. Darfur, the international border of which was not only porous but also cut across ancient ethnic and tribal *dars*, did not escape these troubles.

At the same time, the whole trans-African region was experiencing a decades-long drought that, with ensuing desertification and, ironically, the effects of improved human and animal health, was creating an epic demographic problem. Periodic famines, long the price of life in the Sahel, lasted longer; nomads who would once have returned to their deserts of seasonal grasses no longer did so; the breakdown of security and the irresponsible agendas of politicians made matters worse. In 1984–85, a great famine enveloped Darfur, whose people were left to die by their government. In the unsettled times that followed, with automatic weapons selling at a discount in the maelstrom of Libya's campaigns in Chad, local difficulties that had in the past been settled through traditional tribal mechanisms took on aspects of warlordism. The Sudanese government, preoccupied with its long civil war in the south, armed the Arab tribal "militias" of Southern Darfur and set them loose.

By the 1990s, an increasingly chaotic situation in Darfur was imbued with a particularly dangerous variant of Arab supremacism. This monstrous child of the northern Sudanese metropolitan elite and Gaddafi's Arab Islamism was adopted by some Darfur and Chadian Arab chiefs to inspire, and cloak, the activities of what we know now as the *janjawid*. Whereas gradual assimilation of both Arabs and non-Arabs into the "Sudanese" culture as defined in the Nile valley had been progressing for years, suddenly Darfur – "the abode of the Fur" – was proclaimed an "Arab" land, whose non-Arab usurpers could rightfully be dispossessed. The result, in the early 1990s, was race war. When Khartoum failed to protect them, the non-Arab population formed self-defense forces in Darfur – forerunners of the Sudan Liberation Movement. But that movement (and others) was no match for the combined strength – and scorched-earth strategy – of the Sudanese army and *janjawid*, which acted in tandem to subject Northern and Western Darfur to ethnic cleansing.

A Darfur Peace Agreement, stillborn in Abuja in May 2006, owed much to the attention of the outside world. In the absence of such pressure, easily released elsewhere in an era of frequent and instantly publicized terror attacks, tsunamis, and wars, the millions still immured in Darfur's refugee camps remain at risk. When Darfur was the transit route for the slave trade in the 1860s, Europe demanded action; when in the 1890s British imperialists needed popular support at home to conquer the Sudan, they created it through propaganda about the horrors of the Mahdist state; after Europeans and Americans in the 1980s started buying slaves to rescue them and witnessed the plight of the "Lost Boys" from the southern Sudan, they demanded action, and Europe and the United States intervened to help bring about the end of the North-South civil war.

The future of Darfur remains an open question. With U.S. military forces spread thin and those of Europe seemingly in demand in a growing list of global conflicts, the leading role in Darfur has fallen to the African Union and the United Nations. The Sudanese government vehemently opposed UN involvement and, with the indictment in March 2009 of the Sudanese president, Omar al-Bashir, by the International Criminal Court, even operations of foreign relief agencies were shut down. The accession of the Obama administration in the United States has thus far (summer 2009) promised change, but the level of insecurity of the refugee camps continues to fluctuate, even as those camps have begun to take on a permanent character. Negotiations have made little apparent progress since 2006, and have in fact been rendered less likely to succeed by fractionalization of the rebel side. How things got to this point – how a region once so obscure that it was compared to the dark side of the moon has been the cynosure of world attention – is the subject of this book, a history of Darfur besieged.

THE LAND AND THE PEOPLE

The word "Darfur" combines the Arabic *dar* (home, abode) and the name of the principal ethnic group, the Fur, which has inhabited the region since pre-modern times. At every stage of the period with which this book is concerned, however, from the sixteenth century until the present day, the territory has been ethnically mixed; the majority of the population of the Fur state, at times of expansion, may have been non-Fur. But the term Darfur early came to denote the Fur homeland and the territories and peoples over which the Fur state held sway.

The extent of those territories has ebbed and flowed considerably. At its greatest extent, in the eighteenth century, the Fur empire extended from the Nile into what is today Chad, and as far south as the Bahr al-Arab, an area of some 340,000 square miles; but at other times even the nucleus of the Fur state has been all but extinguished as, for example, after its conquest by al-Zubayr in 1874, again during the Mahdiyya of the 1880s and 1890s, and after the Anglo-Egyptian annexation in 1916. Thus, we are here concerned with the territories under Fur political control at any given time and, during periods of foreign control, what had by the mid-nineteenth century been generally considered "Darfur."

That territory, as defined by Turco-Egyptian provincial boundaries dating to the 1870s and subsequently by Mahdist and Anglo-Egyptian provincial boundaries, has remained, after the independence of the Sudan in 1956, "Darfur," despite its most recent division into the "states" known today as Northern, Western, and Eastern Darfur. Whereas the borders of the Sudan, for reasons owing much to foreigners' desire to control and exploit the Nile, today extend into the forests of equatorial Africa, Darfur itself lies entirely in the vast Sahelian belt of desert and semidesert, savanna and oasis. Climate has been the decisive factor in its history. The relative isolation of the territory has been both a boon and a bane, contributing to undoubted lack of development but also to one of the longest histories of independence from colonial rule.

Much of present-day Darfur is a plateau of about 650 to 1,000 meters above sea level.[1] The dominant geological feature of the region is the volcanic range of Jabal Marra, which runs north-south for about 70 miles near parallel 24 degrees east, reaching a height of some 3,000 meters and giving rise to a number of seasonal watercourses and many springs; to its northeast is Jabal Meidob, another volcanic formation that reaches a height of about 1,700 meters. Most of Darfur lies outside the Nile watershed. North of the Bahr al-Arab, Darfur's traditional southern border, there are no perennial streams. Agriculture has been mainly rain-fed or practiced along and in the beds of seasonal watercourses, and grazing has been mainly migratory.

Figure 1. View of Jabal Marra. (Photograph by J. F. E. Bloss. Durham University Library, 888/10/20.)

Climate has largely determined the patterns of settlement in Darfur. The climate is entirely tropical. Rainfall is heaviest in the southernmost parts of the territory (more than 700 mm per year), least in the north (75 mm or less); the rainy season is between May and September. In the otherwise waterless far northern desert, which accounts for about a third of Darfur's territory, the *jizzu* region of late rain-fed vegetation has been an important grazing area for the camels and sheep of migratory tribes across provincial (and international) borders; the declining frequency of the rains in modern times, and consequent failure of the *jizzu*, has had immense economic and political consequences. Exploitation of *jizzu* vegetation has been the seasonal resort of Zaghawa nomads who wintered in the well-fed scrublands to the south. Theirs has been called a "consumers' economy" because they herd and gather but do not produce; hardy almost beyond imagination, the Zaghawa are ultimately at the mercy of the annual rains: they accumulate wealth in the form of animals, to barter, as bride wealth, and for status.[2]

To the south of the desert are dry acacia lands and savanna supporting agriculture near and in watercourses as well as seasonal grazing; the density of acacia increases southward as thorn-land flora merge with savanna grasses. The vast sandy *quz* region of stabilized dunes extending across central and southern Darfur and neighboring Kordofan supports a wide variety of vegetation, from grass to trees, and many food crops, both rain-fed and irrigated, from citrus trees to *dukhn* (bulrush millet, the staple grain), tobacco, and cotton, and even tomatoes and melons. The *quz*, with its greater rainfall and seasonal watercourses, thus provides ample scope for both permanent settlement and nomadic herding. Jabal Marra itself, while enjoying relatively abundant rainfall, has concomitantly suffered from the erosion of its soil, and the terraced farming practiced there both exploited and defended against the action of seasonal rains. The richer agricultural lands to the south and west of Jabal Marra have a long history of human settlement, whereas the even wetter savannas farther south have for centuries supported large numbers of nomadic and seminomadic cattle-herding tribes.

The southern regions of western Darfur, including the area around Jabal Marra and in Dar Masalit, between the highlands and the border with Chad, are some of the richest agricultural lands. Although the streams are periodic, their beds supply water year-round, through wells and in areas cultivated after the floods. Major watercourses, notably the great Wadi Azum, leave in their floods' wake terraced banks with rich alluvial soil that is ideal for agriculture. Both *dukhn* and *dura* (*Sorghum vulgare* or the "great millet," the staple of much of the northern Sudan) are grown, and a wide variety of other crops, including notably maize, *bamia* (okra), onions, cotton, and tobacco, and some fruit trees, citrus, mangoes, and guavas. These lands, with the highest population density in Darfur outside the towns, have witnessed much of the early twenty-first-century devastation.

Because of its remoteness and the failure of the Anglo-Egyptian colonial regime to extend railway communications to Darfur, the region's agricultural products have never enjoyed a large export market: railhead in Kordofan was an arduous journey of four days or more by truck. Long-distance trade in animal products (skins and hides) and live animals, especially camels, however, predates colonial times, notably along the famous Darb al-Arba'in, the "Forty-Days Road" between Darfur and the Nile in upper Egypt. In its heyday, before the Turco-Egyptian invasion of the Sudan in 1820–21, Darfur's principal export along the Forty-Days Road was human: slaves taken from among the non-Muslim peoples of today's southern Sudan, Central African Republic, and Chad; the leading historian estimates that between 2,000 and 3,000 were on average sent to Egypt annually between 1750 and 1830. Other exports included ivory and rhinoceros horn, gum, and ostrich feathers.[3] Manufactures and luxury goods were the main imports exchanged in this

Figure 2. The high interior of the mountain watershed, Jabal Marra, c. 1954. The difficult terrain has made Jabal Marra a refuge throughout Darfur history. (Photograph by J. F. E. Bloss. Durham University Library, 888/11/4.)

lucrative trade, organization and control of which was an important factor in the rise of the Fur state.

The climate of what is now Darfur underwent important changes long before the problem of desertification was understood. Copious archeological evidence confirms the view that the desert regions supported permanent populations in ancient times, and the natural ranges of various large mammals have only recently contracted far southward, a process owing at least as much to extermination through hunting, however, as to climate change.[4] The extent to which those changes were episodic or gradual and continuous is debated, but not the fact that they accelerated during the twentieth century and were exacerbated at least in part by human pressure on the ecosystem.

Estimates of Darfur's population, either now or for almost any time in the past, are subject to dispute. The vast area; transient patterns of some of its peoples, both within and across local and international boundaries; suspicion of census takers and the use to which their findings might be put – these common problems have been both admitted and exploited by successive regimes to misrepresent the population or one or another of its components. A British estimate in 1898 was 1.5 million; another, in 1906, was 270,000; a third, in 1922, purported to recall a population in 1918 (two years after the Anglo-Egyptian annexation) of 274,000 but in 1921 of 524,000. Reports for both 1930 and 1936 list the total as 715,000. A survey published in 1948 lists 734,000, the Annual Report for 1948 "over 900,000," and a medical report of the same year lists 950,000. A document issued by the Sudan Agency in Cairo in 1950 estimated 875,000. The first scientific census of the Sudan gave an official figure in December 1955, on the eve of independence, of 1,329,000. No national census has been completed since then. But the Sudanese government's *Almanac* for 1963 gives, without explanation, a figure of 1.62 million, some 18 percent higher than its official figure of two years earlier. A much-criticized census of 1973 enumerated 2.18 million. The Bank of Sudan counted 3,094,000 in 1983, and a leading expert estimated 3.2 million in 1989.[5] Estimates today hover around 6 million, which, if accurate, would mean that the population increased four-fold during the half century of independence.

Other than the Sahara, there are no geographical barriers to migration into and out of Darfur. The effect has been constant movement of people impelled by events elsewhere to move into the territory or reacting to local changes by moving within or out of it. Even before the upheavals of the past twenty years, this resulted in an ethnographic map of great complexity, with overlays and dispossessions, mass movements and gradual infiltrations, over a long period of time. Several general trends have been identified: from east to west, that is from the Nile valley westward into Kordofan and Darfur; from the northwest; and from West Africa, especially in more recent times.[6]

Although the same caveats that apply to estimates of Darfur's population as a whole must be recalled when assessing its ethnic makeup, some broad outlines are clear. Jabal Marra marks a rough divide between the predominantly Arab (to the east) and non-Arab populations. The eponymous Fur are an African people looking to Jabal Marra as an ancestral home but whose remoter origins are uncertain. Their language, unrelated to Arabic, is unique in the Sudan, and their separate ethnic identity has withstood the assimilative effects of Nilotic Sudanese culture. The Fur are today divided into three main sections, the Tamurkwa, Kunjara, and Karakirit, which in turn are divided into many other groups, the origins and significance of whose titles are not entirely clear.[7] The Fur royal family came from the Keira, a clan of the Kunjara.

The westernmost lands of Dar Masalit and Dar Qimr take their names from other non-Arab peoples with their own languages, of whom others still, of greater or lesser antiquity in Darfur, are the Berti, near Umm Kadada on the road to Kordofan, the Tunjur, the Daju, and the now Arabicized Birgid. In the far northern desert, the principal tribes are the Zayyadiyya and Zaghawa; the region has also been regularly traversed by *jizzu*-seeking Kababish Arabs, whose homeland is in northern Kordofan, and by the Meidob, whose Nubian language attests to origins in the Nile valley. Although it is reasonable to assume that these peoples predate the Arabs in Darfur, in at least some cases, evidence points to later arrivals, through migrations from the west and northwest similar to those of the Arabs themselves.[8]

West of Jabal Marra, the Fur homeland has been shared by the Arabic-speaking Bani Husayn and Bani Halba and, east of the Marra massif, by the camel-keeping northern Rizayqat. Southern Darfur has been the tribal homeland of the Baqqara tribes (Ar. *baqqara*, cow) of Arabic-speaking cattle nomads. Among the largely sedentary peoples of the central *quz* grasslands are the Arabic-speaking Bidayriyya, Dar

Hamid, Jawamaʿa, and Hamar. Darfur has also become home to a large number of so-called Fallata, immigrants from West Africa, who migrated westward for economic, political, and religious reasons and settled as far east as the Blue Nile valley.[9]

Academic controversy over the origins of the Arab tribes of Darfur only recently assumed ideological and political dimensions. Their arrival in the central *bilad al-Sudan* dates to no later than the fourteenth century.[10] A "slow movement by Arab nomads into and across northern and southern Dar Fur between the fourteenth and sixteenth centuries and their gradual coalescence into the modern tribal groupings" has been discerned, the main components of which can be identified by the eighteenth century.[11] The upheavals of centuries have resulted in a patchwork, with tribes and sections of tribes and clans living far apart from each other, among or under others, with fortunes waxing or waning in ways explicable often only by reference to evolving local circumstances. That through miscegenation the Arabic-speaking tribes have acquired African physical characteristics is evident, but patrilineal descent, fortified by Muslim law, has tended to exaggerate Arab identity on this frontier of Islam.

Tribal genealogies, moreover, are concerned with ancestry, and have appropriated connections with Arabia and even with the tribe of Quraysh and the Prophet Muhammad. The Jaʿaliyyin group of Sudanese Arab tribes, for example, predominant along the Nile, and including in Darfur various groups who migrated or were pushed westward, all claim descent from al-Abbas, the Prophet's uncle. The Bidayriyya, Hawazma, and sections of the several Jawamaʿa tribes in turn claim Jaʿali descent, as indeed, matrilineally, did the Fur royal family. A second group, the Juhayna Arabs, find ancestry in the Juhayna tribe of Arabia who, in the armies of early Islam, migrated to Egypt and were instrumental in conquering Nubia in the fourteenth century. The Juhayna group includes the so-called Fazara tribes of the Kababish, Dar Hamid, Zayyadiyya, Bani Jarar, and Maʿalia, and the Baqqara tribes of the Rizayqat, Habbaniyya, Taʿaisha, Bani Halba, and Misiriyya. Hundreds of subtribes and clans can be identified by name; whereas some all but disappeared during war, migration, and hard times, others emerged with the success of a prodigious family. The salient point is of fluidity and change, not stagnation and immemorially fixed positions geographically, socially, or economically.

On the eve of independence in 1956, the first (and last) national census provided an incomplete account of Darfur's ethnic composition. "Tribes of Western Darfur," the category including the Fur, comprised some 758,000 people, or about 57 percent of the total. "Arab tribes" included 375,000 people, of whom Baqqara numbered, in total, about 269,000, Dar Hamid a mere 4,900, Jawama'a-Bidayriyya some 13,300, and "other Arab tribes" about 55,000.[12] In 1980, the Fur population was reliably estimated at 500,000, and people of West African immigrant origins at 30 percent of the province's total population.[13] In any case, genealogical tables, undoubtedly eventful histories, recent prominence, and claims to precedence of one or another tribe or people may well seem disproportionate to its numbers.

Use of the term "tribe" may be briefly explained. A tribe is a group of people sharing or purporting to share a common ancestry and organized accordingly for political and other purposes. Thus, the Bani Husayn or Kababish, for example, all claim descent from a founding father and owe allegiance to hereditary or elected heads of family, subclan, clan, and, finally, the tribe itself. To degrees that vary from tribe to tribe, political, social, and economic life is endogenous, and the tribe deals as one with outsiders, whether individuals, groups, or the state. But exogenous marriage, amalgamation of tribal groups or their separation, and a whole range of pressures, from the climatic and demographic to the external and military, lend a dynamism to tribal existence at odds with the image of changelessness with which Arab tribes in particular have been endowed in fiction. (A "people," for our purposes, is a large group sharing an ethnic identity [not necessarily with a tribal organization] and a language: the Fur are a people, as are, for example, the Finns or Danes.)

In Darfur, socioeconomic and political developments over centuries have contributed to dynamism in group identity. Just as it appears that various non-Fur groups gradually assimilated into Fur culture before the modern period, so the self-identity of "Arabs" has evolved in recent times. The 1956 census put the number of Arabic speakers in Darfur at 725,000, or more than half the population, with the next largest group, Fur speakers, numbering only about 265,000; the remainder of the population (some 1.329 million) spoke Masalit (163,000), Zaghawa (67,000), and a dozen other languages. Yet, although language ascription and even self-identification may be aspects of ethnicity, they are not necessarily so, and there are other variables. Thus, for example, some Fur have "become" Baqqara through socioeconomic adaptations; many nonnative Arabic speakers learn Arabic as their second (or third) language for practical reasons unassociated with identity, just as Germans learn English and Bengalis learn Hindi.[14]

Although tribal organization in Darfur and elsewhere in the northern Sudan has eroded for many years, as centralizing policies and enforcement powers of state authorities and less discernible but no less powerful cultural pressures chipped away at its bases, recent events give ample evidence that tribal identity is far from a homely vestige of simpler times. In 1980 it could fairly be said that ecological factors had rendered some tribal labels of "only a limited ethnic content or stability" as farmers took to herding or nomads settled, and that "changes in political allegiance were later legitimized by changes in one's ancestors."[15] Chaos in Darfur today illustrates, however, not only how tribal loyalties can be called on to provoke violent action but also how these can be confused, both deliberately as justification for outrageous conduct and inadvertently among people with multiple competing identities and interests. The history of Darfur provides ample evidence of other familiar oppositions: between desert and sown, nomadic and settled, even modern and reactionary. Darfur's is hardly the first case of cynical appeals to ethnic loyalty for the purpose of achieving political and economic ends, nor indeed of fading identities revivified against perceived threats.

The indigenous population of Darfur is entirely Muslim. How Islamization occurred, if it may be called a process, remains a subject of academic controversy. Darfur is remote from the centers of Islamic learning in North Africa and the Near East, and even after the advent of modern transport, it sent few students to Cairo or the Hijaz. Islam came slowly, with trade and itinerant missionaries. The trans-African pilgrimage route to Mecca passes through Darfur, and, in the way of things, would-be or returning pilgrims sojourned or settled, enriching the local variant of Islam; evidence suggests that that route was of little significance before the eighteenth-century jihad movements in West Africa. In any case, countless survivals of pre-Islamic belief and custom remained discernible in the culture of Darfur, at times becoming bones of contention, notably during the Mahdiyya of the 1880s and 1890s, when what is sometimes termed "revivalism" sought to return Sudanese to a version of Islam that most of them had never known.

The few non-Muslims in Darfur at the start of the twenty-first century were foreigners or descendants of foreigners, including merchants of Christian Egyptian, Syrian, and Greek origin who settled during the Turkiyya and after the Anglo-Egyptian conquest in 1916.

The spread of the Arabic language may likewise be discussed as a process, and "Islamization" and "Arabicization" have often been described as simultaneous or even synonymous. As we shall see, however, use of the Fur language, even at the royal court, continued until the end of the independent state; close contact with Arabic speakers has resulted, on the other hand, in Arabic's adoption as a lingua franca and even a first language among some Fur. Arabic has been the working language of the Sudan as a whole since before independence, with English, for historical and, more recently, practical and political, reasons, the common second language; there is little incentive for Arabic speakers to learn Fur. The northern Sudan's political elite consider acculturation a one-way street, and official policies have taken for granted a riverain northern Sudanese model;[16] when an Institute of African and Asian Studies was established at the University of Khartoum, for example, it offered language instruction in Hausa, Amharic, and Swahili but in no indigenous Sudanese languages.

To some extent, that model, by which peoples of the Sudan have adopted Arabic, Islam, and cultural norms of the Nile valley, may be seen to inform the catastrophe that engulfed Darfur in the first years of the twenty-first century. In this view, disinclination to assimilate may therefore be seen not only as a futile reaction to the inevitability of a homogeneous "Sudanese" identity but even as irreligious; it is easily depicted as self-serving, allied to foreign interests, and ignorant. From the opposing point of view, even a worm turns: Darfur's rebellion, after generations of neglect gave way to mass murder, is not merely a defense of local rights but also a struggle for existence. One thing is certain: today's "humanitarian disaster" can hardly be understood without some reference to the history of Darfur.

LORDS OF MOUNTAIN
AND SAVANNA

The Origins and History of the Fur State to 1874

Study of Darfur before the nineteenth century is hampered by a paucity of sources and the difficult nature of those that are available. Since the Sudan's independence in 1956, however, great strides have been made in locating, collecting, describing, and interpreting documentary sources. The work of several Sudanese and European institutions and scholars has been particularly important. In some cases that work has had the effect of pointing out the vast amount of further research, not least in archeology, that could, with the requisite interest and finance, be undertaken. Nevertheless, the study of Darfur's history would have been set back immeasurably had not the process of identification and collection taken place before the upheavals of the early twenty-first century.[1]

Through the collection and analysis of oral traditions, critical examination of the few and relatively late Arab and European travelers' accounts, and, most recently, the detailed study of documents from the Fur sultanate, historians have been able to provide at least a plausible picture, in broad strokes, of the Fur sultanate's early history and a more detailed description of certain aspects of its administration. More can be deduced through reasonable comparative analysis of Darfur and other Muslim states of the Sudanic belt[2] and, indeed, through what is known of long-distance trade (and the products it carried and left behind). Still, it remains the case that much of what has been written about the history of the region before the eighteenth century is based on conjecture, however well informed, and lies open to revision.

State formation in the highland zone of the central Sudanic belt that includes both Darfur and Wadai long predates the myth-shrouded rise of the Fur sultanate. According to tradition, the oldest of these states was the kingdom of the Daju, a people or non-Muslim ruling family originating to the east of Darfur, possibly, as in the case of other origin stories, in the Nile valley. Modern claims to Daju descent, linguistic clues in scattered parts of the central Sudanic belt, and the unexamined ruins of ancient settlements all point to the possibility that future research may be repaid at least in establishing solid theories of Daju origins and of the nature of a Daju state.[3] Until then, however, little can be said with certainty. But in the Daju ruling family of Dar Sila, a principality south of Dar Masalit on the Chadian side of the modern border with the Sudan, traditions of an ancient royal house, and an irredentist threat, lived on until the end of the Fur sultanate.

The Daju were succeeded by the Tunjur, about whom there has also been much speculation. Variations on their name may be found in those of modern groups in the Sudanic belt, but which of these are survivals and which are fortuitous is uncertain. The Tunjur established an empire based on long-distance trade, which they ruled from hilltop palaces at Uri, Ayn Farah, and elsewhere. Historians have interpreted various contemporary Arab and European sources as referring to the Tunjur, or at least to an empire with which the Tunjur name has been associated, and to peoples under their sway, but these establish only the presence of those peoples, not that of the Tunjur themselves. Archeological sites connected to the Tunjur have been identified but not scientifically investigated, and no contemporary local documentary sources have been found. There is indeed disagreement with the traditional account of their origins, concerning not only their homeland – variously given as east, northwest, and west of Darfur – but also their ethnicity and even, by a factor of several centuries, the time of their arrival on the scene. How and when they were ejected from Darfur we do not know, but this was likely by gradual dispossession, a process that culminated in the opposition of two royal houses, the Tunjur of Wadai and the Keira of Darfur, whose rivalry dominated the tribal politics of the region until the coming of the Europeans – echoes of which remain today.[4]

THE FUR

With the downfall, or at least the disappearance, of the Tunjur, we arrive at the advent of the Fur state. The possibility of coexisting Tunjur and Fur polities in the fifteenth century has been cautiously advanced.

According to this interpretation, the Keira, a clan of the Kunjara section of the Fur, were vassals in Jabal Marra of the Tunjur, and when the empire collapsed for unknown reasons sometime between 1580 and 1660, the Keira principality "expanded rapidly to fill the vacuum."[5] Other traditions, by which the Keira married into the Tunjur royal house or traced their local origins to a "Wise Stranger," a figure familiar to origin stories, may be entertained but are as likely conflations of various myths – later emphasized more or less for political or social convenience – as they are echoes of historical fact.

The early history of the Fur (or Keira) state is nonetheless shrouded in legend, some of which may be clarified or interpreted through tradition. Even before the mythic earliest kings, the Fur appear to have been expanding, and for some considerable time, to the southwest from a base in Jabal Marra, through perhaps both peaceful and military means. Fur traditions indicate forcible expulsion of other people southward because they were non-Muslims, into what is today Southern Darfur and beyond the Bahr al-Arab where, indeed, the Fur state later raided for slaves. In this scheme of things, Fur expansion is a long historical process, confirmed indirectly by oral traditions of those they are said to have displaced.[6] The historical consensus holds that Fur progress encountered at some point the eastward migration of Baqqara tribes, who eventually occupied or came to dominate the lands between the Fur and the peoples they displaced. This view is currently under challenge by the suggestion of local, probably Birgid, origins, a theory benefiting from consistency with old and continuing local patterns of assimilation into Arab culture. An intermediate region of shifting political control and great ethnic complexity was Dar Dima, which eventually became the southern province of the Fur empire, over which direct control by the sultans fluctuated.[7]

Of these rulers, Daali (called *jadd al-Fur*, or "father of the Fur," and, according to tradition, a law-giver and founder of the Keira dynasty) and Kuuruu are associated with impressive unexcavated stone ruins around Tura in Jabal Marra; Tura retained sanctity throughout Fur history as a burial place for the sultans. Tradition ascribes various feats to these and others in the royal line, but about them nothing is known with certainty before Sulayman, considered by the Fur a second founder of the state, who ruled in the latter half of the seventeenth century.[8] The historian is careful to point out that the traditions, the only evidence of some of these rulers' existence, were first written down some two centuries after the people and events they describe.[9]

It is not with unalloyed relief, therefore, that we encounter the historical Sulayman, for the documentary sources for his life, too, are scanty. Nonetheless, Sulayman's reign marks a turning point, the end of the line of shadowy Keira rulers in Jabal Marra and the beginning of a historical royal house that expanded the kingdom beyond its mountain base. Whether as cause or effect, control of long-distance trade is a salient feature of that expansion, and it is in connection with trade that the Fur state began (c. 1660) to appear in travelers' and traders' accounts. The historian of the Keira cites references by the Dominican Vansleb to the Fur and their trade goods, including ostrich feathers, ivory, and especially black slaves; an apparent reference to the Forty-Days Road to Egypt attests to its probable use before Sulayman's time. In 1689, Franciscan missionaries at the Kharja Oasis, an important way station on the road, mentioned merchants setting off for the Fur kingdom. Theodor Krump, a German Franciscan who traveled to Sinnar on the Blue Nile, capital of the Funj sultanate, in 1701, wrote of its trade with Darfur, and by 1705 there is also evidence of merchants from Dongola, on the great bend of the Sudanese Nile, residing in Darfur.[10]

From the time of Sulayman's reign, there is also increasing evidence of the influence of Islam. The extent to which the Fur had adopted Islam by this time is problematic and open to dispute, but there is ample evidence of foreign Muslim preachers (Ar. *fuqaha*)[11] in Darfur during the eighteenth century; several families of religious notables trace their local origins to Sulayman's time. Sulayman himself is said to have made Islam the religion of the royal court. There is no doubt, however, that adoption of Islamic norms was gradual, and that these coexisted with or subsumed older customs and traditions, as has been common elsewhere. The degree to which Islamization has occurred is always disputed, as we may see today in what are condemned as Westernization, secularism, backsliding, fundamentalism, and other phenomena named by opponents. Thus, in Darfur as elsewhere, Islamization raises the question of what, beyond individuals' stated adherence, in the form of the *shahada*[12] or otherwise, constituted adoption of Islam. In any case, evidence abounds that early Fur rulers conformed to the paradigm of divine kingship common in African states and that customs and traditions, whether of the pre-Islamic Fur themselves or the remoter Tunjur, survived.

The quickening pace of the Fur kingdom's contacts with the outside world, whether in terms of trade or religion, coincided with its expansion. Among the heroic virtues ascribed to Sulayman is prowess as a warrior, and it is assumed that warring and raiding supplied the slaves and other trade goods that burgeoning commerce with the Nile valley demanded. Even the bare outline of his campaigns, however, cannot be discerned historically, and some surviving traditions are far-fetched. There is evidence of raids into Kordofan,[13] but the main themes of the kingdom's wars were subjugation of neighboring tribes and rivalry with the sultanate of Wadai to the west. Sources for the study of these campaigns are few and are now limited to Fur traditions.

EXPANSION OF THE STATE

Notwithstanding the reverence accorded Sulayman, the "second founder," it was during the reign of his grandson Ahmad Bukr (son of Musa, of whom little is known) that the most systematic expansion took place. The Fur remit was extended first to Dar Qimr, to the northwest, and then to the lands of the nomadic Zaghawa, through which the vital trade routes to Egypt passed; through diplomacy, marriage alliance, and military action, the Zaghawa were subdued and allied. When the Wadai sultan threw off traditional allegiance and invaded Darfur, it was only after resort to the Marra redoubt, a struggle of several years, and in alliance with Wadai's western neighbor, Bagirmi, that Ahmad Bukr was able to eject the aggressors. The campaign culminated in a victory evoked in the Fur name of the town that grew up there, Kabkabiyya (*kebi kebia*: "they threw down their shields").[14]

The period following Ahmad Bukr's death in about 1720 witnessed complicated interplay of court intrigue and foreign war. In a pattern familiar elsewhere, successive sultans sought to centralize power in their and their appointees' hands at the expense of traditional authorities within and beyond the royal court. The tensions thus exacerbated gave openings to rulers of neighboring states and to dissident Fur in exile. Ahmad Bukr's successor, his son Muhammad Dawra (ruled c. 1720–30),[15] is said to have killed or imprisoned as many of his brothers as he could lay his hands on and may indeed have murdered his own son after an abortive revolt in order to secure his position. Muhammad Dawra was succeeded by another son of Ahmad Bukr, Umar Lel (ruled c. 1730–39), whose reign was marked by continual struggle with his many uncles, possibly involving perceived diminution of the power of traditional Fur chiefs, whose interests as the state expanded conflicted with those of a centralizing sultanate. In any case, two of Muhammad Dawra's uncles absconded to Kordofan, where they made common cause with the Musabba'at ruler, whose people were descendants of exiles from Darfur.[16] When Umar Lel thereupon invaded Kordofan, one of the uncles stole back to Darfur where, after some success, he was defeated and killed by the sultan. Possibly in retaliation for support of the rebels, Umar Lel invaded Wadai but was defeated and ended his days a prisoner.

There followed a further struggle for control. Abu'l Qasim (ruled 1739–52), another son of Sultan Ahmad Bukr, took the throne but confronted the same problems his brother and nephew had faced. An early challenge by the Musabba'at of Kordofan ended in Abu'l Qasim's victory at Ril, near Nyala. The logic of the sultan's position had not changed, however, and, even more than his predecessors, Abu'l Qasim sought to build up the institution of the sultanate as against the traditional notables and military leaders of the state by relying on slave troops rather than Fur levies and by appointing outsiders, without independent standing, to high office. Simmering discontent culminated when Abu'l Qasim invaded Wadai and was deserted on the battlefield by his own army. With the support of the Fur notables, yet another son of Ahmad Bukr, Muhammad Tayrab, became sultan; Abu'l Qasim, who, though wounded, had escaped and returned, was executed.[17]

Muhammad Tayrab's long reign (1752/3–1785/6) is remarkable for several related reasons: his success in the centralizing policy initiated by weaker predecessors, relative peace with Wadai, the conquest of Kordofan, and expanding connections with the Nile valley. Whether because of the strength of Wadai and the evident weakness of Sinnar, its western and eastern neighbors, respectively, or because of the Nile valley's increasing importance to Darfur commercially and culturally, the orientation of the sultanate changed. Conquest had altered the ethnic makeup of the kingdom, as more and more non-Fur elements had come under its sway. During successive reigns, the sultan's *fashir*, or encampment, had moved from west of Jabal Marra to its east; Muhammad Tayrab's move to Ril in about 1770 marked the decisive shift, and his successor completed the process by establishing a permanent "camp" or capital, El Fasher. Although this shift hardly marked abandonment of the ancestral homeland, it indicates the ever-increasing eastward emphasis of political, religious, and commercial relations. Even the object of Muhammad Tayrab's unsuccessful campaigns from Ril against the powerful Rizayqat cattle nomads in the south may have been greater control over the supply of slaves from the territories beyond to feed the trade with Egypt. He had more success against the Birgid, rule of whose lands he parceled out to favorites. But his greatest feat was the conquest of Kordofan, the vast territory between Darfur and the Nile: the Funj sultan's grip had weakened, giving scope to the troublemaking Musabba'at, but the gum, gold, and slaves of Kordofan and its southern hinterlands were reason enough to invade. With a huge army, Muhammad Tayrab ejected the Musabba'at, defeated the Funj, and annexed Kordofan. He died on the return journey to Darfur in 1786–87.[18]

In pursuing a policy of consolidating royal power within the expanding Keira dominions, Muhammad Tayrab had been unable to solve the succession problem so familiar in Islamic history. Famous examples range from the Ottoman "Law of Fratricide" (a solution Muhammad Dawra appears to have favored) and the subsequent (arguably worse) system of immurement to the current Saudi method of consensual nomination of a crown prince by a new king, a system observed with worldwide trepidation. Lacking a principle of primogeniture, the Fur sultanate was no exception in this regard, as the contested accession of successive brothers indicates; the uxorious Fur sultans produced scores of sons, so many that they constituted a special class or, as we may say, an interest group. It is unsurprising, therefore, that the demise of Muhammad Tayrab, in his war camp in Kordofan at the end of a long reign, was attended by much intrigue and that the eventual successor, his brother Abd al-Rahman, was able to solidify his position only after a three-year civil war.[19]

At least two visitors to Darfur during the reign of Abd al-Rahman (1787/8–1803) and the early years of his successor, Muhammad al-Fadl (1803–38), have left accounts: the Englishman William Browne, who lived there from 1793 to 1796, and Muhammad Umar Sulayman al-Tunisi, who spent eight years (1803–11) at the Fur court. Their books[20] are historians' most important sources for the period and provide useful information about earlier times. Together with an increasing number of documents from Darfur and its trading partners, they allow a much clearer picture to emerge of the organization and administration of the Fur state during and after its period of greatest expansion.

The succession problem was but one symptom of tensions – or, at any rate, of increasingly obvious contrasts – between the African and the Islamic as the Fur polity expanded into a multiethnic empire encompassing an area of more than 300,000 square miles. The traditional institutions of the Fur monarchy were incompletely equipped to deal with the challenges thus begotten. The late eighteenth and early nineteenth centuries were therefore a period not only of great expansion but also of the institutional changes that this necessitated. These began at the top, at the court of the sultans, which, from the time of Abd al-Rahman, was at last fixed at El Fasher.

ROYAL GOVERNMENT

Whether traveling or in his capital, the sultan was surrounded by elaborate ritual, reflecting ancient custom and, increasingly, with Islamic glosses. His person was sacred, his diet prescribed, his panoply infused with ritual meaning and taboo; his accession and death were marked by ceremony, and he alone was called on to perform various seasonal and religious rites, all of them heavy with symbolism. The account of Gustav Nachtigal, from 1874 but with historical information collected at court, provides copious detail. A huge royal household, with fulsome titles and perquisites, surrounded the sultan; the layout of the royal enclosure reflected his and their places in the hierarchy, combining practical function with ritual significance. In its central zone were the private quarters of the sultan, his principal wife, and his concubines, whose care was in the hands of slave girls and eunuchs. Elsewhere in the compound, the sultan held court, rendered judgment, received petitioners and foreign embassies, and accepted tribute.[21] The royal mews; quarters for the bodyguard and eunuchs; a "cadets' school," recruited from among both slaves and freeborn youths to supply the court bureaucracy and royal guard; and other accouterments of state business and the convenience of the sultan were also housed there.[22]

Whether there was a "chancery" there before the restoration of the sultanate in 1898 is unknown. The number of surviving documents originating at court increases with time from the early eighteenth century onward, giving ample evidence of official activity in various spheres, and even some royal scribes can be identified by name, but it appears that outgoing documents were not copied. Papers received, whether simple petitions, tax receipts, or royal correspondence, have not been preserved in a corpus that would indicate any system for registering or even keeping them. Examples of the sultans' correspondence, however, are numerous. Literacy had come to Darfur with the *fuqaha*, and although Fur remained the language spoken at court, its written language was Arabic.[23]

Because the sultans took so many wives and concubines, the "royal family" at any given time was enormous. Proliferation of ambitious sons and brothers was a problem not only at the end of a reign; the interests of princes could easily conflict with the policies of the sultan, and riotous behavior apparently made them a nuisance. Several female members of the sultan's family held office or, at any rate, bore titles, most notably his mother, principal wife, and favorite sister, the *iya basi* (Fur: "royal mother"); instances are recorded of maneuvers for – and even exercise of – royal power but, in the way of things, at the cost of their lives. After his visit in 1874, Nachtigal reported that the recent decline in the sultanate's prosperity was in part owed to the extravagance of the *iya basi* and the dowries the sultan provided his many daughters, cousins, and granddaughters. Royal women did not practice strict purdah and, in general, Fur women enjoyed greater freedom (as they do today) than women in riverain Sudanese society.[24]

In describing the main offices of state, historians carefully point out the static nature of even the best sources and thus remind us that the relative importance of titles and offices changes over time. A once-significant role may be reduced to little more than its grand title, whereas the holder of a seemingly minor honorific may be a person of great importance. In the Fur state, as perhaps in all others, an eminence grise or secretary, a spiritual adviser or confidant, carried unfathomable weight, and the force of personality and its interplay with circumstance might propel or diminish both offices and officeholders. Thus, detailed descriptions by al-Tunisi and Nachtigal fail to distinguish fully actual influence from apparent or titular seniority. Analysis of the imperial hierarchy, based on Fur and other documentary sources, allows not only descriptions of roles and functions but also some sense of change over time. In any case, the sheer plethora of titles, some grand, some now amusing, and some with corresponding functions still unknown, has made court life and administration much more difficult to describe in detail.[25]

The administration of the sultanate, between the time of Abd al-Rahman and the death of Sultan Ibrahim Qarad in 1874 may, however, be briefly summarized. The *orrengdulung*, or majordomo of the palace compound, was both a military commander and territorial chief. The *ab shaykh dali*, a eunuch and chief of the sultan's slaves, likewise held territorial office and performed administrative functions during interregna. The *abbo fore* or *kamni*, also with military rank, was the "shadow sultan" who, according to tradition, was in early times executed upon the death of the sultan; the *abbo umo*, *aba diimang*, and *takanawi* all commanded portions of the army and were hereditary governors of regions. Nachtigal listed many other court titles and the duties that went with them, some of which are reminiscent of the vapid protocol of European courts; the widespread use of the word *malik* (Ar. "king"), as in *malik al-asal* ("king of the honey") and *malik murunga* ("king of the horsefly," the personage in charge of delousing the sultan's horse),[26] attests to the caution needed in assessing the significance attached to nominal rank.

A feature common to premodern Muslim (and other) royal courts was employment of slaves in a wide variety of functions, including positions of great responsibility. At the Ottoman court, slaves taken in the *devshirme* system famously ascended to the highest office of state, the grand vizirate, second only to the sultan himself and in practical terms much more powerful; in the Mamluk kingdom of Egypt, the sultanate itself was reserved for slaves (Ar. *mamluk*: "owned"). In a process difficult for many Europeans and for Americans familiar only with the plantation slavery of the New World to understand, employment of slaves in important or sensitive positions appealed to rulers as an alternative to relying on potential rivals or territorially based subordinates; slaves had no families or ethnic ties to fall back on: they owed allegiance only to their master. Eunuchs therefore were ideal slaves in a sense because, in addition to their obvious qualifications for employment in the harem or family quarters, they could have no ambitions for offspring. The history of the Fur sultanate offers several examples of slaves who competed for and wielded great power, even as kingmakers – but never as kings.[27] Such figures were exceptions; the vast majority of royal slaves served as soldiers or in other capacities. Slave raiding in the non-Muslim lands to the south was a highly organized enterprise, licensed by the sultan, which fed both domestic demand and the lucrative export market.

The territory of the Fur state was divided into four great provinces, Dar Diima, Dar Abbo Umo, Dar Daali, and Dar al-Takanawi, which corresponded to the four officeholders mentioned earlier. When Kordofan was annexed in 1785, the borders of the northern and eastern provinces of the empire were at first extended to encompass it. The provinces were divided into *shartayas*, each under an appointed *shartay* and each consisting of a number of *dimlijiyyas* (sing. *dimlij*), or chieftaincies. Origins of this system remain subject to speculation.[28] The *shartays* were the sultan's district representatives, with military, judicial, and financial responsibilities; *shartay*-ship was prestigious, and *shartays* maintained miniature courts that emulated the sultan's. The *dimlij*, on the other hand, whose *dimlijiyya* might consist of a few villages, was effectively only the *shartay*'s local agent. At the village level, a headman intermediated, and a literate *faqih*, if there was one, could deal with anything in writing. Early in the nineteenth century, the sultans began to appoint *maqdums* to command special military campaigns, usually against the nomads of the north and south. In the north, the position soon became hereditary; in the south, decades of intermittent conflict with powerful Baqqara tribes, beyond whose territory were the pagan slave lands, rendered the position that of roving warlord. *Maqdums* of the south emerged as powerful figures, overshadowing hereditary provincial hierarchs.[29]

Central to the administration of the kingdom was the *hakura* (estate) system of land tenure, by which the sultans exercised sovereignty by appropriating and awarding rights in land to favored individuals. Such grants varied in type and size. Rights in a defined community or tract involved exemptions from taxation; high offices of state carried with them responsibilities for and privileges in whole regions. Hints of feudal arrangements lie in the reciprocal relations of the sultan and such officeholders, whose rights in land and obligations at time of war are suggestive. The extent to which estate holders legally taxed, withheld tax due the sultan, illegally imposed their own obligations on tenants or communities, and upheld or conflicted with the authority of the local *shartay* must have varied according to time and place. Rights in land were hereditary, alienable, closely defined, and used by sultans to encourage the opening up of undeveloped or abandoned territory. There is ample evidence of absentee landlordism – obviously in cases in which great nobles held multiple estates – and of the beginnings of local dynasties, as when a religious notable was the grantee and his descendants constituted gentry; members of the huge royal family also dispersed in this way. Through continuous occupation, repeated confirmation of charters, and the force of tradition created by patterns of use and privilege recognized through neighbors' consent or acquiescence, the *hakura* system survived into the twentieth century.[30]

Even at the level of *shartaya*, it is worth pointing out that administrative divisions were not based on the ethnic identities of inhabitants nor, in most cases, could they have been. For its part, taxation depended on distance from the capital (and thus the extent of the sultan's direct control) and the nature, whether settled or nomadic, of a district's economic activity. For a variety of reasons, some tribal areas retained semiautonomous status. These included Dar Qimr and Dar Tama in the northwest; the Zaghawa, Meidob, Zayyadiyya, and Berti to the north; the Birgid in the east; and the Bigo and Daju to the south. The sultan's relations with these lands and peoples were pragmatic, tailored to suit the circumstances of each. Tribute, marriage alliances, the elaborate reciprocity of gifts, the Fur sultan's award or revocation of ceremonial drums, intervention in tribal or clan affairs when leadership was at issue, and ultimately resort to arms were all aspects of the sultan's administration, by which a rough balance between central control and local independence was maintained.[31]

THE MILITARY

In the end, the state's authority depended on its ability to use force. Because the remote origins of Fur military institutions are unknown, what historians have derived from travelers' accounts and other sources applies mostly to the era *after* expansion had ended. Speculation about earlier formative periods focuses on institutions common to the central Sudanic belt and on particular geographic circumstances of the Fur homeland. The early Fur army may have been drawn from *jurenga*, groups of as-yet-unmarried men organized by district and armed with spears, shields, and throwing knives. As the state expanded, these infantrymen were supplanted in importance by cavalry.

The effectiveness of heavily armed and, above all, highly mobile forces in eighteenth-century Darfur still echoes today; it was mobility rather than weaponry that gave them a decisive advantage. The examples of sixty horsemen on a punitive expedition against two tribes and of only 200 men sent to repulse an invading army from Kordofan illustrate the point. Despite the huge expense of continuously importing horses from the Nile valley – those bred locally were inferior[32] – cavalry were therefore cost-effective; arms, and armor for both rider and horse, were imported along the Forty-Days Road from Egypt, whereas other equipment was made locally. The historian of the era evokes "heavily armoured *fursan* 'horsemen' (but with something of the same overtones as 'knights') who terrorized the farmers, raided for slaves and upheld their honour in single combat";[33] Darfur would witness again the terror and raiding of old – though hardly the bravado of single combat – in the *fursan* of the twenty-first century.

After the conquest of Kordofan, when the Fur state approximated its greatest extent, the size and nature of the army changed. At the center, at court, were several ranks of royal bodyguards recruited from among slaves. Regiments were stationed near El Fasher, and levies of *jurenga* could be called up as needed. When in the 1840s attempts were made to bring to heel the Baqqara nomads of the south, however, the sultan's forces were inadequate. The Rizayqat and Habbaniyya were expert at guerilla tactics suited to their homelands and used ambush and withdrawal to fend off invaders. Several catastrophic defeats punctuate the period. In dilatory response to this growing challenge, the Fur sultans began to equip their forces with the sort of modern firearms the Baqqara were acquiring from Arab traders infiltrating Equatoria from the Nile valley.[34]

COMMERCE AND THE SLAVE TRADE

This challenge was not solely or even mainly military. Darfur's was a slave-owning and slave-trading society in which religion, ethnicity, and economic interest combined to create attitudes that survived long after slavery was officially abolished.[35] Access to non-Muslim peoples of the south – called collectively Fartit – fed both the sultanate's own demand for slaves and the trade with Egypt. The taxing of easily portable and high-value-added products such as ostrich feathers, tamarind, sism (*cassia absus*), gum, camels, rhinoceros horn, ivory, natron, and animal by-products remained lucrative, but these were never as important as slaves. The sultanate largely depended on the foreign slave market to satisfy its demand for imported luxury goods from Egypt and beyond, including horses, donkeys, arms and armor, textiles, ready-made clothes, perfume, spices (such as sandalwood, cloves, and musk), small implements (notably razors and files), copper scraps, tin bars, paper, beads, semiprecious stones, shells, soap, sugar, and coffee. Slavers, licensed by the sultan to raid in specific localities, entered into contracts with merchants for supplies and trade goods and enlisted men to accompany them. Slaves might be captured or acquired as gifts from chiefs, who were made presents in return; those acquired might well have been slaves already. Subordinate peoples on the southern fringe of the sultanate's control paid regular tribute in slaves. But even in the early eighteenth century, raiders went far beyond, into regions of the upper Oubangui and what are today the Central African Republic and Congo (Kinshasa).[36]

Slaves were exported mainly along the Forty-Days Road from Kobbei, northwest of El Fasher, through the oases of Bir Natrun, Laqiyya, Salima, al-Shab, Baris, and Kharja, to Assiut in Upper Egypt, a 1,110-mile route that dates at least to the late sixteenth century and is probably much older. Kobbei itself existed solely for the trade: its inhabitants were a self-governing community of merchants from the Nile valley with whom, however, the sultan maintained the closest relations, because control of the town was an essential element in the prosperity of the Fur state. Not only did he license the caravans and levy customs duties: so determined was the last sultan, Ali Dinar, to control trade that he ordered his subjects to set upon any unlicensed merchants entering Darfur. Imports from Egypt were assessed and taxed at Suwayni, before caravans reached Kobbei; exports were taxed by the sultan's representative at Assiut: slaves died during the journey, which, of course, they made on foot. European sources from about 1800 estimate the annual export of slaves at 5,000 to 6,000; the scope necessarily depended on supply, demand, and political conditions at both ends, but in general it may be said that demand in Egypt was never fully satisfied.[37] There is evidence of a Fur trading presence in Cairo and, of course, of Nilotic Sudanese and Egyptians living as merchants beyond Kobbei in Darfur; the sultanate was not closed to foreigners. Indeed, a theme in nineteenth-century history is of increasing contacts, in a variety of ways, between Darfur and the Nile valley.

The Forty-Days Road was not Darfur's only long-distance trade route. Another connected the sultanate to the Mediterranean via the Fezzan, and a third crossed the continent from western Africa, through Wadai (then onward to the Red Sea and beyond). This last acquired cultural significance as the "Sudan Road" of pilgrimage to Mecca and may date to the earliest days of Islam in West Africa. Favored (over the trans-Saharan and Mediterranean route) by poorer pilgrims or those moving en masse for political or economic reasons, the "Sudan Road" certainly predates the eighteenth-century West African jihad movements that, in turn, further stimulated it. There is ample evidence of West African settlement in Darfur, both by individuals and tribal groups, throughout the history of the sultanate. J. L. Burckhardt, a Swiss who visited the Nilotic northern Sudan in 1812–14, gave a surprisingly detailed account of pilgrims from Darfur of West African origin he encountered in the Nile valley, some of whom were trading en route. Such east-west trade might involve many middlemen, carriage over both short and long distance, and much less formality, encompassing as it did a spectrum of traders who ranged from individuals on pilgrimage to tribal migrations.[38] Darfur's trade with Tunis and Tripoli, via the oases of Waiti, Sarra, and Kufra, is poorly documented.

The caravan trade was but one source of the sultanate's revenue. The *abu'l-jabbayyin*, or head tax collector, superintended an army of officials throughout the sultan's domains. Until late in the period under review, taxes were collected in kind. The main taxes were the Islamic *fitr*, a head tax, and *zakat* or, in local usage, the *ushur* or tithe, paid in grain or animals (and in the latter case called *jebe*). The *takkiyya* or cloth tax, a term that refers to the means of payment, not the subject of the tax (which is uncertain), was also collected; cloth was a unit of exchange, so regardless of the method of assessment, its collection provided the state with "cash"; slaves, beads, and copper or tin rings were also media of exchange. Nachtigal reported a so-called *diwan* (Ar. to list, register), a species of wealth tax levied every four years and paid in animals, slaves, grain, cloth, tobacco, honey, salt, and, in large amounts from the Baqqara, butter. Other taxes, fees, fines, and dues were collected; a list of thirty-seven has been compiled from surviving charters, but the nature of many is unknown and of those that can be discerned, most appear to be fines for criminal infractions rather than taxes.[39] Because taxes were paid mostly in kind, they were assigned largely to local payment for services rendered or as part of the patronage relations the sultan maintained with local notables. Slaves likewise paid to the sultan as tribute or tax could be disbursed as marks of favor or put to work in capacities ranging from the royal household to agriculture; the royal estates worked by slaves paid annual tribute to the sultan and were exempted from the control of local officials.[40]

RELIGION AND THE STATE

That a large number of the sultan's exactions – whether taxes or fines – were unknown to orthodox Islam may indicate the degree to which the Fur state was in transition during the period from which documentary sources have survived. The limitations of those sources, however, and the ample evidence of increasing contact with the Nile valley in the eighteenth and especially the nineteenth centuries, may tend to obscure important and continuous "Islamization," the vexed nature of which we have alluded to. Leaving aside degrees of orthodoxy, it makes sense instead to notice the introduction of certain Islamic norms and the replacement or desuetude of local ones, and the increasing influence of Muslim experts in the law and ritual observance. Excepting a few foreigners or families of relatively recent foreign origin, everyone in Darfur today calls himself a Muslim. But as late as 1874, Nachtigal reported countless examples of pre-Islamic religious survivals, some puzzling and inconsequential, others shocking even to him;[41] MacMichael in the 1920s reported vibrant pagan traditions and superstitions, including talking snakes, human metamorphoses, resurrections, and the like, not unfamiliar to other monotheisms.[42]

The spread of Islam appears inseparable from the expansion of the Keira state. The sultans were nominally Muslim from the time of Sulayman (c. 1650–80) if not before; acquisition of the elaborate Muslim genealogies his successors displayed obviously came later. By the end of the first sultanate in 1874, the Fur rulers had adopted, at court, many forms and accouterments of the Muslim state; some of the sultan's titles were worthy of a Mughal emperor. It is ironic, therefore, that, unlike the rulers of other Sudanic polities, the Fur sultans maintained the aura (and many rituals) of African divine kingship alongside profession of

Figure 3. Tombs of the Keira sultans at Tura. (Durham University Library, A4/92.)

Islam and adoption of some of its norms. In any case, the arrival of Islam cannot be dated. It came with trade and for political, social, and no doubt personal reasons; from the north, east, and (notably, perhaps earliest) from the west, with itinerant missionaries or "holy men" (*fuqara*)[43] who accompanied (or were themselves) traders. Historians have pointed out that here, as on other frontiers of Islam, proselytizers adapted to or even professed worldviews anathematized in the centers of Islamic learning. Islam in Darfur, even today, incorporates earlier custom and belief and favors that side of religion – the esoteric, the sufi – that emphasizes a personal bond between the human and divine rather than the Law. In this variant, holy men, through healing or other miracles, have become cult figures whose grace (*baraka*), moreover, is heritable. Scions of such families were among the *fuqara* who migrated to Darfur, and a number of new "holy families" had sprung up by the early eighteenth century at the latest.[44]

It was natural that itinerant holy men would gravitate toward the court of the sultan, who might make use of their services. The *fuqara*, like slaves, came without local clan or territorial connections that complicated a ruler's reliance on others. Sultans therefore favored *fuqara* with grants of land and legal and financial privileges and exemptions. A *faqih* failing to impress, or who for other reasons bypassed the court,

might nonetheless settle somewhere as a local holy man, uniquely qualified by literacy and ascendant or otherwise according to his effectiveness
in fulfilling local needs. Immigrant *fuqara* were desirable as settlers: they
often came with families and even followers and, once granted land,
attracted others. They functioned as Qur'anic teachers and imams; a
few of their students even reached al-Azhar. In spite or perhaps because
of the settlement and local influence of itinerant *fuqara*, even at the
end of the twentieth century some of what might locally be termed
"Muslim" would have been unfamiliar or disdained elsewhere in the
Muslim world.

This was most evident in law.[45] At the local level, customary law
coexisted with the *Shari'a* and was administered by the *shartays*, sometimes in consultation with *fuqara*, sometimes not. Imprisonment was
almost unknown: infractions were punished by fines; the usual punishment for homicide was payment of blood money, but there are examples
of offenders sent to the sultan's court and executed. Fines, paid in kind,
usually in grain or animals or their equivalent in cloth, were an important source of official revenue. In civil matters, reference was perhaps
more commonly made to the *Shari'a*, but custom continued to prevail
in certain areas of the law and no doubt to greater or lesser degrees
depending on time and place. It is important to bear in mind that,
beyond security, ordinary people expected little of what today we call
government: differences within a family were settled at home; within a
tribe or clan by its *shaykh* and elders; between tribes often by negotiation; in extreme circumstances, miscreants and nonconformists, then
as now, made off.

The sultan, sitting in judgment, was the final court of appeal.
Although surviving documents tell us that he buttressed his rulings
with the sanction of his *ulama*, his authority was no more restrained
by them than was that of any other Muslim king: notwithstanding a
common impression today of imperious "Muslim clerics," the *ulama*
are famously docile in the face of strong civil authority. During the first
sultanate, there was apparently no hierarchy of *qadis* (judges), despite
titles (*qadi al-qudat, shaykh al-Islam*) that seem to indicate one; at
the local level, *fuqara* might assume the judge's role, and *qadis* were
appointed to the staffs of great provincial officials and the royal court.
Evidence points to experts in the *Shari'a*, whatever their honorifics,
wholly in the service of "secular" state authority, not in opposition to

it. It is, however, reasonable to speculate that deference to the *Shariʿa* might have waxed and waned, depending on the character, views, and circumstances of each sultan; several were noted for their piety: Abd al-Rahman (d. 1803) was himself a *faqih* before ascending the throne, and Muhammad al-Husayn (ruled 1838–73) was initiated into the Tijaniyya order of sufis. Similarly, at the local level, a *faqih*'s functioning as a judge might depend on his own prestige, his *shartay*'s predilections, and relations between the two.[46]

EXTERNAL THREATS AND INTERNAL WEAKNESS

Any description of the Fur sultanate in the nineteenth century runs the risk of misrepresenting its strength, wealth, administrative sophistication, and, indeed, the nature of its cultural complexity. Terminological precision can mislead: the Fur ruler inherited the same title as the Ottoman – "sultan" – and addressed others accordingly;[47] in his own milieu, he was indeed a formidable figure, but the military strength of the sultanate was insignificant compared with that of even contemporary North African states, and its greatest weapon was geographic isolation. The sultan's court, likewise, with all its panoply, was no Topkapi: although an offhand description of Sultan Muhammad Tayrab as "reigning . . . in barbaric splendor" seems doubly wrong, the outermost enclosure of the sultan's compound was a *zariba* (Ar. corral, stockade) of straw, brush, or (finally) brick and his residence a series of hutments,[48] the "palace" at El Fasher of Ali Dinar, the last sultan, as indeed the ruins of Muhammad Tayrab's palace at Shoba, impressed foreigners who may have expected less. And although taxation and the slave trade provided the sultan and elites with imported luxury goods and relative comfort, this was probably inferior to that of provincial centers in Egypt. The rich array of noble titles the sources report may conjure images from elsewhere in the Muslim world that bear no resemblance to reality in Darfur, just as may the obligations of and deference due the titleholders. Finally, standards at court tell us little about the everyday life of commoners even in the towns and the central lands of the sultanate; what today's international media depict as penury is in some cases merely normal.

The weakness of the Keira state in military terms was revealed in several ways during the nineteenth century: the loss of Kordofan in

1821, the threat from the south beginning in the 1840s, and finally the destruction of the sultanate in 1874.

Darfur's contacts with Egypt were mainly commercial before the nineteenth century, but in the late Mamluk period there were hints of Egyptian interest in cutting out some middlemen; long-distance trade stimulated both Darfur's receptiveness to external influences and Egypt's interest in Darfur.[49] With the consolidation in power of Muhammad Ali Pasha as the Ottoman ruler of Egypt, that interest increased. Muhammad Ali's political ambitions in the eastern Mediterranean required an army and, like his predecessors, he was loath to recruit from the Egyptian peasantry. The Sudan's reported riches in gold, ivory, and especially manpower proved irresistible, and the weakness of the Funj sultanate in the Nilotic northeast promised quick victory. In 1820, a two-pronged invasion was launched, with Sinnar, the Funj capital, as one objective and Darfur the second; the Pasha may have been egged on by Muhammad Abu Madyan, a Fur prince in Cairo whose claims had been thwarted by the accession of Sultan Muhammad al-Fadl. In any case, along the Nile, the invaders encountered little difficulty at first, and Sinnar, by then a grossly disappointing village, was "entered" in June 1821.

Under Muhammad Bey Khusraw, a son-in-law of Muhammad Ali, the Darfur invasion force, some 3,000 men with 13 artillery pieces, thereupon set out, from al-Dabba on the Nile in July 1821. Although he received warning of an Egyptian advance, the Maqdum Musallim, a slave eunuch governing Kordofan on behalf of the sultan, adopted a defensive posture and awaited the invaders. In the sole battle of the campaign, before Bara on 19 August, the superior arms of the Egyptians won a crushing victory. Meanwhile, however, a revolt along the Nile persuaded Muhammad Ali to defer the conquest of Darfur. Despite the Ottoman sultan's presumptuous award of Darfur to Muhammad Ali in 1841 and preparations for another campaign, the offensive never resumed.[50] For his part, the Fur sultan, Muhammad al-Fadl, after apparently sending a relief expedition that "disintegrated" en route,[51] pursued an isolationist policy. But the damage was done: the sultanate lost not only the rich province of Kordofan but also control of the trade routes that traversed it; events in the southern borderlands were soon to give evidence of the threat Egypt posed from another direction.

Having harvested the ripe fruit of the northern Sudan, the Egyptians bowed to the logic of their position and pushed southward up the Nile. The unexpected poverty of the Funj only increased the importance of extracting slaves from the Upper Nile. Exploration southward and southwestward therefore began immediately, along the White Nile and its western tributaries. This phenomenon, far more important and complex than mere travel – the Egyptian object was not the Mountains of the Moon, King Solomon's Mines, or the source of the Nile – involved Turco-Egyptians, northern Sudanese of the so-called diaspora, and European adventurers of various stripes; the slave trade, whether sanctioned by Islam or condemned by liberals, was a dirty business. To an extent imperfectly realized, the opening of regions where now the southern Sudan, northeastern Congo (Kinshasa), and the Central African Republic meet was the work also, perhaps mainly, of the Baqqara tribes of southern Darfur, whose slave raiding supplied their own domestic needs and fed external markets. It was in response to those activities in the region, increasingly facilitated with firearms obtained from the Nile valley, that the sultanate was forced to embark on a series of costly military campaigns beginning in the 1840s. Thus, the advent of Egypt in the Sudan was destructive for the Keira sultanate in two ways and in two regions: by costing it Kordofan and by imperiling its slave trade.

The sultans had never been able to control the Baqqara. The southern borderlands were a frontier zone of migration, acculturation, and accommodation, through which both sides, the sultanate and the Baqqara, ultimately profited at the expense of a third party, the people they raided for slaves or the slaves who were passed along northward through middlemen. By the 1860s, the Baqqara had slave soldiers of their own, with modern arms. Thus, while traders infiltrated the region of the Bahr al-Ghazal and began to pass slaves along the return route to the Nile, the importance of modern arms to the sultanate itself increased. These were obtained mainly through illicit trade in the south or with the Nile valley (in contravention of a ban imposed by the Egyptians) and from deserters, who also provided instructors in the use of firearms.[52] Unfortunately for the sultan, however, firearms could not cancel the nomadic Baqqara advantage of fighting in – and the ability to withdraw from – their homeland when attacked.

Figure 4. Al-Zubayr Pasha Rahma Mansur in old age (c. 1903–13). Al-Zubayr, a Northern Sudanese trader and slaver, carved out an empire in the Upper Nile and Bahr al-Ghazal in the 1860s and conquered Darfur in 1874. (Durham University Library, 1/22/71.)

The third and final military threat to the sultanate sprang from its failure to overcome the first two. By the 1860s, the slave trade had changed in several ways. Access from the Nile valley to "Dar Fartit," a term that for practical purposes had come to mean "the land of those legally enslaved," had shifted some of the trade eastward, beyond Darfur's control. In the Bahr al-Ghazal, foreigners had become merchant princes, with networks of trading stations and slave armies. At the same time, European interest in the Upper Nile had grown apace for a number of reasons: imperial rivalries in what would be called the Scramble for Africa were brewing; explorers, whose exploits provided headlines at home, vied to discover the source of the Nile; humanitarians exerted increasing pressure on European governments to act against the slave trade that the explorers so vividly reported. Pressure to curtail the slave trade therefore fell on Khedive Isma'il of Egypt, Muhammad Ali's grandson, providing a good excuse for European interference; Egypt itself, even before the Suez Canal opened in 1869, was where Europe and its Asian empires met, and one of the most glittering prizes of European imperialist competition. All of these developments had ramifications for Darfur.

THE FALL OF THE FIRST SULTANATE

The most famous and successful of the merchant princes in the Bahr al-Ghazal was al-Zubayr Rahma Mansur, a Sudanese Arab of the Ja'ali tribe who, by the mid-1860s, was so powerful that he could forestall the Darfur sultanate's raiding and trading. Al-Zubayr is the villain in many accounts by European travelers and administrators employed by Egypt to satisfy the antislavery movement.[53] When al-Zubayr became a focus of attempts to control the slave trade in the Nile valley, he arranged with the Baqqara tribes of southern Darfur for his slave caravans to pass through their territory northward, bypassing the Nile. By 1873, provoked by the double-dealing of some Baqqara, who at the sultan's behest had attacked his caravans, al-Zubayr was strong enough to move against the sultanate itself,[54] a decision made easier by a succession crisis at El Fasher.

On his deathbed in early 1873, Sultan Muhammad al-Husayn, who had acceded to the throne in 1838, failed as some of his forebears had to win acceptance for a nominee, and only after much intrigue did his

son, Ibrahim Qarad, succeed in April. Following impertinent ultima-
tums, al-Zubayr invaded. In early 1874, the sultan sent Ahmad Shatta
and Sa'd al-Nur against him with an army, which he defeated near
Shakka. Having called up reinforcements from his slave stations in
the south, al-Zubayr then marched on Dara with 7,000 men. Alarmed
by the prospect of a Sudanese parvenu in control of Darfur, Khedive
Isma'il of Egypt declared war on Sultan Ibrahim Qarad and ordered
the governor-general of the Sudan, Isma'il Ayub, to invade the sultanate from Kordofan. Meanwhile, Sultan Ibrahim tried and failed to
relieve Dara and retreated toward El Fasher, but al-Zubayr caught
up with him at Manawashi, where Ibrahim, heroically charging on
horseback with his few remaining retainers, was defeated and killed
on 23 October. Al-Zubayr thereupon marched into El Fasher. The
Egyptian army arrived from Kordofan after the fighting was over and
played no role in the campaign,[55] but Isma'il Ayub began to establish
an Egyptian administration. To protest this abrogation of his rights,
al-Zubayr went to Cairo in 1875. The Khedive kept him there.

THE ENDS OF THE
TURKISH WORLD

EGYPTIAN RULE IN THE SUDAN

A Government of Exiles

Al-Zubayr's conquest of Darfur, and its subsequent annexation by Egypt, might at first glance appear to have continued, or even completed, a long process by which the sultanate came into the orbit of the Nile valley as part of Egypt's expanding African empire. There are, however, many ways to interpret the events of 1874. Sudanese refer to the period of Egyptian rule, from the conquest of 1821 until the fall of Khartoum to the Mahdi in 1885, as the *Turkiyya*. While this reflects a view of foreigners as "Turks," it also denotes the facts that Egypt was a province of the Ottoman Empire and Egypt's governing class, although ethnically diverse, was culturally Ottoman Turkish. Muhammad Ali himself was of Albanian origin, and the language of his family remained, until the time of King Farouk in the mid-twentieth century, Turkish. The records of the regime in the Sudan were kept in Turkish, and although the use of Arabic gradually increased throughout the period, there was little sense that the regime was "Egyptian." Historians disagree over terminology; we refer herein to the Egyptian (rather than to the Ottoman or Turco-Egyptian) regime in the Sudan as a matter of convenience.[1]

To the outside world, extension to Darfur of Egypt's empire may have seemed another chapter in a half-century march into *bilad al-Sudan* that had begun with Muhammad Ali's invasion of Sinnar and Kordofan in 1821. The intervening decades had witnessed almost continuous expansion to the east, south, and southwest, so that by 1874 Egyptian claims (if not meaningful rule) reached almost to the equator and from the Red Sea littoral and Ethiopian highlands to Wadai in what is today Chad. Although commerce with Egypt had been a major factor in the history of Darfur in the period 1821–74, the sultanate had, as we have seen, been slow to respond to the political challenge posed by Egypt and by the traders, slavers, and indeed technology associated with Egyptian expansion.

Following the conquest of 1821, Muhammad Ali had immediately set about extracting the wealth that had attracted him – notably, gold and slaves. Unwilling to await results of raiding southward, the new regime levied on the riverain Sudanese taxes so high as to be payable only in the slaves and animals on which the local economy depended. Disaffection turned to rebellion when Isma'il Pasha, the Egyptian commander, and his retinue were murdered – burned alive – at Shendi in the autumn of 1822. Much of the region from Berber southward rose in a revolt that remained uncoordinated; the Defterdar Ibrahim, commanding forces inferior in number to the locals but better equipped and more experienced in war, was able to suppress the revolt in stages, with great brutality and loss of life. The country of the Ja'aliyyin was devastated and their lands given over to colonization by the Shayqiyya tribe, whose cavalry, after initial resistance in 1820, had become an irregular arm of the regime. Many towns were destroyed and depopulated. By the time order was restored in 1824–5, epidemic, drought, and famine stalked the land.[2]

In the wake of these disasters, the Egyptians wisely adopted a policy of conciliation and acted quickly to establish rudimentary administration. Success was in large part owed to Mahu Bey, commander-in-chief until June 1826, and his successor, Ali Khurshid Agha (as governor of Sinnar and, from 1834, of Dongola, Berber, and Kordofan). Soliciting and following the advice of local chiefs, notably *Shaykh* Abd al-Qadir wad al-Zayn, Khurshid gave amnesty to Ja'ali, Araki, and other refugees and gave tax exemptions to their chiefs and religious leaders, enticing them to resettle abandoned lands. Resisting calls from Cairo for more revenue, Khurshid encouraged commerce and cleared the trade routes. The strategic importance of the confluence of the Blue and White Niles – a place called al-Khartum, "the elephant's trunk" – was recognized, and it soon became, at first unofficially, the capital of the Egyptian Sudan. Khurshid's efforts to extend the empire's borders met with less success:

on the White Nile, despite raids as far as the mouth of the Sobat River, the Egyptians were beaten back by local Shilluk and Dinka, and in the east, attempts to subdue the wild borderlands with Ethiopia failed badly.

It was under Mahu Bey and, especially, Ali Khurshid that foundations of Egyptian administration evolved from the purely military rule established at the time of the conquest. Provincial divisions followed upon those of military districts, each under an officer (*ma'mur*). In 1835, Ali Khurshid was named governor-general (*hukumdar*) of the Sudan, and the *ma'murs* were raised to the same title as provincial governors in Egypt proper, *mudir*. The number of provinces, their borders, their arrangement into groups, and their responsibility to report to Khartoum or directly to Cairo varied over time. (All high officials in the early administration were Turco-Egyptian officers: the first Sudanese were appointed to provincial governorships only in the 1860s, although a gradual increase of the number of Sudanese in lower posts has been discerned throughout the period; a black soldier reached the rank of brigadier general [*mir liwa*] in 1867.)[3] The provinces were divided into districts, and settled areas were subdivided further. After the revolt of the early 1820s, Sudanese notables were taken into the system; *shaykhs* and elders intermediated with district officials, thus in theory saving money and making administration more responsive. But the implication of bureaucratic control is misleading. The functions of early-nineteenth-century government – and not only in *bilad al-Sudan* – were limited, and even a reasonable degree of security, law, and order in exchange for a reasonable level of taxation was an ideal seldom realized; "social services" belonged to the future. Such medical and educational establishments as existed were for officers, officials, and their families.

Egyptian innovations nonetheless had wide social and economic effects. Currency was introduced. Taxes were payable in cash, although in remoter areas, barter and payment in kind remained the norm. Herds, crops, and land were taxed, as were waterwheels along the Nile. New towns sprang up. The Egyptians imposed civil and military legal codes and established a hierarchy of *shari'a* courts. They built mosques. Craftsmen from Egypt were attached to provincial governments to set up shop. Harvesting of gum, ivory, and ostrich feathers was encouraged, and goods were marketed through government agencies (and taxed: customs duties were collected on exports as well as imports);

government monopolies were abolished only in the 1840s. New crops were introduced, including sugar cane, citrus fruits, and opium poppies. The sugar and fruit did well, the poppies did not; domestication of wild indigo failed, at great cost financially and in forced labor. With improved conditions, trade with Egypt greatly increased, as did trade within the Sudan: petty merchants dispersed throughout the country, caravan routes were secured, and wells were improved. Slaves were always in demand; Egypt's market for animals (especially camels), skins, and hides was insatiable; and even the export of wild animals – elephant, hippopotamus, rhinoceros, and colorful birds – was not overlooked by a government always in need of money.[4] Failure to find important quantities of gold in the Sudan was a bitter disappointment.[5]

The term of Ahmad Pasha Shamli (called "Abu Adhan," or "Big Ears"),[6] who succeeded Ali Khurshid as governor-general in 1838–39, was eventful in several spheres. Although generally following the policy of his predecessors, he instituted financial reforms to combat corruption and increase agricultural production. Landowners were ordered to cultivate or risk confiscation and distribution of their land to settlers willing to farm it; he granted tax exemptions for bringing fallow land into cultivation. Other exactions led to local revolt; the availability of the Ethiopian marchlands as a ready refuge for tax-dodgers led Abu Adhan to undertake a series of campaigns in the east. Although he failed to reduce the Hadanduwa tribe to tributary status, establishment of Egyptian control at the village of al-Khatmiyya (later called Kassala) laid foundations for domination of the whole Red Sea coast, with its Ottoman ports of Suakin and Massawa. The Hadanduwa would be dealt with later, by Abu Adhan's successor, Ahmad Pasha Manikli, whose campaign against them earned him the local honorific of al-Jazzar, "the Butcher."

At least equally important as eastward extension of Egyptian authority was sponsorship of explorations to the south, up the Nile. Earlier attempts had failed, beaten back by the fierce resistance of the Shilluk and Dinka. In 1839–40, however, the first of three expeditions under a Turkish naval officer, Salim Qabudan ("Captain Salim"), reached a point on the White Nile at about 7 degrees north latitude. A second expedition, in 1840–41, sailed 100 miles up the Sobat, then up the White Nile as far as Gondokoro, near today's Juba. Salim's final expedition, in 1842, like the second, ended at the Nile rapids at Rejaf.[7] The opening of the Upper Nile and its tributaries would take time and, indeed, in some respects (notably establishment of administration by successive Khartoum regimes) it was hardly completed a century later. Outside interest in these vast regions was purely exploitative, with the notable exceptions of some European missionaries and explorers: commerce in ivory and slaves, almost the only reason for Egyptian interest, did not require – and, indeed, might even make redundant – settled administration.

In any case, the period between Ahmad Abu Adhan's death at Khartoum in 1843 and the accession of Isma'il Pasha as ruler of Egypt in 1863 was one of administrative fits and starts.[8] Abu Adhan's success gave rise to speculation that Muhammad Ali himself, fearing revolt, had had his governor poisoned,[9] a theory bolstered by ensuing ambivalence over a suitable administrative structure for the Sudan. Twice the governor-generalship was suppressed and twice reinstituted when intervening direct control from Cairo proved chaotic. Worse, few of the governors sent to Khartoum remained long enough to make an impression: there were eleven in the two decades following Abu Adhan's death. Cairo's interest had waned. The Sudan had not produced the gold that had enticed Muhammad Ali in 1820; attempts to exploit other minerals had failed; and the supply of slaves had always disappointed, nor had they proven wholly suitable as soldiers in Arabia and the Levant. The Sudanese territories by the late 1840s seemed unlikely ever to repay Egyptian investment, let alone enrich their rulers. Under Muhammad Ali's successors, the Sudan became a place of exile for criminals and troublemakers.

Traders and Slavers

The expansion southward and southwestward of Egypt's African empire coincided with increased European interest in the eastern Mediterranean, setting the stage for conflict that would reach a dramatic conclusion with the British occupation of Egypt in 1882.

Abolition of monopolies in the Sudan was compelled by the Europeans in accordance with treaties foisted on the Ottoman Empire, of which Egypt and its empire remained a legal, if tenuous, possession. There followed an influx of European traders to Khartoum and beyond, and in their wake missionaries and adventurers, all of whom enjoyed certain privileges under the Capitulations.[10] European consuls were accredited to Khartoum, explorers passed through, companies established offices to cut out local middlemen. The roles of businessman, diplomat, and slave trader were not discrete; Khartoum in the 1850s was more Dodge City or the Klondike than it was a stage on the route to King Solomon's Mines. The Upper Nile was worse: Catholic missions there all failed, mainly because of the death rate among the missionaries.[11]

Ivory was very valuable, and although European traders in Khartoum could never get enough of it, they failed to establish lasting relations with the Bari and other tribes of the equatorial Nile who supplied it.[12] Trade gave way to raids. Permanent stations were established, and slaves were taken as porters, concubines, and even as a medium of exchange and were made soldiers to protect the traders, guard the depots, and enforce demands. Tribes were enlisted against each other. The Europeans' heyday was brief: the lion's share of profits from ivory and slaves accrued to those who financed expeditions and to well-connected middlemen who marketed them. By the end of the 1850s, most of the Europeans were gone, discouraged by poor returns and official interference or dead from local diseases. And although as late as the mid-1860s Europeans were caught red-handed hauling slave cargoes down the Nile, most of the trade had been taken up by their agents, partners, or others and had shifted to the land route farther west.[13]

It was at this point that the river route westward from the Nile, up the Bahr al-Ghazal, was discovered, allowing expansion of the ivory trade into the far interior and thus into the slave-raiding lands of the Darfur sultanate. Just as the Europeans had in Equatoria, so in the basin of the Bahr al-Ghazal the traders, mostly Egyptians and northern Sudanese, came to rely on slaves as laborers and soldiers. Al-Zubayr was the most successful of these traders, establishing what amounted to an empire of his own based largely on trade that bypassed Darfur through Kordofan. In this, he and his ilk directly challenged the Darfur sultanate's supply of slaves both for its own military and civilian purposes and for its trade with Egypt. This economic challenge soon brought in its wake a political one, which destroyed the sultanate.

The success of the slave-raiding enterprise had attracted the attention of European humanitarians and missionaries (and, through them, their governments). This shocked Muhammad Sa'id, the Egyptian viceroy (1854–63), into action. On his orders, the public slave market at Khartoum was shut down, and importation of slaves from the Sudan into Egypt was banned. But the trade continued, not least because of continuing demand in the northern Sudan and Arabia as well as in Egypt. Muhammad Saʿid therefore extended his attempts at suppression to the source of supply, the southern Sudan: posts were established and boats heading north made subject to search and seizure. But caravan routes through Kordofan circumvented the Nile, and the government's scarce resources combined with official halfheartedness to effect little (if any) diminution of the trade.

The Sudanese slave trade – and policies pursued to suppress it – may indeed be seen as a preeminent theme in the reign of Muhammad Saʿid's successor, Khedive Ismaʿil. Famous outside Egypt for his affinity with European culture and for the glittering episodes that punctuated his reign, Ismaʿil set the stage for the twin disasters of European occupation of Egypt and Egypt's loss of its African empire. The failure of his predecessor's efforts showed that suppression of the slave trade would depend on extension of Egyptian political control. From the beginning of his reign, therefore, Ismaʿil took steps to reform and extend administration and to combat the slavers, including a tripling of the head tax on merchants' personnel heading up the Nile. A force of river police was established to intercept smugglers. After some initial success, this policy failed because of the slavers' countermeasures, including bribery, evasive tactics, and loopholes in the law.[14] The very expense of the feckless Egyptian government in the Sudan, with its large standing army and inefficient taxation, budget deficits, and arrears in pay, encouraged officials to turn a blind eye to slaving, which enriched all involved in it. Why else were they there? Mere accretion of new territory would do little to eradicate the slave trade if officials appointed to the task profited from it themselves.

It was for this reason that Ismaʿil decided to recruit foreigners and make them responsible directly to him. Europeans and Americans – as well as Armenians, Syrians, and others – had already been employed in many capacities in Egypt; the end of the American Civil War saw an influx of both Union and Confederate officers, appointed to the Egyptian army and other services.[15] The first of the European cadre was Samuel Baker, who in 1869 was appointed to annex the lands of the upper Nile basin, suppress the slave trade, and establish a chain of posts. But despite Ismaʿil's munificent support, Baker's task was nigh impossible in the face of almost universal local opposition; it was not only traders and officials who profited from a trade that was sanctioned by Islam, was a basic factor in the northern Sudanese agricultural economy, and indeed had become important to local economies in Equatoria. Baker was thus able to barge in, through force of arms, and establish posts, but the trade continued, not least because the Nile route northward was increasingly circumvented by traders in the Bahr al-Ghazal, who sent their caravans along the inland route through Kordofan.

Isma'il's attempt to establish administrative control in the vast territory of the Bahr al-Ghazal ended in ignominious failure when in 1872 his ambitious governor there, Muhammad al-Hilali, a trader himself, was defeated in battle by al-Zubayr, then killed by al-Zubayr's famous lieutenant, Rabih Fadl Allah. Isma'il thereupon regularized al-Zubayr's position by constituting the Bahr al-Ghazal as a province and appointing him its governor in 1873. That this put the fox in charge of the chickens was obvious, but other analogies suggest themselves, not least in reminding us that a nominal subordinate was preferable to a rampaging rebel in a region obviously beyond Egypt's direct control. It is in this context that we should view al-Zubayr's conquest of Darfur in 1874.

Gordon Pasha

At this point, the history of the Sudan intersects the career of General Charles Gordon. Famous for his exploits in China, Gordon was appointed in 1874 as governor of Equatoria to succeed Baker, whose policy he continued by strengthening the Egyptian posts along the Nile and establishing a provincial capital at Lado. After resigning in 1876, he was appointed in the following year as *hukumdar* – governor-general of the Sudan – thus placing in control of the entire administration a European Christian who had already exhibited the idiosyncrasy that would make him world famous a decade later.

In Gordon's appointment in 1877 there is a hint of Isma'il's desperation. Egypt's empire had expanded enormously during his reign but at great cost and with little to show beyond imperial pretensions: unnecessary military campaigns against Ethiopia had failed disastrously, the Bahr al-Ghazal was in chaos, and Darfur, as we shall see, was already in revolt. Moreover, Isma'il was increasingly beset by the growing crisis of his finances and the partly consequent interference of the European powers, whose interest in Egypt had only grown since the opening of the Suez Canal in 1869. Thus, as Gordon achieved some impressive initial successes in the Sudan, the essential support of the Khedive rapidly ebbed. In 1879, at the behest of the European powers, the Ottoman sultan deposed Isma'il in favor of his son, Muhammad Tawfiq, who from the start was a puppet of the Europeans. Gordon resigned in 1880 and was succeeded as *hukumdar* by Muhammad Ra'uf Pasha, who would reap the whirlwind of the Mahdist Revolution.[16]

EGYPT IN DARFUR

Conquered but Ungoverned

In light of these developments, it is easy to understand why al-Zubayr's conquest of Darfur did not lead to rapid establishment of Egyptian administration. Having killed Sultan Ibrahim and his chiefs on the battlefield of Manawashi on 24 October 1874, al-Zubayr, ignoring orders from the governor-general of the Sudan, Isma'il Ayub, marched on El Fasher and took the town. Five days later, Isma'il Ayub arrived with an army that had contributed nothing to the victory. The two fell out immediately. Isma'il Ayub proposed dividing Darfur into four parts; the southern territory roughly corresponding to the Maqdumate of the South, with its ungovernable Rizayqat, would be annexed to the Bahr al-Ghazal province under al-Zubayr. But al-Zubayr had not conquered Darfur for Isma'il Ayub or, indeed, for the Khedive except in a formal sense: he wanted to rule it himself. It was under these circumstances that al-Zubayr went to Cairo in June 1875 to present his claims and was detained there.

It was during the last stage of Egypt's imperial expansion then, and as the crisis of its own independence approached, that administration of Darfur was undertaken. In the historical memory of Darfur's people, initial resistance to the Egyptians never really ceased. This is the era of the "Shadow Sultans" who, from the ancestral redoubt of Jabal Marra, maintained a kernel of independence and held out the promise of revival.[17] The territory over which the pretenders exerted authority – as opposed to the extent of their raiding – was always small; the history of Darfur during 1874–81 is not that of the Keira royal family.

Historical sources for their exploits, and for the period in general, are poor. Local documents are few. Accounts by foreigners, notably Europeans appointed to the Egyptian government, are less perspicacious than those of earlier travelers, are more prone to special pleading, and often retail secondhand information of dubious accuracy. Few administrative records have come to light, and more historical sources may have been lost than were created.[18] Official sources have not been fully exploited. Results of a lengthy reconnaissance in 1874–76 by two American officers of the Egyptian general staff have long been reported lost;[19] another American sent to El Fasher in 1876 died there.[20] Poor communication and the unsettled state of Darfur meant that its affairs were not subject to the same level of reporting as those of the riverain Sudan. European consular records, aside from reporting rumors of disturbance in the far west, concern mostly the central government in Khartoum and its effects on trade. Na'um Shuqayr's monumental account combines redactions from official and private papers, details of which, however, vary from those of versions found elsewhere. Diaries, letters, and memoirs of European officials offer insights and anecdotes; diary entries and letters home of General Gordon remain the most important source for some events of the period. Little in the secondary sources focuses specifically on Darfur.

Keira resistance to Egyptian occupation was not passive. Upon the death of Sultan Ibrahim at Manawashi in October 1874, members of the royal family fled to Jabal Marra. Al-Zubayr went after them and succeeded in winning the submission of Hasab Allah, an uncle and nominal successor of Sultan Ibrahim, and of Ibrahim's brother, Abd al-Rahman Shattut, both of whom were sent off to Cairo. Bosh Muhammad al-Fadl, another son of Muhammad al-Fadl (ruled 1803–38) and uncle of Ibrahim, succeeded to the royal title. Betrayed to al-Zubayr, he and his brother Sayf al-Din fled to Kabkabiyya where, in a last stand in 1875, they were killed. Bosh's son, Muhammad Harun al-Rashid, then became the nominal sultan.[21] The legitimacy of successive soi-disant sultans must have been based on consensus and the relative strength of character of various potential claimants. But the prestige that accrued within the Fur homeland from such recognition was cruelly outweighed by lost glories, and the neighborhood teemed with unsettled scores.

Meanwhile, Isma'il Ayub's plan for Egyptian administration of Darfur was adopted. The territory was divided into four provinces, each under a governor responsible to a general-governor (*mudir amm*, as distinct from the title of the governor-general – *hukumdar* – of the Sudan) at El Fasher. The western province, including Dar Masalit, Dar

Sila, and Dar Tama, was centered on Kabkabiyya and later Kul Kul; the headquarters of the southern province was at Dara; and the eastern province had its administrative center at Fogia; the district of El Fasher itself comprised a province or, at any rate, a *mudiriyya*. The provinces were subdivided into *qisms* that took account of tribal boundaries. The southern district, for example, comprised five *qisms*, centered on al-Tuwaysha, Kirshu, Giga, Sirga, and Aribu.[22]

Because the Turkiyya in Darfur lasted less than a decade and was marked throughout by great unrest, enormous local variation, and rapid succession of officials, it may be considered an interregnum. Although the royal court ceased to exist in all but name, and titles and privileges of the old order were abolished or ignored, the Egyptian regime failed to establish itself before it too was overthrown. The limited scope of intended change may be inferred from the practice of government in the eastern Sudan. Its goals were security, resuscitation of commerce, collection of taxes, and suppression of the slave trade. The nascent administration therefore confirmed or acquiesced in the continuation in office of those tribal *shaykhs* and village elders who made their submission and was content to rule through them. But the new government was as often a pawn in intertribal feuds as it was an arbiter of them. Attempts to extend to Darfur even those meager services it provided in the older provinces were hampered by insecurity.[23] The degree to which the new regime, once established, would have proven more or less beneficent than its predecessor cannot be known, but the Egyptians came to rule, not to revolutionize.

Commercial records have hardly been exploited, but certainly trade resumed during the Turkiyya. Some important changes occurred. Throughout the nineteenth century, and especially after the Egyptian conquests of the 1820s, there was steadily increasing participation of riverain *jallaba* in the local – as well as long-distance – trade of Darfur. The meaning of the word itself evolved: whereas previously *jallaba* were Sudanese engaged in the caravan trade with Egypt, in the nineteenth century, with increasing migration from the northern riverain Sudan of Ja'aliyyin, Danagla, and other sedentary tribesmen, the term came to include everyone from long-distance (and large-scale) merchants to resident peddlers, and in modern usage it still includes an implication of foreignness.[24] The diaspora, too, under way for centuries owing to population pressure on irrigable land along the Nile, accelerated because of related Egyptian demands for increased agricultural production and taxes and also because of opportunities afforded by Egyptian rule. Small traders dispersed southward and westward from their homeland, taking advantage of established networks and creating new ones through family and tribal connections. By the 1860s, *jallaba* dominated the trade of the southern and western Sudan, were resident in all the large towns (and in many small ones), and engaged in commerce of all types, including the slave trade. In this context, big traders in ivory and slaves, such as al-Zubayr, were *jallaba* writ large, although merchant princes no more considered themselves *jallaba* than would a modern commercial magnate see himself as a rag-and-bone man. They were, in other words, a class – viewed locally as a foreign class – of merchants who had spread the interests of their tribal homelands into all corners of the Sudan.[25]

The importance of *jallaba* in the commercial life of Darfur increased after al-Zubayr's conquest in 1874. The Egyptian regime's complicated relations with them, however exceptional, illustrate the point. One prominent merchant, Ilyas Umm Birayr, was actually appointed governor of Shakka early in the Egyptian occupation and was later made governor of all Kordofan. For all his rage against slave traders, Gordon himself repeatedly appointed merchants to positions of authority, including even the despised Sulayman al-Zubayr. In this was an element of desperation, but it is important not to confuse substantial businessmen with itinerant peddlers: although their interests may often have coincided, the very prominence of the great merchants, and their deep knowledge of affairs, lent them a claim to authority that Egyptian (and European) officials lacked. In any case, in 1879, in his last attempt to disrupt the slave trade, Gordon ordered the *jallaba*, who supplied the slavers with guns and ammunition, to clear out of southern Darfur. When they failed to do so, he let the local Baqqara tribes loose on them: wherever they were found, the *jallaba* were sent off penniless and even naked, while the Arabs divided their possessions and trade goods, including slaves. Although this gave Gordon grim satisfaction, any effect on the slave trade was ephemeral, not least because the anger of the *jallaba* would factor into the overthrow of the Egyptian regime a few years later.[26]

The collapse of government authority in Darfur during the early 1880s and the propaganda employed later to justify the Anglo-Egyptian conquest of the Sudan in 1896–98 have led to a general assumption that Egyptian rule in Darfur must have been oppressive, at least in comparison with the rule of the sultans before it. Yet, general disorder rather than onerous exaction is the overarching theme of the period. And although some far-flung or relatively strong groups managed to avoid subordination – meaning taxation – altogether, how much more would those have been willing to pay who were reduced to penury by the rapine of successive royal pretenders, greedy or incompetent officials, and marauding tribesmen? Meager evidence supports a view of confiscatory taxation only in episodic circumstances, not as policy. In western Darfur, for example, the total poll tax was based on local rulers' own estimates of their population: how accurate those estimates, and to whose benefit inaccuracy accrued, the people's or the *shaykhs'*, we cannot now know.[27] In southern Darfur, Gordon encountered in 1879 a "self-constituted Collector of Taxes of the Egyptian Government,"[28] and it is unlikely this gentleman was unique. Unlucky indeed were those through whose villages and lands passed a rebellious tribal leader, angry slave trader, or government posse. In mid-1879, Gordon calculated that since 1875 some 16,000 Egyptians and 50,000 natives had died during the violence in Darfur.[29] Even granting the license due an emotional writer, insecurity rather than overtaxation was clearly the hallmark of the era.

The remit of the new government from the beginning was therefore to pacify. The first general-governor was Hasan Pasha Hilmi al-Juwaysar, a Circassian soldier of long experience in the Sudan, who had been governor of Kordofan before the conquest of Darfur and had accompanied Isma'il Ayub to El Fasher. Then personally commanding one of two columns sent against Muhammad Harun in Jabal Si, Hasan Pasha lost two-thirds of his force of 1,300 and had to retire; he went to Egypt on sick leave in 1877 and did not return. (The other column, of 800 men, led by Zakariyya Bey, was annihilated.) Attached to Hasan Pasha's command, Gordon's former private secretary, Tuhami Jalal al-Din Bey, had better luck, defeating a rebel force under the former *maqdum* Sa'd Argun at the Hayyaya wells north of El Fasher. Whether inspired by Muhammad Harun's success or spontaneously, risings occurred in the major towns, including Dara, Kabkabiyya, and Kul Kul. In El Fasher itself, forces loyal to the sultan twice attacked the Egyptian fortress and were driven off only with difficulty. A relief expedition had to be sent from Khartoum under Abd al-Razzaq Haqqi Pasha, who had been acting governor-general of the Sudan during the absence in Cairo of Isma'il Ayub. Appointed as acting general-governor of Darfur, pending the arrival of Hasan Pasha's successor, Abd al-Razzaq advanced through Kordofan, gathering forces en route, and at Burush on the road between Umm Shanqa and El Fasher inflicted a heavy defeat on the rebels. He went on to relieve the garrison of El Fasher and set about suppressing the rebellion, while Muhammad Harun again withdrew to Jabal Marra.[30]

If the Egyptians could not hold the towns, what chance had they in the hinterlands? The historian of Dar Masalit writes of the Bani Husayn and others "being a tribe again," of each tribe negotiating its own modus vivendi with both neighbors and the government. Uncertain of the outcome between the old regime and the Egyptians, local people were harassed by both, plundered or "taxed," their agriculture despoiled, and their commerce disrupted. Soon after the fall of the sultanate, a small Egyptian force sent to reconnoiter in the far west appears, from the little known of it, to have shown the flag and taken what it could in "taxes" but did not establish a permanent presence: it marched on Umm Dukhn and Tumayd and made a camp at Kereinik, then moved on through Mogurnei and Shabaki and along the Wadi Kajja to Dar Erenga and then away again. Two years later, after the governorate of western Darfur had been set up, with headquarters first at Kabkabiyya and later at Kul Kul, a post was finally founded at Mogurnei, and a year later still, another at Abu Qurayn near the Masalit border with Dar Tama, each with a small military force. It was under these circumstances that the sultan of Dar Qimr threw in his lot with the Egyptians and that Hajjam Hasab Allah of the Masalit, while doing duty to the new regime, had a free hand in forging his people into a political unit by force of arms. The ruler of Dar Tama, however, whose principality had long been tributary to the sultans of Wadai, openly admitted that he would support whichever side emerged the ultimate winner, the Keira or the Egyptians.[31]

Gordon in Darfur

Owing to Darfur's rebelliousness, in 1877, almost three years after the defeat and death of Sultan Ibrahim, an Egyptian army of some 16,000 men was still stationed there, ineffectively and at great expense. The garrisons were under siege, and the countryside was unsafe for the passage even of large contingents of soldiers. In the chaotic south, moreover, at Shakka, Sulayman, the young son of al-Zubayr left in charge of his father's affairs and in command of his army, was restive. Only two weeks after his installation as governor-general of the Sudan on 5 May 1877, therefore, General Gordon left Khartoum for Darfur. Convinced that the people had risen in revolt because of Egyptian oppression, Gordon determined characteristically to settle affairs himself.[32] Reinforcements had preceded him by three months, and he brought with him another 2,700 men. He intended to relieve al-Tuwaysha, Dara, and Kajmur, then proceed with their garrisons against Sultan Muhammad Harun, whom he hoped to subdue by a show of strength, at the same time removing from those areas the principal cause of local people's disaffection.[33]

"It is indeed a nice imbroglio, this Darfour!" So Gordon wrote on 3 July 1877. He had traveled on camels via El Obeid and on the night before reached al-Tuwaysha, the principal town of eastern Darfur. There he found that the Egyptian garrison, "some 500 armed with flint-lock muskets,... a mere set of brigands," had not been paid for three years; he sent the lot back to El Obeid to be disbanded.[34] He relieved Dara on 12 July, finding a situation he compared to the siege of Lucknow: there had been no news for six months, and food was selling "at famine prices."[35] Allying himself with the powerful local Rizayqat, who had wearied of incessant encounters with the slavers, Gordon put down a continuing threat from the Mima and Khawabir nearby.[36] He then marched on El Fasher and relieved the garrison, forcing Muhammad Harun to pull back again to his base of operations in Jabal Marra. Although Gordon reasoned that as long as the sultan was alive the resistance would continue, a plan to pursue him had to be postponed when word reached El Fasher that Sulayman al-Zubayr was threatening Dara.[37]

Gordon's earlier successes at Dara and El Fasher had illustrated, rather than concealed, the weakness of the overall Egyptian position in Darfur. Gordon himself was well aware of it: he pondered outright evacuation of the former sultanate even as he rushed hither and yon trying to create order. He trusted no one, despised his subordinate administrators, and "hated" the local Arabs; everywhere was corruption, the worst of which was the slave trade.[38] As soon as Gordon had left Dara for El Fasher, Sulayman and his plundering slave army had moved north from Shakka and waited for the right moment to attack. When news of Sulayman's advance reached him, Gordon, in a feat noteworthy even of one whose record-breaking treks were legendary, rushed south and, in an incident much remarked at the time and later, went with only a few guards to Sulayman's camp. In what amounted to a series of bluffs, Gordon ordered Sulayman to return to Shakka, followed him there, and completed the rout by refusing him the titles and honors – and the arrears in pay – that he demanded.[39] Word arrived of renewed "panic" at El Fasher – where the garrison still numbered 5,000 – and Gordon remarked disgustedly that the slave dealers would rescue them.[40] Force of personality, reckless courage, and seeming ubiquity were not a policy, and upon returning to Khartoum, Gordon left behind a province nominally subordinate but largely out of control and seething with disaffection.

In the north, there were three reasons for the Egyptian regime's inability to deal with Sultan Muhammad Harun once and for all. In pitched battles, its superior forces with modern arms won the day, but the Egyptians lacked mobility and were unfamiliar with the countryside, poorly led, and outmatched in guerilla warfare. Second, the nascent administration's attempt to levy taxes approximated mere collection of tribute; owing to the regime's weakness, payment was avoidable: in nomadic areas, the old system of tribal assessments, which *shaykhs* were responsible for collecting, was maintained, but with only the threat of military action to enforce it. Third, Jabal Marra always loomed as a haven for the Fur sultan, where he could at least hold out and inspire revolt.

Even after successive defeats, Muhammad Harun thus ensconced himself in the Tura region, whence he raided and where his independence taunted the heavy-handed Egyptians. Nor were all of Gordon's decisions likely to dishearten the sultan: after abandoning plans to campaign against him, Gordon gave orders for reduction of the army of occupation, as an economy measure.[41] In October 1878, the Sudan's budget for the last financial year showed a deficit of 72,000 pounds, "all through Darfour," as Gordon put it, and an accumulated debt of 327,000 pounds.[42] The regime had clearly failed to establish itself, and Gordon, ever willing to throw over one bright idea for another, brooded over alternatives that included abandonment, indirect rule through a Fur prince, and, although never stated as such, an administration of Europeans.

When a year earlier, in September 1877, Gordon had humiliated Sulayman al-Zubayr and instead appointed Idris Abtar (another slave trader) as governor of the Bahr al-Ghazal, he could hardly have expected that province's affairs, or its relations with Darfur, to be finally settled. The slave trade, which with his own eyes Gordon had seen thriving all around him, resumed with a vengeance; in common cause with the other traders, Sulayman duly revolted, massacred an Egyptian garrison, and drove off the governor. In Khartoum, Gordon persuaded Romolo Gessi, a peripatetic Italian he had known from Equatoria, to undertake an expedition against Sulayman. Marching west from Shambe on the White Nile with 1,400 troops reinforced en route, Gessi, through a strategem, occupied Daym Idris (Ganda) in December 1878, where he was attacked by Sulayman's much larger forces. Twice these were driven off, and while Sulayman awaited reinforcements from (and, apparently, coordinated risings among) the slave traders in southern Darfur, Gordon, informed of the predicament, set out for Shakka, along the way encountering in Kordofan one slave caravan after another, as proof of his failure.

Gordon reached Shakka – "this den of iniquity"[43] – in early April 1879, determined "to make a clear sweep of the slave dealers."[44] So positive were reports from Gessi that Gordon mulled an early departure to the north, to deal once and for all with Sultan Muhammad Harun. Taking a page from the traditional statecraft of the region, wherein dissident uncles and cousins were held in readiness at neighboring courts, as pawns or protagonists in kingmaking, he telegraphed the Khedive to request that a Fur prince, sulking in Cairo, should be dispatched to Darfur at once; the administration was so rotten that the "only hope" was "to restore the old regime as soon as possible."[45] Until that pretender arrived, a regency council of two former officials of the sultanate would hold the fort, and Muhammad Harun would be told to retire quietly or come in and assist Gordon until the new sultan arrived. This scheme, like so many others, came to naught; the Fur prince never left Cairo.[46]

Meanwhile, Gordon swept all before him, intercepting slave caravans, releasing their human cargo – only to see them snatched up by local Arabs – arresting dealers, and confiscating their goods. He captured some of Sulayman's officers and had them executed. From El Fasher, he moved west to rendezvous with 2,000 government troops at

Kul Kul whom he had ordered to El Fasher months earlier but had not heard from since. His own column was raided near Kabkabiyya and attacked in force near Kul Kul, which he found "a prison," whence the garrison had not ventured for two years; the surrounding countryside had been lain waste. Gordon sent some soldiers back to Khartoum, then returned to El Fasher, where messages awaited him: one from the Khedive ordering him to Cairo, the other from Gessi announcing victory over Sulayman al-Zubayr who had, however, escaped. Gordon rendezvoused with Gessi at al-Tuwaysha, plotted strategy for the final destruction of the slavers, then returned to Khartoum, and in July Gessi managed to surround Sulayman's camp at Gara and forced his surrender without a fight. When, it was later said, Sulayman plotted an escape, Gessi had him and his lieutenants executed by firing squad, earning for himself, and for Gordon, the costly and lasting enmity of al-Zubayr.[47] Nor, of course, did the end of Sulayman mean the end of the slave trade or the beginning of peace in southern Darfur.

As we have seen, Gordon was only the most notable European appointed to the Sudan. He had governed Equatoria after Baker and had been succeeded there by the Americans Henry Prout and Alexander Mason, and finally by a German, Eduard Schnitzer (later famous as "Emin Pasha"). As governor-general, he continued the policy in Darfur whereby men of varying quality were promoted to the highest offices for little reason other than their availability and his disgust with Egyptian officers. Thus, in 1879, he made Karl Friedrich Rosset, an obscure trader, part-time consul, and sometime official, the general-governor of Darfur; he died three days after arrival in El Fasher. Rosset's successor there was Giacomo Messedaglia, a Venetian officer of the Egyptian general staff and former governor at Dara; to succeed him at Dara, Gordon appointed Charles Rigolet, a French soldier, who was succeeded, in turn, by Francesco Emiliani dei Danziger, who reportedly knew no Arabic (a deficiency he must have shared with many others). As deputy governor-general of the Sudan, Gordon appointed Carl Giegler, the German in charge of the telegraphs.[48] In the South, Gessi's successor, in 1880, was the Englishman Frank Lupton. There were others.[49] Although the last years of Egyptian rule were notable for incompetence, the serial appointment of Christians and Europeans to positions over Muslims and to suppress the slave trade was at least tactless and perhaps hypocritical. Some were brave and resourceful, but few showed brilliance either militarily or in administration, and European officials continued to hold slaves, to recruit slaves for the army, and even to favor the use of slaves as currency in the payment of taxes.[50]

The most famous of these officials, after Baker and Gordon, was the Austrian Rudolf Slatin, whose rise to prominence was particularly fortuitous. After visiting the Sudan as a teenager in 1874–76, Slatin received in July 1878 a letter from Gordon who, sight unseen but on others' recommendations, invited him to join the government. Slatin accepted but disliked his work as a financial inspector and soon resigned, only to be appointed, at the age of 22, governor of Dara, capital of Southern Darfur and one of the most sensitive positions in the country. He had no relevant experience beyond brief military service in Austria, he could hardly have known Arabic, and, by his own account, he looked like a child.[51] Within weeks he was ordered by Messedaglia, at El Fasher, to take the field against Sultan Muhammad Harun, an effort that ended in fiasco: with about 300 men, Slatin marched via Manawashi to Kobbe, then into the Marra mountains to Muhammad Harun's headquarters at Niurnia, which Slatin occupied unopposed because the sultan and all his people had left. While Slatin waited there, Muhammad Harun turned the tables, attacked Dara itself, and set about raiding at will. Slatin caught up with him and won a victory, but Muhammad Harun escaped on horseback to Dar Qimr, and Slatin, his force depleted and exhausted, retired to Dara. A few days later, in March 1880, al-Nur Bey Muhammad Anqara, a former lieutenant of al-Zubayr and, since 1878, owing to one of Gordon's better appointments, governor of the western province at Kabkabiyya, commanding ex-slave soldiers Gordon had sent there, ambushed the sultan at Abtar in Dar Qimr. Muhammad Harun was shot dead, his force dispersed, and his head sent as a trophy to El Fasher.[52]

Not even this put an end to Darfur's resistance, which as we have seen had never been limited to the royal family. The title of sultan fell to Abdallah Dud Banja, a grandson of Sultan Muhammad al-Fadl and cousin of the late Muhammad Harun, and he continued to hold out in Jabal Marra. The southern borderlands with the Bahr al-Ghazal remained chaotic even after the death of Sulayman al-Zubayr. Slatin, writing[53] a decade and a half after the event, only touches upon the confusion: Sulayman's slave troops at large among the Baqqara tribes, dispossessed *jallaba* clamoring for restitution, recalcitrant tribal *shaykhs* and conniving clerks, the intrigues of jealous officials. Nevertheless

Figure 5. Rudolf Slatin (1857–1932), an Austrian adventurer, was made general-governor of Darfur in the dying days of the Turkiyya and surrendered the province to the forces of the Mahdi in 1884. Shown here in Cairo after his escape from captivity in 1895, he became famous in Europe as Slatin Pasha. (Durham University Library, 453/700/4.)

describing the district as "perfectly tranquil," Slatin went off in January 1881 to Khartoum, leaving Muhammad Khalid Zuqal in charge, with consequences we shall see.[54]

Meanwhile, in the wake of Khedive Isma'il's deposition in 1879, Gordon had finally resigned and left the Sudan and been succeeded by Muhammad Ra'uf Pasha, archly described by one historian as envied "for his skill at baccarat."[55] Within days of Slatin's arrival in Khartoum, Muhammad Ra'uf shuffled Gordon's deck and had Slatin appointed to succeed Messedaglia as general-governor of Darfur; Gordon had made an enemy of Muhammad Ra'uf who, we are told, relied on the advice of Giegler, who hated Italians.[56] At any rate, Slatin, learning, he later wrote without apparent irony, that "matters in Darfur had not been progressing very satisfactorily," set out at once for El Fasher, which he reached on 20 April 1881.[57]

The new *mudir amm* now purported to find the government in El Fasher in shambles, spiced by insubordination and intrigue. Corrupt officials were suing each other. The former governor, Sa'id Juma, against whom there were charges pending, was indispensable, so Slatin reappointed him. The governor of the west, al-Nur Muhammad Anqara, was a "villain": Slatin sent him to El Obeid, where he was dismissed; he would be heard from again. Slatin's own account barely mentions attempts to settle affairs in the capital and, typically, as soon as possible he went off on trek, dispensing justice and receiving local notables as if to the manner born. While so engaged, Slatin received a message to the effect that the forces of Rashid Bey Ayman, governor of Fashoda on the White Nile, had been annihilated at Jabal Qadir in southern Kordofan. The Mahdist Revolution had begun.[58]

4

DARFUR AT THE END
OF TIME

The Mahdiyya, 1885–1898

THE MAHDI OF ISLAM

By the 1880s, Egypt's empire had become an expensive nuisance. Reeling from the pressure of its European creditors, the Khedival government had begun a process of withdrawal from its most distant possessions in Equatoria. Costly wars with Ethiopia had ended in failure. Annexation of Darfur had not halted the slave trade but had added greatly to Egypt's financial burden. Discontent, born of various grievances, simmered in the towns of the Nile valley, while in far-flung outposts, where government failed even to provide security, authority had been openly defied. In the absence of any overarching identity, however, the idea of a general rising of the heterogeneous "Sudanese" would have been fanciful, until 1881, when a leader arose to unite them.

Sunni Islam, like Judaism and Christianity, carries within it a concept of messianic deliverance from the evils of earthly existence. Elements of that concept may be seen as survivals of older religious traditions and as accretions as Islam spread. These elements have been buttressed by Traditions (sing. *hadith*) of the Prophet Muhammad and Ali b. Abi Talib that seem to foretell the circumstances of deliverance and the attributes of its agent. By the time of Ibn Khaldun (1332–1406), disparate ideas had coalesced into a doctrine of the Mahdi, or divinely guided one, who would restore justice, unite the Muslims, and signal the end of the world. Claimants to the role have arisen from time to time but even in their success have confronted what the historian of the Sudanese Mahdiyya calls the "dilemma of history": continuing disunity of the Muslims, the prevalence of injustice, and evident postponement of the Last Day. Even seemingly failed movements have accrued mystical significance as

60

elements in long drawn-out historical dramas, however, or as necessary prologues to the final act of existence. Thus, expectations have lived on, while messianic claims have waxed and waned.[1]

Although Mahdist movements have arisen throughout the Muslim world, they have been particularly noteworthy on its frontiers, in Africa and Asia. Several factors may account for this: the lesser influence of orthodox *ulama* in such regions; a frequent and perhaps concomitant greater influence of Sufism (Islamic mysticism), with its emphasis on human agency to interpret or show the way toward divinity; and the more robust survival or more recent memory of pre-Islamic traditions and beliefs that lend themselves to synthesis with concepts in Islam.

Popular receptivity of a claim to Mahdi-ship presupposes both specific proofs of legitimacy and general conditions indicating that the time is ripe. The logical point for restoration of justice might seem to be when injustice is most rampant; the need to unite the Muslims is most obvious when they are most fragmented. In this context, the rise of the Sudanese Mahdi is easier to understand. By the late 1870s, the legitimacy of the Egyptian regime seemed in question: its failures even to maintain law and order were obvious, its corruption manifest, its policies – notably in combating the slave trade – at odds with Islam, and indeed its local agents were increasingly European Christians. The Sudanese were not concerned with comparisons between Ottoman provincial administration and British India or Leopold's Congo: their world was ruled by Egypt, and Egypt's rule was corrupt, increasingly arbitrary, and, lately, seemingly in ever more unjust conflict with the interests of the Sudanese.

That this perception was formed by important and otherwise quite distinct groups of Sudanese is important and nowhere more so than in Darfur, where effects of Egypt's attempts to suppress the slave trade were especially wide ranging. Among slaves themselves, those enlisted into the private armies of al-Zubayr and other merchants were an important element; manumission would mean the drudgery of conscription into the ragtag Egyptian army or the penniless "freedom" of detribalized highwaymen; military slaves shared with their masters an interest in promoting, not suppressing, the slave trade. For their part, restive Baqqara tribes of southern Darfur, who had fought the Fur sultans to a stalemate, had no interest in suppressing a trade that had enriched them or in propping up an administration that was trying to tax them. Finally, the Fur resistance, from the redoubts of Jabal Marra, benefited from any government action that weakened the Egyptian grip on the province: suppression of the slave trade had no appreciable effect on the soi-disant Fur sultan, now Abdallah Dud Banja, but he could hardly have devised a better means of whipping up opposition to Egypt's occupation. Although Egypt had therefore given many elements of Darfur's population ample reason to revolt, it would take a Sudanese to unite them.

This was Muhammad Ahmad Abdallah, son of a boat builder from Dongola on the Nile, who in 1881 declared himself the Mahdi. Born in 1844, Muhammad Ahmad was a pious sufi of the Sammaniyya order who, even before he settled in 1870 at Aba Island on the White Nile, had begun to attract attention for his holiness. That reputation survived, and was perhaps enhanced by, a breach with his *shaykh*, after which Muhammad Ahmad transferred allegiance to another, al-Qurashi wad al-Zayn. When that *shaykh* died in July 1878, Muhammad Ahmad went to al-Masallamiya on the Blue Nile for the construction of a tomb and there met the man who would be known to history as the Khalifa Abdallahi. Muhammad Ahmad then traveled to Kordofan, where he contacted local dissidents and extended his reputation for piety.

The historian of the Mahdiyya discerns in the encounter with Abdallahi an impetus to Muhammad Ahmad's subsequent declaration of Mahdi-ship. Abdallahi hailed from the Ta'aisha Baqqara of southern Darfur, but more remotely from farther west, whence his great-grandfather had come on pilgrimage and settled and married into the Ta'aisha. With his father, a tribal *faqih*, Abdallahi became caught up in the affairs of Southern Darfur on the eve of al-Zubayr's conquest. There is ample evidence of widespread messianic expectation during that time of disorder, which Abdallahi famously epitomized when he asked al-Zubayr if *he* was the Mahdi. Setting out for Mecca, Abdallahi met Muhammad Ahmad and became his disciple. In March 1881, Muhammad Ahmad revealed himself to Abdallahi and other confidants, and in June, at Aba Island, he made public manifestation as the Mahdi. From there he dispatched letters calling for *hijra*, or flight, from among the wicked, one of many ways in which the Mahdi consciously reenacted the early days of Islam. The Egyptian governor-general ordered him to Khartoum. When he refused the summons, a military force was sent against him, which the Mahdi ambushed and routed; he then led his disciples into Kordofan, while word of his seemingly miraculous victory spread far and wide. The Mahdist Revolution had begun.

The Revolt Spreads

In the critical early days of the Mahdiyya, the government's incompetence played a decisive role. Its tactics at Aba had been inept. Now in Kordofan another government force was ambushed and annihilated, providing not only large quantities of arms and ammunition but also apparent further evidence of divine mandate. Sudanese flocked to the Mahdi's banner. A third army was assembled from various posts and, on 30 May 1881 near the Mahdi's headquarters at Jabal Qadir in southern Kordofan, was surprised and utterly destroyed. Momentum was now with the Mahdi, and the numbers coming in grew apace, as the Hamar, Bidayriyya, Hawazma, Ghudiyat, and Jawama'a tribes rose up. The Mahdi gradually reduced Kordofan to submission, one post at a time, until only Bara and El Obeid, the capital, held out. Conditions in both places favored the rebellion and, after initial attacks were beaten off with heavy losses, the Mahdi laid siege. On 6 January 1883, Bara surrendered. At El Obeid, a fifth column had been active, and spirits were low among defenders, who were starving owing to the siege; after negotiations, on 19 January the Mahdi led his forces into the town and completed the conquest of Kordofan.[2]

Response to the Mahdi's success had already been widespread, from the Gezira in the east to Darfur in the west. He had dispatched letters to religious and tribal *shaykhs* urging adherence to his divine mission and a rising against the Turks, whose officials, Muslim and Christian alike, were denounced as infidels. From among the Baqqara of Southern Darfur, groups and individuals came in. By early 1882, the Rizayqat, Habbaniyya, and Ma'alia were in open revolt, although this probably reflected decline in the government's prestige more than it did adherence to the Mahdi. Complicating the position was the fact that Muhammad Khalid Zuqal, a wealthy merchant and governor at Dara, was a cousin of the Mahdi. More serious was a dispute over leadership of the Rizayqat tribe: this had resulted in 1881 in deposition of Madibbu Ali as chief, who thereupon had gone east and joined the Mahdi. Madibbu was duly sent back to raise the revolt among the Rizayqat, who by mid-1882 threatened Dara. The attachment of the Darfur Rizayqat to the Mahdiyya is a good example of the way in which the spread of an explicitly religious (and universalist) revolution benefited from local political, economic, and, indeed, personal circumstances.[3]

The Reduction of Darfur

Even before the fall of El Obeid, the government's position in Darfur had thus seriously deteriorated. The Baqqara were seething; between El Fasher and El Obeid, the Humr besieged the important town of Umm Shanqa; reinforcements and supplies could not get through, and Slatin, the general-governor, had to send messages concealed in agents' shoes or in hollowed-out sticks. He therefore made his headquarters at Dara, but the surrounding countryside was completely up in arms, and he found himself, with ever-diminishing reserves of men and arms, pulled in all directions. Madibbu Ali wiped out a government force outside Murrai, near Shakka. In October 1882, Slatin moved southward with some 2,000 men armed with rifles, and more than 7,000 irregulars from among the Begu, Birgid, Misiriyya, Zaghawa, and others hostile to particular Mahdist tribal leaders; the intention was to retake Shakka, build a fort there, and make it a headquarters from which to subdue the surrounding tribes. En route, however, Madibbu Ali's Rizayqat attacked him at Umm Waraqat and won a decisive victory, wiping out or making prisoners of almost the entire government force. Slatin retreated to Dara with great difficulty, only to find that news of the disaster had preceded him. He wrote to Lupton, the British governor of the Bahr al-Ghazal, asking for diversionary attacks on the Rizayqat from the south: security was such that Slatin sent the message in a dried-up pumpkin.[4]

At Dara the government's position was complicated by news from abroad. Word had reached El Fasher of the Urabist movement in Egypt, which had been gathering support against the khedival regime and the European powers behind it. Precisely when the news filtered in to Darfur of the Urabist defeat at the battle of Tel al-Kabir, and of the subsequent British occupation of Egypt in September 1882, is uncertain, but that the government in Cairo was fully occupied with its domestic affairs is obvious. The sense of abandonment, long a grievance of Egyptian officials in Darfur, must have become almost palpable. Sudanese Arab tribesmen were not the only ones susceptible to Mahdist propaganda:

who, trapped in an Egyptian garrison at Shakka or Kabkabiyya, could have failed to wonder whether the hand of God was behind the success of the Mahdi?

It was under these circumstances, moreover, while he undertook operations against the Mima and the Khawabir Ma'alia, that word reached Slatin of the fall of El Obeid to the Mahdi. This news would create a sensation, and Slatin took steps to counteract it. He ordered establishment of positions at Fafa and Woda in the Mima territory to maintain communication between El Fasher and Dara, whither he returned at once to prepare for a siege. There, he became aware of his own officers' disaffection and of a draining away of his authority in small but unmistakable ways: rumor had it that his own dismissal had been ordered but not yet officially received; hitherto loyal *shaykhs* now pleaded inability to attend; reinforcements were regrettably unavailable; camels for transport could not be found. His order for the evacuation of Umm Shanqa was defied. In one particularly ominous episode, Slatin discovered that six Fur noncommissioned officers were plotting a general mutiny, after which they intended to abscond to Abdallah Dud Banja, the "shadow sultan" in Jabal Marra; Slatin had them executed by firing squad and then made his famously expedient profession of Islam.[5]

The Egyptian government's position in southern Darfur continued to deteriorate, however, and outside Dara and a few outposts, the tribes were in open rebellion. Slatin made the most of rumors from the east of a large government force tasked with the reconquest of Kordofan – this, the so-called Hicks expedition, did not even set out from the Nile until September 1883 – and resorted to sending himself fake messages about government victories, which were duly broadcast to encourage the troops. In another attempt to buy time and remove from the scene a potential source of great danger, Slatin sent Muhammad Khalid Zuqal, the Mahdi's cousin and outwardly loyal governor of Dara, on a mission to Kordofan, ostensibly with the dual aim of discouraging a Mahdist attack on Darfur and, if all else failed, assisting in an orderly transfer of power there; Zuqal's family were kept at Dara as hostages.[6] Slatin then undertook operations against the Bani Halba, whose *shaykh*, Bashiri Bey wad Bakr, was raiding the local Misiriyya. Outnumbered but with superior arms, Slatin routed the Bani Halba, who rejected their own *shaykh*'s peace terms. Apparently egged on by his father-in-law, *Shaykh* Tahir al-Tagawi, Bashiri returned to the fray and, in a headlong charge accompanied only by a servant, was killed a few days later. Slatin advanced on Roro, Tahir's village, which he looted and burned, then returned to Dara. He meanwhile loosed a lieutenant, Muhammad Bey Tia, and his cavalry on the Bani Halba and sent word to the neighboring Ta'aisha that if the Bani Halba sought refuge among them, they, the Ta'aisha, could seize their flocks and herds with impunity. The resulting devastation of the Bani Halba and division of the spoils among the loyalists did little to relieve the general deterioration of security in the province.[7]

"We had brushed them off as one drives flies off meat" was how Slatin's later account described an ensuing success against Madibbu Ali of the Rizayqat, allies of the Bani Halba, but he might have referred to his entire strategy in southern Darfur.[8] In the north, the Fur sultan, Abdallah Dud Banja, had like clockwork seized the opportunity to come down from Jabal Marra and whip up the tribes around El Fasher. The Mima cut off communication between Dara and El Fasher, wiping out a government garrison in the process. A relieving column of 750 men sent from El Fasher was mauled by a motley force of Mima, Khawabir, Birgid, and Manasir. The Mima *shaykh*, Abo Bey, advanced toward Dara and ambushed and destroyed yet another force Slatin sent against him.

Meanwhile, Madibbu Ali and the Rizayqat, together with sections of the Ma'alia, Berti, Bani Halba, and Habbaniyya, tightened the noose around Dara, and even those sections of the Misiriyya that had hitherto sided with the government were, for their own sake, abandoning the few loyal *shaykhs* and bringing their families into Dara for protection. For Slatin, who had contemplated evacuating Dara and concentrating the entire government defense on El Fasher, it had become too late. To buy time, he sent word that he was willing to surrender and parleyed with the chiefs (except Madibbu Ali, who opposed negotiation) outside the fort. An armistice was arranged, under which Slatin would send a message to the Mahdi offering to surrender to his delegate and, pending a reply, the tribes would cease their attacks. Only Madibbu Ali seemed to suspect the obvious, that Slatin was merely stalling until the Hicks expedition reconquered Kordofan. While correspondence with the Mahdi pended, word reached Slatin that Hicks's army had been utterly destroyed.[9]

At the time of the surrender of El Obeid to the Mahdi in January 1883, the government in Cairo had already become subject to the dictates of British occupation. The complexities of foreign control need not detain us here. But the British refused to take any responsibility for the Sudan, let alone to intervene directly there, while the Khedive, Muhammad Tawfiq, and his ministers were loath to relinquish their empire without a fight. Elements of the newly defeated and demoralized Egyptian army were therefore sent to the Sudan, under Sulayman Pasha Niyazi and with a British officer from India, Colonel William Hicks, as chief of staff. The governor-general of the Sudan, Abd al-Qadir Pasha, was recalled and replaced by Ala al-Din Pasha Siddiq. The ill-assorted responsibilities of these officials were one factor in the delay that dogged the government at Khartoum in the months that followed. After much infighting, Hicks was made commander-in-chief in August 1883, and in September, he and Ala al-Din finally set out with a force of some 10,000. From its first day, the expedition suffered from incompetence and disarray; the chosen route proved short of water, and Mahdist tribesmen shadowed every move. Finally, on 5 November, the Mahdist army annihilated the expeditionary force at Shaykan, south of El Obeid; Ala al-Din Pasha and Hicks were both killed, and of their men and camp followers, only about 250 survived.[10]

Word of the battle of Shaykan, the psychological impact of which can hardly be exaggerated, quickly reached Darfur. It was immediately obvious to both sides that the Egyptian regime there was at an end; what would follow in its wake was wholly unclear. After Shaykan, the Mahdi had appointed Muhammad Khalid Zuqal as commanding general (*amir umum*) of Darfur, and he set out immediately from Kordofan to take up his new position.[11] Umm Shanqa submitted, and on 23 December Slatin surrendered Dara. Al-Sayyid Bey Jum'a, the commander at El Fasher, decided that with a thousand armed men in a strongly fortified position, he had the means to resist. But the government garrison at Kabkabiyya in western Darfur had gone over to the Mahdi, and it now reinforced Muhammad Khalid at El Fasher. After a week's siege during which his sorties failed to break the Mahdist hold of the wells on which the garrison depended, al-Sayyid Jum'a capitulated on 15 January 1884.[12]

The Conquest Completed

Following Shaykan, the British government had altered its policy of non-interference in the affairs of the Sudan, demanding instead that Egypt abandon the territory. To carry out the evacuation of the thousands of Egyptians, civil and military, and to leave behind some semblance of order there, General Gordon was appointed. The fateful error of this appointment and the partly consequent differences over Gordon's precise role have been much regretted and ably described.[13] It suffices in the present context to note that even before he arrived at Khartoum, again as governor-general of the Sudan, the stage had been set for the famous disaster in which Gordon played the leading role in January 1885.

One of Gordon's schemes for combating the Mahdi or, at the least, for leaving the Sudan in order, involved restoration of local notables to positions made redundant during the Turkiyya. He therefore invited one Abd al-Shakur Abd al-Rahman Shattut, a grandson of Sultan Muhammad al-Fadl of Darfur, to accompany him to Khartoum, whence the prince would be sent to claim his patrimony at El Fasher. Orders were duly sent to hand over the province to him, orders that Slatin received in captivity after the surrender of Darfur. In any case, Abd al-Shakur fell out with Gordon and never reached Khartoum, let alone Darfur; if he had, his cousin Abdallah Dud Banja, the established claimant to the sultanate, would likely have seen that this episode had a less comical ending. That Gordon later made similar offers to al-Zubayr Pasha, and even to the Mahdi himself (to whom he offered the governorship of Kordofan), illustrates the degree to which he misunderstood the nature of his enemy.[14] His schemes and devices all came to naught, as is well known; holing up in his palace and defying the British government to risk the outcry that his abandonment would entail, Gordon died famously in the wreck of Khartoum in January 1885. The Mahdi himself died in June, in Omdurman, the new capital he had decreed on the left bank of the Nile opposite Khartoum, as he was planning the conquest of Egypt.

THE KHALIFA ABDALLAHI AND DARFUR

The Succession

The death of the Mahdi precipitated a crisis. The crisis would have occurred even had his regime been purely secular, but the divine basis of the revolution was inevitably called into question by the death of its raison d'etre. The Mahdi had appointed four *khalifas*, not as deputies or representatives in the common sufi sense, nor as serial successors to himself, but as spiritual successors to the first four caliphs of Islam.[15] First among equals from the start was Abdallahi, less because of his style as "successor" to Abu Bakr, the first caliph, than because of his proven abilities, commanding personality, and the leading role played in the Mahdist victories by his Baqqara tribes of southern Darfur. His personal military command was the Black Flag division, comprising mainly Baqqara and numerically superior to those of the other *khalifas*. Upon the Mahdi's death, he received the oath of allegiance, with differing degrees of enthusiasm, from the principal officers of state, a succession buttressed by reference to prophetic visions. One such was related specifically in a letter the new sovereign wrote to the people of Darfur, in which he revealed the Mahdi's testimony that "all the divine secrets" had been reposed in him, Abdallahi, who bore a physical mark in proof.[16]

In writing to Darfur, the Khalifa Abdallahi had good reason to emphasize his rights. The Baqqara tribesmen who had played such an important part in the collapse of Egyptian authority in southern Darfur had loomed large in the overall military success of the Mahdist movement throughout the Sudan. But he of all people would be aware of the depth of these tribesmen's religious conviction; they had needed no divine call to rebel and plunder the towns, and any attempt to bring them to heel faced obvious difficulties. With little real devotion to the Mahdi, how much less attachment were they likely to feel to Abdallahi, a Taʿaishi tribesman? The history of the Mahdiyya in Darfur would be marked by the Khalifa's attempts to impose central control over tribes that had just thrown it off. And in the Mahdiyya's relations with the borderland principalities to the west, the era rivals seventeenth-century Germany in the complexity of its politics and diplomacy and in the bloodiness of its almost incessant war.

Muhammad Khalid Zuqal's tenure as general commander in Darfur was brief. From El Fasher, he sought to extend his own authority to the corners of Darfur both peacefully and through force of arms. According to a contemporary source,[17] his army consisted of 1,400 regulars and as many as 20,000 Arab tribesmen. *Shaykhs* of northern and western Darfur sent messages of allegiance, as did even the sultan of Wadai, but diplomatic recognition of the new regime was hardly the same as submission to its dictates. The historian of Dar Masalit, for example, states that Muhammad Khalid's relations with the western border regions of his domain were those of an ambassador rather than administrator.[18] The Fur "shadow sultan," Abdallah Dud Banja, rejected calls to present himself, and the amir Adam Umar besieged him in Jabal Marra, where he held out for two months before capitulating; in Omdurman, the Fur prince threw himself on the mercy of the Khalifa and died fighting for the Mahdist cause at Gallabat in 1889.[19] Muhammad Khalid dispatched another force under Umar Darhu to Jabal Marra to put down Fur resistance, with devastating effect: many Fur were killed and much booty taken, in goods and captives. But on news of the Mahdi's death, Umar Darhu planned to rebel himself; when his followers declined to join, he accepted Muhammad Khalid's offer of clemency and went back to El Fasher, where he was treacherously executed.[20]

The most pressing threat to the Khalifa in Darfur during the early days of his reign seemed to come from the governor, Muhammad Khalid Zuqal, who had been appointed by the Mahdi. Because he was a prominent member of the *ashraf*,[21] the Mahdi's large extended family, his potential for dangerous combination with relatives disaffected by the accession of the Khalifa was obvious. Whether fully aware of their plots, which were real enough, he was adept at testing the wind; as he had at Dara in the days when the success of the Mahdi hung in the balance, so Muhammad Khalid temporized and straddled. When the Khalifa repeatedly called him to Omdurman to pledge allegiance, Muhammad Khalid stalled until, in December 1885, he finally set out – with his army in the vanguard. His progress was sluggish, and the Khalifa used this time for adroit political maneuvers. In these, Hamdan Abu Anja, the trustworthy Ta'aishi commander of the *jihadia*,[22] who had already won prominence in battle, played a leading role. In Omdurman, the Khalifa acted to disarm conspirators: the personal military resources of the junior khalifas, the ever-loyal Ali wad Hilu and the feckless Muhammad Sharif (a nephew of the Mahdi and leader of the *ashraf*), were put under the command of the Khalifa's brother, Ya'qub. Finally, at Bara, Hamdan Abu Anja's forces surrounded Muhammad Khalid's, and the governor of Darfur submitted and was imprisoned.[23]

The Khalifa and the Tribes

The Khalifa's writ in Darfur was still weak. In December 1885, Darfur had five administrative districts, each under a local appointee: of the western borderlands, the parvenu Isma'il Abd al-Nabi, a Masalati *faqih*, was put in charge; of both El Fasher and Kabkabiyya, none other than Yusuf Ibrahim, a son of Sultan Ibrahim, with a high-blown Mahdist title; of Dara, Adam Kunjara; and at Umm Shanqa, Hasan Umm Kadok.[24] Soon after Muhammad Khalid departed, Yusuf Ibrahim threw off allegiance to the Mahdiyya. At Shakka, in the south, the Mahdist agent was Muhammad *Shaykh* Muhammad Kurqasawi, a Dongolawi whose brother Karamallah had occupied the Bahr al-Ghazal in 1884 and been made governor there by the Mahdi. Madibbu Ali, the *shaykh* of the Baqqara Rizayqat who had done so much to bring down the Egyptian regime in southern Darfur, had no intention of submitting to another foreigner at Shakka or to a Fur prince at El Fasher. Thus, in the whole of Darfur, Mahdist authority was nominal. With Muhammad Khalid out of the way, the Khalifa was better equipped to impose his will, but he had few local weapons other than the disunity of his enemies.

Circumstances dictated dealing first with the dangerous Rizayqat and Bani Halba. Madibbu Ali sought to strengthen his own position by recruiting mutinous *jihadia* who, after revolting at El Obeid in the autumn of 1885, were a year later still holding out in the Nuba Mountains. This came to nothing, and Madibbu, deserted by the Bani Halba, was caught by the Kurqasawi brothers. Karamallah came up to Shakka from the Bahr al-Ghazal with a large force, and when Madibbu refused a summons, Karamallah took the field against him. In a battle, Madibbu was defeated, fled north, and was finally captured and delivered to Yusuf Ibrahim, who in turn handed him to the Kurqasawis. Passing through Kordofan as a prisoner en route to Omdurman, Madibbu Ali fell into the clutches of Hamdan Abu Anja; the two had crossed swords before, and Abu Anja executed the Rizayqat chief and sent his head to the Khalifa.[25]

With the Rizayqat temporarily off balance, there remained two centers of power in Darfur: the Kurqasawi brothers in the southern borderlands and Yusuf Ibrahim at El Fasher. The danger posed by a resurgent

Fur sultanate was obvious, but the threat from the Kurqasawis seemed greater. Karamallah and his brother, as Dongolawis, were presumed equally inimical to Baqqara hegemony in Omdurman as to Baqqara rebellion in Southern Darfur. Moreover, they had forces at their disposal, at a great distance from the seat of Mahdist power and with easy avenues of escape. Therefore, when Yusuf Ibrahim complained that the Kurqasawis were demanding taxes the depleted province could not pay, Hamdan Abu Anja, in Kordofan, as *amir al-umara*, ordered Karamallah to withdraw to the Bahr al-Ghazal and leave Darfur to Yusuf Ibrahim. The Khalifa followed this up with the familiar call to the Kurqasawis to present themselves in Omdurman. This they failed to do.

The Rizayqat and other Baqqara, undeterred by the fate of Madibbu Ali, regrouped and continued to assert their independence, as did Yusuf Ibrahim. In several encounters with the Rizayqat, Karamallah was worsted. Forced back on Shakka, the Kurqasawis petitioned the Khalifa for help. Yusuf Ibrahim had meanwhile become increasingly open in his own designs to revive the Fur sultanate: assuming the title of sultan, he restored members of his family to positions of honor at El Fasher and sought to reimpose in the vicinity aspects of the pre-Egyptian administrative system. He, too, failed to obey summonses to Omdurman. Several bloody clashes with the Kurqasawis resulted in stalemate, and both sides prepared for more. It therefore behooved the Khalifa to assert Mahdist rule by force.

In the early autumn of 1887, the Khalifa launched a major campaign in Darfur. To lead it, he appointed Uthman Adam (sometimes called Uthman Janu), a young Ta'aishi relative who had succeeded Hamdan Abu Anja in Kordofan and shown ability against the recalcitrant Kababish tribe there. Uthman set out on 10 October with an army he numbered at more than 17,000, leaving in Kordofan only the garrison of El Obeid. Marching to Shakka, he accepted the submission of Muhammad Kurqasawi and sent for Yusuf Ibrahim, who did not respond. Reinforced by the troops of the Kurqasawis, the Mahdist army marched on Dara. Yusuf Ibrahim had succeeded in raising the Zaghawa, Birgid, Mima, and other northern tribes, but after three fierce encounters, Uthman took Dara on 27 December. He then defeated a force sent out against him from El Fasher and headed for the capital. Yusuf Ibrahim, in time-honored Keira fashion, decamped for Jabal Marra and, following another battle in late January 1888, Uthman entered El Fasher. By a decree prepared in advance of the expedition, he was declared agent-general (*amil umum*) of the west. Later, in March, a force under another Ta'aishi amir, al-Khatim Musa, succeeded in tracking down Yusuf Ibrahim, whose head was sent to the Khalifa at Omdurman. Yusuf's brother, Abu'l-Khayrat, assumed his titles and role in the Marra redoubt. According to Slatin, Uthman Adam took steps to arrest all male members of the Fur royal family and treated the females as booty to be doled out as concubines, with the exception of two elderly sisters of the late Sultan Ibrahim.[26]

Uthman Adam's conquest of Darfur may well be seen as the first real imposition of Mahdist rule there, so varied had been the motives of the tribes ejecting the Turco-Egyptian regime five years earlier and so mixed the results of attempts to administer the province thereafter. But there was still no peace. For, as master of Darfur, Uthman Adam set his sights on extending the Mahdiyya's domains to the west, where propaganda had already reaped some results and promised more. Perhaps partly in response to the prospect of aggression but certainly also with other motives, there arose, in western Darfur, arguably the greatest internal threat the Khalifa Abdallahi faced during his entire reign. This has usually been referred to as the rebellion of Abu Jummayza, the suppression of which induced far-reaching changes in the administration of Darfur.

THE MAHDIYYA AND THE WESTERN BORDER LANDS

Westerners' grievances against the young Mahdist state, although difficult to quantify, may be briefly described. Since the collapse of the Keira sultanate in 1874, local peoples had enjoyed a degree of independence that they were reluctant to give up, least of all to a regime that seemed, in its local variant, in many ways a continuation of the Turkiyya. Some local rulers' allegiance to the Mahdi had been cost-free and formal; the appearance of Mahdist tax collectors brought home the reality of a new regime. Worse, the chaotic 1880s witnessed the crisscrossing of Darfur by large armies with even larger numbers of camp followers, all of whom had to be provisioned from local sources. This was accomplished through widespread expropriation. Furthermore, the puritanical side of the regime went down badly in a region where the version of Islam had happily tolerated alcohol, among other heterodox enormities. Nor was the Khalifa willing indefinitely to accept protestations of fealty from borderland sultans: his demand that they come personally to Omdurman, with their retinues, to swear allegiance was rightly seen as an aspect of policy rather than a formality; not all who made the trip returned; some were replaced during their absence, others were held hostage. Stalling thus gave way to a stark choice: to submit or to resist.[27]

That rebellion began in the territories west of the Darfur heartland is significant. The lands of Dar Tama, Dar Qimr, Dar Masalit, Dar Sila, and Dar Zaghawa, which today straddle or abut the border between the Sudan and Chad, had generally maintained varying and uneasy degrees of tributary independence from their larger, more important neighbors, Wadai and Darfur. As governor, Muhammad Khalid Zuqal had begun to extend Mahdist authority to these districts where, moreover, Fur exiles and other dissidents had found refuge, even if, in many cases, only to be enslaved. After mopping up Fur resistance around Jabal Marra in 1887, however, Uthman Adam encountered growing opposition and an unlikely sense of common cause among the westerners. When he summoned the rulers of the Mahamid, Qimr, and Tama to El Fasher, they failed to appear; Isma'il Abd al-Nabi of the Masalit submitted in the spring of 1888, only to be sent to Omdurman never to return. But the sultan of Wadai, Yusuf Muhammad Sharif, having closed the pilgrimage routes into Darfur and improved his defenses with arms imported from the Fezzan, moved east to defend his border with the Mahdist state. Sultan Abu Risha of Dar Sila barred Mahdist envoys from his dominion, while Sultan Idris of Dar Qimr was in touch with the latest Fur pretender, Abu'l-Khayrat who, having been forced to flee, was taken in by the ruler of Dar Sila. Uthman Adam therefore attacked, in turn, Dar Qimr, the Zaghawa Kobe in the north, and, in August 1888, Dar Tama; Sultan Idris found refuge at the court of Wadai, but the aged Sultan Ibrahim of the Tama was taken prisoner and deported to Omdurman.[28]

Abu Jummayza

When the Mahdi had appointed his four *khalifas*, one of them, the *shaykh* of the Sanusiyya sufi order of Cyrenaica and the Fezzan, had not responded. Then, in 1888, a certain Muhammad Zayn, a young *faki* among the Mahriyya nomads of northwestern Darfur, appeared to assume the mantle. Thus, ostensibly as either the Sanusi *shaykh*'s son or his nominee, he did not reject the Mahdiyya but adhered to it, claiming, however, the vacant Khalifa-ship and preaching against the Khalifa Abdallahi as a usurper. His local reputation as a miracle worker is attested in his having been called Abu Jummayza, after the *jummayza* (fig) trees under which he preached – or from one of which he was said to have sprung; some sources less colorfully associate him with a place in Dar Tama called Jummayza al-Hamra. In any case, after successfully leading an attack by Tama tribesmen on a Mahdist post in September 1888, he attacked the *Ansar* camp at Abu Qurayn in Dar Erenga while most of its garrison was looking for him elsewhere. Victory enhanced his prestige, and people from the neighboring *dars* flocked to the rebel banner, which for reasons of his own attracted also the Fur pretender Abu'l-Khayrat. A Mahdist army of some 16,000 under Muhammad Bishara sent out from Kabkabiyya against the rebels was heavily defeated on 11 November. At El Fasher, Uthman Adam concentrated his forces amid reportedly widespread alarm and demoralization.[29] Then Abu Jummayza died.

Abu Jummayza's death, reportedly from smallpox, robbed the movement of its central rallying point. That even before his death some of his motley following had begun to drift away leads to the conclusion that they had been motivated more by a desire to eject the *Ansar* than to reform the Mahdiyya under a righteous Khalifa. But that those closest to the rebel leader sought to conceal his death speaks also of his essential role. As the westerners dithered, Uthman Adam drew in reinforcements from the east, which, by the time of the decisive battle of Shawai outside El Fasher on 22 February 1889, numbered more than 36,000. By then the rebel army was composed mainly of Fur, under Sultan Abu'l-Khayrat, Daju under Bakhit Abu Risha, and Masalit under Sultan Abbakr. The *Ansar*'s better discipline and arms won the day. Abu Jummayza's brother and would-be successor, Sagha, was killed, while Abu'l-Khayrat took the well-worn escape route to Jabal Marra, and thence to Dar Sila. Attempts to maintain a united front among the westerners failed.[30]

Both Mahdist and Anglo-Egyptian intelligence sources[31] skewed the nature and scope of the rebellion in Darfur. Local Mahdist commanders described the movement in mostly religious terms, condemning its leader as a charlatan and his followers as dupes; no allowance was

made for the possibility of legitimate grievances. After the death of
Abu Jummayza, moreover, the Mahdist leadership assumed, or pur-
ported to believe, that direction of the movement had passed to Abu'l-
Khayrat, the Fur prince. The intelligence department of the Egyptian
Army, either misinformed (and misinforming) or a victim of wishful
thinking, first identified Abu Jummayza with the Sanusiyya and later fic-
titiously as Abbakr, the son and successor of Isma'il Abd al-Nabi of the
Masalit, bent on avenging his father. The British, moreover, ascribed
to the movement the potential not only of ejecting the *Ansar* from
Darfur but, because the whole Sudan was supposedly groaning under
the Khalifa's oppression, also of overthrowing the regime. There is,
however, no evidence that Abu Jummayza's revolt won adherents in
the central or eastern Sudan. Indeed, while the unwonted unity of the
westerners under him was remarkable, it was also short-lived and not
without discord.[32]

Uthman Adam sought to consolidate his victory by moving against
Sultan Abu'l-Khayrat in the north and the Rizayqat and Bani Halba
tribes of Baqqara in the south, who had taken advantage of the Abu
Jummayza revolt to reassert themselves. In this Baqqara rebellion may
be seen a reaction to the Khalifa Abdallahi's policy of enforced migration, itself a logical, if extravagant, extension of the policy of requiring
the *hijra* of tribal potentates. The Mahdiyya had succeeded in raising
whole tribes against the Egyptian regime, but the Mahdi's call had
no tribal basis nor did it recognize tribal divisions and identities. The
Khalifa likewise couched his appointments, and his summonses to various tribal *shaykhs*, in religious terms, and failure to obey took on a
religious as well as a political or merely personal character. He was free
to confirm or depose recognized tribal leaders and to appoint outsiders.
Some fence-sitters were left in place, others forced to come down on one
side or the other, depending on the circumstances of time and place and,
in no small order, diplomatic skill. *Shaykh* Hamid Yahya ("Turjok")
of the Bani Husayn survived successive regimes; Sultan Idris's reign of
fifty-six years in Dar Qimr spawned (in the 1930s) the Anglo-Sudanese
word "tagility," from the Arabic *tajil*, to forestall.[33] Internal tribal
divisions were exploited and endemic fraternal rivalries seized upon;
sworn Mahdists with no other claim to tribal leadership won appointments, which they brandished as a new kind of legitimacy; hard-nosed
frontier politics often trumped a millennial certitude that, with time,

proved repeatedly susceptible to traditional local methods of fight and flight.

Migration of the Tribes

The Khalifa had acted even before the death of the Mahdi to bring in his own Ta'aisha tribe to Omdurman.[34] Although contemporary and some later European sources saw in this a wish to reward them with the high life of the capital, while relying on them to cow the effete townsmen chafing under his personal rule, in fact his intention was probably to keep an eye on them. In January 1888, just before the outbreak of the Abu Jummayza revolt, the Khalifa told Uthman Adam in El Fasher to send in the Rizayqat, Habbaniyya, and Ta'aisha, among other troublemaking tribes. The Habbaniyya suffered greatly: en route to Omdurman their *shaykh*, Bishara Taj al-Din, was murdered and the tribe split, with the majority continuing to the Nile and bedraggled remnants making their way back to Darfur. The *shaykh* of the Ta'aisha, al-Ghazzali Ahmad Khawwaf, on the other hand, shot the messengers summoning him, and Abdallahi responded by deposing him, ordering the tribe to abandon him, and setting a rival, Salih Hawa, against him. Finally, the Khalifa told Uthman Adam to adopt a scorched-earth policy if necessary. In May 1889, al-Ghazzali and his chiefs surrendered to an expeditionary force, and the Ta'aisha were sent on in groups to Omdurman. That this *hijra* was exile rather than reward is evident: after a mass defection of Ta'aisha to Darfur in 1890, al-Ghazzali was imprisoned; and when he himself escaped, he was hunted down and killed.[35]

When other Baqqara Arabs of Southern Darfur took advantage of the Abu Jummayza rebellion to revolt, Uthman Adam, the governor, adopted a change in policy. To be sure, in March 1889, with a force he numbered at almost 18,000 men, he swept all before him in the Bani Halba country, and punitive patrols would continue, especially in the far south of the province. But *hijra* could not be termed a success if it depopulated the province. Uthman therefore held a grand conclave of tribal leaders at Dara, under a flag of truce, and promised what amounted to the lightest touch of Mahdist administration: the appointment to each tribe of an official to enforce religious conformity and tax only according to the law; loot already collected by the *Ansar* would be returned.[36] The tribes' willingness to retire and Uthman Adam's assurances regarding taxation were both likely responses to the great Sudanese famine of 1888–90 that, moreover, coincided with the forced migration of the Ta'aisha to Omdurman. But the policy of forced migration had its effects, both locally and in the Sudan generally. By the later years of the Khalifa's regime, the Mahdist armies depended ever more heavily on Baqqara and *jihadia*, with Baqqara – and indeed Ta'aisha – officers preponderant in the most important and sensitive military commands.[37] Several of those Ta'aisha amirs who survived the Mahdiyya became prominent at the court of Ali Dinar.

MAHDIST ADMINISTRATION IN DARFUR

The historian of the Mahdiyya has distinguished between "military" and "metropolitan" provinces of the Mahdist state and included Darfur in the former category along with districts bordering Egypt, the Red Sea, and Abyssinia. The governors of these provinces were officers who combined military and administrative functions, commanded forces of *jihadia* and tribal irregulars in their capitals and important outlying posts, and maintained provincial treasuries. Under Uthman Adam and his successor, Mahmud Ahmad, Darfur was combined with Kordofan as the *imalat al-Gharb* or "province of the west"; Kordofan had a deputy governor at El Obeid. In contrast, the "metropolitan" provinces had no standing armies, and their governors' functions were fiscal rather than administrative.[38] In the central provinces, the administration of the Mahdi and the Khalifa tended strongly toward centralization through bureaucratic means, whereas in the border regions, and especially remote Darfur, where a degree of autonomy was unavoidable, central authority would be exercised through tight personal control of trusted lieutenants.

The administration of justice in Darfur was in theory directed from Omdurman. As in other regions, at the conquest most pending litigation was suspended; the Khalifa Abdallahi decreed a further suspension upon his accession. Emergency laws were enacted from time to time by the Mahdi and the Khalifa. There was a variety of such legislation concerning, for example, marriage and the status of women, ownership of property, interest, and the proscription of various local customs and beliefs as un-Islamic. During his lifetime, the Mahdi was supreme judge, with judicial powers delegated to the *khalifas*, the governors of frontier provinces (including Darfur), and others. When, as governor of Darfur, Muhammad Khalid Zuqal informed the Mahdi of some judgments recently made with the approval of local *ulama*, he was chastised: the body of Islamic jurisprudence had ceased to exist; judicial decisions must henceforth be based only on the Qur'an, the *sunna* (custom) of the Prophet, and the decrees of the Mahdi. Muhammad Khalid was ordered to constitute a small board of judicial deputies (*nuwwab*) to render unanimous decisions on that basis.[39]

The Mahdist state's judicial hierarchy included a *qadi al-Islam* who likewise derived his authority from that of the Mahdi. Ahmad Ali, a *qadi* at Shakka in Darfur who joined the Mahdiyya before the conquest of Kordofan, was appointed to this post in 1882 and remained in it until 1894, when he fell from grace and was imprisoned. His successor, al-Husayn Ibrahim al-Zahra, soon followed him, after which the office was apparently left vacant. The Omdurman court had both local and appellate functions, rendering decisions on cases referred to it from all over the country. In Darfur, the governor was the chief judicial official, subject to overrule from Omdurman, to which cautious reference was frequently made, but vast distance and consequent slow communication made detailed consultation impractical. The governor himself appointed both the provincial board of deputies and judges. When Mahmud Ahmad was made governor of the west in 1890, he was accompanied to El Fasher by a four-man judicial commission for the purpose of reorganizing the provincial judiciary. But even these officials were subject to him and acted to appoint a new chief judge, termed *na'ib umum Dar Fur*, only after consulting him; Mahmud Ahmad appointed local judges himself, including typically religious notables of the old regime who had embraced Mahdism, and some of these indeed would later serve in similar capacities under Ali Dinar.[40]

The practical effect in Darfur of Mahdist judicial policy and appointments is difficult to gauge. What is true of the social history of Darfur as a whole[41] is also likely true of its legal history: in a theocratic state born of jihad against its predecessor, arrangements made under enactments of the infidel regime were ipso facto illegitimate. The position of a tribal *shaykh* and the ownership of property were alike, theoretically open to

79

question and subject to the new dispensation. The local impact of the new regime in legal affairs is therefore unclear, but it is likely to have depended on several variables, including distance from an administrative center, the economic and social structure of each tribe or locality, the relative strength of tribal custom and pre-Mahdist reference to the *shariʿa*, the predilections of local chiefs, and the character and methods of judges.

The borders of Darfur, and thus of the Mahdist state in the west, were never fixed by treaty with either the neighboring states or the encroaching European powers. It was, indeed, mainly in western Darfur that the limits of Uthman Adam's policy of conciliation are clearest. In 1890, he invaded Dar Masalit, ostensibly as punishment but perhaps for the more practical reason of obtaining food for his army as famine took hold elsewhere. He traversed the *dar* and the Masalit fled before him, but before long, amid torrential rains, a devastating epidemic of cholera struck, which locals attributed to divine intervention. The remnants of the army withdrew to El Fasher, where Uthman Adam himself died upon arrival. Under his successor, the amir Mahmud Ahmad, a cousin of the Khalifa Abdallahi (nicknamed Mahmud *Asal*, or Mahmud Honey, in contrast to his predecessor, whose rhyming local sobriquet was Uthman *Basal* – "onion"), Darfur as a whole experienced a period of relative calm born of catharsis: successive invasions, calls to arms, famine, and disease had left the province exhausted.[42] But the western borderlands – corresponding to today's border between the Sudan and Chad – remained in almost constant turmoil.

One achievement of Mahmud Ahmad's governorship was the eclipse of the shadow sultanate of the Keira, although this hardly resulted from any action of his. After the collapse of Abu Jummayza's revolt in 1889, Sultan Abu'l-Khayrat and some of his men took refuge with the sultan of Dar Sila but quarreled and had to leave. They operated as virtual bandits around Jabal Marra until Abu'l-Khayrat was killed in 1891: differing versions ascribe the deed to his own followers, possibly slaves, and even to his successor, Ali Dinar, a grandson of Sultan Muhammad al-Fadl. The new claimant, duly recognized at least by his own men, then adopted the same policy toward the *Ansar* as did the borderland sultans: he temporized. When Mahmud Ahmad repeatedly summoned him to El Fasher, Ali Dinar replied with various excuses, couched in an obsequiousness bordering on sarcasm. Indeed, he purported to blame his very loyalty to the Mahdiyya for attacks on him by the Masalit whose leader, however, hardly needed this reason to oppose the Fur dynast. In any case, in October 1891, he finally submitted to Abd al-Qadir Dalil, Mahmud Ahmad's deputy (and, to Ali Dinar's undoubted dismay, a former slave of his aunt) at El Fasher. Abruptly ceasing to style himself "sultan," Ali Dinar was sent to Omdurman to swear allegiance to the Khalifa, saw service in the Mahdist armies, then returned to El Fasher in 1894 where, apparently, he lent his own weight to the Mahdist government's call for dissident relatives to submit. Eventually, he went back to Omdurman, still adhering to the Mahdist cause (with what degree of sincerity has since been debated), and he was still there in 1898 when the regime collapsed.[43]

There was thus an element of prevarication in Mahmud Ahmad's early claims of complete tranquility. Peace in depopulated tribal lands was perhaps nothing to brag about. Besides, the militant Mahdist state should by its divine mandate expand; the tribes and principalities of the far west were a logical target for jihad. A biographer describes Mahmud Ahmad as "brave but stupid"; the kinder historian of Dar Masalit dubs him "optimistic" and credulous.[44] In any case, tranquility was easily maintained when gauged only by flattery and written assurances of fealty; actions spoke louder than words. The governor's repeated summonses failed to bring in the border-state rulers, and Mahmud Ahmad's prolonged absences from the province only encouraged them to renew their internecine aggression and encroach on tribal territories in Darfur itself.

It took a real threat from El Fasher to unite even temporarily the fissiparous border sultans, to whom wariness was second nature and temporizing a cardinal virtue: in 1893, Mahmud Ahmad prepared an expedition against them, accompanied by a claque of rival claimants to the local thrones; under these circumstances, the sultans refused requests for supplies and readied themselves to resist or flee. The submission of Ali Dinar had ironically emboldened them, for it seemed to mark the end of a permanent fact of central Sudanic political life, the ancient Fur sultanate, and thus to open the way to ambitious successors.[45] The Wadaians, who had established a forward base in Zaghawa country, were expelled by the *Ansar* in July 1894, and subsequently Mahmud Ahmad marched into Dar Qimr and Dar Tama and chased out their rulers in favor of disloyal relatives; it was not for nothing that Sultan

Idris of the Qimr was nicknamed *sirayju barra* ("he whose saddle is waiting outside"). But recalling Uthman Adam's disastrous rainy season campaign in 1890, the Khalifa Abdallahi ordered a halt. The newly installed pro-Mahdist sultans in Dar Qimr and Dar Tama were expelled, and Dar Masalit, Dar Sila, and indeed Wadai were spared from the wrath of Mahmud Ahmad, who returned to El Fasher via Zaghawa country. In 1896, amid western Sudanese diplomacy that was complex even by the Byzantine standards of the era, and as the Mahdist *amir* prepared to launch a massive invasion, the Anglo-Egyptian advance up the Nile toward the heart of the Mahdist state began. In November, Mahmud Ahmad was called to Omdurman, and the campaign in the west never took place.[46]

That the patience of Mahmud "Honey" had worn thin was due in part to the provocative outrages perpetrated by the self-appointed sultan of Dar Masalit, Abbakr, son of Isma'il Abd al-Nabi. In the aftermath of the Abu Jummayza revolt, Abbakr acted to establish by force his claims to a sultanate of Dar Masalit. Feared by neighboring rulers as an aggressor but disdained as a commoner, Abbakr was sui generis, unable to depend on either brotherly sultans or the Khalifa who had carried off his father and would support a rival, Hajjam Hasab Allah, against him. In 1895, when Mahmud Ahmad occupied Dar Qimr, Abbakr gave refuge to the Qimr sultan, Idris, only to rob him of all his possessions. He made his renegade position clear by raiding *Ansar* positions in Dar Qimr itself, where his men captured much booty and killed the Mahdist commander. Thus in 1896, when Mahmud Ahmad's planned invasion was canceled, Abbakr's neighbors, readied for battle with the *Ansar*, took the opportunity to turn on him instead. Sultan Yusuf of Wadai and Sultan Abu Risha of Dar Sila invaded Dar Masalit, defeated Abbakr's brother Taj al-Din, and even captured their mother, with great insult. Abbakr himself fled and was saved only by the threat of Mahdist intervention, which was enough to frighten off the Wadaian and Silawi forces and allow him to regroup.[47]

From the time of Mahmud Ahmad's recall to Omdurman in 1896 until the collapse of the Mahdist regime two years later, Darfur's administration was in the hands of three acting or deputy governors based at El Fasher, Kabkabiyya, and Dara, an arrangement presumably meant to signal the temporary nature of Mahmud Ahmad's absence and possibly to preclude rebellion by a single acting governor while the bulk of the province's army was elsewhere. At El Fasher, he left Umbadda al-Raddi in charge; at Dara, Fadlallah al-Daghur; and at Kabkabiyya, Sanin Husayn,[48] an Arab whose grandfather had settled in Dar Tama and who would long survive the collapse of the Mahdist regime. Relations between the Mahdist commanders and what has been called "the western front" of borderland sultans and tribes reached stalemate as the commanders themselves, notably Sanin, became effectively local rulers in their own right.

In events on the western borderlands we may glimpse several themes. First, as before the Mahdiyya so during it, Darfur faced a strong and determined rival in the sultanate of Wadai. As the Mahdists sought to extend their writ westward, Wadai not only resisted through various means but also probed for opportunities to extend its own power eastward; far from the cringing acceptance of the millennium, we see continuity, however chaotic normality had been in Darfur since the early 1870s. Second, this rivalry between the "big" powers of Wadai and Darfur was fought out to some extent in and by the intermediate principalities; it took military strength, deft diplomacy, and not a little luck for these states to remain independent, but the very fact that they did so served Wadai's purpose of maintaining a buffer with its powerful eastern rival. The small sultanates paid a price, in tribute and in having to accede to Wadai's wishes in their relations with each other. Third, contention for political control was complicated by the issue of legitimacy and succession, which in turn had a religious dimension: the Mahdiyya recognized no dynastic rights, so each sultanate's internal, and even external, affairs involved rival claimants and factions, not least in El Fasher. This complication was particularly serious but also opportune for Abbakr of the Masalit in the quest to build up an independent sultanate under his own rule,[49] but there are many other examples in the Arab and other tribes as well as within the sultanates. Finally, as fascinating as the complicated diplomatic and military history of the era is, there is a risk of losing sight of the forest for the trees: this was an era of great uncertainty, of changes so rapid that change seemed a constant, of dislocation and upheaval in almost every way. Comparison with, say, the Thirty Years' War may be especially apt in reminding us that the Mahdiyya was in its origins a religious movement, and that tens of thousands of its adherents, in Darfur and elsewhere, believed in its mission.

THE ECONOMY

That this is so is perhaps no better proven than by reference to the survival and, indeed, flourishing of Mahdism long after its military defeat in 1898. In this as in other respects, Darfur may serve as an example, for in purely political terms Darfur suffered as much as any other part of the Sudan. The economy of Darfur during the Mahdiyya was dominated by war and insecurity. Sources of information are incomplete and often impressionistic, but the decade or so of unsettled Turco-Egyptian rule and the wars, dislocation, migrations, droughts, and famines of the Mahdist period undoubtedly greatly impoverished the region. Looting that accompanied the Mahdist campaigns destroyed or transferred much portable wealth. The forced migrations of the Baqqara left their homelands depopulated, and although after the collapse of the Mahdist regime repatriation took place, many thousands had died in the wars.

During the Mahdiyya, long-distance trade was disrupted throughout the Sudan, and what remained was redirected: the Forty-Days Road to Egypt was effectively closed and Darfur's trade reoriented eastward, to Omdurman; the region continued to export salt, cloth, ostrich feathers, slaves, and lead and to import arms, ammunition, and some luxury goods.[50] Whereas Anglo-Egyptian statistical reports of goods trickling between the Sudan and Egypt and through the Red Sea ports indicate only trade that was officially recognized, western Sudanese products such as gum, animals, and animal by-products required reasonably settled conditions for trade of much extent, and the import of manufactures, especially war materiel, was contraband. But even the pilgrimage route to Mecca was closed; when in 1891 spies were discovered to have infiltrated those small groups who appeared anyway in Darfur, the pilgrims were arrested. Because of all this, trade between western Darfur and Wadai became more important. To be sure, it too was disrupted by political insecurity, but the trans-Saharan route to the Mediterranean remained open, and slaves, ostrich feathers, and ivory continued to be exported.[51] An almost constant state of war in the western Darfur borderlands indeed helped to enrich the sultan of Wadai, who clearly took advantage of his smaller neighbors' exposure to the Mahdist jihad to extort tribute from them and was able to use his local control of foreign trade to impose his political will.[52]

Both settled and nomadic populations were prey to the armies of the Mahdiyya and of their indigenous neighbors. Although the Baqqara, for example, had a history of raiding and retreating, cattle actually restricted their mobility and made them relatively easy targets for determined, well-armed soldiers. The fate of cultivators was potentially worse, of course. The rich farmlands of western Darfur were tempting targets at all times, not only when famine prevailed elsewhere; when Uthman Adam swept through Dar Masalit in 1890, virtually the entire population fled, and what his army did not eat, they took away with them, leaving returning locals with nothing but what they had taken with them, including their slaves.

The Sudan in general experienced several periods of severe drought and famine, and several epidemics, during the Mahdiyya. These were nothing new to Darfur, but to natural disaster as causes or accompaniments was added man-made insecurity. There is no doubt that wartime conditions, including the concentration of large numbers of fighting men and camp followers with little or no medical resources and at times living off the land; the depredations suffered by the civilian population through whose lands the armies marched; the forced migrations of the Baqqara; and the food shortages and consequent greater vulnerability to disease of townspeople when agriculture and trade were disrupted played their parts in making the entire period from the fall of the Turco-Egyptian regime in 1874 until the accession of the Anglo-Egyptian Condominium (described later) in 1916 one of almost unparalleled disaster in popular memory. The population of Darfur may have declined by as much as half. Several of the famines of the period were bad enough to be named: that of 1873–74 is *Karo Fata* or "White Bone."[53]

No disaster surpassed that of the great famine of 1888–92 (the *Sanat Sita*, or "Year Six," because it began in 1306 of the Muslim calendar), which affected most of the northern Sudan. In the east, the cause was drought. In Darfur, the causes were partly political: the revolt of Abu Jummayza and the enforcement of the Khalifa's policy of tribal migration to the east. Those areas where food was plentiful, notably the western sultanates, became prey to Mahdist armies; conditions may have been made even worse by a locust plague in 1889. In any case, the ground prepared by food shortages was exploited by disease. The cholera virus, which was already known to spread particularly easily along trade and pilgrimage routes and, once established, to pose a devastating threat to troop concentrations, struck first. Across the whole of the northern Sudan and Ethiopia the epidemic raged, with great loss of life; statistics are lacking, but anecdotal evidence from eyewitnesses is abundant. The same period witnessed what may have been the nineteenth-century Sudan's worst outbreak of smallpox, which numbered Abu Jummayza among its many victims. In the aftermath of famine and disease, moreover, survivors were more vulnerable than usual to further challenges; rainfall was poor in 1894, and plagues of locusts were common.[54]

5

BETWEEN AN ANVIL AND A HAMMER

The Reign of Ali Dinar, 1898–1916

ALI DINAR AND THE BRITISH

In November 1896, the Khalifa Abdallahi ordered Mahmud Ahmad, governor of the west, to bring his army east to help defend the Mahdist state against Anglo-Egyptian invasion. Since the fall of Khartoum in January 1885, powerful forces in Britain and Egypt had looked to "reconquest" of the Sudan as the only outcome consonant with British imperial interests and worthy of British dignity. Others had just as firmly opposed all-out war, preferring to adopt a defensive posture and await events. The European – and, indeed, African – diplomatic background to the decision finally to make a limited advance along the Sudanese Nile in March 1896 is part of the final chapter in the Scramble for Africa, one that would end only in 1916 with the annexation of Darfur.

European opposition to British occupation of Egypt had not ceased in 1882. Egypt's strategic position and glamorous place in the European imagination rendered it a special case, one further complicated by the fact that, at least until 1914, Egypt remained legally a province of the Ottoman Empire. The anomalies of British occupation have interested scholars far more than they did British proconsuls in Cairo,[1] but they affected every aspect of British policy in Egypt and of British and Egyptian policy toward the Sudan. This is not the place to delve again into Bismarck's *realpolitik* or the legal ramifications of the Capitulations, the *Caisse de la Dette*, and the Mixed Tribunals. It suffices here to note that Darfur had been territory ruled by Egypt while Egypt was a province of the Ottoman Empire, that Britain and Egypt for purposes of their own therefore treated the Mahdist state as lands in rebellion rather than as a sovereign entity, and that what was decided in Paris,

Berlin, or Cairo would redound in Wadai and Darfur, whether or not the Sudanese liked it.[2]

It was for several reasons therefore that, from its inception, what would be known as the "Anglo-Egyptian Sudan" was an unequal partnership. Successive khedives and the old Turco-Egyptian ruling elite chafing under British occupation saw in recovery of the Sudan a partial restoration of lost prestige. Successive British governments, overseeing a three-dimensional African chess match in which worldwide rivalries and interests were advanced or checked, were loath to take control of huge new territories that might upset balances and prove costly to administer. A powerful British administrative and military elite in Egypt, with useful alliances in business circles and the home press, publicly obsessed about avenging Gordon, relieving the agonies of the Sudanese, and removing the Mahdist affront to civilization, while privately warning about French, Belgian, and other gambits from the east, west, and south threatening the Nile, the key to Egypt. The solution was a classic example of ad hoc imperialism: Britain would supply troops to "reconquer" the Sudan and officials to administer it, while Egypt would foot the bill and, as nominal co-ruler, shield Britain diplomatically against European complaints. Thus, the anomalies of internationalism that annoyed the British in Egypt could be used to their advantage in the Sudan.

The Anglo-Egyptian campaign, once begun, proved inexorable. The conquest of Dongola was achieved by September 1896. After months of careful preparation, the advance continued, and Abu Hamad, commanding the great bend of the Nile, was captured in August 1897, thus allowing completion of Kitchener's railway from Wadi Halfa. The Mahdist commander, Mahmud Ahmad, fresh from Darfur, proved dilatory and inept. Anglo-Egyptian forces occupied Berber in September 1897, and a forward base was established at the mouth of the Atbara. Short of food, Mahmud's army began to disintegrate, then to starve. But determined to fight rather than conduct a strategic retreat, he marched his army to the Atbara where, on 8 April 1898, Kitchener's Anglo-Egyptian force routed it; Mahmud Ahmad was taken prisoner and the remnants of his army fled. While the British prepared for the final phase of the campaign, the Khalifa Abdallahi held back with a huge army, awaiting the invaders. When Kitchener set out again in August, therefore, he met no opposition until he reached the Karari Hills a few miles north of Omdurman. While his gunboats bombarded the

Mahdi's capital, Kitchener's army, equipped with machine guns against the charges of *Ansar* cavalry and spearmen, routed the Mahdist host on 2 September; as many as 11,000 *Ansar* were killed and some 16,000 left wounded; the Anglo-Egyptian army suffered only 48 dead. Kitchener entered Omdurman, and the Khalifa, having fled, was finally cornered and killed at the battle of Umm Diwaykarat in November 1899.

Mopping up from these cataclysmic events and creating a new regime on the ruins of the Mahdist state would occupy the British for years to come. Their troops began to leave within days of the battle of Omdurman; suppressing Mahdist resistance, occupying – and even exploring – the far-flung provinces of the Sudan, setting up and staffing an administration, and achieving a modicum of security would be the work of the British-led Egyptian army, fortified (and watched) by a small British garrison, and of Egyptian, British, and other foreign administrators. The "constitutional" framework of the regime, two Anglo-Egyptian conventions that, together, came to be called the Condominium Agreement, was laid down in January 1899.[3] The wars, droughts, famines, and migrations of the Mahdiyya had doubtless taken a heavy toll, and the local resources the new regime had available were meager. Under these circumstances, decisions taken regarding Darfur – and the whole of the southern Sudan – are easy to understand. Indeed, the latter region, after flag-raisings and border demarcations, would undergo almost three decades of "pacification."

At about the time of the battle of Omdurman, Ali Dinar, the erstwhile Fur sultan, and a few tribal notables raced westward from the Mahdist capital to reclaim his patrimony. He had good reason to hurry. Although not counted as shadow sultans, other pretenders had emerged after his submission in October 1891; the Fur sultans reproduced prodigiously, and Ali Dinar himself was not the son of a sultan but only one of countless grandsons, a point relevant in precedence. A certain Ahmad Abu Shak, known from a single documentary source, aspired to the throne in the early 1890s; there must have been others. Ibrahim Ali, a grandson of Sultan Ibrahim Qarad taken up by Kitchener and allowed to go west after the battle of the Atbara, dawdled, and Ali Dinar, setting out later, beat him to El Fasher where, however, he found another cousin, Hussayn Abu Kauda, already ensconced. With followers he had picked up en route, Ali Dinar took over the capital. The feckless Ibrahim Ali pleaded for British help; Kitchener, now governor-general of the Sudan, told him that the race belonged to the swift. Ali Dinar's men, near Umm Shanqa, routed Ibrahim Ali, who fled; Abu Kauda submitted. Ali Dinar took pains to assure Kitchener of his loyalty, the British ignored Mahdist-era evidence to the contrary, and a modus vivendi was established. All of this took place before the death of the Khalifa Abdallahi in November 1899, while the nascent Anglo-Egyptian regime was fully occupied.[4]

Despite the ease with which Ali Dinar had reclaimed his throne and come to terms with the British, he never fully mastered the task before him. During the Mahdiyya, Darfur had suffered as much as any part of the Egyptian dominion; it had known no peace since the early 1870s, and to the effects of war and famine had been added the forced exodus of the Baqqara. The great-power rivalry of Darfur and Wadai had given way to particularism. The French and Belgians were advancing from the south and west and Anglo-Egyptian forces from the east: the latter occupied El Obeid, capital of Kordofan, in December 1899. Once it found its footing, the Condominium regime was bound to take an interest in Darfur, whose border with Kordofan meant nothing to the tribes and whose trade would depend on routes beyond its control. Although in the end Ali Dinar, and Darfur itself, fell to European imperialism, the wonder is that he survived for as long as he did.

Ali Dinar's main assets in doing so were the weakness of the Anglo-Egyptian regime – which soon became known blandly as the "Sudan Government" – and the very remoteness of Darfur. Despite the titles and panoply of Kitchener and Sir Reginald Wingate, who succeeded him as governor-general in 1899, the last word on major issues – and on many minor ones – rested with the British agent and consul-general in Cairo, Lord Cromer. He had acted as a brake on British officers – none more than Wingate, director of military intelligence for the Egyptian army during the Mahdiyya – who had pushed, prodded, and cajoled to "avenge Gordon" and conquer the Sudan. For Cromer, the only reason for a British presence in the Sudan was the security of Egypt. Once he had acquiesced in "reconquest," his objective was staking out Anglo-Egyptian borders at the least cost to Egypt's treasury. He knew little and cared less about Darfur, and if Ali Dinar could keep it quiet without British or Egyptian men and money, the sultanate would approximate his ideal African dependency. In this attitude we may see an extreme

Figure 6. An embassy from Sultan Ali Dinar of Darfur in Khartoum, 1907. Ali Dinar, the last sultan, maintained generally correct relations with the encroaching Anglo-Egyptian authorities until the First World War. (Durham University Library, A30/35.)

version of what would later be enshrined as an ideology of benign neglect.

As much as the soldiers would have liked to adopt a "forward" policy, they came to appreciate the necessity of Cromer's line in light of their meager resources. When Wingate launched a trial balloon about raising British and Egyptian flags in Darfur, Cromer shot it down. Officers' "earth-hunger and prestige mania" only increased his vigilance; Ali Dinar should be held by "the lightest of threads." Successive titles used in addressing him are therefore an index of Wingate's thwarted ambition rather than of the Fur prince's status: from Wingate's "agent" he evolved into a "ruler," "Emir Ali Dinar, Acting for the Government in Darfur," "Emir Ali Dinar, Managing Darfur Affairs," and finally "Sultan Ali Dinar." The substance of Wingate's communications was more liberal, for although plain reference was made to Ali Dinar's vassalage, and a token payment of five hundred pounds a year was assessed, he enjoyed a free hand in the sultanate's affairs. Nor should the obsequious language of his own messages to the Sudan Government obscure their real intent: when he begged for "orders," he was probing for concessions. And when Wingate proposed sending his inspector-general – the ubiquitous Slatin Pasha – to Darfur for consultations, Ali Dinar resorted to "tajility," stalling until Slatin, already in western Kordofan, gave up. No senior British official entered Darfur during Ali Dinar's reign.[5]

Ali Dinar's relations with the Sudan Government therefore approximated those of a remote Indian prince with the British Raj. London was concerned only with issues that impinged on sovereignty: Darfur's relations with neighboring territories subject to European encroachment; international commerce, including trade in slaves and arms; and tribal affairs along Darfur's borders with Kordofan and the Bahr al-Ghazal. (Published annual reports on the Sudan mentioned Ali Dinar only in passing: his "attitude" was reported in 1903 as "eminently satisfactory"; the 149-page report for 1904 devoted two sentences to Darfur, under "Frontier Affairs.") Khartoum's policy toward the slave trade was ambiguous, officially intolerant to fend off European critics but in fact pragmatically laissez-faire. Frightened Darfur *shaykhs* or dispossessed *jallaba* who petitioned the Sudan Government were ignored or told to take up their complaints with the sultan. In 1905 Slatin assured Ali Dinar in writing that the Sudan Government would "return by force all those who flee from Darfur" for any reason.[6] It was only during the First World War, when Ali Dinar's "attitude" turned hostile and the world's attention turned elsewhere, that Khartoum purported to discover intolerable atrocities in Darfur.

OPPOSITION

Mahdist and Tribal Resistance

Ali Dinar's subjects were more difficult to deal with than the British. Mahdist resistance had not ended at Karari. In Darfur, it took several forms: bitter-enders, who would have to be suppressed by force; those loath to give up positions to which the Mahdiyya had raised them; and true believers who, temporarily discombobulated by events, would later reemerge as the rank and file of "neo-Mahdism."

An example of the first was the redoubtable Ta'aishi amir Arabi Dafallah who, having been forced in 1897 to evacuate Equatoria by Belgians advancing from the Congo, had made his way into southern Darfur. After clashing with forces sent by Ali Dinar and Kitchener, Arabi settled eventually in Dar Kara in the far southwest, where he lived as a virtual bandit. It was only in 1902, after heavy defeats at the hands of the encroaching French, that he and his men surrendered to Ali Dinar.[7]

Figure 7. The mosque at Kabkabiyya, 1919. (Durham University Library, A16/28.)

Much more serious was the resistance of Sanin Hussayn, who in 1896 had been made acting governor of western Darfur when Mahmud Ahmad and his army went east. From his seat at Kabkabiyya, Sanin, whose mother was a Tamawi, was virtually independent and a powerful player in the war and politics of the borderland sultanates. After the fall of the Mahdist state, various die-hard elements gravitated to him. His relations with Ali Dinar in the days when the latter was a fugitive had been poor. In 1900, the sultan sent a large force against him, which was twice defeated. Sanin appealed to Khartoum as a loyal servant, but if the flimsy documentary record is to be trusted, he hardly needed help: in 1901, he scored another victory against Ali Dinar's troops and in 1903 two more. In 1907, the sultan mounted a huge campaign, sending two armies under the famous commander, Adam Rijal, and Ali Dinar's own most trusted nobleman, Mahmud Ali al-Dadingawi. Instead of forcing battle, they surrounded Sanin's camp. The siege lasted an astonishing eighteen months, and most of Sanin's starving fighters gradually deserted. Finally, in January 1909, Sanin's *zariba* (fortified camp) was stormed. He and his lieutenants were killed and their heads sent to decorate the market at El Fasher.[8]

Although Sanin proved the most formidable challenger to Ali Dinar's authority and prestige, he was by no means the last. The southern tribes, those that had remained during the Mahdiyya and those that had survived it in the east and, with the encouragement of the Sudan Government, were returning, had long histories of violent relations with the sultanate. In 1900–01, Ali Dinar settled scores with scattered remnants of the Bani Halba, despoiling the tribe and killing its *shaykh*. After reporting to the Sudan Government that the Rizayqat and Ma'alia had plundered traders from the west, rustled livestock from neighboring tribes, burnt villages, and carried off women and children, Ali Dinar routed the Ma'alia in September 1901; the Rizayqat fled south. Musa Madibbu, the Rizayqat *shaykh*, went to El Obeid to plead his case and was told to go home and follow the sultan's orders: he did so and came to terms. It was only when Ali Dinar's forces, taking on the eastern hill people of Kaja Seruj, pursued fleeing survivors into Kordofan and threatened Foja that the Sudan Government took any action. Posts in western Kordofan were lightly reinforced, and Ali Dinar backed off. As his biographer makes clear, however, "there was no sanction short of outright conquest, that could be applied to Ali Dinar, and both sides knew it."[9]

Thus, clashes between the sultan and tribes on the Kordofan side of the border tended to be resolved by negotiation. Ali Dinar thought nothing of writing directly to tribal chiefs and provincial officials there, presumably reasoning correctly that their bringing his threats and complaints to Khartoum's attention would be more effective than doing so himself. He sent forces in hot pursuit deep into Kordofan and reacted with indignation or apology, depending on the circumstances, when he was warned off. Such problems were unavoidable even with the best of wills: the border was poorly defined, ran through tribal *dars*, and was meaningless to nomads whose periodic migrations depended on rainfall and grazing. Besides, it was in the sultan's interest to keep the peace with the tribes of Kordofan, notably the far-ranging Kababish, with whom Darfur's relations ebbed and flowed throughout his reign; the Kababish wanted the Sudan Government to occupy Darfur and regulate the affairs of the tribes that neighbored their huge nomadic *dar*. Thus, the difficulties that arose should not be seen as trumped up for small advantage or, if they were, to have been so by Ali Dinar rather than by the *shaykhs* or renegades along the wild frontier.

The Western Borderlands

Largely because of such problems, an attempt was made in 1903 to define the borders of Darfur. Anglo-French agreements in 1898–99 had referred to respective spheres of influence in terms of the Nile-Congo watershed and the historical border between Wadai and Darfur (as the latter had been constituted as a province of the Egyptian Sudan in 1882). When in 1903 Slatin parleyed at al-Nahud with an envoy of Ali Dinar and a description was rendered of Darfur's frontiers (notably with Kordofan), this left Darfur's western borders unclear:[10] the problem was not susceptible to technical solution by surveyors, for it consisted of the Darfur and Wadai sultans' competing claims to sovereignty over the intermediate *dars* of the Tama, Sila, Masalit, Qimr, and Zaghawa. The arrogant offhandedness of 1898 began to assume troubling political dimensions when the French steadily advanced eastward in the early years of the twentieth century and Ali Dinar sought to impose his rule in the west.

Seen in this light, the enormous campaign of 1907–09 against Sanin Hussayn at Kabkabiyya is easier to understand, for much more than pride was at stake. Whatever claims Paris and London would concoct for the western borderlands, Ali Dinar knew these belonged to him. Relations between Darfur and Wadai, and with the petty sultanates between them, had entered a new and, as it happened, final phase with the arrival of the French. In April 1900, the French defeated and killed the extraordinary empire-builder Rabih Zubayr and established a protectorate of Chad, which brought them into direct contact with Wadai. Sultan Yusuf of Wadai had died in 1898, and from the ensuing succession struggle, in which the French found opportunities to interfere, Muhammad Salih (known as Dud Murra, or "Lion of Murra") finally emerged in June 1902 as sultan. Moving steadily eastward, establishing fortified posts as they went, the French had by 1907 advanced to within a hundred miles of the Wadaian capital at Abeshr.

The French conquest of Wadai brought to a head the problem of Darfur's western borders. The situation was reminiscent of that in 1874 when Darfur had been annexed to the Egyptian Sudan. France's hold on its vast new conquests was weak, lines of communication were long and tenuous, a shadow sultan (in this case, the dethroned Dud Marra) remained at large, and the neighboring sultanate, now Darfur, posed a potent and unpredictable threat. The French, moreover, in keeping with the ethos of the Scramble for Africa, laid claim to all territories that had ever been subject to the sultans of Wadai and immediately sent out patrols to show the flag. This constituted aggression when seen from Darfur, for Ali Dinar's claims over the border sultanates had strong historical roots that he had cultivated since the end of the Mahdiyya. His relations with Sultan Bakhit of Dar Sila conformed to the old pattern: he married a Silawi princess and, at first, caravans from Dar Sila passed peacefully through Darfur. After 1906, however, for reasons unknown, there was a falling-out; Ali Dinar kept the upper hand by virtue of his control of Dar Sila's trade to the east. Likewise, Ali Dinar treated Sultan Idris of Dar Qimr as a vassal and, when disrespect was shown, repaid it tenfold by plundering the *dar* and putting the old man to flight.[11]

Ali Dinar's relations with Dar Masalit were more complicated. This was the most powerful of the border states; to Ali Dinar, and indeed to his fellow rulers, it was not a sultanate at all but rather an illegitimate by-product of the Mahdiyya, during which its ruler, the parvenu Abbakr, had arrogated to himself and his *dar* a status to which they were not entitled. Mutual wariness in the early days of Ali Dinar's reign soon gave way to open hostility. In 1905, Adam Ali and Mahmud Ali al-Dadingawi defeated the Masalit at Shawai and captured Abbakr, who was paraded through El Fasher with the spoils of war. While he remained a hostage, leadership of the Masalit passed to his brother, Taj al-Din, but the Fur were too much for him, and for a time it appeared that Ali Dinar might break up the *dar* and rule it directly through *maliks* and *shartays*. Any such plan was forestalled by fierce Masalit resistance. But their defeat of another Fur army cost them their sultan when, in vengeance, Ali Dinar executed the hostage Abbakr. Taj al-Din succeeded him and in 1907 made peace with Ali Dinar.

The sultan's motive in coming to terms with the Masalit may well have been concern over the continuing French advance from the west. In any case, in early 1908 the French defeated the Wadaian army twice near Atya and, in June 1909, after inflicting further humiliating defeats on Sultan Dud Murra, a French column entered Abeshr. Dud Murra fled, and the French installed his cousin, Adam Asil, as nominal sultan. In the aftermath of this stunning development, the French turned their attention to the border states and, through Adam Asil, called on the sultans to recognize the new regime. A column entered Dar Tama and replaced Sultan Uthman with a puppet. Sultan Bakhit of Dar Sila and Sultan Idris of Dar Qimr both offered to concede, received French embassies, and signed treaties establishing protectorates over their *dars*. There followed, at the end of 1909, French reconnaissance into Dar Masalit, already stricken after the hostilities with Darfur.

Ali Dinar watched these events with alarm. It behooved him to remind the Sudan Government of that aspect of their relations to which both sides had paid lip service: Anglo-Egyptian sovereignty. In a barrage of angry letters, he asked what Khartoum intended to do about French aggression into territories long subject to Darfur and that, by submitting to France, were in rebellion against him. In one reply almost sure to raise ire, Slatin, whose broad remit was "native affairs," wrote appeasingly that "the boundary of Darfur" was "well known to the French Government, and you must not be afraid that France will encroach on it." In a further missive, Slatin warned Ali Dinar not to enter into direct negotiations with the French. No scion of the Keira could have failed to detect European collusion, and Ali Dinar decided to raise the ante.

In this resolve, the sultan was buoyed by a French disaster. Apparently expecting the same passivity that had greeted their arrival in the other *dars*, the French reconnaissance force in Dar Masalit let down its guard and on 4 January 1910 was ambushed and wiped out at Kirinding. A week later, Ali Dinar brashly informed the British inspector at al-Nahud that, in light of French aggression, he was preparing to take the field himself. At this point, London and Paris became engaged, but with little effect on the ground: orders relayed to Ali Dinar to respect the border were meaningless when there was no border. Nor could he ignore local developments, news of which reached El Fasher very quickly; the Sudan Government's bland pronouncements must at the very least have appeared out of date. When Slatin, writing from Khartoum – or Vienna or Scotland – counseled patience and respect for borders, French columns were laying waste to Dar Masalit and overthrowing sultans whom Ali Dinar (and, in Egyptian days, Slatin himself) had considered tributary to Darfur.[12]

Table turning was the law of nations in this part of the world. Risings in the other sultanates coincided with Darfur's intervention. The French were ejected from Dar Qimr and Dar Tama, while the Darfur army, under Adam Rijal, raided deep into Wadai. Yet, by May 1910, Adam

Rijal's army had been defeated by a much smaller but better-armed French force, the French puppet-sultans had been restored in Dar Tama and Dar Qimr, and Dud Murra had fled to Dar Masalit, whence Sultan Taj al-Din, undeterred by his allies' setbacks, continued to raid into Wadai. During the ensuing rainy season, French reinforcements were brought up, and in November they advanced into Dar Masalit. On the 9th, at Daroti, the Masalit launched a surprise attack, which was beaten off only after heavy casualties on both sides, including Sultan Taj al-Din. In military terms, this battle was indecisive, but the French could not tolerate the status quo. In January 1911, a French column marched through Dar Masalit, winning bloody victories and destroying the capital, Darjil. While the French were thus occupied, Ali Dinar sent raiding parties into Dar Tama, causing great destruction and taking much booty. Threatened with another French invasion, the new Masalit sultan, Abbakr's son Endoka, expelled Dud Murra, who finally surrendered to the French in October 1911. With their position solidifying, in 1912 the French deposed their puppet in Wadai and assumed direct rule. Of the other sultanates, only Dar Masalit emerged with independence intact – but with a third of its territory lost and with deep divisions within its ruling elite: the sultan of Dar Sila accepted French suzerainty, while the French, having killed the sultan of the Zaghawa Kobe, Abd al-Rahman Firti, installed their own man there, Hajjar Toke.[13]

By the eve of the First World War, Darfur had thus come to occupy between the French and British colonial empires a position analogous to that which the petty sultanates had occupied until then between Darfur and Wadai. European diplomacy would thereafter decide the fate of the borderlands and their people: Anglo-French relations were too important to be left to the whims and fancies of Ali Dinar, let alone of shadow sultans and disgruntled cousins; and although British and French soldier-administrators were reluctant to give up even a mile of scrubland, their superiors were less willing to endanger the *Entente Cordiale*. In essence the positions of the two sides were compatible. French claims to the borderland *dars* were weak, and they had no claims at all to Darfur; France pressed for early delimitation that would force the British to control and therefore to occupy Darfur. The British were reluctant – because without commitment of major military, financial, and administrative resources, they were unable – to do so. Slatin, a ready (if out-of-date) reference for all things Darfurian, was relied on to imagine a factual basis for Anglo-Egyptian claims to Dars Tama, Qimr, and Masalit at least; many of his opinions were obviously written by Wingate.[14] Even al-Zubayr Pasha, of all people, was called in retirement to testify. But any border claim, like any border, has two sides, and in this case old travelers' accounts, sketch maps, sultanic correspondence, even lists of goods sent and received by rulers – were these gifts or "tribute"? – were dusted off and subjected to palaeographic examination in the respective foreign ministries.

British qualms, almost entirely financial, were thus adumbrated in high-sounding references to the precedent need for France to recognize Anglo-Egyptian sovereignty in Dars Tama and Masalit – and to the breach of faith with Ali Dinar that occupation of Darfur would entail. The French held to the view that delimitation without occupation would result in a border respected by only one party to the agreement, themselves. The weakness of each position – the empty claims of France versus the empty treasury of the Sudan Government – is evident in the dilatoriness of the diplomacy that ensued. On the British side, a note from Paris to London had to be referred to Cairo, then Khartoum, then Wingate (in Dunbar or Baden or Equatoria), then Slatin (similarly at large), with draft replies exchanged by each pair of correspondents before anything could be dispatched to Paris; on the French side were similar, if less attenuated, channels. In May 1912, the British proposed a conference in Europe to settle the issue in early autumn when both Wingate and Slatin would be on leave. In July, Paris agreed but suggested December, when officials from Equatorial Africa could attend. The British accepted December but only in Khartoum, not Europe, because Wingate and Slatin could not leave their posts then. The French declined Khartoum, with its echoes of Fashoda, so in August, the British suggested Cairo; in December, the Quai d'Orsay demurred that colonial officials' work in Paris, and their *health*, would not permit their traveling to Cairo![15]

In ensuing intramural correspondence about the possibility of arbitration, the British seemed in 1913 to adopt a new line, which may also have been evident in – or even caused by – Kitchener's appointment as British representative in Cairo. In any case, he ruled that Ali Dinar's "appointment" as sultan of Darfur "strictly prohibited" his involvement in foreign affairs; if after delimitation he abused the frontier with French territory, the Sudan Government would be justified in stepping in to stop him and would, in any case, establish border posts. But such an evolution in thinking by colonial men on the spot was irrelevant at this point because Paris and London were unable to agree on details of the proposed arbitration: by the outbreak of the First World War, these had not been settled, and in January 1915 the British suggested deferring the whole issue until after the war.[16]

ALI DINAR'S DOMESTIC POLICY

The Tribes

Ability to conquer but inability to rule might have been the epitaph of successive regimes in Darfur. Under the first sultanate, the Baqqara of the south gave constant trouble; the Egyptian regime could patrol and extort tribute but never administer; the Khalifa had resorted to forced migration, the peace of virtual imprisonment. Ali Dinar fared no better: behind the panoply of Sudanic kingship and the bluster of an autocrat was a kingdom in almost constant revolt. Reference has been made to the difficulties posed by the Kababish camel nomads of northern Kordofan, whose seasonal migrations across Darfur were fraught, even with the best wills in the world, with potential for disturbance. Both sides appealed to the Sudan Government, which preferred, in the absence of general hostilities or unwonted interest from the outside world, to let them sort out their own problems in time-honored fashion. When it came to the tribes of Darfur, Ali Dinar was on his own.

Relations with the Baqqara tribes were a constant preoccupation. Ali Dinar granted clemency to the Rizayqat chief, Musa Madibbu, in 1899, but they were always at odds, and in 1913 Ali Dinar told Slatin he intended to destroy the unregenerate Musa, not only for the usual catalogue of murder, rustling, unpaid tribute, warring on neighboring tribes, harboring wanted fugitives, and other enormities but also because the Rizayqat were in treasonous contact with the French. The sultan's campaign against them, at the end of October 1913, ravaged Dar Rizayqat but met unexpected reverses, and his army under Ramadan Ali was forced to retreat. This only postponed the day of reckoning; Musa Madibbu went to Kordofan and begged for British intervention, but had not Slatin once wanted help from Musa's father, Madibbu Ali? Musa was told to submit to the sultan or go into exile. He submitted.

The Sudan Government's deference (or dereliction) in the matter of revolting tribes reached its apogee in 1913 with the Zayadiyya. For reasons hotly disputed at the time, a section of these camel nomads fled to Kordofan, where other sections of their tribe were already settled, and asked for permission to remain. British opinions differed, but Slatin had the last word: the tribe must either go back to Darfur and submit to the sultan's rule or be resettled far away from the border and their kinsmen. They chose the latter option. After a year of extreme destitution – and the outbreak of the First World War, which cost the Sudan Government the services of Slatin, an Austrian – they were allowed back to live with the Kordofan Zayadiyya.[17] The biographer of Ali Dinar contrasts this case with that of the Bani Halba, the long-troublesome neighbors of the Rizayqat, whose rebellion early in 1914 Ali Dinar put down; some rebels absconded to Dar Sila with their loot, and Ali Dinar complained to the French in Wadai, with no results.[18] Subsequent cross-border tribal flare-ups took on new significance; even minor incidents in the most remote localities of the Muslim world would be examined through the lens of the Great War.

As hard as the Sudan Government's policy toward Darfur refugees appears, and indeed as fatal as noninterference may have been for various dissidents and rebels, such results were inherent in the sultanate's autonomy. Moreover, all incidents – not only before the First World War but also during it, when Khartoum suddenly became more attentive to the plight of the injured – should be seen from both sides. Tribal *shaykhs* had a long history of pitting one overlord against another. And it was in Ali Dinar's own interest to keep the tribes content, at least to the extent of keeping them in Darfur; depopulation of the province, with concomitant loss of production and revenue, served no purpose.[19] Was Ali Dinar's rule oppressive? By whose standards should it be judged? To answer these and related questions, we turn to the nature of the revived sultanate under him and thus to the policies Ali Dinar adopted to establish and maintain his rule.

Restoration and Legitimacy

The ability of successive shadow sultans to hold out against the Egyptians after 1874 and during the Mahdiyya indicates the strength of the Keira ruling clan's legitimacy in the eyes of the Fur and others. That these princes were reduced to the status of refugees did not destroy that legitimacy, and the return of Ali Dinar to El Fasher was in a literal sense a restoration. But he was one of many with equal claims to the throne: Sultan Muhammad al-Fadl, his grandfather, was survived in 1838 by forty-six adult sons, and Ali Dinar's father, despite posthumous titles, never ruled.[20] Thus, both by birth and by virtue of the interregnum, he needed to buttress his rule by reference to tradition and right and by demonstrating success. Toward his many uncles, cousins, and nephews, the *awlad al-salatin*, he was neither as draconian as some of his predecessors nor as feckless as others, but judicious: Husayn Abu Kauda, the pretender he ousted upon his return from Omdurman in 1898, was given a minor post at court; another cousin, Husayn Ibrahim Qarad, was said to have been immured for three years. Among his wives were princesses of the neighboring sultanates' royal houses, to which, in turn, were sent in marriage high-born Keira ladies; nor did Ali Dinar depart from the old sultanic custom of hospitality for overthrown or aspiring princes of those *dars*.

In restoring forms and usages, however, Ali Dinar was flexible and pragmatic and, although neither an antiquarian nor a modernizer, he adapted ancient custom to suit current needs. This flexibility knew few bounds: it ranged from such orthodox sovereign commonplaces as endowing mosques and at least several times sending a *mahmal* (a cover for the *Ka'ba*) to Mecca under elaborate escort; to jaw-droppingly heterodox claims of miracle working, including rainmaking, cures, and mind-control, accounts of which appeared in the British press. Gilding the lily of the Keira sultans' stupendous genealogy, Ali Dinar had himself described as "the Hashemite," "the Abbasid."[21]

During his entire reign, Ali Dinar never left Darfur, did not campaign, and rarely ranged far from El Fasher, where he lived in Sudanic state. He restored the grand pre-Mahdist nomenclature at court but, as we have seen in the evolving relations of officeholders and titleholders in the nineteenth century, circumstances and ability meant more than old (or new) titles.[22] Far from suppressing Mahdism, he borrowed freely from its terminology and practice. He received at court ex-Mahdists and confirmed in or appointed to office servants of the late regime. Many had collaborated under duress, and his personal knowledge in such matters must have been immense; but some never abandoned the cause.[23] Among prominent Mahdists, or ex-Mahdists, in Ali Dinar's service were the *amirs* Arabi Dafallah, Adam al-Nur Jahi, Ali Sanusi, and Jumʿa wad Jadayn; some who won his favor later lost it.[24] An early historian went so far as to state that Ali Dinar "did nothing to revive the older system"; "he had been brought up under the Mahdia and he believed in military and personal government," but this goes too far. Necessity was the mother of his innovations, and judging the extent to which "the older system" was revived or not presumes greater knowledge of it than sources allow.[25]

Yet having seen the power of religiously inspired dissent, Ali Dinar acted cautiously in dealing with heterodoxy. His relations with the powerful Sanusiyya order of sufis, which during the nineteenth century from its base in Cyrenaica and the Fezzan had spread its influence into the central Sudanic lands, were checkered: early warmth, inspired by common commercial interests, gave way to hostility over Sanusi activities in Wadai; relations were later restored, and a Sanusi lodge was apparently established in El Fasher. The equally prominent Tijaniyya was allowed to recruit, but by joining it himself he ipso facto became Darfur's most prominent member. He came down harshly on self-proclaimed messiahs – he executed a Mahdi, a Jesus, and a reincarnation of the Prophet Muhammad – but at court kept favorite *faqihs* around him. In the provinces, he restored estates to established religious families and sought, as much perhaps for economic as religious reasons, to settle *faqihs* on abandoned lands. A novelty entirely in keeping with his justifiable fear of religious pretenders was Ali Dinar's organization of Darfur's *faqihs* by district and their required presence annually in El Fasher for Ramadan.[26]

Personal Rule

Pragmatism extended to territorial administration. The office of *maqdum*, on which in the nineteenth century perhaps too much had depended for Ali Dinar's liking, was diminished, with the partial exception of the *maqdum* of the north, Muhammad Adam Sharif, to whom, personally, Ali Dinar also restored family estates. Even he was reportedly kept on a short leash.[27] *Maqdums* were appointed in the south on an ad hoc basis, and none served for long: four *maqdums* (including Mahmud al-Dadingawi) in succession administered Dar Diima and Dar Kerne during one ten-year period. The powers of the even older

Figure 8. Maqbula bint Nurayn, granddaughter of Sultan Muhammad al-Fadl of Darfur (d. 1838), widow of the Mahdi, and mother of Sayyid Abd al-Rahman al-Mahdi. (Durham University Library, 747/6/4.)

provincial hierarchs, the *abo dali*, *abo dima* (*dimangawi*), *takanawi*, and *abbo umo* (*umangawi*), were not revived, although some of the titles and honors these had accrued survived. In administrative terms, Ali Dinar reverted instead to direct rule over lesser territorial and tribal chiefs. These answered to the sultan through *manadib* (sing. *mandub*) or agents, who had no traditional claim to authority, could be transferred, and thus posed little threat of rebellion.[28] For historians of the period, as for the Anglo-Egyptian regime after the overthrow of Ali Dinar, the result was difficulty in sorting out the apparently overlapping responsibilities of the territorial and functional offices that had survived. One has only to consider the discordant nomenclature, constitutional powers, and real authority of offices in the modern European or American state to realize the potential for misrepresenting aspects of Ali Dinar's system.

In practice, Ali Dinar relied at the center on a few officials appointed for their loyalty and competence rather than through claims to inherited rights. As *wazir* (vizier), he appointed successively a certain Kairan, a Baqqara Arab; Tayrab Sulayman; the Takruri Adam Rijal, who married Ali Dinar's daughter; and Ramadan Ali, his former slave at Omdurman. They acted at times as commander-in-chief or chief minister, although Adam Rijal seems at least on occasion to have performed both functions, until he fell from grace in 1911. Even in the military sphere, a commander-in-chief may have been supreme only by title. The position of chief adviser appears to have been filled informally by Mahmud Ali al-Dadingawi, the lifelong right-hand man who had returned from Omdurman with Ali Dinar and repaid the sultan's trust with scrupulous loyalty. Tibn Sa'd al-Nur, as *malik al-nahas*, reportedly deputized on occasion in the sultan's absence. The grandly titled *majlis al-maluk* ("council of kings") was wholly advisory, a gathering in one place of important officials and cronies. Again, a comparison with the modern British cabinet system, and still more with the American one, may help in understanding a divergence of practice from theory.

As in most traditional Muslim states, the judiciary was subordinate to the executive. For the first time, a chief judge (*qadi al-qudat*) sat at El Fasher but by all accounts was under the sultan's thumb; the Dongalawi Idris Abdallah occupied the position throughout Ali Dinar's reign. A council of *ulama* advised the sultan when he sat in sovereign judgment. The chief *qadi* appointed district *qadis*, who ruled according to the *Shari'a* and, in the opinion of a British observer disinclined to praise the system, with considerable sophistication and probity. At least some of these *qadis* and their deputies (*na'ib*) were holdovers from Mahdist days. In any event, the vast majority of legal disputes would have been dealt with locally, within the family, clan, or tribe; or between tribal *shaykhs*, and according to custom rather than by reference to a *qadi*. An important source of *shaykhs'* and *shartays'* income was the fines levied under customary law.[29]

The sultan's sources of revenue were in type much the same as those of his predecessors, but the proportion and amounts accruing from each may have changed considerably because of the disruption of long-distance trade. The turmoil of the intervening years had undoubtedly impoverished Darfur, not least in terms of population; those estimates that exist are notional or biased. And famine, resulting from bad weather or civil unrest, took its toll, in human and financial terms. As before the Turkiyya, taxes included both the Islamic and the customary: *ushur* or tithe payable on crops; the *fitr* or head tax; *zaka*, in practice a herd tax levied on camels, sheep, cattle, and goats; and the annual tribute called *takkiyya*, payable in lengths of cloth (*takkiyyas*) by each tribal unit. From time to time, the sultan requisitioned goods and slaves and, in a nod to the Mahdiyya, cash. Import and export taxes and market dues were imposed on merchants and traders. Tribal and other notables were expected to make substantial gifts. The historian of the sultanate concludes that the proportion of taxes paid in to the state treasury at El Fasher was greater under Ali Dinar than it had been before the Turkiyya and gives anecdotal evidence of the burden imposed by the sultan's exactions on nearby communities.[30]

Many types of coin circulated in Darfur, including Ali Dinar's own issues: foreign coins included the Maria Theresa dollar, Turkish *majidi*, and Egyptian piastre, which was copied locally and repeatedly adulterated. Ali Dinar's coinages were in small numbers, originally of very high intrinsic value but thereafter also repeatedly debased. Most taxes were paid in kind, either (in areas nearer the capital) to officials sent out directly to assess and collect them or, in remoter parts, to local chiefs who passed up the share prescribed or negotiated. The *hakura* system that had supplied the sultanate with armed men in return for rights in land had, by the fall of the first sultanate in 1874, apparently ceased to return much revenue to the center, and its bases in wealth – productive land – had by Ali Dinar's time greatly declined in value owing to depopulation and the disruption of the trade in slaves, on whose labor production relied.

Figure 9. View of the sultan's palace, El Fasher, c. 1920. The palace of the sultans remained the center of government under successive regimes. (Durham University Library, 1/24/20.)

The sultan's rule ultimately depended on his coercive power. Published descriptions of Ali Dinar's army are based mainly on contemporary British sources. This was estimated in 1903 at 6,000 infantry and 1,700 cavalry, organized into *rubas* (divisions) and consisting of regulars armed with rifles and stationed at El Fasher and a few other permanent posts, and of irregular spearmen on call in their home territories. A 1910 intelligence report listed three main divisions under Adam Ali, Adam Rijal, and Mahmud al-Dadingawi, divided into units of a hundred each under a commander, *ras miya*. A report prepared shortly before the Anglo-Egyptian invasion in 1916 estimated that total strength had declined to about 5,000, divided into nine or ten *rubas* of varying size and with widely varying constituent units all under strength. Anecdotal evidence suggests that even among the most loyal of Ali Dinar's officers, command of more than a few hundred was highly unusual. The army was equipped with spears and shields, chain mail, muzzle loaders, double-barreled shotguns, Carambils, Martinis, and especially Remingtons, which had been acquired through trade, raids, and Egyptian disasters. Ammunition was manufactured locally but in very small quantities. Soldiers received no pay but were fed; booty remunerated the successful.[31]

THE FALL OF THE DARFUR SULTANATE

Whether Ali Dinar's army had been depleted by design, because the internal affairs of the sultanate had by 1914 achieved a degree of stasis, or by a need to economize, it was sufficient for his purposes until the final crisis of the regime. At that point, in 1916, only rearmament wholly beyond the capability of any contemporary African state would likely have saved him; the Anglo-Egyptian conquest of Darfur was carefully planned, expertly prepared, and carried out with attention to detail worthy of a much stronger opponent. The campaign, in the midst of a world war, was from Europe's vantage point a sideshow of a sideshow, but it was a tidy triumph for the impresarios of the Anglo-Egyptian regime and would have long-term consequences for the people of Darfur.[32]

We have seen how by 1914 the British and French had reached a diplomatic stalemate over the border between their colonial spheres. With weak claims to territory they did not occupy, the French were in no hurry to make permanent the old armistice lines of the sultans of Darfur and Wadai. Adding another huge territory to the enormous and unremunerative Sudan held little appeal for the British: with Ali Dinar, they had their cake and ate it. But Wingate, in civil and military command of the Sudan since 1899, had "land hunger": leaving Darfur unoccupied was Britain's and Egypt's policy, not his. The tone changed noticeably with the arrival of Kitchener as British agent and consul-general in Cairo in 1911. His very appointment, amid nationalist stirrings, signaled a less forgiving attitude toward subject peoples. Kitchener became secretary of state for war in August 1914 and was succeeded in Cairo by the seat-warming Henry McMahon, who was no match for his own British officials let alone for the cunning Wingate. Forgotten in an imperial backwater, Wingate devised his own western front.

War under Cover of War

In August 1914, sleepy colonial border regions suddenly became potential war zones. The French and British empires had many millions of Muslim subjects, and the anticipated entry into the war, on Germany's side, of the Ottoman Empire provoked fear of popular risings, spontaneous or inspired, in favor of the Turkish sultan, who had arrogated to himself the caliphate of Islam. The British in Khartoum had long claimed both constant danger from a "fanatical" uprising and unique competence for having prevented one. What effect would deposition of the Egyptian khedive and declaration of a British protectorate over Egypt in December 1914 have in the Sudan, with its Egyptian garrison? How would Sudanese react to an Ottoman call to jihad against the British? Wingate, with long experience in military intelligence, took the matter in hand. Preemptive measures, both large and small, were taken, including arrests, deportations, censorship, propaganda, and conciliation of local religious leaders. This last included, famously, collaboration with Abd al-Rahman (a son of the Mahdi by Maqbula, a princess of Darfur and first cousin of Ali Dinar), until now a pariah, who toured the country drumming up support for the Sudan Government.[33]

At the very least, the war required Khartoum to review the policy of benign neglect toward Darfur. There, in the middle of the continent, was the last independent Muslim state in northern Africa, whose people had no reason to favor the British and French over the Germans and Ottomans and whose ruler had chafed at feckless British defense of his interests against the French. Might he take advantage of Britain's preoccupation? Or might Wingate? In invective Ali Dinar was a match for anyone; in diplomacy, he proved an amateur compared to the man whose propaganda campaign had helped bring down the Mahdist state. As early as September 1914, Wingate worried that Ali Dinar might suspect Anglo-French collusion and rise against the Khartoum regime before it was ready to deal with him. While privately priming London – but not Cairo – through "back channels," Wingate wrote to the sultan, enclosing letters from Sudanese religious notables supporting the British war effort and urging loyalty.

By the spring of 1915, the Sudan seemed secure from German-Ottoman intrigues and the local population quietly uninterested in the war. Wingate purported to discern disaffection among the tribes of Kordofan, "got at" by agents of the Turks who had implausibly infiltrated via the Sahara. In reinforcing border posts, Wingate brushed aside private criticism of dangling "bait" for potential raiders from Darfur – in other words, a setup. Despite expert military conclusions that Ali Dinar planned no hostilities, in June the governor of Kordofan, R. V. Savile, recommended invading Darfur as soon as possible. His justification: "the military axiom that the best defensive is a vigorous offensive."

Savile's importuning allowed Wingate the mantle of reluctance, even as he maneuvered in private correspondence with London; Cairo's interference had prevented occupation of Darfur in 1898, and Wingate feared that political and financial objections from British officials there might stymie him again. He therefore told Savile to be patient while the ground was prepared in both Britain and Darfur: when they marched on Darfur, it must be as "champions of the people (at any rate the Arabs) against the present Sultan and his clique."[34]

Wingate thought of everything. To minimize any danger of a religious reaction, he proposed a rival candidate for the sultanate and admitted a need to "increase the unpopularity of Ali Dinar." This he would do through "secretly support[ing] ... the various forces of sedition and opposition," including the Baqqara. Under cover, a political officer (H. A. MacMichael) would be sent to Kordofan to gather intelligence. There had long been British spies in El Fasher; aggrieved individuals would now be contacted. The French in Wadai were asked, and they agreed, to supply information.[35] What Wingate hoped to avoid was the sort of imbroglio that, eighty years later, would envelop the Americans in Iraq: "you," he wrote to Savile, "are inclined to depose the Sultan immediately and by force of arms. This course of action has the merit of simplicity.... Its disadvantages ... are that its execution involves a march of a relatively small force under Christian leaders into a little known country against a population inclined to bouts of fanaticism ... and of whose attitude towards an invading force we cannot be certain."[36] Wingate began secretly to arm the Arab tribes of Darfur: in September 1915, the son of Musa Madibbu of the Rizayqat visited al-Uddaya in Kordofan and went away with the promise of 300 rifles and 30,000 rounds of ammunition; in December, 200 rifles were approved for the Kababish, the nomads of northern Kordofan long at odds with Ali Dinar.

Even the weather turned against Darfur. Drought in 1913 and a poor Nile had afflicted the whole of the northern Sudan and resulted in famine. North of Khartoum, the government earned much moral capital by providing relief, which placed it in good stead when the war broke out. In Darfur, however, relief was unavailable, and the sultanate was unsettled. Tribes migrated far afield and across international borders: Zaghawa moved well into southern Darfur, and Fur far west, where, however, conditions were no better; some of the destitute were enslaved, a fate better than death. Northern sections of Dar Masalit lost as much as two-thirds of their people to migration, and its ruler, Sultan Endoka, abandoned his waterless capital for a new one, El Geneina. Grain at El Fasher reportedly fetched twenty times its 1908 price and three times that at Omdurman. Ali Dinar waived some taxes, but the famine, locally named *Julu* ("Wandering," from its effect on the tribes), was one of the worst on record. British intelligence confirmed the disaster, about which Ali Dinar was candid in his communications with the Sudan Government.[37] But, then as now, people ground down by natural disaster might be less inclined to resist a change of regime.

To what extent were British preparations for war – and steps to provoke it – justified by Ali Dinar's actions? Evidence of Turkish attempts to suborn the sultan came to light after the Anglo-Egyptian conquest in 1916, but the earliest of these, letters from Ottoman officials, appear not to have reached El Fasher before the middle of 1915. (Invitations implicate the sender, not the recipient; Queen Victoria's reply to the Mahdi's request that she submit to Islam has gone unrecorded.) The Ottomans were more successful in winning over the Sanusiyya leadership, who by late 1915 were indeed openly helping the Turks in the western desert of Egypt. Claiming apprehension that the Sanusis would turn Ali Dinar,[38] and brandishing a threatening letter from the sultan in November 1915, Wingate increased his troop deployments in western Kordofan. Reconnaissance was stepped up. Obviously in response, in February 1916 Ali Dinar sent forty cavalry and ninety men "riding two to [a] camel" to reinforce Jabal al-Hilla, the main town on the Darfur side of the border between Kordofan and El Fasher. At the same time, letters addressed to "the Governor of Hell in Kordofan and the Inspector of Flames at Nahud," calling them various names, were duly sent on from Khartoum to Cairo as evidence of the sultan's disturbed state of mind. (A letter to the Sansusi *shaykh* in early 1916, alerting him to Ali Dinar's imminent declaration of jihad, exists only in English translation.)[39]

By then Wingate was ready to act. Citing the menace of the "large Darfur force" (referred to earlier) at Jabal al-Hilla but in full knowledge (supplied by MacMichael) that Ali Dinar was not preparing even to raid, Wingate could no longer delay sounding out Cairo; he was, after all, in theory responsible to the government of each co-dominus and, in practice, to London through the intermediation of the British representative in Cairo. He told McMahon as little as seemed necessary to get his way while allowing cover (and reinforcements) if things went wrong. Assuring Cairo of an advance only to Jabal al-Hilla and Umm Shanqa, he also sent a final "warning" to Ali Dinar, promising honorable treatment if he surrendered and grants of clemency to all Darfur forces that submitted. It was at this late date, with his army already occupying Jabal al-Hilla and the important town of Abiad fifty miles northwest, that Wingate encountered the European political objections he had long feared and had acted so carefully to forestall.

These took several forms. The French, having for years pressed for British occupation of Darfur, now viewed this as inopportune: their garrison in Wadai was small; what would happen if Ali Dinar fled west with his forces? Wingate replied disingenuously that no advance was contemplated but that the future was impossible to control. McMahon, blind in the labyrinth of Anglo-Cairene politics, took up the French cause (and that of Wingate's personal enemies) and chimed in with other objections, including financial ones: who would pay for the campaign? Egypt could not: no military advance should take place before London ruled on this and related matters. Wingate had no intention of ending the sole Sudanese campaign of the Great War as Viscount Jabal Hilla. Using carefully cultivated private channels, he contacted Kitchener, who provided the necessary permissions without reference to Cairo. And taking a page from his well-thumbed book as chief propagandist during a quarter century of Anglo-Egyptian intrigue, Wingate "privately" told an American journalist that, in only his latest atrocity, Ali Dinar, with a large mortar and pestle, had pulverized a baby and forced its mother to eat the resulting mess: "This is the gentleman," he wrote, "to whom the Kaiser's agent is sending a considerable quantity of arms and ammunition."[40]

The End of the Sultanate

The conquest of Darfur proceeded according to plan. In a novel tactic, airplanes were sent to drop leaflets on El Fasher on 12 May, denouncing Ali Dinar and promising justice and religious freedom once he was gone; clemency and confirmation in office for all tribal chiefs who submitted;

Figure 10. Ali Dinar Zakariyya Muhammad al-Fadl, sultan of Darfur, 6 November 1916. His army defeated outside El Fasher, Ali Dinar fled and was later ambushed and killed by Anglo-Egyptian forces. (Durham University Library, 588/1/159.)

and relief for the Arabs who had suffered under the Fur sultan's oppression. On the 15th, the Darfur Field Force advanced from Abiad. The decisive battle was fought on the 22nd at Biringia, twelve miles from El Fasher. Ali Dinar's army attacked and was repulsed with 261 left dead on the field as against 5 for the Anglo-Egyptian force. The sultan, who had stayed in the town, at first tried to regroup. During the night, many of his followers slipped away, and he fled to the southwest with a small retinue. El Fasher was thereupon occupied on 23 May without difficulty.

Taking to the hills of Jabal Marra, in the way of his ancestors, Ali Dinar held out for another five months, waiting for another turn of the Darfur kaleidoscope. As he had with the Mahdists in 1890, he entered into correspondence with the Sudan Government. In this, he blamed everything on subordinates, renounced the sultanate, and offered to surrender if he and his family were promised safe retirement to his lands. Wingate would not countenance that last suggestion: Ali Dinar and his family must go into exile. For this purpose, Wingate contacted the sharif of Mecca. But he eventually came to share his officers' view that Ali Dinar was stalling, intent on salvaging a state within a state, as his predecessors had tried to do during the Turkiyya.[41] When in October 1916 the sultan moved to Kulme, southwest of Jabal Marra, an Anglo-Egyptian force went after him. On 6 November, he was tracked down, ambushed, shot, and killed.[42]

Figure 11. Members of the Fur royal family and other notables surrendering to Anglo-Egyptian forces, 23 November 1916. (Durham University Library, 12/3/50.)

In an oft-quoted passage written immediately after the occupation, MacMichael described Ali Dinar's palace as

a perfect Sudanese Alhambra. . . . There are small shady gardens and little fish ponds, arcades, colonnades, store rooms, and every type of building. The floors are strewn with fine silver sand, the thatch on the roofs is the finest imaginable and looks as if it had been clipped with scissors. The walls are beautifully plastered in red, and the interiors of the halls covered with great inscriptions from the Koran in handsome caligraphy [sic] or with chess board designs. . . . Trellis work in ebony is found in place of the interior walls and the very flooring in the women's quarters, under the silver sand, is impregnated with spices.[43]

Such was the estate of the barbarian tyrant now overthrown, Ali Dinar, last sultan of Darfur.

6

"CLOSED DISTRICT"

Anglo-Egyptian Colonial Rule in Darfur, 1916–1939

REACTION WITHOUT MODERNIZATION

When Anglo-Egyptian forces entered El Fasher in May 1916, the history of Darfur entered a new phase. But in describing and evaluating this period, we recall that the Condominium regime in Khartoum had begun its formal existence in 1899; immediately upon its occupation, Darfur became a special case, and it would remain one until the Sudan's independence in 1956. Few territories in Africa experienced a shorter period of colonial rule.

By 1914, the Sudan Government had become complacent. The north had been pacified after the upheavals of the Mahdiyya, and the Egyptian army and British garrison easily quelled the incidents of crypto-Mahdism that arose from time to time. The colonial regime conciliated both orthodox Muslim leaders and leading sufi *shaykhs* and left tribal rule in place in the vast rural areas. Legal codes, adapted from India and Egypt, had been enacted, but the *Shari'a*, applied by government-trained and salaried *qadis*, regulated personal and family matters. Taxes were low, but thanks to loans and annual subventions from Egypt, basic infrastructure had been put in place: a railway system extended from Wadi Halfa to Khartoum, the Gezira, El Obeid, and, on the Red Sea, the new Port Sudan; government steamers plied the Nile to Uganda and into the Bahr al-Ghazal; the telegraph connected even the most remote regions to Khartoum, Cairo, and Europe. Fearing Sudanese wrath and mass vagrancy, the government discouraged slave trading while largely ignoring slavery: owners were renamed "masters" and slaves "servants"; reports of progress were sent to England to placate busybodies, while the watchword of policy was gradualism. Basic social services, including primary education and rudimentary health care, were put in place. The southern Sudan, from which nothing was expected, was given little: international borders were fixed, posts built, and missionaries gratefully allowed to establish themselves, while well-heeled European and American tourists passed as through a zoological garden.

This happy state of affairs was disturbed by events in Egypt, the nominal co-dominus under British control. Egyptian nationalism had deep roots but, at the turn of the twentieth century, new shoots began to appear, partly in reaction to British occupation. The declaration of war in Europe in 1914 greatly accelerated this process. From the status of an Ottoman province, however fictive, Egypt was transformed at a stroke, unilaterally by the British, into a "protectorate." Moreover, the war was costly for Egypt: to man the front with the Turks to the east, the British impressed Egyptian labor; price controls were imposed, animals and food requisitioned, political advances reversed. At the end of the war, pent-up Egyptian national feeling exploded, with much violence. The stage was set for the long and reluctant British departure from Egypt, the first phase of which was visible on the horizon already in 1918 and was reached in 1922, when Britain declared Egypt independent but remained in occupation. At that time, four "Reserved Points" were left to future negotiation, one of which was the Sudan.

Repercussions up the Nile were impossible to avoid. Long before 1918 the British saw Egyptians, especially of the educated official and commercial classes, as a potential fifth column; the Egyptian army, stationed in the Sudan, was deeply suspect, as were the hundreds of Egyptian officials, teachers, and salaried employees. It became an object of British policy not only to minimize Egyptian influence – an unspoken goal since 1899 – but also to reduce dependence on Egyptian personnel. This could be achieved in two ways: by training Sudanese – Europeans were expensive – and by obviating altogether the need for bureaucracy by extending and regularizing the authority of tribal rulers. This view of future political and economic development would deeply inform British policy toward Darfur even before the conquest of 1916.

The people, if consulted, would in any case have agreed that what they needed most was peace and security. To appreciate the dire condition of Darfur, it is unnecessary to rehearse the diatribes with which each recent regime had seen off its predecessor and justified itself. The deliberate way in which the British had planned the conquest gave considerable scope for postwar administration. The solutions arrived at would be fateful, for Darfur became a laboratory for testing policies' applicability elsewhere. At the outset, however, the Sudan Government had three basic objectives: to pacify the territory, to establish an administration that was both cheap and adequate for maintaining law and order, and to resolve with France the long-standing border issue.[1] It was the tragedy of Darfur's people that, once these objectives were met, little more was attempted.

The pacification of Darfur had worried Wingate and his officials in Khartoum. Attending to their own propaganda, they did not discount the possibility of fierce resistance, whether "fanatical" or merely defensive. In pretending to make Darfur a front of the First World War, they wanted a quick and easy victory. In the event, the submission of El Fasher after Ali Dinar's flight symbolized the exhaustion of the sultanate: recovery from the drought and famine of 1913–14 had been slow because of the depth of the disaster. British propaganda, aimed not only at the capital but, more subtly, at the tribes, had emphasized the futility of resistance and the promise of a new day; communication between religious figures in Darfur and the eastern Sudan may have played a part, as tribal and personal contacts certainly did, in suggesting a wait-and-see attitude. It would anyway soon be clear that the new regime was insistently reactionary and determined to rule through "traditional authority" even where there was none.

Even before the campaign was launched in March 1916, the British had decided, mainly in order to save money, that Darfur would not be subjected to the same "bureaucratic" government as the rest of the Sudan. As early as September 1915, MacMichael, as Darfur intelligence officer, even suggested the possibility of appointing a new sultan who, on a model then much favored, would rule with the "advice" of a British resident, an idea Wingate vetoed. But as the European war dragged on, there were fewer British personnel and distrust of Egyptians grew. MacMichael therefore propounded a "conservative policy that would leave the power of the existing sheikhs, 'shartais,' 'meliks,' and 'salatin' over their people unimpaired as long as they behaved themselves." Wingate saw this as a temporary measure to overcome any initial impulse to resist the new regime; MacMichael, imbued with the lessons of experience among the tribes of Kordofan, had the longer term in mind. By March 1916, these ideas had crystallized, and a whole system had been outlined by which "traditional" local rulers would be left in place "unless and until it was thoroughly demonstrated beyond doubt that" they were "either disloyal or consistently unjust when judged *by native standards*"; Egyptians would be dispensed with; taxation would be imposed collectively and justice supervised by a grand *qadi* sitting in El Fasher. After the conquest, this basic policy, which encapsulates the colonial ideology of Indirect Rule, was ratified.[2]

The skeletal structure of provincial administration was soon in place. At the top was a governor (*mudir*), as elsewhere in the Sudan an officer who also commanded the military district. The first governor, Colonel P. J. V. Kelly, had led the advance into Darfur and was duly installed in Ali Dinar's palace, with his desk in front of the sultan's throne; his successor, from May 1917 until 1923, was Colonel Savile, an old Sudan hand who had been governor of the Bahr al-Ghazal (1908–09) and, as governor of Kordofan (1909–17), had urged the conquest of Darfur. Many officials of the old regime had submitted upon the surrender of El Fasher and, without missing a beat, had been put to work for the new one. The province was divided into districts, each under a British inspector (*mufattish*) and each subdivided under *muawins* (rather than Egyptian *ma'murs*); these divisions in Darfur's case were huge.

The administration of justice in Darfur under the Condominium regime would follow the pattern established elsewhere in the Sudan but with local amendment. The codes and ordinances of the Sudan would apply, as would the *Shari'a*. A provincial *qadi* (Shaykh Isma'il al-Azhari) was appointed immediately, succeeding Ali Dinar's chief judge, Idris Abdallahi, who was made *mufti* of Darfur, an office that in practice meant little but attested to an eye on continuity and respect for Islam; the *mufti* of the Sudan took precedence, so Idris, whose loyalty was to government, not governors, functioned in effect as head of the local religious establishment, the *ulama*.

The same solicitude that had informed MacMichael's prescriptions for Darfur's administration guided the Sudan Government's approach to delimiting the western border, which, as we have seen, the British and French had decided to defer until after the war. For all his collating of genealogies and rendezvous with spies, MacMichael[3] had before the occupation known little about the regions west of El Fasher. In recent years, the sultans of Dar Qimr and Dar Masalit had established close relations with the French who, by 1916, had clearly decided, for reasons of their own that have yet to be satisfactorily elucidated, to cede their claims to those territories. After the fall of El Fasher in May 1916, the French advised Sultan Idris of the Qimr to submit to the British, and he duly went to El Fasher, got the royal treatment, and returned to his *dar* loaded with gifts. But London was still in no hurry: anticipating postwar negotiations with France over worldwide colonial claims, the Foreign Office wondered whether a separate agreement over Sudanese boundaries might waste a bargaining chip. No British post was established at Kereinik on the eastern border of Dar Masalit until March 1918. A highly unsatisfactory status quo continued until March 1921, when an Anglo-French convention was finally ratified, leaving Dar Masalit and Dar Qimr in Darfur.[4]

Because rumor had it, naturally enough, that the British had come in 1916 to take over Dar Masalit, they were soon despised for not having tried to do so. Sultan Bahr al-Din (Endoka), whose personal encounters with the British are ludicrous examples of reciprocal prejudice,[5] gave them a cool but not overtly hostile reception. Rebuffed by the French, however, Endoka visited El Fasher in January 1920 and entered into discussions about the nature of his relations with the Sudan Government. As a result, he remained sultan, but on the model of an Indian rajah or Nigerian emir: he would pay annual tribute and disband his army; his judicial powers would be regularized; and commerce in slaves, arms, and alcohol was forbidden.[6] Before this agreement went into effect, however, the biggest uprising of the entire Condominium era, deeply implicating the sultan and his people, broke out at Nyala in Darfur.

THE SECOND COMING OF MAHDISM

In a land that had recently survived the Mahdiyya, Abu Jummayza, several self-proclaimed prophets, and a miracle-working sultan, the rising of 1921 had a familiar ring. On 26 September, 6,000 Baqqara, Fallata, and Masalit attacked the government post at Nyala: forty-one officers and men were killed, including the British inspector, before the attackers were beaten back with heavy losses. Their leader, Abdallahi al-Sihayni, a Masalati who had declared himself the Prophet Jesus,[7] was soon handed over, tried by court-martial, and hanged. But it would be several months before pockets of resistance in southern Darfur, Dar Masalit, and elsewhere were cleaned up. At Kutum, 200 armed Zaghawa – having heard

Figure 12. Bahr al-Din (Endoka) b. Abbakr Isma'il, sultan of Dar Masalit, on the arrival of Anglo-Egyptian forces, 1916–17. Endoka's long reign (1910–51) spanned the period between the Fur sultanate and Sudanese self-government. (Durham University Library, 1/10/12.)

of a titanic sword falling from Heaven – were stopped by government police from raiding the cattle of the local Fur. The sedentary Berti were similarly upset by wild rumors until their *malik*, Adam Tamin Bishara, cut down the holy tree under which they had gathered.[8] The worst episode occurred in October when Mahdist tribesmen surrounded the government post at Kereinik, spoiling for a fight; Sultan Endoka's intervention and the threat of government machine guns deterred them. Endoka nonetheless fell under suspicion for having encouraged the rising and was forced to acquiesce in a government patrol's procession through the *dar*, occupation of El Geneina, and payment of a fine. He, in turn, jumped on the government bandwagon and blamed all on the baleful influence of Sayyid Abd al-Rahman al-Mahdi.[9]

The Nyala rising illustrates two related themes of the colonial era in Darfur: Indirect Rule and Mahdism. Although there was strong evidence of economic and political reasons for the revolt, officials focused on Mahdist revivalism to explain it and exculpate themselves. A boundary dispute between the Masalit and Habbaniyya had given offense; taxes were too high, in some cases confiscatory, and had provoked rumors of worse to come – that "houses and even dogs" were slated for appraisal. Nor had assessments been modified on account of a disastrous outbreak of cattle plague; most tribes had been affected, the Rizayqat alone reportedly losing two-thirds of their herds. (Sudanese explanations for this latest act of God included His wrath at the tribes' "intercourse with infidels," namely, the British.) Although officials came up with countless other explanations – Franco-Sanusi intrigue, communism, "world-wide . . . unrest" – and privately blamed the slain inspector at Nyala, Tennent McNeill, for incompetence,[10] the focus of their wrath, perhaps even an excuse for it, was the presumed resurgence of Mahdism.

The cult of the Mahdi had indeed survived all reversals, including his death, destruction of his regime, and occupation of the Sudan by the Egyptians and British. The early Condominium government reacted almost with panic to hints of "fanaticism," hunting down and stringing up "prophets," often with enthusiastic help from local people who had had enough of it all. Surviving Mahdist notables had been kept in prison, under house arrest, or exiled. The large family of the Mahdi was under the greatest suspicion: his son by Maqbula of Darfur, Abd al-Rahman, had gained acceptance as bearer of his father's legacy. Just as various aspects of the Mahdi's call had won adherents to his message, so Abd al-Rahman's appeal would vary: in the tradition of Sudanese holy families, he had inherited his father's *baraka*, or charisma, and as scion of *abu'l-istiqlal* – the father of independence – he would symbolize a time when Sudanese had vanquished and expelled the very powers that ruled them now, Britain and Egypt. Abd al-Rahman's assumption of this role was ironically hastened by the British themselves.

Much would later be written about that change in British policy but, even if mistaken, it recognized a fact: Sudanese showed little interest in the orthodox *ulama* imposed by their governors; they looked for leaders instead among sufi *shaykhs* and *fuqara* – and nowhere more than in Darfur, where orthodox cult officials had no influence outside the towns, but individual holy men had played a multifarious role. In 1926, one British official referred to Mahdism as "the only definite current in the sea of [Darfur's] native thought."[11] Defenders of the new policy argued that Sayyid Abd al-Rahman (or "SAR" as the British called him) was not himself "fanatical" or disloyal. His service during the war proved his worth, it was better to cultivate his friendship than earn his enmity, and his movement had evolved into something like a sufi order. Sudanese who thought this way were not the problem, argued British opponents of this view: the mass of Mahdists were ignorant and superstitious, awaiting "a sign" from the sayyid to rise in jihad. And most of those unreconstructed Mahdists were in the West, in Kordofan and Darfur.

Almost from the beginning of the new regime in Darfur, therefore, the "conservative" ideology that informed its administration was meant to solve all of Khartoum's problems at once: by relying on tribal chiefs, it would be cheap; it would keep out Egyptian (and educated Sudanese) personnel, the despised "effendi class"; it would thereby insulate the populace from disturbing foreign trends – nationalism, other "isms"; and it would combat homegrown Mahdism, which most of Darfur's tribal chiefs considered a threat to their own authority. But in panacea we discern a placebo: some officials saw empowerment of local aristocracy, others a bulwark against modernity, others still the roots of local government, and, at the extreme, "the beginnings of democracy"; one high official – forty years later – denied that Indirect Rule had been aimed at Abd al-Rahman at all.[12] But these prognoses all glossed an underlying necessity of living within the government's limited means.

Weakened by the disasters of recent decades – decimation in battle, the execution of *shaykhs*, forced migrations, drought, famine, and disease – the tribes were perhaps more susceptible than ever to a religious appeal. Even before restrictions were lifted in 1914, SAR had extended his influence in Omdurman and from the hallowed Aba Island, which he had been allowed to reoccupy. Tribesmen returning from the Mahdist wars, pilgrims on hajj routes reopened by the Condominium regime, and, his detractors noted, agents (*manadib*) sent by the sayyid spread his name throughout the west. Pilgrims diverted from the hajj – or with him as their object – began to come in, as did tribesmen at odds with their *shaykhs*, and were settled on agricultural estates in Aba and adjacent lands. Ominously, in time-honored fashion, ex-*shaykhs* and second sons were said to be flocking to SAR and looking to the future. Thus, to western tribal *shaykhs* and their British exponents, the appeal of Abd al-Rahman was not an effect but a cause of Darfur's problems. The extent to which tribesmen went absent without leave is impossible to gauge: official numbers were always guesses and usually of arrivals at Aba not departures from Darfur. Such men were called "exiles" (*muhajarin*), a term redolent of Mahdist ideology.[13]

All of this both worried and incensed officials in the west. Had Britain not conquered the Sudan to destroy Mahdism? Yet, everywhere they saw evidence of SAR's growing popularity: in northern Darfur, it was said, belief in the Mahdi had been "almost non-existent" in 1916 but by 1922 had "gained a firm footing"; in Dar Masalit, "nearly everyone" was "a supporter of the Sayyid"; among the Baqqara, Mahdism had "an amazing hold." SAR's *manadib* were not secret agents: he was required to list them. In 1923, there were officially four in Darfur, including Adam Hamid in El Fasher, and they appointed *imams*, collected *zakat*, and created alternatives to local *shaykhs*. The government ordered him to recall or renounce these agents and stop collecting *zakat* (a restriction later relaxed). The real pot-stirrers, however, were not official agents, and recall of *manadib* allowed SAR to shift the blame when troubles arose. One old Mahdist was found touring the west, preaching that the British were the Antichrist and SAR the Second Coming. There were others. In May 1923, Khartoum's director of intelligence reported that in "the whole of the Baqqara country" and "throughout Darfur" people were "on the tiptoes of expectation for the Second Coming." When confronted, SAR infuriated officials with plausible denials: his influence in the west was a force for stability; he took every opportunity, he said, to denounce "prophets" popping up there, who were as antipathetic to him as to the Sudan Government.[14]

British panic over Mahdism began to subside after SAR helped calm the waters of the "1924 revolution." Western officials continued to cry wolf, but Khartoum had other priorities: in the same year (1926) that Reginald Davies, SAR's archenemy, complained about Mahdists in Sudan Defence Force (SDF) units stationed in Darfur, SAR was knighted. To be sure, when a self-proclaimed Mahdi, known locally as Fiki al-Muhajir, arose in 1927 in the Western District of Darfur, he was tracked down and killed, but for his few bedraggled hangers-on, clemency made sense. (Several notables, including the sultan of Dar Masalit, were implicated in the affair, at least through inaction, and local discontent over taxation, delousing procedures, and other policies was well known.)[15] Even the hoary issue of slavery came into play: economic development in the east had made paid labor scarce, and the influx of "pilgrims," whether to SAR or Mecca or just runaway slaves, was encouraged by British officials there, while those in Darfur fulminated.[16] As one put it: "Every [British] inspector has his own ideas and acts in accordance with them alone; one will go to any lengths to recover runaway Sudanese, another is rabidly 'anti-slavery,' others steer a course between these two policies and others have no consistent policy at all."[17] Omdurman and the Nile were magnets pointed toward Darfur and farther west. That "God took away our slaves but sent us the Fallata" (West Africans) was a cliché of Sudanese landowners. The security provided by the colonial regime made travel easier, and paid work in the east for impoverished westerners made migration both attractive and necessary.

Thus, both tradition and modernization favored the ascent of SAR. His assistance to the government in 1931, when students of Gordon College went on strike, reinforced the impression that his movement had evolved: although western tribesmen would remain a source of mass support, his attentions would increasingly focus on the "intelligentsia" of the towns in his endless duel with Sayyid Ali al-Mirghani ("SAM") of the Khatmiyya. In July 1934, the governor-general, Sir Stewart Symes, an old hand who had never subscribed to venomous anti-Mahdism, removed most restrictions on Abd al-Rahman. The ban on agents in Darfur remained, but it is only in his repeated attempts to have it lifted that we discern any evidence of its effect. SAR instead ran what amounted to a Darfur Office at Omdurman and Aba, entertaining visitors from the province, supporting private schools there, subsidizing financially embarrassed notables, and, eventually, operating through the machinery of the Umma Party (discussed later).[18] And "unofficial" agents meanwhile carried on, "mixing politics with religion" and competing unkindly with the Tijaniyya tariqa.[19]

INSTITUTIONALIZED NEGLECT: INDIRECT RULE AS PANACEA AND PROBLEM

Legislating against the Future

Policy toward Mahdism was but one front in a war over the Sudan's political future. Exponents of Indirect Rule – the "conservative" policy of governing through tribal chiefs – used many foils for their case, including the "detribalizing" influence of Mahdism. But those who saw the colonial mission as training Sudanese for responsible roles in a modern bureaucratic state were not necessarily supporters of SAR. There were other straws in the wind. The Milner Mission, sent to investigate the bloody uprising in Egypt in 1919, had made recommendations for the Sudan as well, and these (largely the work of Sudan Government officials) included the possibility of "a system like that prevailing in Northern Nigeria," which would obviate "the necessity of creating an effendi class." Debate continued while a "dual policy," the work of Wingate's successor Sir Lee Stack, of empowering *shaykhs* in sparsely populated regions while creating local government in settled areas, bought time. In 1922, the first legislation to promote Indirect Rule was enacted. The Powers of Nomad Sheikhs Ordinance, which recognized and regularized the administrative and judicial authority of several hundred *shaykhs*, was limited to nomadic tribes, where such power – and more – was already wielded. This made sense.

The appeal of Indirect Rule became irresistible only in 1924. As Anglo-Egyptian negotiations over the Sudan and other issues made no progress, anti-British incidents in Khartoum and elsewhere increased tension. Sudanese "effendis" – and soldiers – demonstrated against Britain and for Egypt, mutinies occurred, and "sedition," much of it imitative and mischievous, became widespread; the British organized for self-defense, and memories of General Gordon were evoked. Catharsis came in November when Stack was assassinated in Cairo. Rather than accept a British ultimatum, the Wafd government of Sa'd Zaghlul resigned, and London unilaterally imposed solutions to several unrelated problems. These included evacuation from the Sudan of the Egyptian army, during which some Sudanese in Khartoum resisted; a violent showdown ensued. The near-fiction of "condominium" was retained, however, for its value in future relations with Egypt. The SDF was established, under British officers, and most Egyptian officials were dismissed.

After this – the 1924 Revolution in Sudanese historiography – opponents of Indirect Rule were routed. With hundreds of Egyptians suddenly removed from administrative positions but Sudanese effendis now proven unsuitable to replace them, the way was clear for "bold experiments" with tribal chiefs. Reaction was most pronounced in two related areas, education and administration: in student numbers and curriculum, the government cut back, no longer preparing Sudanese for increasingly responsible positions but avowedly for ones subordinate to tribal chiefs. In 1927, The Powers of Sheikhs Ordinance granted statutory authority to territorial *shaykhs* and those of sedentary tribes. More ordinances followed. Now, even among acephalous peoples in the south, attempts were made to identify chiefs and powers that could be officially recognized, with mixed and confusing results. In the north, large towns had no tribal identity, *shaykhs* were often mere civil servants, and educated urbanites were unwilling to submit to patriarchal worthies whose "traditional" authority no one recognized. They were not alone: British officials in the towns ridiculed Indirect Rule and stalled.

But in the west, especially in Darfur, exponents of Indirect Rule acted as if time had stood still or, where it had led to inconvenient developments, might even be turned back. In 1922, a proclamation under the Closed Districts Order declared Darfur (among other areas) off limits to anyone without a government permit; the Sudan's borders were sieves, but the law might deter – and allow summary ejection of – Mahdist agents and effendis. No law was needed to dispense with education. New British officials were indoctrinated about "Egyptians, Bolsheviks and Mahdists" and the "fanatical Baqqara of Darfur."[20] The governor-generalship of Sir John Maffey (1927–33) marks the high-water mark of the ideology, although in some ways and in some parts of the country,

Figure 13. A conference of Darfur tribal chiefs, 1934. Shown are (left to right) *Shartay* Adam Ya'qub of the Birgid; Abd al-Rahman Adam Rijal of the Fur; Muhammad Ibrahim Dabaha of the Bani Halba; Ibrahim Musa Madibbu of the Rizayqat; Ali Sanusi of the Ta'aisha; al-Ghali Taj al-Din of the Habbaniyya; and al-Sammani al-Bashir of the Fallata. Conferences were an important regulator of intertribal affairs and gave hope for future peace. (Durham University Library, 637/15/3.)

it never ebbed. Maffey, from India, saw native potentates as the only bulwark against forces – whether "babus" or effendis – conspiring to overthrow British rule everywhere. He advocated "wild experiment," trial and error, and the sacrifice of oppressive "efficiency." But despite the radical language, only three Native Administrations in Darfur (Dar Masalit, the "Zalingei Emirate," and the Rizayqat Nazirate) had budgets of their own on the eve of the Second World War.

The Sultan of the Masalit

The most notable of the Native Administrations was Dar Masalit, where Davies, the regime's ideologue, was appointed in 1922 as Resident. Influenced by Lugard's theories (but not his practice) in Northern Nigeria,[21] Davies treated the *dar* as a "miniature Lugardian emirate." The historian of the sultanate suggests that the goal was to make it "loyal, just and progressive, cheap and efficient, possibly in that order."[22] Possibly not: loyalty came first, then cheapness, with justice required to the degree that it kept people loyal and efficiency sacrificed to ideology: "native" administration was *by definition* inefficient. In Dar Masalit, the contradictions inherent in European imposition of "traditional" inefficiency were soon evident. Because the object was to rule through Sultan Endoka, government officials – if there had been any – must not poke their noses into rural administration. But Davies could not abide disorder: he wanted things in writing, he "advised" reduction and amalgamation, abolition and creation; he even codified and made clear who had the last word while bemoaning the sultan's "weakness." Some innovations took hold, others did not. Rapacious princes of the royal family had their personal *dars* abolished by decree in 1921, then predictably carried on as before, with double-taxation the result. In 1926, the assistant resident, convinced of Endoka's double-dealing over Mahdism, recommended a spy to get reliable information. In 1934, a "taxpayers' strike" finally revealed the Sudan Government's ignorance of a dynamic system in which positions, titles, blood relations, and personality interplayed and in which the theoretically aloof Resident, like a bumbling anthropologist, was a major factor. Endoka knew what was happening and resented it but recognized the true nature of his position more clearly than the British did.[23]

Nevertheless, through trial and error and adaptation on both sides, the Dar Masalit "experiment" appeared by the 1930s to have borne fruit. The Native Administration had its own budget, courts, and prison, and the Resident had moved from El Geneina to the fort outside town. Taxes were coming in, in cash. The sultan, on a salary and with a privy purse, was described as like "an eccentric English country-gentleman, self-confident, fond of horses, and the proud owner of a two-seater Ford." There were other views: Margery Perham, the theorist of African administration, passed through in 1938 and reacted with disgust. Endoka's idiosyncracies became aspects of administration: he always ran a surplus and ignored budgets; he had a *qadi*, but his own judgments were final. Khartoum's rationalizing impulse, especially after the heyday of Indirect Rule had passed, was to put Dar Masalit on the same footing as other Native Administrations, but Endoka himself was an institution, and change was put off until the next generation. Because he died only in 1951, on the eve of the Sudan's independence, Dar Masalit remained a special case.[24]

The Maqdumates of the North and South

Two other experiments revived old titles. In 1928, the administration of southern Darfur under a so-called *dimangawi* was judged a failure.

Abd al-Hamid Ibrahim, a Fur prince living obscurely at Kosti on the White Nile, was therefore installed as "Maqdum of the South." Early signs were good. In 1930, he was officially styled "emir." His Azharite *qadi* was sound, and there was even a slightly absurd reference to a "foreign policy" when he met Sultan Endoka of the Masalit.[25] But the success was personal, as his sudden death proved: by 1934, his son Muhammad, the new emir, was already contemptibly judged a complete failure, with "half-baked-effendi ideas picked up amongst second-rate, semi-educated colleagues in a commercial firm at Sennar." He had run up debts, squandered advances, and almost died from his excesses. There was talk of a "regency" if, after "some really glaring and unforgiveable series of atrocities," Muhammad had to be deposed. The administration descended into chaos as unchecked *shaykhs* stole property, extorted money, and instilled terror through floggings and beatings. A soldier, Hugh Boustead, was brought in as Resident but acted like a rival: Muhammad's writ was curtailed in 1936, and when he burned down his own treasury to hide a theft, he was dismissed. In April 1938, the governor appointed a *shartay*, Sese Muhammad Atim, to the on-again, off-again *dimangawi*-ship. But Boustead was the real boss.[26]

Attempts to revive the Maqdumate of the North proceeded similarly. Yusuf Hasan, son of the last titleholder under Ali Dinar, was installed in 1926, only to be dismissed by his own *shartays* for unspecified enormities: he had, in the governor's memorable phrase, "failed to re-absorb in his person the traditions of the past."[27] While options were weighed, a "Shadow Magdumate [*sic*]" awaited someone to run the local court. In 1930, Yusuf was reinstated, with his brother in the wings in case of relapse. More successful, by all accounts, was the court established at El Fasher under the presidency (from 1928) of the *umda* (mayor), Salih al-Dadingawi, whose glittering genealogy and reputation for probity lent much-needed prestige. Until his death in 1939, the British considered him the head of the local Native Administration, but his role was neither traditional nor very different from one in local government in the east. Nor was it universally popular: in 1933, a fatal affray between his Dadinga and members of the defunct royal clan led to installation at El Fasher of a son of Ali Dinar, Sayf al-Din, as paterfamilias. His personal habits proved disappointing, however, and after reopening hostilities with Salih, he was sent away.[28]

Shaykhs and Nazirs

Nomadic tribes were, in theory, best suited to Indirect Rule. But, as in the case even of the Kababish of Kordofan, the government's favorite tribe, the British could not leave well enough alone. In Darfur, nomad *shaykhs* enjoyed unfettered despotism after the collapse of the sultanate in 1916, when the British were preoccupied. With adoption of Indirect Rule, the statutory establishment of courts and enumeration of powers thus *reduced* tribal chiefs' authority. *Nazir* Ibrahim of the Rizayqat and his brothers, sons of the redoubtable Musa Madibbu, had, for example, resumed their independent ways. Province officials steered clear of their *dar* except on special occasions and with police escorts. Yet Darfur's governor, C. G. Dupuis, as ardent an Indirect Ruler as there was, detected "defects" in their method, for example, "over-centralization," insufficient (legally recognized) judicial authority, and inadequate pay. In 1928 warrants were drawn up to regularize the *nazir*'s powers under relevant ordinances; whatever was the effect in practice, legally his authority was diminished. (An ambitious attempt to centralize rule of all the Rizayqat, north and south, under Ibrahim was abandoned in 1928, and the five northern sections went their own way, under their *shaykh*, Mahdi Hassaballah.)[29]

British officials paid great attention to intertribal relations. Carefully staged palavers of *nazirs* and *shaykhs* in Darfur took on aspects of state visits, with elaborate ceremonies and shows; some of these were annual affairs, at which, building on tribal traditions, outstanding issues could be resolved with or without the presence of a British District Commissioner (DC) and witnessed by thousands of tribesmen. Not all tribal disputes were treated equally: fallings-out in settled and relatively populous areas were treated seriously; raids into Dar Zaghawa from French territory were reciprocated with little notice. Rizayqat relations with the Malwal Dinka in the Bahr al-Ghazal were periodically vexed: a Grazing Agreement in 1935, brokered by provincial officials, proved susceptible of amendment as needed; British intervention was required when the Dinka sold slaves to the Baqqara. Rizayqat relations with the Berti were also reduced to formal agreement, after years of difficulty, in 1938. British patience with the Rizayqat was tried to the point where plans were made to depose Ibrahim Musa, but so important a cog had he become in the local machinery that these were never carried out. The

Figure 14. *Shaykh* Ibrahim Musa Madibbu, *Nazir* of the Rizayqat, 1928. *Shaykh* Ibrahim's family has played a leading role in the history of southern Darfur for generations and has been prominent in efforts to keep the current fighting from enveloping that region. (Durham University Library, 760/7/6.)

lowland Fur and Masalit, neighbors along the Wadi Azum, required frequent mediation. To the east, in scenes from Hollywood, Baqqara cowboys drove their cattle into Fur cultivations, farmers took the law into their own hands, and the British DC, like Judge Roy Bean, had to settle matters; the comparison is not strained by reference to the cavalry – the provincial police and SDF – which everyone knew could be relied on to restore order on the government's terms. Formal meetings of tribal *shaykhs* along the border with Kordofan were routine. British and French officials likewise exchanged visits and cooperated in cases of cattle rustling and fugitives from justice.[30]

In 1949, the governor of Darfur, G. D. Lampen, described the Native Administration of the 1920s – when he had been a DC there – as "an orgy of fining and imprisonment," when "the most flagrant injustice and nepotism and selling of posts were allowed."[31] Khartoum's voluminous files support him. *Shaykhs* were routinely appointed because of their lineage and despite personal disqualifications. But a corrupt official was easy to dismiss; a tyrannical *shaykh* was not. Every time an officer interfered, the theoretical basis of government suffered. Even serious abuses were "winked at" lest removal of a *shaykh* or *shartay* weaken his office and the system. When in 1928 Karam al-Din Muhammad of the Birgid was convicted of abusing power, he was merely deprived of authority for a year.[32] Despite the personal failings of Muhammad Ibrahim Dabaka of the Bani Halba, he was judged suitable to head a court, the regularized powers of which would, it was hoped, help to restore discipline.[33] A "hoary old reprobate" who "took bribes shamelessly," *Nazir* Ghali Taj al-Din was "probably the sort of nazir" the Habbaniyya deserved.[34] Double taxation was common, irregular exactions too numerous to report, fear of reporting abuses almost universal: British reluctance to annoy the *shaykhs* encouraged abuse of power.[35]

One reason Native Administration was cheap is that it provided so little. But instead of creating territorial units big enough to support civil servants, ideologues tried to create tribes from a dog's breakfast of left-over clans and families. After decades of dislocation, many of Darfur's tribal units were unviable alone and dispersed from their original *dars*. "Avoid division into separate tribal entities where they are ceasing to exist to keep our units as large as possible" was how the governor put it in 1938: "amalgamate as opportunity occurs." But appointing *shaykhs* over people who happened to be at hand did not make them a tribe, let alone give them a government. The result was inevitably accession of supra-tribal overlords endowed with powers considered suitable and necessary. The difference between this and a normal local government ultimately reduced to the method by which officials were appointed.

Examples abound. In the Baqqara subdistrict of southern Darfur, presidency of a joint court for the Habbaniyya, Masalit, and Fallata in 1929 went to Adam al-Nur of the Jimaa because the tribes could not agree on one of their own: his "foreign" status was taken as a harbinger of impartiality. For two years, officials tried to amalgamate the nomadic Ma'alia with the sedentary Rizayqat Ma'alia, but this ended in total failure thanks to the *shaykhs'* abuses. The Khalifa Abdallahi's Ta'aisha in southwestern Darfur could not be brought under the jurisdiction of any court. When *Nazir* Muhammad Uthman of the Nyala Misiriyya lay dying, it was decided that each tribal unit in his *dar* would be reassigned to whichever overlord it preferred. One leftover Humr section in Darfur had nowhere to go but Kordofan.[36] In Umm Kadada district, detailed proposals included detaching a *dar*, amalgamating others, and setting up another "maqdumate."[37] But fancy titles rarely appealed as much to the tribes as to the British and caused confusion through differing memories of what those titles meant. And if Native Administration came down to self-rule of a clan and its participation, through its head, in judicial and administrative bodies, then it was merely local government without elections.

EDUCATING "PEOPLE WHO MATTER"

The worst feature of Native Administration in Darfur was failure to provide for the future. Where Indirect Rule seemed to thrive, its conservatism and ability to combat external influences implied rejection of education and economic development. Whereas by the mid-1930s the perceived danger of "fanatical Mahdism" had waned (not least because of vastly improved communication, notably by air), other "isms," in the decade of the Great Depression, seemed more fearsome than ever. The idea that Sudanese should acquire literacy for its own sake was widely dismissed, but even Native Administration needed people to keep books, register taxes, and record judgments. Bringing in trained people from outside the tribe would empower dangerous and despised effendis. The solution arrived at was to educate a few tribesmen and only to the level required to support the chiefs. But because even that courted the danger that clever parvenus might overawe bumpkin *shaykhs*, it was to *shaykhs'* sons themselves that the government's meager educational effort would be devoted.

The Sudan's education system had evolved in any case into an adjunct of administration. By the end of the period under review (1939), the vast majority of Sudanese boys still received no formal education at all, as did far fewer girls. In the north, the structure was broadly pyramidal. Locally, private *khalwas* of untrained, often barely literate *faqihs* taught rote memorization of the Qur'an; in the 1920s, the government, in its zeal to combat modernism, began to subsidize some of these. Primary education consisted of four-year elementary vernacular schools (*kuttabs*), of which by 1933 there were ninety (with about 9,000 boys) and, above them, eleven four-year intermediate schools (with about 1,000 boys). At the top was a single secondary school, Gordon Memorial College. In all of the northern Sudan, thirty-five years after the Anglo-Egyptian conquest, about 4 percent of boys received primary education.[38] (Figures for the south, where education had originally been left to missionaries, were very much lower.) Various training schools and higher programs of medicine, science, veterinary medicine, agriculture, nursing, teacher training, *Shari'a*, and other technical subjects produced practical specialists. A small but flourishing system of private education was provided by and largely for foreign and minority communities. Allocation of scarce places was not based on merit: sons of the prominent got preferential treatment; selection by examination was deemed – as late as 1939 – "undesirable," and when there were too many applicants for the seats available, the children of "people who mattered were moved up the list."[39]

When Darfur was occupied in 1916, the bias against modern education had already set in and, by 1919, when Egypt exploded in nationalist revolution, that bias solidified. British officials in Darfur, apprehending multiple and potential threats to order, thought they still had time to "save" the province through a two-pronged policy of Indirect Rule and noneducation. Twenty years later, when groundwork was laid for postsecondary education in the riverain north, Darfur thus languished behind even the dismally backward south. As late as 1929, not a single student in the government secondary school was from Darfur, whereas there were 218 from Khartoum, 93 from Blue Nile, 41 from Kordofan, and even some foreigners. In 1934, Darfur had one student at the college. The annual report for 1936 boasted that two boys from the province had been sent to the teachers' training college.[40]

In its heyday, when the theory of Native Administration was most sophisticated, access to modern education in Darfur was a potent tool of social policy, wielded to widen the gap between the masses and their "natural" rulers. Education was for the "aristocracy"; government *kuttabs* were abolished. Nor was this exclusionary policy hidden. In 1938, the governor explained: "The educational policy in Darfur is not haphazard but has been carefully thought out with a view to the education of the sons of tribal chiefs." Entry had been "very strictly controlled to the virtual exclusion" of "sons of low paid ghaffirs [guards]," "petty merchants and police." He backed this up with statistics. More than twenty years after the conquest – and less than twenty years before independence – Darfur, a province of 750,000 people, had three elementary vernacular schools, at El Fasher, Nyala, and Umm Kadada. At Nyala, a *khalwa* replaced the modern *kuttab*, thus signaling a conscious reduction in the level of education available locally. Zalingei and Kutum each had a "Native Administration school"; El Geneina had one "subgrade" school with one "subgrade" master; the whole of Southern Darfur District had one – "subgrade" – government school. There was no intermediate school at all, and the governor was dead set against having one: some chiefs' sons could be sent, as some already had been, to El Obeid for intermediate education. By 1945, the governor wrote, there should be one elementary vernacular school in each district, with two in El Fasher and Northern Darfur and "one and a half" in Southern Darfur, after which the "pace" would "slow down"![41]

Quantity was not sacrificed for quality. The few schools were poor. After external examination of its education system and as part of the post-1924 reaction in general, Khartoum had increased the number of so-called subsidized *khalwas*, purportedly as "a *useful adjunct to the educational system* [my emphasis]," through which pupils might learn their ABCs and how to count, memorize bits of the Qur'an, and so forth. In this way, annual reports boasted of expanding education while the amount offered was reduced, and in Darfur the *khalwa* virtually took the place of the "system" to which it was meant to be an "adjunct." Such schools did little: surveys in Khartoum in 1933 showed that a year after leaving, few pupils could write more than their own names. Meanwhile the slightest evidence of learning was trumpeted in Darfur as signifying progress, and reports glowed with news of pupils occupied in manual labor rather than book learning. But even Darfur abhorred a vacuum: many *khalwas* were run by Mahdists.[42]

Where ideology failed, the Depression was invoked. A new British DC in the Southern District wrote in 1933 that since *khalwa* teachers were illiterate themselves, the future seemed "hopeless"; he asked the governor to reopen the suppressed *kuttab* at Nyala, only to be told there was no money.[43] In 1936, the Resident in Dar Masalit reported that the Sultan's "advanced *khalwa*" failed even in its "chief purpose, which is to educate the sons of local chiefs."[44] At Zalingei in 1932, the acting

Resident reported difficulty in getting a teacher to abandon "visions of red brick buildings and . . . furniture" and realize that he was "educating future rulers."[45] Southern Darfur suffered financial loss because no one could add and subtract, but the official pointing this out thought that eighty *shaykhs'* sons who could "read, write and add up" was all the district needed: limiting education to *shaykhs'* sons would avoid their "being swamped in class by the sharper-witted sons of merchants." Besides, it would be "the greatest of pities" if the local elementary school "developed into something . . . more than the district needed or deserved."[46]

Long after the bloom had faded from Native Administration, British officials in Darfur fought a rearguard action against the Education Department in Khartoum, echoes of which could still be heard half a century later. In 1935, the director of education called attention to the grim statistics. The government was spending a grand total of 1,200 Egyptian pounds (£E) per year on education in all of Darfur, less than the salary of one senior government official. For the whole of the Northern District – about 150,000 people – there was, in educational terms, literally nothing. The director asked for £E55 more and was turned down.[47] British officials in Darfur thumbed their noses at Khartoum and boasted about it. "The education of chiefs' sons is proceeding apace" is how the 1938 province report's one paragraph on education stubbornly begins.[48] The single paragraph on education in Darfur in the Sudan Government's consolidated report for the three years 1939–41 reads as follows:

The first girls' school in the province was opened in Fasher in 1939 and there were 200 applicants for the 80 places. Ten of the girls in the school were daughters of notables sent from other districts. The Fasher boys' school was doubled in size. With the guidance of a life convict, trained in Fasher prison as an expert bricklayer, and a few prisoners, the Umm Keddada schoolmaster and boys built a boarding house for which no funds were available. Nyala school recovered from the disorganization caused by the death of its headmaster in the autumn of 1938. The Fur-speaking headmaster of Zalingei was temporarily exchanged with Kordofan to give him a change of milieu. The Kutum school continued to prosper. The policy of associating local Fekis with the boys' elementary and sub-grade schools was maintained. Two new sub-grade schools were opened in southern Darfur at Tullus and Deradir. The Sultan's school in Geneina was raised to elementary status by the secondment to his administration of a teacher from the Education Department as headmaster. The number of pupils rose to 59, of whom 19, sons of outside chiefs, were boarders.[49]

That was all.

UNDERDEVELOPING DARFUR

Even with a missionary zeal to bring Darfur into the modern world, provincial officials would have been hamstrung by the Sudan Government's economic policies, which, regardless of administrative fashion, heavily favored the riverain provinces. This, even more than Darfur officials' reactionary certitudes, explains the lack of progress, for a determined central government could have enforced its will. Bias is evident in every area and illustrated in every annual budget. The resources devoted to outlying regions in human and veterinary health, agriculture, animal husbandry, and communications were meager compared with those reserved for the center. Darfur, often subsumed statistically with "the North," arguably suffered even more than the famously neglected south.

We have noted that in its early years the Sudan Government benefited from Egypt's annual subventions and development loans. These allowed the building of a modern communication system, including the Sudan Government Railways and Port Sudan, and the rebuilding and embellishment of Khartoum, among many projects far exceeding the country's ability otherwise to afford. British officials disliked this reliance on Egypt, but it was only the specter of political objections in Egypt itself that led the British to reduce and then eliminate the annual grants. Given the limits of the Sudan's economy, it became necessary to find new sources of revenue. Thus was born the Gezira Scheme, an enormous irrigation project south of Khartoum designed to supply cotton to the British market and that by the time it was inaugurated in 1926 had cost many millions in British-guaranteed loans. In its first few years it was hugely successful, producing ever-increasing cotton yields and revenues, but the coincidence of the Great Depression and crop failure in the early 1930s plunged the Gezira – and the country's finances – into desperate straits. Whereas the riverain Sudan had gained most from government investment in infrastructure and services, the peripheral regions – including the south and Darfur – would suffer most when investment dried up.

The revolution in communications the Condominium wrought in the Sudan left Darfur far behind. After the occupation in 1916, the telegraph system was quickly extended but railhead reached the province only after independence. Economic development was thus severely handicapped by the high cost of transport and consequent low profitability of most local products. "Roads" were in fact routes – tracks improved by fitful attention to scraping, ramping, and culverts – always difficult and, during the rains, impassable; long distances from productive areas to eastern markets, notably across the 200-mile sandy stretches of the route to El Obeid, were never overcome. Animals and animal by-products perforce remained the province's main exports throughout the period, and even these were modest except by the standards of the regime's early years. Cattle, camels, sheep, skins, hides, and clarified butter were also imported from French territory for reexport. Darfur's hides were of poor quality: horn-raked and thorn-scratched from night-time corralling in *zaribas*, usually flayed from beasts dead through disease, and often inexpertly cured, before transport these were already destined to achieve poor returns. Even so, competition from regions closer to the point of sale often priced Darfur's products out of the market. Worse, the intense variability of demand hardly seemed to reward even good technique: official exports of hides, for example, fell from about 297 tons in 1929 to almost nothing a year later. In 1930, with the onset of the Depression, live cattle and camels often could not be sold for export at any price.[50]

Indirect Rule, touted for cheapness, seemed suited for poor places during hard times. The "retrenchment" of the Depression era was uncalled for where little or nothing had been budgeted in the first place. Nonetheless, Darfur's personnel budget, including police, was reduced from about £E41,000 in 1931 to £E32,800 in 1932; the number of police officers fell from 491 in 1926 to 301 in 1932. One sensible innovation involved transfer in 1932 of the Baqqara nomads from poll and herd taxes to "tribute," assessment of which was easier to align to changing circumstances – in this case, collapse of the export market and depletion of the herds by rinderpest. In 1934, wholesale reduction in taxes was necessary. Despite considerable government attention, which included quarantine stations, inoculation, and vaccination, rinderpest remained a constant problem. The 1927 epidemic killed an estimated 40,000 head of cattle; another outbreak in 1930 was even worse, and one in 1931 worse still, with the Rizayqat alone losing 20,000 to 30,000 head. Outbreaks continued sporadically, especially among the Baqqara, notably in 1936.

The Depression allowed prolongation of Indirect Rule in Darfur even after it had stalled in the east, and militated against the pressure to modernize that Khartoum – or London – might have exerted if times had been better. If Darfur could pay for its own administration, law and order be maintained, epidemic diseases be combated, and the effects of droughts and famines eased, then Khartoum was relieved to leave well enough alone. The province's income was indeed meager, even by Sudanese standards: in the bumper year of 1928, Darfur's revenue stood at only £E57,575, out of total government revenue of about £E6 million.[51]

FAMINE AND DISEASE

The historical trio of drought, famine, and disease continued to stalk Darfur. In 1926, most of the province experienced drought, and consequent food shortages and high prices resulted in famine, which was followed – and exacerbated by – a catastrophic outbreak of relapsing fever, the first such epidemic recorded in the Sudan. The disease came to Darfur from West Africa and established itself in Jabal Marra, whence it spread in all directions. Infection rates exceeded 50 percent, and mortality an astounding 60 to 80 percent when the disease went untreated. Whole villages were wiped out. By one estimate, as many as 25 percent of the Fur died from the disease; sober government reports estimated 15,000 dead, but many cases must have gone unreported and some affected areas unexamined, so the numbers were speculative. A disquieting element is the possibility of government neglect for political reasons: in responding to a memorandum about Mahdism in Dar Masalit, the governor, R. A. Bence-Pembroke, wrote that if the epidemic's mortality rate there was as high as it had been in Zalingei, and the Masalit, on the advice of their *faqihs*, resorted only to traditional remedies, "then the epidemic by itself" would "remove large numbers of troublesome persons and so save us a lot of trouble." In Khartoum, science prevailed: investigations at the Wellcome Research Laboratories confirmed that the disease was louse-borne, and this set the stage for efforts to combat it in Darfur. Systematic delousing was undertaken and quarantine measures prevented free movement of people and goods; disinfecting stations were set up along the border with Kordofan to prevent the disease's spread eastward.[52]

The emergency steps taken in Darfur to combat this epidemic laid the groundwork for the province's system of dispensaries. This came too late to combat a 1928–29 smallpox epidemic, but it is likely that Darfur's first outbreak of cerebrospinal meningitis since the occupation, in 1935–36, would have been much worse without that basic infrastructure. As it was, more than half the cases reported in the Sudan were in Darfur, and of almost 10,000 reported cases in the province, more than 7,000 proved fatal.[53]

A plague of locusts in 1929 resulted in complete destruction of crops in some parts of northern Darfur and at least some damage throughout the province; another infestation a year later, first of the common desert locust (*Schistocerca gregaria*) but then, for the first time in forty years, by the rarer tropical (or migratory) African locust (*Locusta migratoria migratoriodes*, sometimes grotesquely called in the Sudan the hairy-chested locust) was reported as the worst in memory. At the height of the cycle, heroic measures, combining intense local effort and experimental methods introduced by British officers, mitigated the disaster, but losses were heavy and demand for food, including from Wadai, where the invasions had catastrophic effect, resulted in high prices and shortages; hardest hit were the nomads. After the poor crops of 1929 and 1930 and the late rains of 1931, famine conditions prevailed; a particularly good season for wild *mukheit* berry (*Boscia octandra*) was credited with saving thousands of lives. Huge areas were planted in 1931, but another locust invasion required enormous effort to control; some areas had to be planted three times, and some continued on the edge of famine through 1932. Subsequent years were better, but a major infestation occurred in 1938. Only through enlisting almost the entire machinery of government and population within affected areas were the effects of locust plagues mitigated.[54]

Despite reaction, Depression, lack of investment, drought, famine, and plague, the 1920s and 1930s witnessed some economic progress. Standards of living were judged by the market prices of food and consumption of sugar: increasing food prices meant reduction in the standard, and increasing sugar consumption meant that people were doing well. Thus, for example, sugar consumption recovered to some 10,600 sacks in 1929 from a lowly 4,223 in 1927 and surprisingly fell only to 8,340 in 1932 and 5,492 in 1933, when the province was gripped by Depression; it recovered its 1930 level only in 1936.[55] Government efforts to diversify agriculture to improve diet and stimulate a cash market were sporadic and, by all but local standards, unambitious. These included planting citrus in Jabal Marra; encouraging native tobacco farming; experimenting with olives, dates, varieties of melons, and other fruit; and importing seeds. Poisoning campaigns against local pests, notably baboons, were undertaken. Tree farms of *gambil* provided wood for local furniture and other uses. Wage labor, employed mainly by the government, was a tiny factor in the economy in terms of both the amount of demand and the miserly wages paid, and indeed had to compete with that of prisoners, Native Administration tribesmen working off dues, and even foreigners (from French Equatorial Africa, where wages were lower still).[56]

A problem imperfectly understood but already assuming economic and political dimensions in the 1930s was what would later be called desertification. This was noticed first not in spectacular encroachment of dunes in areas of habitation but in the drying up of water supplies. El Fasher itself had for long depended on its *fula* (lake) for water, which supplied wells through seepage. The lowest *fula* level ever recorded was in 1938, after which boring operations began to tap the lower aquifer. Government geologists identified sites throughout the province for new wells, and tribal or convict labor was enlisted to do the dangerous work of sinking them. Evacuation of villages owing to the drying up of water supply became more common, however, and there had long been ample evidence – although not conclusive as to long-term implications – that both Dar Zaghawa's seasonal rain-fed grazing and its wells were drying up.[57]

Aside from emergency provisions in times of plague, medical advance was likewise measured statistically, but in Darfur as elsewhere numbers were misleading because increased attendance at clinics and hospitals may mean either declining health or increased availability of service. In 1930, Darfur had three hospitals – at El Fasher (with 129 beds), Nyala (48), and El Geneina (35) – and eight dispensaries, and some 160,000 outpatients were treated.[58] But the Depression brought retrenchment even to this area: in 1932, the Nyala hospital was reduced to dispensary status, and the author of the annual *Report* thought it noteworthy that "medical treatment has the greatest possible administrative value"; the dispensary at Zalingei was singled out for praise as "run extraordinarily cheaply" – the patients grew their own food.[59] The number of dispensaries gradually increased throughout the period: there were nineteen by 1934. About standards we know little.

Medical provision compared poorly with that of eastern provinces of similar or even smaller populations: in 1940, for example, Darfur had only ten trained midwives, whereas Kassala, with 422,000 people (compared with Darfur's 715,000) had twenty-six, and the Northern Province (535,000) some eighty-three; by 1949 the numbers had improved to twenty-one, thirty-four, and ninety-eight, respectively. Of 503 El Fasher schoolchildren examined in 1940 by the central government's School Medical Service, 47 percent were infected with bilharzias (the highest rate in the Sudan) and 43 percent with trachoma; at El Geneina, where 63 children were examined, an astounding 92 percent were found to be infected with trachoma. Moreover, Darfur had special call on medical services owing to its location on the pilgrimage routes: it had long been recognized that pilgrims from the west and tribal interchanges along the border with French Equatorial Africa exposed Darfur (and the rest of the Sudan) to constant threat of epidemic outbreaks of smallpox, cerebrospinal meningitis, and other diseases. Yet, although health measures were taken at borders, including quarantine and delousing, plans to vaccinate the entire population of Darfur against smallpox were made only in 1938. In 1940, Darfur accounted for some 28 percent of the country's hospital admissions for syphilis and 22 percent for amoebic dysentery. A survey of 11,000 people in Darfur in 1949 found 18 percent infected with schistosomiasis (*S. haematobium*).[60]

The Depression came upon the Sudan with suddenness and force as great as anywhere else in the world, and upon its poorest regions – those always closest to the line between sufficiency and want – it fell hardest of all. The value of the country's trade fell from £E13,665,000 in 1929 to £E5,646,000 in 1931, and revenue (excluding reserve funds) from £E4,835,000 to £E3,360,000. In Darfur, the disastrous combination of poor rains, locust invasions, cattle disease, and poor market prices for animals created enormous hardship, including famine conditions

in some areas. In general, the nomads suffered more than the sedentary population. With grain prices exorbitant and demand for animals
low but with nothing else to sell – and the animals they had beset by
rinderpest – the nomads faced ruin.[61] In 1932, the Zaghawa, already
reeling, experienced what one report called a "colossal visitation" of
locusts;[62] their meager plantings and even grazing were wiped out by
drought in 1933: Dar Zaghawa had by then had one good crop in eight
years. Demand for the province's exports all but dried up, and money
became very scarce. The provincial government resorted to a form of
import substitution, buying up local produce instead of rice and lentils
for prisoners and using local homespun (*damur*) for their clothes, as a
way of injecting (what must have been a very small amount of) cash into
the economy; the homespun was rejected for hospital clothes because it
was too coarse. It is pathetic to read of attempts to establish an export
market for local string, some of the profits of which paid for the care
of the lepers who made it.[63] Better weather and lower incidence of
cattle plague improved living conditions by the mid-1930s, but export
prices took longer to recover and for some commodities reached pre-
Depression prices only with the onset of the Second World War.

Darfur's exports of any importance continued to be limited to animals, animal by-products, and gum. The effect of the Depression is eas-
iest to gauge on gum because its export was registered: in 1928 some
973 tons of Darfur (*hashab*) gum were sold at the El Obeid and Nahud
markets; in 1930, 1,505 tons; in 1931, 1,325 tons; but, in 1932, only
411 and in 1935, 256, after which the market began to recover. The
value of the Sudan's exports of cattle and sheep, which, with wartime
demand had reached £E1.15 million in 1918, fell to below £E50,000
in 1932. Even when demand picked up, prices fluctuated widely, and
Darfur's export, of poor quality, went mainly to other Middle Eastern
countries.[64]

7

UNEQUAL STRUGGLES, 1939–1955

...we are really a bit behind hand in everything here – Education, Health, Agriculture, Town Amenities. The sad thing is that while we can manage the important things, such as public security and Local Government, we cannot get departments to help us in our very modest departmental proposals. Modest they have to be: we are remote and have a skeleton staff.

> G. D. Lampen, governor, Darfur, to the civil secretary,
> Khartoum, 23 February 1946[1]

DARFUR AND THE SECOND WORLD WAR

Touchdowns and Landings

Although the Sudan played no role in the First World War, its position, sandwiched between Italian colonies and upstream from Egypt, made it a front for a time during World War II. And although the occupation of Darfur in 1916 was a footnote in the history of the First World War, the province would play an important supporting role in the Allies' defeat of the Axis Powers of 1939–45. The overall impression of the war years in Darfur, however, is of political and administrative stasis and, indeed, of continuing neglect by Khartoum and the emerging Sudanese political elite.

The Sudan's position when Britain and France declared war on Germany in 1939 was extremely vulnerable. The 6,000-man Sudan Defence Force (SDF) was designed and organized for internal security rather than national defense, its famous Camel Corps and other units well trained and resourceful but hardly a match for a modern army. It was seemingly such an enemy, Fascist Italy, that from 1936 lay on the eastern borders, in occupation of Eritrea and Ethiopia, a short haul from Khartoum. The Italian buildup there and in Libya was so enormous, and the Sudan's defensive measures so casual, that British officials in Cairo suspected defeatism. They were right: London had decided that the Sudan was not of essential strategic importance.[2] Left almost alone in a dangerous neighborhood, Khartoum took what steps it could as the European crisis deepened, recalling officials, transferring military units, organizing civil defense, restricting exports, fixing prices, dealing with enemy aliens, imposing censorship. After Britain and Italy went to war in June 1940, Symes, the governor-general, was forced to resign and a soldier, Sir Hubert Huddleston (who in 1916 had hunted down Ali Dinar), was brought in to succeed him.

The situation he faced was grim. Sporadic Italian air raids, although doing little damage, had shown the weakness of the Sudan's defenses. Port Sudan was wide open to attack from the air and susceptible to occupation by a swift mobile force. Italy had more than 200,000 men in East Africa (and another 215,000 in Libya); counting the British garrison, the Sudan had about 10,000 in arms, no tanks, and no artillery. In July 1940, the Italians occupied Kassala and Gallabat and stood 270 miles from Khartoum across terrain ideal for mechanized forces. But no number of tanks and men could compensate for dithering and poor intelligence; the Italians halted their advance, probed, and harassed, but never regained momentum. While the British rushed reinforcements from India, the SDF, aided by cobbled-together units of local irregulars, managed greatly to exaggerate its strength. In the upper Blue Nile, Upper Nile, and eastern Equatoria, the SDF and local guerillas under British officers and hastily commissioned civilians also did their part, improvising in utter obscurity. At the end of 1940, a counteroffensive was launched; Sudanese, British, and Indian troops, with recently acquired armor and air support, drove back the Italians, reoccupying Kassala in January 1941. The invasion of Eritrea and Abyssinia ensued, and Addis Ababa and Massawa were occupied in April. By the end of May 1941, the fighting had ended in complete Italian defeat.

The perceived threat from Italian Libya never materialized. Before Italy entered the war, some gung-ho British and French colonial officials were as keen to invade Libya as others were fearful of an Italian thrust southward into Chad and the Sudan. The mood changed after the fall of France, when the British focus in Khartoum and Darfur shifted to defense. The loyalties of French Equatorial Africa, whether to Vichy or the Free French, were uncertain and all-important, and agents of both sides flew to Chad to sway opinion. Officials in Darfur did what they could by visiting their counterparts and praising de Gaulle, arranging joint meetings of Darfur and Chad tribal groups, and supplying Khartoum with information. A joint patrol of the Ennedi Groupe Nomade and irregular Darfur scouts to Merga Oasis in December 1940 gathered intelligence. Under armistice terms with Italy, the French had withdrawn from the Chadian posts of Tekro and Bardai, leaving Erdi and Ennedi, adjacent to northernmost Darfur, unoccupied; the governor of Darfur pressed unsuccessfully to arm his own Zaghawa to fill the vacuum. Although the Italians sent reconnaissance flights over Darfur from Sarra in southern Libya, the terrain over which an advance into Chad and Darfur would have to pass was so vast and inhospitable – and the potential return on such an investment so negligible – that cool heads were unconcerned. When the Chad Territory declared for Free France, the danger on Darfur's thousand-mile border with French territory also dissipated.[3] A Dad's Army, organized at El Fasher in three units – Greeks and Syrians, "effendis," and "merchants and market riff raff" – never saw action.[4]

The famous North African campaigns, culminating at El Alamein in October 1942, were fought along the Mediterranean littoral, far bypassing Darfur. Still, French colonies in West and North Africa loyal to Vichy posed a threat: if the Germans decided to occupy them, Allied supply routes would be cut, and the position in Chad would be endangered. Sudan officials could do little to avert this, but they continued to give the royal treatment to their Free French counterparts in Chad, exchanging official visits and sending expensive gifts. On 1 March 1941, a small French force from Chad took the Italian base at the strategically important Kufra Oasis. That position was thereafter held by the SDF and British troops, who had to be resupplied from railhead at Wadi Halfa on the Nile, 700 miles across the desert.[5] Kufra became a base for the British Long Range Desert Group's activities farther north and was targeted in German bombing raids, but it held. The potential consequences of even a lightning raid were great: in early 1942, a single German plane bombed the airport at Fort Lamy in Chad, destroying 90,000 gallons of aviation fuel that had been brought overland by truck from Nigeria.[6]

It was in supplying the Allies in North Africa and the Middle East that the Sudan would make its greatest contribution. Routes crisscrossed the country: the Congo-Nile; the African Line of Communication from South Africa through the Southern Sudan and down the Nile; through East Africa; from Port Sudan to Shallal in Egypt; and the Western Air Reinforcement (WAR) route through Darfur, where facilities were constructed for the Royal Air Force (RAF) and U.S. Army Air Force. The value of the WAR route (and the tracks beneath) increased until the North African campaign wound up in 1943, but the route remained in use until 1945. A confidential report of August 1942 referred to the WAR route as a "vital life-line to Alamein for war-planes, and probably the Sudan's most important job for Middle East forces." Funding for communications in Darfur, until then derisorily parsimonious, flowed freely. In 1942, runways at El Fasher and El Geneina were extended to handle very large aircraft; control towers were added at both airports in 1943. At the RAF's request, extensive work raised the main provincial roads (El Geneina–El Fasher–Nyala–Nahud) to all-weather status before the 1942 rains, for aviation fuel had to be trucked in from the east; the Nyala-Nahud link remained a problem.[7] Much air traffic was of short-hop fighters and bombers, and tales of unscheduled stops in outlandish places, pilots lost, rescues, incognito luminaries (including General de Gaulle), and disaster punctuate the period. When the war ended, the province inherited excellent airfields of which little use was made: as late as 1952, there was only weekly service through El Geneina.[8]

Harbingers of Environmental Disaster

The WAR route emphasized the need to maintain popular support for the government in Darfur. No serious danger of Axis propaganda or sabotage was apprehended, but reaction to policy had to be gauged, as did the potential for wider trouble growing from intertribal or cross-border fractiousness. Allied air and ground traffic affected the local economy: demand for food (and water) raised prices, and construction and maintenance increased demand for wage labor. Even a terrible series of crop failures brought no widespread disaffection. Serious locust invasions in 1939 and 1943 caused considerable crop loss; the 1940 harvests were disastrous: the millet crop in the north and rain-watered wheat in Jabal Marra failed completely. Again in 1941, the northern grain crop failed, and yields were halved elsewhere. In 1942, when famine conditions prevailed in much of the province after two years of poor rains, the government imported 400,000 liters of grain. Even so, prices for grain and animals skyrocketed, benefiting the rural population but hurting townsmen. The 1943–44 harvests were only adequate and prices remained high; only in 1945 did the province return to a grain surplus. When controls were lifted at the end of the war, export prices for the province's animals and animal by-products shot up. But the primitive state of the economy is illustrated by the 1945 *Report*, which devoted attention to an increase in elephant hunting in the south owing to the higher world price of ivory.[9]

Transport was at the heart of the problem. In the early years of colonial rule, it was taken for granted that Darfur would never compete in most areas and that even its animals sold on the hoof in Kordofan would be priced out of the market from time to time. By 1945, the cost of a "car" (meaning a truck) trip between El Obeid and El Fasher still priced most products out of eastern markets. Tobacco, gum, and melons were the only cash crops that repaid export; other fruit and vegetables did not survive the trip. Grain prices in Kordofan rarely reached levels that made export of Darfur's occasional surpluses profitable; trade with Chad was more likely to bring a return, especially when the French colony's links to the west were cut during the war. Extension of railhead to Darfur and more all-weather roads were needed before investment in agriculture for export would make sense. Meanwhile, officials routinely complained of too much cash circulating in the province: during the war, sugar, tea, and cloth, the principal imported luxuries, were rationed, and in rural areas there was little demand for anything else. When asked what they spent their money on, tribesmen always reportedly answered, "more animals."[10]

That comment, regarding the need to stimulate demand, was inadvertently ominous. During the war, climatic pressure in Darfur and its consequences began to be appreciated in a scientific way as a long-term problem of great potential magnitude. Anecdotal evidence had been previously noted as probably fortuitous or possibly cyclical. Thus, when failure of the 1940–41 crops and grazing brought migration southward of the northern tribes, officials noted what was assumed to be the normal response to a harsh environment that nomads had adopted since time immemorial. By 1945 they considered the migration a permanent trend. "Lack of water in the north and easy living in the south" was how the 1945 *Report* summarized the causes; concern was raised about the tribes' disintegrating "into independent and uncontrolled family units" unless better water supplies could be provided in their home-lands.[11] Thus, ironically, before scientific studies, some consequences of the phenomena they would describe began to prey on the minds of administrators.

Human action had already sped up imperfectly understood but insid-ious and gradual natural processes. Throughout Darfur, a variety of tactics were employed to improve water supply: deep boring, well lin-ing, exploration for new well fields, construction of water yards (*hafirs*) for villages and along cattle-export routes, and so forth. The empha-sis was on the short term. In 1942, the governor-general appointed a Soil Conservation Committee to review the presumably related prob-lems of soil erosion and rural water supply and to propose a five-year plan for conservation after the war. Each province submitted recom-mendations. The committee's report, in April 1944, warned of already uncontrolled degradation in the central Sudan owing to woodcutting (for fuel), expansion of cropped areas, and increased well digging. In pastoral areas, where wealth was measured in animals, demand for water and fodder must eventually outstrip supply, and the replenish-ment of aquifers, especially in areas of negligible rainfall, was probably slight or nonexistent. There was, in other words, a hidden environmen-tal time bomb ticking, with those detecting it unable to direct policy and those in its blast area unable to postpone its explosion or mitigate its effects. Some individuals and groups, like the Okies of dust-bowl America, were already moving.[12]

Straining the metaphor, we may discern in the Soil Conservation Committee's report both an early warning and the reasons this warn-ing went largely unheeded. Overgrazing was the biggest factor in soil degradation, with long-term or even irreversible effects; the commit-tee recommended limiting herds. Cutting scrub for fuel contributed to desert creep; the report suggested that an existing ban should be enforced and that firewood be provided from commercial forests. The main focus was on detailed planning at the local level. Where there was already overpopulation, people should be moved: an optimum number of people and animals a village could support should be established, then enforced. Enclosure for crop rotation and grazing paddocks was needed to conserve soil and protect forest plantations. To carry out such recommendations would have required a degree of government direction and control that few areas of the Sudan had experienced or would tolerate. The short-term increase of water supply was much easier.[13]

Paramount Chiefs and Nationalist Politics

A notable political event of the war period was inauguration of the Darfur Province Council in 1944. Under Symes, the practical limits of Native Administration had become clear to all but die-hards. At the same time, Anglo-Egyptian rapprochement in the face of global tensions had led, in 1936, to a treaty by which units of the Egyptian army returned to the Sudan. These changes reopened competition between the co-domini for the support of educated Sudanese, whose political consciousness had been further stimulated by their rulers' condescension. Impetus for liberalization also came from within, notably from Douglas Newbold, who as governor of Kordofan (1933–38) and civil secretary (1939–45) made a mark in colonial administrative theory. In effect, the government reverted to the dual policy of the pre-1924 era, by which a modern bureaucratic regime would be extended in the towns (under the Local Government Ordinances of 1937) and the limits of Native Administration recognized. Local governments thus established had very limited powers, however, and progress was slow during the war.

In 1938, alumni of Gordon College founded a Graduates' General Congress to represent their interests. British hopes that this would concern itself mainly with social issues – and act as a bulwark against Egyptian nationalist influence – were dashed when the congress turned to overtly political matters. In 1942 it issued a declaration calling for Sudanese self-determination immediately after the war. This lent urgency to an idea that had been floated as early as the 1920s: a national advisory council. Although some British officials saw this as an outlet for aspiring politicians, others hoped it would empower conservative tribal leaders who, after all, "represented" most of the population. The gap between the local and national was filled first, under a 1943 ordinance, by creation of province councils in the north, which in turn drew members from district councils established for the purpose; the south was ruled incapable. Darfur's province council, purely advisory, was composed of *shaykhs*, their representatives, and a few officials, under the presidency of the governor. The governor-general appointed the Advisory Council of the Northern Sudan from among members of the province councils: from Darfur came Sultan Endoka of the Masalit, Ibrahim Musa of the Rizayqat, and Hamid Effendi al-Sayyid, chief clerk of the provincial administration.[14]

Although Darfur's representatives had predictably little impact in Khartoum, reforms undertaken under the local government ordinances before the war and under the advisory council ordinance of 1943 began to take hold within the province. G. D. Lampen, who had come to the Political Service from the Finance Department, succeeded Philip Ingleson, the longtime (1935–44) governor and Indirect Ruler. A new structure, incorporating much of what was in place but adding features of local government at the town and district levels (whence members of the province council were chosen), was erected. Outside the towns, Native Administrations – tribal governments – would remain, with authority technically devolved from the districts of which they were resident rather than from the (British) District Commissioner (DC) but with the powers and functions of *nazirs* and *shaykhs* intact. District governments, with councils and budgets, were established.

Some reform was made easier by the failure of Native Administration. The old Zalingei Emirate already had the rudiments of local government, and failure to incorporate it with the Southern Maqdumate, a wartime improvisation, led to establishment of a council of *shartays* under the *dimangawi*. This was supposed to be an "interesting experiment in combining the autocratic system inherent in Fur rule with dependence on a council," but the real autocrat was Hugh Boustead, newly returned from the war. Advantage was likewise taken to reform Southern Darfur: moribund structures would be pruned and a new single-district government established, which in turn would devolve powers to four regional agencies roughly coterminous with tribal boundaries. In northern Darfur, four regional units were likewise created, but the failure of the northern Maqdumate to evolve into an "emirate" and amalgamate tribal units resulted in an unworkably large number of independent entities. The poor and sparsely populated

Eastern District had an informal council. At the death of the *malik* in El Fasher, the administrative and judicial powers he had long wielded were separated, and work began to create a council with specialized committees for education, rationing, and public health. In October 1945, a district council was formed, with members elected by "120 leading citizens" and the rural population represented by government nominees.[15]

In this tentatively progressive atmosphere, the surviving sultans seemed more than ever relics of the heroic age. In Dar Masalit it was said that Sultan Endoka continued "to exercise his benevolent autocracy": he shelved a plan for his own advisory council, instead relying on an informal *majlis* – his "daily lunch party." He was incapable of delegating. But his autocracy was not such as to mislead informed passersby as to where sovereignty actually lay. In 1945 Sultan Hashim Idris, unlucky thirteenth in his line in desiccated Dar Qimr, a distinct polity since the seventeenth century, died, and the sultanate was amalgamated into Dar Masalit. By then there was little left to the royal family, the governor wrote, except "determination . . . to batten on a rapidly emigrating population." During an interregnum of direct British rule, the late sultan's son, Mustafa Hashim, succeeded to the title, but the role was akin to that of paramount chief in a dust bowl.[16]

Tribal relations continued to receive much attention. The intercourse of the Kababish and Meidob required constant notice, as did that of the Baqqara and Dinka. Old enmity between the Fur and Masalit flared from time to time in cases of theft and drunken homicide, but the personal relations of the chiefs, with British support, held things together. Periodic eruptions southward by the Zaghawa required police patrols, arrests, rulings, and compensation; the Zaghawa court assumed international significance when, in 1944, under the auspices of the DC at Kutum and the commandant of Faya in Chad, disputes over tribal boundaries, grazing rights, and access to watering places were settled. In 1940, a gathering of all the Baqqara of southern Darfur was held at Abu Salaa, and its ability to deal with outstanding issues encouraged hopes of "confederacy": a court combining the Bani Halba, Fallata, Habbaniyya, Rizayqat, Ta'aisha, and several much smaller tribes was duly established in 1941, with Ibrahim Musa of the Rizayqat as president, but the tribes continued to vary widely in their degree of self-government.[17]

Old Attitudes, New World

As the war drew to a close and, unimagined by all but the most ambitious Khartoum politico, with independence a mere decade away, Darfur's development gap continued to widen, and in no way more seriously than in education. At its first session, in May 1944, the Advisory Council for the Northern Sudan discussed a report by the director of education that illustrated Darfur's situation: while national and regional statistics were reeled off and plans for ever-wider and ever-higher education were discussed, Darfur remained unmentioned, its representatives silent.[18]

Ambitious educational goals laid down in 1938 were not achieved during the war. The number of boys' elementary schools in the Sudan increased between 1939 and 1946 from 106 (with 15,509 pupils) to 127 (with 22,015), of boys' intermediate schools from 11 (with 1,317 students) to 13 (with 2,027), and there remained but one secondary school in the whole country, with 517 boys. Toward the end of the war, however, plans were afoot to move the secondary school from Gordon College and use its buildings as the nucleus of the university college that eventually emerged as Khartoum University. It was only in 1945, therefore, that the Sudan had two secondary schools, at Wadi Saidna, north of Omdurman, and at Hantub, across the Blue Nile from Wad Medani. The sharpening rivalry of the co-domini added impetus to development and another element to the educational mix: whereas for centuries Sudanese students had gone to Egypt, the numbers now increased dramatically, and Egyptian schools, including a secondary school, were established in the Sudan.[19]

In Darfur, education lagged. In 1941, there were 715 boys in elementary school, and in 1945 about a thousand. In 1941, a grand total of seventeen boys were admitted to post-elementary schools outside the province (there were none in it): six to intermediate schools, five to the teachers' training school, and six to technical schools. Not one boy from Darfur was admitted to secondary school. Even in El Fasher's elementary school, the most advanced in the province, handicrafts and vocational training dominated the curriculum. Small wonder that the 1942–44 *Report* found elementary schoolboys "either unwilling or unable to pass into the El Obeid [intermediate] school." A private Ahlia intermediate school, financed in part by the Graduates' Congress, opened in January 1945, with a first intake of forty-eight boys selected by competitive examination. But only 3 percent of the boys in Darfur received any formal education at all, and despite anecdotal evidence of schools bursting at the seams and demand doubling or tripling the seats available, the official view was that the "slow pace of increase [in student numbers] was due to the sturdy resistance in many tribes to educating one of the most useful members of the family, the young cowherd or shepherd." Demand for cowherds did not delay a census "of the sons of notables of educable age" to "keep the boarding house full" at El Fasher boys' school.[20]

In 1944, Darfur's province council endorsed a ten-year plan to increase the number of elementary schools from seven to sixteen and the number of boys receiving formal education – including in "sub-grade schools" (the number of which would increase from fifteen to ninety-six) – to about 14 percent. Of girls, as the 1945 *Report* put it, an "infinitesimal percentage" got any education at all; a girls' school opened at Umm Kadada in 1945, in grass buildings of a former convoy rest house. Although some might still wonder why a rural society needed "book learning," British administrators recognized that in discrete ways the low level of education militated against even basic administration. At the end of the war, for instance, fewer than 15 percent of the province's police were more than semiliterate, there was an acute shortage of trained midwives, the number of teachers was insufficient to staff even the sub-grade schools, and of other technical staff there were few or none at all.[21] Because boys sent east for technical training did not return and riverain effendis disdained relocation, apprenticeships had to do.[22]

NATIONALISTS AND COUNTRY COUSINS: THE RUSH TO TRANSFER POWER, 1945–1955

Hurrying to Stay Behind

In the aftermath of independence in 1956, earlier predictions that the Sudanese would not prove ready to rule themselves seemed to objective observers – Sudanese as well as British – to have come true. Coups, civil war, economic deterioration, and financial crisis had cruelly repaid the bold rhetoric of the mid-1950s and, in some cases, engendered rueful appreciation of the colonial era's law and order.

In the last decade of the regime, events at the center, inextricable from the anomalies of Condominium, continued to dominate political development. During the war, Anglo-Egyptian relations had deteriorated. Even die-hard imperialists recognized that British occupation of the Suez Canal Zone, as well as the scope for intervention in Egyptian politics, had entered a new phase. Would London sacrifice the Sudanese for Suez? Egypt's claims in the Sudan were historical, buttressed by geography and culture; aside from "right of conquest," hardly a useful rhetorical device, Britain's depended on the presumed acquiescence of the Sudanese. Nationalist politics thus developed in a unique and unhealthy way: one strain, whose slogan was "the Sudan for the Sudanese," supported the British to keep out the Egyptians; the other, proclaiming "the Unity of the Nile Valley," purported to favor Egyptian claims at least until the British were ejected. Both sides, evolving from cliques in the Graduates' Congress, found it necessary to identify with one of the Sudan's great, mutually antagonistic religious figures for mass support: the pro-Independence group, whose party was the Umma, with Abd al-Rahman al-Mahdi; the Unionists with Ali al-Mirghani of the Khatmiyya sufis.

Unionism had a tactical advantage. British credibility depended on demonstrable progress toward independence. At every stage Unionists demanded more than the British offered, thus garnering prestige among the educated elite and branding Sayyid Abd al-Rahman and his supporters with the stigma of collaboration. British protests about Sudanese incapacity were seen as self-serving – indeed, self-fulfilling – as well as insulting; Muslim, Arabic-speaking Egypt, itself suffering from British imperialism, had by far the easier case to make. And what attraction had "the Sudan for the Sudanese" if it entailed a Mahdist monarchy? In the event, what Newbold and others hoped would be steady progress toward self-government became a headlong rush, marked by statutory milestones that to the Khartoum political elite, both British and Sudanese, were best judged by their distance from complete self-determination.

In March 1947, a highly contested Administration Conference recommended steps toward full self-government. These included replacing the Advisory Council with an elected legislative assembly for the whole country and an executive council functioning as a cabinet for the governor-general. Egypt and the Unionists rejected these proposals, which were enacted as the Executive Council and Legislative Assembly Ordinance in June 1948. No one was happy with the results: speaking for British administrators, the civil secretary, Sir James Robertson, no Newbold, wrote: "90 percent of tribal and illiterate country men" considered these "something mad the Ingleez are doing and say that all they need is their Nazir, their Mufetish [DC] and their Mudir [governor]."[23] Because most assembly seats were filled through indirect election by provincial "colleges" of notables, the Unionists boycotted it. In Darfur, the "colleges" comprised government councilors, and these sent to the assembly two tribal *shaykhs*, Ibrahim Dau al-Bayt (a *shartay* in the Eastern District) and Ibrahim Musa Madibbu of the Rizayqat; Abd al-Rahman, son of Sultan Endoka of the Masalit; Abu'l-Qasim Ali Dinar, a son of the late sultan; al-Malik Rahmatallah Mahmud of the Central District Council at El Fasher; and Abd al-Hamid Abu Bakr Ibrahim, a Fur *umda*.[24]

The Legislative Assembly's composition was its downfall: although in some sense it "represented" the Sudan, it provided insufficient scope for the educated elite that dominated political discourse. Doomed from the start, it had little to do, and the government's attempts to persuade opponents to join merely offended those who had already done so. Domination of the assembly tarred the Umma and SAR as stooges, leading them to press ever harder for progress. In December 1950, the assembly passed by one vote an Umma motion calling for self-government within a year. The close vote allowed the governor-general, Sir Robert Howe, to ignore it, and he instead appointed an Anglo-Sudanese "constitutional amendment commission." Challenged by its own erstwhile supporters, the government had to agree to membership almost entirely of educated townsmen, a concession it knew would skew the results against it.[25] Meanwhile, Egypt, frustrated by lack of progress in negotiations over the canal, unilaterally abrogated the 1936 Anglo-Egyptian Treaty and the 1899 Condominium Agreement.

Regardless of legality, Egypt's drastic action quickened the pace of events in the Sudan. Both blocs welcomed abrogation, for obvious reasons. A draft self-government statute for the Sudan was presented to the Legislative Assembly in April 1952. The British sought Egyptian approval but balked at the terms, which would have recognized Egyptian sovereignty over the Sudan. Egypt thereupon opened negotiations directly with the Sudanese. In July, the Egyptian revolution paved the way for a breakthrough. The new government reached agreements with the Sudanese parties, including, crucially, the Umma, recognizing the Sudanese right to self-determination after a period of self-government. Attempts by Robertson and others to sabotage these agreements failed, and the British had little choice but to fall in line. Thus, in February 1953, a new Anglo-Egyptian Agreement prescribed a three-year transitional period of self-government leading to self-determination, during which the Condominium would be liquidated. The British, playing up, staged celebrations throughout the Sudan, including even in district headquarters in Darfur.[26]

The province played only a minor role in these events. Including the south in the self-government arrangements had been a British concession to the nationalists, for until then, loose talk of a separate political future had crystallized in demands for regional "safeguards," the very mention of which was taken in northern political circles as an insult; in the event, there would be none. No such demands were made for undeveloped northern areas such as Darfur; the presumed divide, however oversimplified, was between an Arabic-speaking Muslim north and a multilingual non-Muslim south. But before examining the constitutional arrangements enforced during the period of self-government, we turn to the development of administration and politics in Darfur before the parliamentary elections of 1953.

The More Things Change

The government's *Report* for 1948 noted, as it might the appearance of a rare bird, "a small political demonstration in Fasher, the first of its kind in the province" in connection with the opening of the Legislative Assembly in Khartoum. Until the end of the war, the impact of nationalist politics in Darfur had been largely indirect. But there were local grievances akin to those in the east: price controls, rationing, and inadequate housing had strained British relations with the small Sudanese official class. Rather than conciliating those most liable to turn against the regime, the government tended to take them for granted. And Darfur's geographic isolation was a double-edged sword, delaying some trends from the center but rendering more acute some local effects of central problems. A strike by the railway union in 1948, for example, had its repercussions in shortages and prices in El Fasher and in merchants' accumulation of goods for export.[27] In general, however, the large Mahdist population of the province, and its mostly rural and tribal character, made Darfur a poor field for the Omdurman intelligentsia. When the time came for a showdown, Darfur could be counted, perhaps to its detriment, as firmly pro-Independent or at least virulently anti-Unionist.

Meanwhile, development of provincial administration continued at a leisurely pace. The advisory Province Council met infrequently. By 1949 the boundaries of local government had all been defined except in the problematic areas of the poor Northern District and Dar Masalit. It was only in 1948 that Sultan Endoka agreed to decentralize his judicial system and, in 1949, his imperium was extended by formal inclusion of Dar Qimr, the literal dead end of Darfur. Endoka died in April 1951. His son, Abd al-Rahman, an enthusiastic modernizer who was already a member of the Legislative Assembly, succeeded, with his half-brother Muhammad, already with long experience in finance, assuming informally the role of chief minister. But for all the panoply and terminology, Dar Masalit was ever less a sultanate and ever more an administrative unit like any other: the Resident still held major courts, and he was involved in many lesser cases requiring "boundary courts" that involved other districts. The "emirates" and "maqdumates" were by now dead letters; one of them, Zalingei, would in 1949 have a Sudanese DC.

Within the constraints of Native Administration, a committee system was developed at the provincial, district, and, where needed, municipal levels, for finance, health, education, markets, general purposes, and so forth, but the scope of local government continued to be hampered by the general underdevelopment of the provincial economy. Districts had their budgets, but the budgets had little money. Recognition of Native Administration's logical limits had come grudgingly, with the failure of the "emirates" and subsequent amalgamations. The committee system allowed appointment to local government units of educated experts, where there were any, as either advisors or even executive officers; outside the towns, judicial and "tribal" affairs remained necessarily the purview of *shaykhs* and *shartays*. The catalogue of their abuses continued unabridged. As always, much depended on individual character and British willingness to intervene. The southern Maqdumate had failed when its founding "emir" died in 1931; the northern *maqdum* had never emerged from the batch of *shartays* and princes he was meant to rule, and after the war his authority was reduced to the vicinity of Kutum; a putative eastern maqdumate was never inaugurated; and the grand Baqqara confederacy was downgraded to a joint court. The future lay in development of a civil service.[28]

The combination of Native Administration and local government in Darfur had only a few years under British tutelage. Later criticism of successive regimes' local government reforms paid insufficient attention to the brevity of the system's existence and its improvisational nature, ancient titles notwithstanding. It was only in 1947 that Southern Darfur's district council, comprising the regional administrations of the Kalaka, the old maqdumate, the Rizayqat, and the Western Baqqara, was inaugurated. In 1948, the Western District's council of *shartays* was established, with the *dimingawi* as chief executive. In the same year at El Fasher, a Joint Town and County Council was inaugurated. The poor Eastern District would make do with a rural council, and its offices were opened with fanfare in March 1953. The council for the Northern District, the runt of the litter incorporating Kabkabiyya, the Meidob, Mellit, the northern Rizayqat, the Zaghawa, and remnants of the maqdumate, was finally recognized in 1951.[29] It was only by terms of the Local Government Appropriation of Taxes Ordinance in 1954 that revenue from the main local taxes, the *ushur*, animal tax, and poll tax, was assigned to the councils. An irony of the forty-year Condominium regime in Darfur was not the conservatism of enshrined traditions but rather the constant innovation required to maintain their vestiges.

There is an element of pathos in Darfur's late colonial regime, where perhaps more than anywhere in the Sudan British DCs deserved their reputation as "jacks of all trades." As late as 1947 El Fasher's normal complement of political officers was two: the governor or his deputy and the DC. Zalingei and El Geneina had one DC; Kutum and Nyala had one each. When the Resident in Dar Masalit was on leave, his stand-in was a *ma'mur*. There were no British staff at provincial headquarters for emergencies. Major courts, which still required a British official, could not be held for much of the year. Even allowing for wartime transfers and secondment, at full establishment the British administrative presence in Darfur was very slight. There were no province judges or education officers, so such duties as these performed elsewhere fell to the DC who, even had education been a priority, had no time to devote to it. Some areas were simply let go: Dar Qimr was left to the ravenous uncles of its hapless sultan, perhaps the better to complete its depopulation.[30] Indeed, the provincial administration was rich only in the metaphors of poverty: run on a shoestring, pared to the bone.

During the last decade of the Condominium, Darfur's western frontier remained volatile. In the immediate postwar period, British and French officials stayed in close touch, continuing the custom of exchanging visits and holding both regular and extraordinary meetings as needed. Smuggling was rampant, extradition routine. The area of greatest difficulty was in the north, along the marches of Dar Tama, Dar Qimr, and Zaghawa country, where government relied on the Western Arab Corps to show the flag and keep the peace but where intertribal affrays over animals and grazing often assumed an international character. (Cross-border contretemps were least likely when times were hardest because then the northern nomads migrated southward rather than east or west. In 1948, for the second year running, there was no *jizzu* grazing in the northern desert, and the nomads headed south to buy grain and graze their animals. Then and in other years, police statistics showed that Zaghawa grain theft and rustling peaked as the tribesmen started to head north again. A record *jizzu* in 1950–51 proved the point: police patrols on the Wadi Hawar were even discontinued, but trouble flared across the international border, as was usual in years of luscious grass; the tribes on both sides went where the grazing was best, regardless of the border.) An informal Anglo-French policy of "hot pursuit" ended in 1950 after some Sudan police and a French gendarme, having brought in to Biltine four murderers, were arrested and fined by local authorities, and the murderers released, before French administrators could intervene. With changes of personnel, collaboration resumed; a meeting at Tini in November 1951 resulted in agreement over grazing, tribal compensation for recent enormities, and settlement of outstanding cases. In a related development, Darfur and Northern Province negotiated an agreement so that all the *jizzu* grazing area would be in Darfur.[31]

Although Fur and Masalit relations with the Zaghawa and Bani Husayn required constant attention, they always had; whether there were incidents depended as usual mainly on economic prospects as foretold in rainfall, *jizzu*, and grain prices. Incursions by Bani Halba into Dar Masalit were likewise problematic but routine. Conditions in general were such in 1950–51 that Kababish, Kawahla, and Hamar ranged as far south as the Bahr al-Arab. As usual, such migrations, especially when relatively peaceful, were seen in two ways: evidence of immemorial custom as modified by colonial law and proof of an ever-closer Malthusian disaster.[32] In 1951–52, when unusually large numbers of Kordofan tribesmen moved westward, various plans were mooted to regulate future relations, but, as one report put it:

These palliatives would do more harm than good if they simply resulted in the reduction of the [Darfur] grazing grounds to Kordofan level. This is one of the problems which used to be settled by battle or the decimation of stock by disease or famine. Northern Kordofan is in fact carrying far too much stock and no answer can be satisfactory which permits the increase to continue at the expense of the grazing further west.

In the same report's section on Kordofan, we read: "The opening up of new grazing areas by the provision of fresh water supplies is now an urgent necessity."[33]

Indeed, the agriculture of Darfur, on which much else depended, was itself highly dependent on the rains. By the 1950s, the government had become accustomed to an annual emergency in one part or another, and great alarm was shown only when, as in 1949, the crops were poor in the granaries of the province, Dar Masalit and Zalingei. The postwar political climate focused British attention on potential consequences of – and the need to alleviate – food shortages. A quick way to judge the "Darfur year," politically as well as economically, might in fact have been to ascertain the going rate for grain in the principal towns. In 1949, the price at El Fasher reached unprecedented levels, and elsewhere there were days when no grain could be had at all; the government's contractor defaulted. A dole was established for El Fasher's poor, and in rural areas, diet was reduced to berries. Khartoum expected political agitation – not in Darfur but on Darfur's behalf among the Omdurman intelligentsia and Egyptian propagandists.[34] Although the usual mass migration of tribesmen provoked official concern, this was accompanied by the customary fatalism: "one can't really blame them," the governor wrote of the Meidob, off to Aba after two years of drought, "with conditions so bad at home."[35]

A FAILING ECONOMY

The cotton-growing Gezira Scheme, financed by huge loans, became world famous for its scope and innovations and generated much academic controversy over definitions of "development." During the Depression, it almost bankrupted the country, and Khartoum thereafter adopted a much more conservative approach to major government investment. Even after the war, old prejudices and insistent turf protection skewed planning. For political as well as economic reasons the center won and the periphery lost out; those who had, got more. In pursuing Darfur's interests, its officials were simply no match for their competitors in other provinces and the departments of central government.

An early harbinger was the Sudan Government's allocation of a £E2 million postwar development grant from Britain. Of this, fully half went immediately into an endowment for Gordon College, with another £E250,000 designated for new secondary school facilities elsewhere. Of the rest, £E300,000 would be devoted to a new hospital in Khartoum, £E120,000 to agricultural schemes in Kassala and Kordofan to increase food production; and £E40,000 for a tuberculosis campaign. Most of the remaining £E290,000 was assigned to public works, "including rural water supplies." But the fine print shows that even of that amount, £E93,000 would be devoted to plant and equipment for water and electricity supplies in Kosti on the White Nile, £E15,000 for water projects at El Obeid, and £E6,000 for a related scheme nearby at Khor Taggat.[36]

Making the Rich Richer: The Five-Year Plans

The Five-Year Plan for Post-War Development[37] adopted in 1945 similarly revealed an official mind oriented almost entirely to those sectors of the economy and those regions of the country already most developed. Of some £E11.5 million budgeted for the central government, the politically powerful Sudan Railways[38] would get £E2.5 million, agriculture and forests £E1.85 million, irrigation £E1.575 million, and public works £E1.72 million. In contrast, education got less than £E1 million, health just over £E0.7 million, and veterinary services £E0.85 million. Local government would get £E1.05 million.

The railway administration had long exercised a veto over development in transportation. In 1934, the aptly named Carriage of Goods by Motor (Control) Ordinance actually *forbade* road-haulage competition with the railways.[39] Under the Five-Year Plan, its program included new headquarters offices and a new station at Atbara, new housing and offices elsewhere, renovation of Khartoum Station, improved passenger carriages, a start on other station improvements (waiting rooms, toilets), and an office in the center of Khartoum. "Feeder" roads would meet Darfur's desperate need for connection to railhead, with transport left to private enterprise. The relatively large sum budgeted for public works (£E1.72 million) included only £E250,000 for roads *for the whole country*, of which an unspecified sum would be allotted to improving fifty miles of the main Kordofan–Darfur road (part of the so-called A5 between Omdurman and Chad) and upgrading some "secondary roads." Kordofan and Darfur would share £E87,500 for water yards. Meanwhile, the public works line provided £E500,000 for a new police headquarters in Khartoum, a prison for the criminally insane, and new offices and staff housing in several provinces; £E680,000 would go to the Car Allotment Committee to improve departmental and provincial mechanical-transport fleets.

The plan's provisions for irrigation and agriculture exhibited the same mind-set. The £E1.575 budgeted for irrigation was entirely for the Gezira Scheme and related projects, and most of the £E1.85 million designated for agriculture and forests was devoted to big projects elsewhere: £E665,000 for Equatoria (mainly for the Zande Scheme); £E360,000 for mechanized farming in Kassala; a dozen small projects in Kordofan, the Nuba Mountains, and Port Sudan; and even a few items arguably misplaced (a creosoting plant for railway sleepers, a match factory, the Atbara dairy). Horticulture got £E6,000. The plan included £E340,000 for the program of rural water supplies and soil conservation. How much of this went to Darfur is unknown. The plan's award for veterinary services was disappointing: of £E85,000 budgeted, £E64,000 would be spent in Khartoum – on a new headquarters, animal hospital, and other facilities – whereas £E4,800 would go to developing a livestock export market, £E12,000 to disease control, and £E2,000 to breeding. After a new veterinary laboratory opened at Nyala in 1947, Khartoum pressed Darfur to squeeze more money out of cattle herders, who were already paying twice the prewar tax.[40]

Similar skewing – in defining "development" and in the projects funded and regions favored – may be seen in the other categories of the plan where, moreover, the amounts budgeted were modest to begin with. "Health," for example, would get £E716,000 under the plan, £E260,000 of which was for the new hospital in Khartoum and £E350,000 for hospital buildings elsewhere. El Fasher would split £E6,000 with three towns in other provinces on new X-ray equipment and might get a share of £E15,000 designated for clinics. Of £E986,500 for education, £E500,000 would go to Gordon College. Of £E665,000 for communications, £E527,000 was for telephone service; the plan raised the issue of radio telephony for "provinces like Equatoria and Darfur" before rejecting it as too costly. A final, omnibus line was for local governments, which were to get some £E1.05 million. Of this, fully £E586,000 was for Khartoum (including £E100,000 for a town hall), £E204,000 for Port Sudan, and £E64,000 for Wad Medani, arguably (with Atbara, the railway headquarters) the most "developed" towns in the country. No funds were designated for Darfur.

Darfur's British officials reacted mildly. Whether because of chronic staff shortages and overwork, a lack of sophistication, the ability of officials at the center to outmaneuver them, or simply a low opinion of what Darfur "deserved," the governor, Lampen, and his DCs had responded to the call for proposals with little imagination or detail. In the drafting stage, Lampen had discerned problems even where Darfur appeared to be getting something, for example, in its "being lumped in with Kordofan . . . for new water yards": Kordofan had forty water yards, Darfur five. Darfur had but two elementary vernacular school buildings and the lowest establishment of government vehicles of any province, including the south.[41] He disliked complaining but had hoped for more. There is no evidence that anyone paid attention to such gentlemanly comments, but in his defense the importance of propinquity to the capital should be noted. As the governor put it in 1949: "I am rather out of touch . . . after five years in Darfur."[42]

What would prove to be the last Five-Year Plan (for 1951–56) of the colonial regime was similarly unhelpful to Darfur.[43] Initially set at £E24 million, the plan eventually called for £E34 million in capital expenditure. Of this, about 27 percent was budgeted for communications, 23 percent for "productive schemes," 15 percent for utilities, and 20 percent for social services. Fully £E4.5 million would go to the Sudan Railways but less than a quarter of that for extending track (from Sinnar up the Blue Nile to al-Rusayris); the rest would be spent on engines, rolling stock, port facilities, buildings, and river craft. What did the country as a whole get from this spoilt child? Its subsidized passenger services were famously pictured on postcards and extolled in government propaganda. It carried the Gezira's cotton to Port Sudan. Its workshops at Atbara were a showplace of the tiny modern economy. But it was a classic creation of colonialism. As an economist not under its spell put it, "the railway system is rudimentary.... [It] collects produce from convenient centers and hauls it off to export: it was not built to move goods or passengers extensively within the Sudan. Much of the system had no purpose other than to link producing areas with [the] seaport."[44]

It was Darfur's misfortune that the world's demand for gum, unlike that for cotton, did not increase at astronomical rates during and after the Second World War, although it did increase to a degree. In any event, even of the remainder of the communications budget, only a small percentage could be said directly to benefit the far west: of £E1.1 million for trunk roads, about £E400,000 would be devoted to improving the road from Omdurman to El Fasher and £E50,000 for the road from El Fasher to Kabkabiyya. By comparison, some £E900,000 was devoted to telephony (almost all of it in major towns and to connect the Nuba Mountains to Malakal), £E160,000 for post and telegraph offices (£E70,000 of it for Omdurman), and £E480,000 to airports (£E435,000 of which would be spent on Khartoum and Port Sudan). Of the £E5.1 million for utilities, more than 80 percent would be spent in the capital region and Wad Medani.

Of the plan's £E7.85 million for "productive schemes," the lion's share went to cotton production and manufacturing and related irrigation works. Some £E2.875 million was devoted to rural water supply and soil conservation, most of which (£E2.5 million) was for bores, wells, *hafirs*, and other surface storage; fully half of that amount was for *hafirs* in six provinces, including Darfur. Veterinary services were allotted £E250,000 to promote better grazing, combat disease, and develop livestock. A Grassland Experimental Center would be established in Darfur to study conservation and rotation, and one of three Livestock Improvement and Animal Industry Centers would also be sited there. Six experimental agricultural centers were set up in 1954.

The province would benefit from work conducted elsewhere, for example, in the Research Station for the Central Rainlands funded at Tozi in the Blue Nile Province. But even there, most of the money was for staff housing rather than research, and the suspicion arises that outlying provinces had to be given something from the vast "productive schemes" budget simply to keep them quiet. As a British economist in Khartoum wrote at the time, "On any test, other than money value, rainlands production is far more important [than cotton crops grown under irrigation]: most obviously in that it provides subsistence and an income directly for perhaps half the Sudan's population." Yet it continued "in the same primitive fashion as for generations past." (His writings were suppressed.)[45]

The 1951–56 plan called for £E6.9 million for social services. Some £E4.1 million of that was earmarked to expand a ten-year education plan for the northern Sudan that, under pressure, the Education Department had revised in 1949. This increased the rate of expansion at every level. To supply staff, much greater emphasis would be placed on teacher training. At the elementary level, twenty new schools would be opened in 1950, with thirty more per year thereafter. The number of schoolmistresses for girls' schools would rise from 60 per year in 1950 to 150 by 1956, with 10 new girls' schools per year until 1953 and 20 in 1954 and 1955; the total reached 211 by 1956. The country's first girls' intermediate school opened only in 1940; two were added in 1946, and eight more were planned by 1956, including one at El Fasher. Of fifteen new intermediate boys' schools planned, Darfur would get two, with boarding houses: the first, at Nyala, had been open only a few months when its students went on strike in 1951. The number of boys' secondary schools would be increased to five, but by independence Darfur would still have none. It would be cause for cheer that, in 1949, the (private) Ahlia intermediate school in El Fasher sent five boys to the government secondary schools in the east and three to other post-intermediate courses. Plans for creation or expansion of programs in technical and vocational training centered around government departments, and thus little affected Darfur: the new Senior School of workshop training would be in Khartoum, as would a new Technical Institute. Provision would be increased for study abroad, mainly in Britain and Egypt, for postgraduates.[46] For the northern Sudan as a whole, these were ambitious plans, but in conception they shortchanged the marginal regions and in implementation they widened the gap between the sophisticated center and the backward periphery.

Similarly, of the plan's £E2.4 million for health services, another new hospital in Khartoum (£E850,000), new equipment for it (£E200,000), and a special tuberculosis hospital there (£E100,000) accounted for almost half, whereas Khartoum would also share in the various lesser expenditures on, for example, staff housing. Eight provincial centers were to get new 100-bed hospitals, but a ninth, at Zalingei, would be created by upgrading its dispensary. It need hardly be said that a poor country could not afford health care on a European scale, but such concentration of resources in the capital was "development" for the national elite rather than of the rural poor. Indeed, the plan called for more expenditure on prisons and police stations (£E330,000) than Darfur was likely to reap from the entire budget. (In this context, the budget did call for £E25,000 for prison labor camps in Darfur and a new police station in El Fasher.) The bias toward developing the developed lasted until the end of the regime (and beyond): in October 1955, it was estimated that of £E90 million needed to meet the (reduced) costs of planned development over the next eight years, some £E42 million would be taken up in extending the Gezira Scheme and building a dam at al-Rusayris; already there was need to retrench.[47]

Water

Regardless of Khartoum's plans, the now-permanent search for water in the west awaited no budget surpluses. Under the Soil Conservation Committee's program of 1944, two drilling rigs, one north and one south, had initial success but by their final year (1951) had often been looking in vain for water where it was needed rather than where it was expected to be found. Much more emphasis was placed on providing *hafirs*. Under the second Five-Year Plan, funds were allocated for a large number of new ones – some 500 by 1956 – and, as important, for clearing fire lines. There was no overall plan behind this: recommendations for bores and *hafirs* were solicited and made, approved or not, on a variety of grounds that included political influence and "common sense," and although administrators of Darfur may not have lacked the latter, they had very little of the former. Thus, ironically, in Darfur technical expertise may have been brought to bear more often than elsewhere. In 1950, a concerted effort was begun in Dar Rizayqat for comprehensive pastoral development, arguably the only such scheme before independence in which water supply was a major component. The scheme, which would supply cattle to a processing plant at Kosti on the White Nile, involved building some thirty-six *hafirs*; much water was supplied, but the export plan failed.[48]

It was very late in the colonial day, and some unpalatable recommendations of the Soil Conservation Committee went predictably unheeded: forest reserves and nurseries were local affairs, uncoordinated from the center; the problem of erosion through cutting for firewood (and brick kilns) had not been systematically addressed; and the continuing destruction of forests was simply not taken in hand. There is evidence too of working at cross-purposes by Soil Conservation and Rural Water Supplies officers and between them and the Geological Survey. In this as in other areas, chronic staff vacancies – from the level of British political officers down to local Sudanese *ma'murs* and departmental cadres – also played a part. Such efforts at conservation as were made were more difficult because they found no natural constituency among the Sudanese; and even among British authorities, the arguments for providing more water were intuitively stronger than those for soil conservation.[49]

In the supply of water, El Fasher – and the 40,000 people who lived within twenty miles – remained only one step ahead of crisis. In 1947 the government completed a dam at Mellit, the chief town in the Berti country, northeast of El Fasher, just in time to avoid catastrophe as El Fasher's *fula* dried up; its reservoir watered 40,000 camels, 72,000 sheep, and 95,000 head of cattle a month at the height of the 1948 dry season. Building in El Fasher ceased in the summer of 1948 owing to water shortage, and the cultivated area continued gradually to decline as wells had to be dug ever deeper. A plan to build a dam and reservoir at Wadi Golo and to pipe water 8 miles to El Fasher was inexpertly carried out and finally completed only in 1951. New *hafirs* were constantly added around the town. Annual shortage had long been normal.[50]

Elsewhere in the province, the government continued boring new wells and establishing permanent water yards, but again almost all anecdotal evidence is of hurrying to keep from falling further behind. Officials continued to report, without always seeming to recognize, the looming contradiction between growing demand for water and increasing wealth measured in animals. In 1949, some 35,000 head of cattle were exported from the Southern District of Darfur alone; mass immunization held down disease but ran the risk of overstocking and consequent scarcity of water. These fears were realized when an approved plan to dig new *hafirs* was postponed. Attempts to restrict herd size failed; animals were hidden, counts were inaccurate, reports were lost. News that water was found, at a depth of 1,025 feet, in 1951–52 after more than three years of work at Umm Sauna, was reported as a victory for perseverance rather than a sign of desperation. There was an insistent insouciance about water in the government's plans to improve grazing and inoculate all cattle, and thus to increase the quantity and quality of cattle.[51] The last Five-Year Plan states:

Numbers are increasing now that the effect of disease is checked, but an equally serious limiting factor is the prevailing low level of animal feeding in the dry season when... grass is poor and scarce. It is this poor feeding which is largely responsible for the slow growth of animals to maturity, their poor milk yields, low rate of births – and, indeed, heavy losses from starvation.[52]

Too Little, Too Late

The relative backwardness of Darfur during the period leading up to independence is evident in every way. Even when development budgets were relatively large, shortages of materials and personnel, red tape, foot-dragging, and old habits created long delays. The attitude persisted that money was wasted on roads where there was no traffic or on water where there was no agriculture. In 1946, the civil secretary told the governor of Darfur he could not have an agricultural inspector because there were too few to go around and provinces with a vacancy took precedence over those that had never had one! Kordofan had five, and even urban Khartoum had one; Darfur finally got its first in 1953. The governor had to recruit SDF engineering troops in 1947 to cut roads up Jabal Marra; in 1948, the central government assumed responsibility for the main roads connecting El Obeid to El Fasher and El Geneina, and El Fasher to Nyala (a mixed blessing in light of the Public Works Department's reputation). El Fasher's merchants were at the mercy of long-distance truckers from Kordofan: price-gouging led in 1949 to boycotts and shortages, and investigation showed that prices of some commodities in Darfur were almost double those at El Obeid. The first regular long-distance "bus" in the province was inaugurated only in 1948.[53] As late as 1952, all but the main towns still depended on camels, runners, and unscheduled cars for mail service.[54]

In the provision of health services, Darfur continued to lag, despite its terrifying medical history. In 1950, for the first time since 1936, cerebrospinal meningitis struck in epidemic proportions; despite development in the meantime of sulfa drugs, some 2,600 of Darfur's 14,100 cases proved fatal – very similar numbers occurred in Kordofan. Official reports ascribed the population's vulnerability to poor nutrition and debility born of a higher than usual incidence of malaria after the heavy rains; scores of quarantines were needed, and trade was severely disrupted. Amazingly, it was only in 1951, after an outbreak of smallpox, that the government approached French officials about joint quarantine efforts on the international borders – these were undertaken in the following year. Political aspects of a line of posts, whether as quarantine stations or border crossings, were not ignored. In the postwar period, the number of West Africans coming east, ostensibly on pilgrimage to Mecca but in fact for many reasons, continued to increase, and they not only brought disease – another outbreak of smallpox in 1949 was traced to them – but also attracted thieves, religious charlatans, and rapacious money-changers. In that year Darfur, still with only three hospitals, had an estimated 4.64 hospital beds per 10,000 people, the poorest ratio in the whole country, worse even than the Upper Nile and the Bahr al-Ghazal. Khartoum had the best, at 23.75, and although by independence the ratio in Darfur had improved (to 5.7), it remained the worst in the Sudan.[55]

SUDANESE POLITICS IN DARFUR

When the Sudan's 1951–52 annual *Report* described Darfur as becoming "politically conscious if not politically active," it referred to tours and propaganda by politicians before the first parliamentary elections in 1953.[56] Officials had habitually described Darfur as idyllically uninfected by nationalist politics, as if claims of provincial somnolence were proof of national incapacity. An administration founded on keeping out "isms" inimical to British rule and local hierarchy had, through Native Administration and correlative education and economic policies, done nothing to associate local people with the drama unfolding in Khartoum. In this way, the stage was set for exploitation of those the British most wanted to defend and the victory of those they most despised.

It had never been possible to quarantine Darfur politically. Making it a "closed district" open only to permit-holders had, as such restrictions always do, annoyed the law-abiding while hardly hampering others. Agents of SAR, peripatetic *faqihs*, proselytizing sufis, even Europeans wandering off the beaten path elicited little comment; western Sudanese – and West Africans – returning from Mecca or from work in the towns and cotton fields brought news and views. Outsiders took an interest: the editor of *al-Nil* visited in 1945 and published a series of articles.[57] Proverbially well-informed *jallaba* did not answer to tribal *shaykhs* and embodied the limits of censorship. Precluding the educated few, whether "servants" of *shaykhs* or teachers and clerks, from aspiring to a political role was myopic; belittling them as a tiny minority spurred them on. Yet even the government's political intelligence branch degenerated, in the heat of Anglo-Egyptian competition, into propaganda, repeatedly reporting the masses' revulsion from politics and unity in wishing to maintain the status quo.[58]

That Darfur was ill prepared for nationalist politics but unavoidably caught up in it was evident first in the field of labor relations. Paid labor still occupied a very small number of people; had it not been for prison labor, much government work – in road maintenance and dam and reservoir construction – would have gone undone. In Darfur as elsewhere, however, government employees were uniquely powerful because so much depended on them. In the east, this power was epitomized by the Railway Workers' Union, which repeatedly disrupted commerce over terms and conditions of employment and in pursuit of political objectives. (Darfur, well beyond railhead, was seriously affected by these strikes because of its already high transport costs.) Local strikes by veterinary workers, "mosquito men," public works employees, teachers, and nurses in 1950, although dismissed as imitative, awakened them and their managers to artisans' and professionals' power; soldiers, police, and scabs kept essential services operating. In another echo of the east, in January 1952, the Nyala intermediate school was shut down when pupils boycotted classes over a demand for recognition of a debating society.[59]

These disturbances heralded the arrival of party politics in Darfur. Previous elections – to the Advisory Council for the Northern Sudan and the Legislative Assembly – had been wholly undemocratic. Three parties contested the 1953 elections nationally: the Umma, whose president was SAR's son, al-Siddiq al-Mahdi; the National Unionists, under Isma'il al-Azhari; and the Socialist Republicans; the Southern Party and various independents also stood. In the absence of opinion polling, there were widely different expectations during the months of campaigning that preceded the elections. Putting their money where their mouths were, the Egyptians gave important support to the National Unionist Party (NUP), the only party with a real organization. Umma leaders, sure of their Mahdist base, were inept and overconfident, whereas their symbiotic but unacknowledged partners, the British, disastrously hedged their bets. With Darfur, Kordofan, and other rural areas in mind, they conjured up the hilariously misnamed Socialist Republican Party (SRP).

The SRP, founded in 1951, seemed to fill an obvious gap in the political landscape. When the Umma proclaimed "the Sudan for the Sudanese," what many heard was "the Sudan under SAR." What choice had those who favored independence *without* a Mahdist monarchy? Many educated northerners were persuaded that the NUP, despite professed unionism, stood the best chance of achieving that. The British, stung by the Umma's 1950 self-government motion in the Legislative Assembly and subsequent willingness to deal with Egypt, devised a plan to rally what they saw as their rural base. Such a party might draw support from the Umma and prolong British rule. Immediately after Egypt announced abrogation of the Condominium Agreement, a group of tribal *shaykhs* in the Legislative Assembly held a press conference in Khartoum and, in a statement prepared by Desmond Hawkesworth, an assistant civil secretary, announced continuing support for the British until the country was ready for self-government. A few weeks later, this nucleus blossomed into a "party." At the pinnacle of the British establishment, there was barely concealed delight over this coup, but what had really been achieved was the permanent enmity of SAR.[60]

In the party's manifesto, Ibrahim Bedri, the party's "secretary-general," blithely claimed to speak for "100 percent" of the people of Darfur (as well as 100 percent of southerners and precisely 83 percent of Kordofan). It upheld a continuing role of the governor-general, opposed wholesale dismissal of British administrators, rejected "a certain local monarchy," and proposed a "socialist republic" (in contrast to the "nearest neighbouring capitalist independent countries" – meaning

Egypt, with a swipe at the arch-capitalist SAR).[61] But rural tribes' presumed abhorrence of politics did not translate into support for a party: money was scarce, and although there were plenty of chiefs, there were no followers. Ibrahim Musa of the Darfur Rizayqat was the party's unlikely financial angel, contributing £E1,000 of the £E3,000 budgeted from tribal notables, some of whom collected money from their subjects but did not hand it in.[62]

In Darfur, where the last British governor, K. D. D. Henderson, was a prime mover behind this "country party," the stage was set for a tripartite showdown of the tribal leaders, Mahdists, and secular nationalists, which the British confidently expected would finish in that order. A "branch" of the SRP, founded at El Fasher in February 1952 under al-Malik Rahmatallah Mahmud – who resigned from the party three months later and was succeeded by *Shaykh* Ali Idris – was duly reported to be "preparing for the elections," but little evidence has been found of any campaign at all. Henderson, a colleague wrote, had "a gift of making the facts fit in with the theories and beliefs which he holds."[63] But Umma and NUP leaders toured Darfur, drawing large crowds; SAR had never been there, so the visit of his son, al-Siddiq, caused great excitement. To the pronounced skepticism – and annoyance – of the British, Isma'il al-Azhari of the NUP came too, and its impressive rallies gave evidence of party organization.[64] After what amounted to a two-year campaign, replete with outrageous propaganda, illegal support of both co-domini for respective favorites, and payoffs, the elections were finally held in November and December 1953.

The results, nationally and in Darfur, were stunning. Robertson, the departing Civil Secretary, had predicted in April that the SRP would win 35 seats (of 97) in the House of Representatives, and the Umma 45; even thirty years later, his protégé, Gawain Bell, claimed that the SRP – "a new and interesting development" – "enjoyed a substantial following." But the Independence vote split, as tribal *shaykhs* stood against Mahdist stalwarts in one constituency after another. The Mahdist-Mirghanist duel degenerated further when followers of a third holy family, the Hindiyya, drew support in the Blue Nile; in Darfur, the Tijaniyya sufis encompassed the resident *jallaba*. Al-Siddiq al-Mahdi was no politician, and the Umma neglected even basic aspects of a modern campaign: electoral officials proscribed illiterate candidates, and others failed to register. The NUP won a clear majority of fifty-one seats, the Umma twenty-two, the SRP a derisory three. (Failure is an orphan: in his memoirs, Robertson not only denied British connections with the SRP but changed its name, to Sudan Republican Party.) In Darfur, the Umma won only six of eleven seats, the SRP one, and the NUP two. The remaining two seats were won by independents.[65]

Although none of Darfur's Members of Parliament (MPs) was a "new man" in the usual nationalist sense, the literacy requirement and destructive competition of the Umma and SRP led to election of several young and relatively obscure candidates.[66] Of the Umma MPs, Uthman Ishaq Adam (Kutum Centre), a Tunjur merchant born in 1921, was a graduate of the local elementary school; Mustafa Muhammad Hasan was a Bornawi merchant and *imam* of a Mahdist mosque at Nyala. Three had important tribal connections: Mahmud al-Tayyib Salih was a brother of al-Tijani al-Tayyib, *shartay* of the Dar Galla Zaghawa; Abd al-Rahman Muhammad Ibrahim, who had trained in veterinary work, was a brother of the *nazir* of the Bani Halba; and al-Malik Rahmatallah Mahmud was head of El Fasher court. The odd man out was most prominent of all: Abdallah Khalil, born in the Nuba Mountains in 1888, who had retired from the army as the first Sudanese *miralai* and had been a founding member and secretary-general of the Umma, won the "safe" seat of Eastern Darfur.

The remainder of the Darfur delegation in Parliament illustrated the split of the Independence vote. The two Zalingei constituencies returned Unionist candidates: Yusuf Abd al-Hamid Ibrahim, son of the late Emir but now, after an undistinguished military career, a lowly clerk, and Arbab Ahmad Shatta Ishaq, son of the *maqdum* (now *shartay*) of Dar Tarbila. Dar Masalit sent two independents: Hasan Jibril Sulayman, the *umda* of El Geneina, and Abbakr Badawi Abbakr, a member of the royal family and lately headmaster of El Geneina elementary school. Completing the delegation was the sole Socialist Republican, Abd al-Hamid Musa Madibbu, scion of the Rizayqat ruling family, who, although presumably a republican, was no socialist.

In the Upper House of Parliament, the Senate, the NUP enjoyed a similar majority. Of Darfur's four members, two – Muhammad al-Zaki Ahmad, lately chief clerk of El Fasher court and a member of the province council, and Muhammad Ali Abu Sinn, an eastern merchant in El Fasher – were elected on the NUP ticket. Ahmad Abu'l-Qasim of Kutum, a merchant, won a seat for the Umma. Hasan, a son of Taj al-Din (d. 1910), once sultan of the Masalit, won as an independent. The governor-general was free to fill appointive seats as he wished, but the lopsided vote precluded packing the house. He nominated moderate unionists, merchants, southerners, and others, none from Darfur; one choice, Abd al-Salam al-Khalifa, a longtime civil servant and lately member of the Electoral Commission, was a son of the Khalifa Abdallahi and thus a Ta'aishi. Also appointed was Ibrahim Bedri, leader of the soon-to-be-defunct SRP.

Darfur and Self-Government, 1954–1955

The election results illustrated the precarious position of Darfur on the eve of independence. Already a peripheral region of *decreasing* economic importance and dominated by a backward-looking administrative system exposed as electorally weak, the province would have little influence in the parliament that would see out the Condominium and determine its successor. At the national level, the period was dominated by the question of union with Egypt or independence. Whichever was determined, Darfur was likely to face uncomfortable challenges.

The first Sudanese government took office in January 1954, with Isma'il al-Azhari, the NUP leader, as prime minister. His relations with the British, always poor, did not improve. Mechanisms to settle disputes were all in place under terms of the 1953 Anglo-Egyptian Agreement, and to these al-Azhari repeatedly resorted. Most notable was accelerated "Sudanization," which was meant to preclude political interference when self-determination was exercised. Loaded with anti-British unionists, the Sudanization Committee set about getting rid of hundreds of even minor and, worse, technical officials. The effect was minimal in Darfur, where chronic understaffing was a hallmark of the regime: by the end of 1952, there were but nine British political officers, and Ali Abu Sinn, the DC at Zalingei and scion of the Shukriyya tribe's ruling family in the eastern Sudan, succeeded Henderson, the last British governor of Darfur.[67] Yet, although all British officials received generous terms, a mood darkened by Egyptian taunting swung back to schemes for bringing down the NUP. In the meantime, SAR made it clear that he would not retire to a contemplative life at Aba Island: he and his minions hinted at – and some openly threatened – armed rebellion, centering on the strongholds of the west.

A showdown occurred when, after a parliamentary recess, a grand reconvening was scheduled for 1 March, with General Muhammed Neguib of Egypt in attendance. Thousands of Mahdist tribesmen poured into Khartoum to protest. At the airport, 50,000 Sudanese cheered Neguib, while Mahdists lined the motorcade route. Alerted, officials ordered a detour, and Neguib arrived at the palace unscathed. There a mob broke through a police cordon, troops were called out, shots were fired, and thirty were left dead, including the British commandant of police. Under duress, SAR ordered his followers to leave the city, and a state of emergency was soon lifted. In the aftermath, some British civilians were evacuated from Darfur. The episode's main effect was to raise awareness of the numerical strength and the depth of feeling of the forces SAR commanded; union with Egypt would provoke civil war. Al-Azhari's real views on this all-important issue may never be known, but those of his tactical supporters, including crucially Ali al-Mirghani, were clear enough: the Sudanese government's job was to liquidate the colonial regime and bring the country to independence.

This it did. With London determined to make the best of things (and, as always, more interested in Suez than the Sudan) and his own support within the NUP uncertain, al-Azhari moved quickly to preside over dissolution of the Condominium. The last potential obstacle intruded in August 1955, when southern troops, disaffected by notice of transfers north and inflamed by unfair Sudanization and wild rumors, mutinied in Equatoria. The ensuing rampage, during which hundreds of people, mainly northern civilians, were killed, briefly threatened Anglo-Egyptian delay. But London had washed its hands of the south, and al-Azhari would not countenance Egyptian intervention. The government restored order but, weakened politically, fairly limped to independence. After rushed parliamentary votes in December and recognition by the co-domini, this was finally attained on 1 January 1956.

8

COLONIAL LEGACIES AND SUDANESE RULE, 1956–1969

DARFUR AT INDEPENDENCE

The Sudan achieved independence in unique circumstances. Most obviously, the cooperation and competition of the co-domini had brought a degree of economic development and speed to self-government that would not have occurred under a single colonial master. But that competition, and the sectarian division that advanced with it, poisoned political development. The parliamentary system, on the Westminster model, empowered the Khartoum elite while providing little scope for outlying regions to compete for resources. Although the familiar theme of postcolonial dominance of center over periphery would, in the Sudan's case, be identified with ethnic and religious differences between north and south, it was evident in relation to all regions.

The rush to self-determination left many aspects of statehood incomplete. These included relations with the former co-domini, ownership of their property, the rights of their and other foreign citizens, terms of service for remaining civil servants, currency, accession to treaties, the Nile waters, informal border arrangements, and much else. The country had no constitution: government carried on under authority of the old regime's ordinances, as implicitly recognized in parliamentary elections; the head of state was a five-man committee. Mutiny and subsequent atrocities in Equatoria in late 1955 hinted at what lay in store there. Development plans mooted in the late days of the Condominium immediately encountered insufficiency of funds. The main political parties, the National Unionist Party (NUP) and Umma, remained organizationally inchoate and ideologically vapid, prey to deeper sectarian, sectional, social, and indeed personal interests: the government that presided at Independence fell apart soon after it.

The transfer of power on 1 January 1956 was a succession rather than a revolution.[1] Within weeks, however, Isma'il al-Azhari was forced to broaden his government. A historic if cynical rapprochement of the two sayyids soon served notice of where power really lay. In June 1956, the NUP split: Members of Parliament loyal to Sayyid Ali formed the People's Democratic Party, then joined a coalition government under the Umma leader, Abdallah Khalil, leaving al-Azhari and the rump of the NUP out in the cold. Opposition to al-Azhari was hardly a program of government, however, and although agreement was easy over technical and ceremonial aspects of the Sudan's new status, maneuvering behind the scenes continued. On the basis of the Sudan's first scientific census, conducted in 1955–56, parliamentary constituencies were reconfigured and their number increased from 97 to 153 before the elections in 1958.

That this census was the last unambiguously to survey the whole country indicates the burgeoning tensions beneath superficial unity even in 1956, for there was political interest in denying ethnic differences within the "North," exaggerating the majority status of Muslims, and underrepresenting peripheral regions, especially the south, in national institutions. The census reported the Sudan's population as 10,263,000. Darfur's 1.33 million ranked third only to Blue Nile (2.07 million) and Kordofan (1.76 million); the six northern provinces comprised about 7.5 million, or 72 percent of the total, and Darfur therefore almost 18 percent of the north's and 13 percent of the Sudan's population. Of females over puberty but of childbearing age, Darfur had the highest percentage of any province – 24.6 percent – and between the ages of five and puberty also the highest – 11.4 percent – ominous statistics in the environmentally degraded west. The census found that a bare majority of Sudanese (51 percent) spoke Arabic at home, followed by Dinka (11 percent). Arabic was also the majority language in Darfur (55 percent): Fur (classified for census purposes as three dialects of one language, North, South, and West Darfurian), was spoken at home by 42 percent (5.6 percent of the Sudan's population), and the rest spoke other languages, none of which accounted for more than 1 percent of the province's total.[2]

In terms of tribe or "nationality," the census found that 375,000 of Darfur's people were Arabs (of whom 269,000 were Baqqara) and 758,000 "Westerners" (Fur, Masalit), figures that indicate, among many things, that Arabic had become the first language of roughly a third of those considered ethnic Fur. Some 86,000 were classified under "Nigerian tribes" (Fallata) and the rest as members of a surprising range of Sudanese and other, mainly central and west African tribes (which included 10,000 people in a subcategory called "unknown"). These and other figures relating to ethnicity, tribe, and language would later assume much more importance.[3]

There was nothing controversial about the census's other findings, which implicitly condemned the defunct Anglo-Egyptian regime. The astounding education statistics are highly relevant to contemporary events. In terms of the highest school attended (by people over the age of puberty), no province of the Sudan, including even the south, had a lower percentage for intermediate school than Darfur: 0.2 percent; the figure for females was 0. Likewise for secondary school attendance, no province had a worse record: the Bahr al-Ghazal and Upper Nile matched Darfur at 0.1 percent. For the Sudan as a whole, 78 percent of males over the age of puberty had received no formal schooling, and 97.3 of females; for Darfur, the figures were 65 and 99 percent, respectively. The surprisingly high (35 percent) number for males having received some education was owed to the province's sub-grade schools and Qur'anic *khalwas*, which 33 percent had attended or were attending; only 1.8 percent had any elementary education, a percentage second worst in the country (to Upper Nile's 1.4 percent) – of Khartoum Province's adult males, 16 percent had some elementary schooling, and of Blue Nile's 20 percent.[4]

Given these figures, the census's findings on employment are unsurprising. Of Darfur's 350,000 males over the age of puberty, 232,000 were farmers, 38,000 nomadic animal owners, and 31,000 shepherds. There were 158 male and 37 female primary and intermediate schoolteachers in the entire province. Among medical practitioners, 2 were classified as "professional" and 281 as "semiprofessional" (including 63 women). There appear to have been 783 policemen and prison wardens (4 of whom were women), 1 professional accountant, and 2 (males) in the field of "entertainment." Most women – 79 percent – were classified as "unproductive," and the only field in which they out-numbered men was "Unemployed, beggars." Of the Muslim provinces, Darfur had the highest number and percentage of men with three or four wives and the highest of all provinces with two; fifty-three men had five wives, and one had six.[5]

The picture painted by the census was thus of a province still over-whelmingly rural, dependent almost entirely on agriculture and animal husbandry, with a very low level of educational and technical attain-ment and with a population likely to grow rapidly in the near future. Detailed analysis reveals that the tiny modern sector of the economy belonged mainly to outsiders – eastern merchants, *jallaba*, truckers, a few Syrian or Lebanese Christians. As sobering as this picture is, it masks even starker realities. For just as national averages hid huge discrepancies between Khartoum and Darfur, there were wider vari-ations within each province: Khartoum had its slums and impover-ished rural villages to be sure, and Darfur its few relatively prosperous and modern towns, where almost all modern economic activity was concentrated.

Native Administration had largely succeeded in limiting education to the sons of chiefs. The census found, for example, that of 131,000 people over the age of puberty in the two Kutum districts, 630 had some elementary education, 69 some intermediate education, and 9 some sec-ondary; 94 percent in Kutum Centre had no education at all (including 99.9 percent of females). Coincidentally, interim reports for eastern Darfur and the eastern part of Nyala Baqqara district were filed at the same time as that for the city of Khartoum, and these reduce almost to absurdity the handicap Darfur suffered. Almost half of Khartoum's 61,000 adults had some education, 9,600 some elementary school, and fully 7,300 had attended secondary or higher school. In Nyala Baqqara East, with about the same number of people (63,100), 109 had some ele-mentary schooling and none had any secondary education. Put another way, in Khartoum, more than 15 percent of adult males had attended secondary school, whereas in both the Nyala Baqqara East sampling area and eastern Darfur, the (rounded) figure was 0 percent. Eastern Darfur had 10 intermediate and primary school *teachers*, the Nyala Baqqara district 6, Khartoum 265; Nyala Baqqara East had 3 book-keepers, Khartoum 705.[6] No wonder the Khartoum elite expressed a right and duty to "speak for" their backward brethren!

PARLIAMENTS AND JUNTAS

Carrying On

Worse than incompetent, the fledgling independent government was unlucky. The last development plan of the colonial era, whether ambitious or inadequate, was based on revenue estimates that proved overly optimistic. This reflected reliance on cotton exports, to which the country had become addicted: development budgets themselves, including that for 1957–62, called for huge investment to expand cotton cultivation, thus increasing the potential for boom or bust. As early as 1956, the Ministry of Finance tightened credit, pressed for import controls, and called for savings in all areas, including government salaries; "nonproductive" areas of development, except the army and national airline, had to be funded by higher taxes or foreign loans; foreign currency balances were dangerously low. The 1957 and 1958 cotton crops were poor, and in a declining world market, the government's marketing board mismanaged sales, with results that echoed the early 1930s.[7] The disharmony of a coalition of party politicians was not relieved by the need for retrenchment, which included suppression of posts, leaving vacancies unfilled, and postponing cost-of-living adjustments.[8]

At the same time, what today seems a curious artifact of the Cold War intruded on the Sudan's parochial politics. In the aftermath of the Suez Crisis of 1956, the United States offered financial aid to the Sudan. Was this a Trojan Horse made in Britain? While some proposed taking the money and running, others, conscious of national dignity and instinctively siding with Egypt in a regional atmosphere of increasing radicalism, preached self-reliance and Arab unity. Disputes over Nile waters and the international boundary complicated that position. None of these issues was solved before the 1958 parliamentary elections. The Umma and the People's Democratic Party (PDP) fought those in continued alliance, thus underlining not a unity of purpose but the absence of any other than continuing in power.

The elections, in February–March 1958, maintained in office the Umma-PDP coalition. Features familiar to electoral politics elsewhere played their part: gerrymandering, a strategic agreement by the Umma and PDP not to compete against each other's candidates, and extension of the franchise – in this case, the naturalization of many Fallata, a factor of particular relevance in Darfur. The so-called graduates' constituency, devised for the 1953 election to send multiple members to parliament based on the educational attainment rather than residency of voters, was abolished. The Umma won 63 seats (of 173), the PDP 26, and the NUP a surprising 44; the remaining 40 went to the Southern Liberal Party, a regional collaboration of southern politicians, most of whom cashed in their chips with one or another of the northern parties. The election confirmed Darfur's loyalty to the heirs of the Mahdi. The Umma took 57 percent of the vote there and increased its bare majority from six of eleven seats to nineteen of twenty-two, and the NUP (with 24 percent) took the other three (in El Fasher, Zalingei, and Dar Masalit).[9] An attempt by disaffected sons of the Khalifa Abdallahi to split the Mahdist camp fared poorly when their candidates – calling themselves the National Liberation Party – were denounced as traitors by Sayyid Abd al-Rahman and failed even to win over their own kinsmen, the Ta'aisha.

Invitation to a Coup

As soon as the new government took office, the rationale for its electoral strategy was overwhelmed by its internal contradictions. The coalition partners publicly criticized each other, and not only over matters of policy: the very orientation of the regime was in play. Negotiations, secret or open depending on the advantages perceived to accrue from rumors or statesmanship, took place between the Umma and NUP and between the NUP and PDP. The dual specters of Mahdist monarchy and Egyptian invasion were revived. That the prime minister himself, Abdallah Khalil, a former officer, now secretly invited the army to overthrow his government emphasizes the artificiality of not only the unwieldy coalition but also the system that produced it. On 17 November 1958, it collapsed: the army chief, General Ibrahim Abboud, declared an emergency and dismissed, suspended, or dissolved state institutions. A Supreme Council of the Armed Forces assumed power, delegating it to Abboud as president, who appointed a cabinet of officers and civilians.[10]

To the outside world, the accession of the military appeared but the latest in a string of takeovers in the Arab and Muslim worlds. Yet although some of the Sudanese terminology echoed revolutionary Egypt, the junta and its policies bespoke law and order rather than radicalism.[11] Flare-ups within the military itself were suppressed, first (in March and May 1959) with kid gloves and finally (in November) with public executions. The regime's foreign policy was officially non-aligned but pro-West. In economic terms, it broke little new ground. The major domestic issue of its six years in power was the crisis of the southern Sudan, where the military's ham-fisted Arabicization and Islamization provoked civil war. Darfur was hardly represented in the senior ranks of the army, just as in the civil service or other institutions, and its allegiance to the Umma was based entirely on that party's embodying the will of Sayyid Abd al-Rahman (and, after his death in 1959, of his successors). In Darfur, the passing of power from parliament to army would be seen mainly in local effects of Khartoum's administrative and economic policies.

The Abboud regime sought a fresh start in Sudanese politics by creating institutions to circumvent political parties and "foreign" parliamentary systems. Legislation in 1960–62 swept away the inherited structure, and established consultative councils at the local, provincial, and national levels. Provincial governors were replaced by Government Representatives, who would preside over legislative councils and administrative authorities. The indirectly elected central council would serve as both legislature and constitutional convention. Striving for an impression of deliberateness, the regime came across as unhinged: the central council could not begin work until the lower councils operated, and elections to these were not held until early 1963. In both spirit and substance, the system resembled institutions of the colonial regime and was widely seen as intended to delay the soldiers' return to barracks.

In Darfur, local government institutions remained in place, even as superficial aspects changed and essential underpinnings were eaten away. The governor at independence, Ali Abdallah Abu Sinn, who had joined the civil service in 1923 and served in Darfur since 1946, was succeeded in August 1958 by Ahmad Makki Abdo and in December 1959 by al-Tijani Sa'd who, under the Provincial Administration Act of 1960, would be Government Representative and Chairman of the Province Authority. When the office of district commissioner was abolished in 1960, inspectors of local government filled the void. Most, if not all, of these officials appear to have been civil servants of standing, and there is no evidence of an attempt to empower Darfur natives in home districts: even southern Sudanese were appointed to the Darfur administration. Within its six districts (North, South, East, West, El Fasher, and Dar Masalit), local government councils, as constituted under the Condominium's ordinances and laws, continued. An experiment in financing local government in part from prorated shares of the sugar monopoly was abandoned after the regime was overthrown.[12]

THE CONTINUITY OF ECONOMIC DECLINE IN DARFUR

Plans for Planners

Only a strong government with clear support from an informed citizenry could have implemented policies to narrow significantly the gap between the Sudan's poorest and richest regions. Neither the civilians of 1956–58 nor the soldiers of 1958–64 had the will or the means. A later commentator wrote that "naturally, constitutional and administrative reform took priority over economic policy for the first few years" after independence,[13] a startling assertion from any perspective other than that of the Khartoum elite. That elite was drawn mainly from the riverain north and had succeeded to the perquisites and priorities of the colonial regime. Its inheritance included a bias toward big "productive schemes," not incidentally in the center, because these promised the returns needed to finance social services, communications, and other development. The regional bases of the political parties' support also tended to shortchange Darfur: the Khatmiyya, aligned with the NUP and later the PDP, was concentrated in Northern Province, the Khartoum metropolitan area, and Kassala; the Umma drew strength from the poor west, but the economic interests of the Mahdi family and its allies were mainly in Dongola and along the Blue and White Niles. That the Umma could count on Darfur's votes made them cheaper.

During the period 1956–69, the Sudanese economy continued to depend on agriculture and underwent no important structural changes. Both parliamentary and military regimes implicitly endorsed a mixed economy, encouraging the private sector but also involving the state in massive development projects. Flirtation with radical economic ideas in 1965 ended in reconciliation of the political system with conservative interests; one vestige of that heady period would be the first income tax. Successive regimes diverged little from the priorities of the late colonial era but were much less adept at controlling expenditure. Compared with its neighbors, the Sudan may have achieved the lowest growth rates in gross domestic product (GDP), the highest contribution of the public sector to GDP, and the highest level of military spending; there is doubt that the economy grew at all on a per capita basis. The reason for slow growth was overreliance on agriculture, especially cotton, and thus relatively low returns from exports. Although agricultural production as a factor in GDP fell from 61 percent in 1955–56 to about 48 percent in the mid-1960s and to less than 40 percent by the end of that decade, only the public and general commercial sectors accounted for more than 10 percent. Agriculture's contribution to export earnings never fell below 90 percent in the 1960s. Import substitution was the stated rationale behind most attempts at industrial development: the country imported nearly all manufactured goods it consumed. Modern manufacturing as a factor in GDP rose from about 1.0 percent in 1956 to only 4.2 percent in 1969, after which it declined. The government ran deficits for almost the entire period.[14]

The first formal development plan after independence continued trends established in the colonial regime's Five-Year Plans. (Instead of another such plan, annual development budgets were drawn up until the adoption, in 1962, of a Ten-Year Plan.) One problem with these was only implicit "prioritization" of projects: the two colonial plans were grab bags reflecting the influence of government departments and bureaucratic bailiwicks. At independence came pressure from politicians – akin to what would in the United States be called "earmarking" – to fund favored projects. The so-called New Schemes program of 1957–61, therefore, ranked long-term projects and gave precedence to a few big ones: the dam at al-Rusayris, the plan to settle at Khashm al-Qirba Nubians displaced by the reservoir behind the High Dam at Aswan, the Managil Extension to the Gezira Scheme, the Sinnar hydroelectric project, and construction of a sugar factory at Geneid. All of these were in the east and, together with similar projects and the ancillary works they required, accounted for an even greater share of development budgets than "productive schemes" had under the Condominium: fully 56 percent of expenditure under the New Schemes program, with only about 10 percent to transport, communications, and utilities.[15]

The Ten-Year Plan (1961/2–1971/2) had as its ambitious goal the doubling of income per head within twenty-five years, which, given an expected population growth rate of 2.8 percent, would actually mean quadrupling national income. Total planned investment was 565 million Sudanese pounds (£S) of which £S337 million would come from the public sector. Yet, although the plan endorsed the need to diversify sources of national revenue (including diversifying agriculture), to encourage exports, and to increase import substitution, some specific goals were unrealistic or contradicted others. For expertise, no less than for soliciting external aid and investment, the government turned to private sources and international agencies; the plan called for £S150 million in external financing and assumed an annually increasing amount of finance from the private sector, presumably as the economy grew and the plan showed success. No mechanisms were proposed to enforce private investment, but incentives under the Industrial Act and Approved Enterprises Act of 1956 (the latter updated in 1968 as the Organization and Promotion of Industrial Investment Act) continued and the Industrial Bank of the Sudan was established to provide credit. To choose projects that would contribute to meeting the plan's goals and to coordinate those selected, a secretariat for economic planning was set up in the Ministry of Finance and, in 1966, a separate Ministry of Industry and Mining was created.

The pragmatic character of successive governments is indicated in the variety of its sources of external financing for development: it is difficult to find a country, bloc (East, West, nonaligned), bank, aid agency, or United Nations fund that went untapped. Institutionalization of aid paralleled and encouraged vast expansion of government bureaucracy, which in turn hampered implementation and ironically became an aspect of (nonproductive) "development" – an end in itself – for the elite. The Ministry of Agriculture had at one point four undersecretaries, each of whom oversaw as many as eight sections or departments, along with fourteen corporations. The National Research Council grouped together departments and agencies with research responsibilities, one of the five specialized components of which, the Agricultural Research Council, had seven committees. The Agricultural Research Corporation, established in 1967 under the Ministry of Agriculture and Irrigation, oversaw (through a board, a general manager and his deputy, and four heads) some ten departments and sixteen research stations, centers, and administrations, any one of which might have as many as twelve further departments and substations, some of which had offices in the capital for "liaison."[16]

A notable aspect of foreign financing during this period was increasing involvement of the United States. Under a bilateral aid agreement, four types of assistance were provided: development grants trained Sudanese abroad, established demonstration projects and feasibility studies (for example, the Khartoum–Port Sudan highway), and paid for buildings. Development loans, provided at low interest rates, fully or partly financed such projects as the Sudanese American Textile Factory ($10 million) and a sewer system in Khartoum North ($3.8 million). "Non-Project Assistance" helped in overcoming difficulties in the country's balance of payments: in 1959–60 alone this amounted to almost $21 million. Finally, Food for Peace sold subsidized U.S. agricultural products in the Sudanese market, with the proceeds accruing to joint accounts for, among other things, development projects and loans to private enterprises with American interests. From its inception until mid-1964, U.S. aid in all these forms amounted to more than $83 million. Effects were felt in many areas because of the sheer variety of projects funded, from crop development to university dormitories.[17]

Despite its ambition, the Ten-Year Plan reflected the conservative orientation of the military regime. "Investment" was defined in its most literal or unimaginative sense as allocation of capital to produce measurable annual returns. Although lip service was paid to social services, the essential connection between these and the "real economy" failed to convince. An addiction to gambling on King Cotton pervaded even aspects of the plan designed to enhance alternative sources of public revenue – for example, rain-fed cotton-growing schemes outside the Gezira. The plan proposed reducing cotton's percentage of total exports from 65 percent in 1951–52 to 61 percent ten years later. Worse, the impression is left of a plan designed to increase rather than shrink the gap between developed areas of the country (and sectors of the economy) and the underdeveloped regions and traditional sectors. Many projects involved neither production nor services: new chambers for the attorney general and offices and houses for his regional representatives; new courthouses; £S1.1 million to take over missionary schools in the south and almost £S1 million for Islamic institutes; housing for officials of the Ministry of the Interior (at £S1.3 million) and for police (£S1.25 million); "V.I.P. Rest Houses"; new embassy buildings in Paris, Washington, Delhi, and Islamabad; and a "film unit," which in 1963 produced such classics as *President Abboud Visits Germany* and *Some*

Advantages of the Revolution. About 50 percent of the plan's total public investment was in projects already approved, and it is arguable that almost every piastre of that except for railway expansion was destined for projects in or serving mainly the capital region and irrigated agriculture.[18] After the overthrow of Abboud in 1964, the plan was abandoned, but it served as a general template for successive annual plans under the parliamentary regime of 1965–69.

Tomorrow Never Comes

The performance of Darfur's economy under parliamentary and military governments may be briefly surveyed. Sources suffer from Khartoum's and some foreigners' habit of treating Darfur and Kordofan together as "the West," with the result that Kordofan appears poorer and Darfur richer than they should. Statistical representation of sectoral performance by province is incomplete. Darfur's economy remained overwhelmingly agricultural and pastoral, the vast majority of its population remained on the land, and growth continued to be retarded by poor infrastructure. Population growth – estimated at about 2.7 percent per annum between the mid-1950s and the early 1970s – probably outstripped the growth rate of the economy, making Darfur's people ever poorer. The effects of development investment are more controversial: analysis of allocation and of the interests observers have discerned to have benefited or suffered from it is now bound up in the political crisis that began in the 1980s.[19]

Although there were valid reasons for the Khartoum metropolitan area's continuing as the focal point for industrial investment, the country's failure to develop the modern sectors of its agricultural economy has no such explanation. The inability of successive regimes to match productive capacity even to local demand – the most expedient form of import substitution – is most clearly exemplified in the case of Darfur's livestock industry. Although the country imported leather, shoes, and dairy products, and malnutrition was common, Darfur grappled with the problems identified in the 1940s: the poor quality of animals resulting from nomadism and inadequate or fitful veterinary services; poor and uncertain pasturage and overgrazing; poor infrastructure, including the old problem of transport to market; and the failure to develop local meat-packing, animal by-product, or dairy industries.

Darfur accounted for about a quarter of the country's herds (including a third of its cattle), but that sector had barely entered the modern economy. By one account, the Ten-Year Plan devoted less than 1 percent of its resources to development of the country's nomadic economy; an unpublished 1971 survey found almost no local industrial exploitation of Darfur livestock. Precisely 134 people were employed in modern manufacturing of any kind in all of Darfur. But when Yugoslavia offered to finance a tannery, it was located in Khartoum, not Darfur. A dairy-products factory financed by the Soviet Union was built at Babanusa in Kordofan (and almost immediately failed). The "big project" delighted alike the foreign grant-makers and local bureaucratic elite; cheap and simple innovation was boring and crucially lacked the panoply of the salariat. Where once ostriches had been killed for their feathers because gatherers had no scissors, the government provided diesel-engine pumps for the wells of nomads who had no mechanics and uncertain fuel supplies. The vast superstructure of post-independence "planning" only made things worse, inviting – indeed, epitomizing – corruption. How often was "inappropriate technology" applied *because* it was foreign and expensive and fundable, or despite inevitable failure after proponents had moved on, or because a minister had an interest in the contract?[20]

Nevertheless, Darfur's cattle wealth, as measured by herd size, continued to increase, even as monetized wealth declined both in gross terms and on a per capita basis, and political pressure mounted to supply more wells and *hafirs*. Disaster loomed. Just before independence, 5 million head of cattle were immunized against rinderpest, using the new attenuated goat vaccine that protected an animal for four years, with the result that the disease was for a time effectively limited to calves. By 1965, the Sudan's cattle stock was estimated at 9 million head, of which 80 percent were in Southern Darfur. In the far north, the Zaghawa, virtually ignored until they made trouble, remained largely outside the modern economy, except when drought forced them into day labor. The drought of 1969–70 brought mass migration, destruction of herds once they reached tse-tse fly territory, and even plans for permanent relocation.[21]

A similar if less dramatic picture emerges of Darfur's major export, gum. The Sudan's share of the world market remained stable at roughly 85 to 90 percent, even as production fluctuated and prices increased.

Gum maintained its place as the country's second or third export earner: in 1958, a year disastrous for cotton, gum accounted for 13 percent of exports by value, and in its worst year, 1962, it accounted for more than 6 percent. An auction system used since 1922 in Kordofan and later Darfur (at Nyala) continued, but at the national level changes were made that did nothing to stimulate production. As a forest product, gum depended on adequate local prices, without which gatherers would not bother with it; extension of the railway to Darfur was undoubtedly important in stimulating production. In 1962 the military regime introduced a system to fix minimum prices at auction and for export. As Kordofan's production declined during this period, for several reasons, Darfur's percentage of the country's output increased, from about 7.5 percent in 1959–60 to about 30.5 percent in 1971–72.[22]

Darfur remained the Cinderella of the north. The Ten-Year Plan provided $2.65 million for a Jabal Marra Investigation Scheme of agricultural expansion (supplemented by the United Nations Special Fund), £S1.6 million for *hafirs* and dams for the entire country, a study of range-land water use, £S153,000 for development of animal skins and hides, a mobile plant for the Department of Agriculture in Kordofan and Darfur, a mere £S62,000 to improve gum gardens, only £8,130,000 for national soil conservation, and a new quarantine station at El Geneina. These projects and amounts were trivial and haphazard compared with those for irrigation and agricultural expansion in the east. New airport facilities were approved, but no daily air service connected Khartoum and Darfur as late as 1963, when there were nineteen flights a week between Khartoum and Wad Medani, a distance of 110 miles.[23] El Fasher was the only place in the province with piped water, and no town had a public electricity supply. The nearest newspaper – a biweekly – was published at El Obeid. Even Juba had a cinema before any town in Darfur.[24] The major achievement of the era was extension of the railway: long mooted but deferred as unprofitable and therefore "unproductive," the line ran from al-Rahad through southern Kordofan via Babanusa to al-Daiem and railhead at Nyala.

Soon after the onset of self-government in 1953, and largely at the behest of western MPs, a committee was established to investigate the Rural Water Supplies and Soil Conservation Board. Despite political pressure, the committee urged a change of emphasis from water supply to soil conservation through land-use planning. Among other things, it recommended herd management to match the carrying capacity of land; measures to protect grasslands from fire and overgrazing; and, most significantly, limiting unirrigated agricultural development to areas where annual rainfall exceeded 400 to 500 mm. The committee also urged a reorganization by which various agencies, including the Darfur Construction Unit headquartered at El Fasher, would amalgamate into a new water department.[25]

The Land Use and Rural Water Development Department, established shortly after independence, should have eased coordination of water-supply work and agricultural development by grouping the main units of government responsible for these in one administrative unit. Although the ensuing period saw an increase in deep-bore well digging and a decrease in *hafir* construction, it is unclear whether this resulted from a change in policy. In any event, it obviously resulted in increased water supply in some areas. More attention was paid to the problem of land degradation in the vicinity of water points; experts continued to recommend decreasing western herds to sizes compatible with what pastureland could carry without degradation. This had been heard before; water had a political constituency, but land conservation did not.[26]

Health services in Darfur hardly kept up with the population growth rate. After independence, the Sudan joined international health and medical organizations, and a ten-year health plan adopted in 1951 was revised and extended. Given the distorting effects of inflation (and unaccounted migration), not much can be concluded from annual increases in government expenditure on health services, but the percentage of government revenue devoted to health actually declined in the decade 1956–66, from 7.4 to 6.5 percent.[27] Darfur's international border, with constant nomadic activity and pilgrimage traffic, was both a blessing and a curse, attracting Khartoum's attention by exposing it to disease. A new Quarantine Law was enacted shortly before independence, incorporating major points of the International Sanitary Regulations regarding the six quarantinable diseases. There were no serious outbreaks of the epidemic diseases in 1956–69.

Of the endemic diseases, malaria – again owing especially to the relative mobility of Darfur people, including workers returning from eastern agricultural districts where they lived in hovels along the canals – remained rampant, infecting a large percentage of the population. Incidence of schistosomiasis in the Sudan increased throughout the period, in Darfur from about 3,800 cases in 1955 to about 11,650 in 1965 (of 91,000 cases nationally). Leishmaniasis (the visceral variety, called *kala-azar* in the Sudan and sometimes dumdum fever elsewhere), a problem mainly in the Gezira and Upper Nile, was first reported in Darfur in the 1930s and became endemic in the region of El Fasher. Untreated, it is fatal within two years in 80 to 90 percent of cases. Because the vector is the tiny sandfly, prevention was impossible, and in the period under review, the etiology of the disease had not been fully understood. The overwhelmingly rural character of the province's population, and the poverty of resources made available to it, remained the greatest stumbling block to improved health: clean water was still a luxury and sanitary waste disposal haphazard at best. Because in 1960 there were only 200 qualified doctors in the entire country, it is unsurprising that Darfur had no medical specialists or surgeons. The province got its first midwife training course only in 1958.[28]

THE OCTOBER REVOLUTION

The military regime of 1958–64 ironically shared one characteristic with the Sudanese Communist Party (SCP), its fiercest enemy: the absence of a constituency. It also discovered gradually a flaw of civilian life that General Eisenhower once called attention to: the mere giving of an order does not ensure it will be carried out. The essential ties between the center and the periphery, in both Khartoum's relations with the provinces and provincial capitals' relations with the districts, had depended in colonial days on broad agreement over irreducible essentials of policy and the maintenance of bureaucratic routines. The shock of self-government and independence had loosened the mortar, and chips, then chunks, began to fall away during the late 1950s and early 1960s. Deterioration in the fabric of government was hastened by the appeal of modern political forces and the latent factionalism that Native Administration had tended to control.[29]

Opposition to the military regime was not long in coming. The attempted coups of its first year had shattered the nimbus of military discipline and solidarity. Political parties, officially banned, continued informally, and in 1960 a "national front," including the Umma but not the PDP, called for early return to civilian rule. Local elections in 1963 and preponderant delegation to the provincial and central councils of conservative tribal leaders and businessmen cemented the junta's association with – or reliance on – establishment cliques, even as opposition grew in discrete centers and for a variety of reasons. Labor unions and the parties suppressed since the coup operated unofficially and increasingly openly, with growing underground support from the illegal SCP. At the other end of the spectrum, the Muslim Brotherhood, unencumbered by the dynastic ambitions of sectarian leaders, preached low-grade opposition to an increasingly corrupt and cynical regime. Opposition coalesced around the issue of the south.

While the time would come for direct connection between what Khartoum dismissively called the "Southern Problem" and the politics of other marginalized areas, the effects in Darfur of growing crisis in the south were in the early 1960s still oblique. Through policies of Arabicization and Islamization, and the ways in which it pursued them, the military regime alienated important elements of southern leadership; claiming a nationalist mantle to reverse British imperialism the generals instead seemed to mimic its high-handedness. They established an Islamic institute at Juba and *khalwas* throughout the south, switched the day of rest from Sunday to Friday, replaced English with Arabic as the language of instruction in intermediate schools, and finally expelled foreign Christian missionaries. Southerners rebelled. Many went into exile, founding a series of organizations to represent their interests, while veterans of the 1955 mutiny took arms as the nucleus of the Anyanya. What southerners viewed as a war born of Khartoum's existential threat to southern culture, the junta purported to see as a breakdown of law and order.

Rumblings of resentment against Khartoum's domination were heard in other regions. Inchoate political groupings and even registered "parties," some of which tried to speak for the Beja, the Nuba, and indeed the Nubians, had surfaced from time to time but tended to fade in the face of sectarian appeals, their leaders' bribed defection, or the apathy of presumed constituents. In Darfur, the period of military rule witnessed two such entities, both underground. Reminiscent of the shadowy groupings of the 1920s, the Red Flame (*Al-Lahib al-Ahmar*) produced leaflets condemning *jallaba* control of the local economy but was otherwise invisible. In 1963 a group called Soony (after a place in Jabal Marra), drawn mainly from among local soldiers, called for a united front against the exploitive *jallaba*. The army command reacted by purging the ranks and more closely vetting recruits. In a pattern familiar in Sudanese regional politics, an organization of educated civilians, the Dar Fur Development Front, then sprang up in Khartoum under the leadership of Ahmad Ibrahim Diraige, avowedly to represent provincial interests at the national level.[30] Several aspects of these developments are notable: a focus on the *jallaba* that indicated resentment of "foreign" – eastern, Nile Valley, Arab – domination; politicization of local soldiers, whose senior officers were likewise outsiders; and the very title of Diraige's group, with an almost plaintive recognition of where Darfur stood in the scheme of things.

Military governments that cannot win wars are seldom popular. By 1964, the Abboud regime was isolated, and old politicians, new groups, trade unionists, students, and others were allied against it. In October, the government failed to suppress huge demonstrations in Khartoum, encouraging what amounted to a general strike. When elements of the army began to defect, the Supreme Council gave up. A transitional government was formed from the so-called Professionals' Front, an omnibus group that had brought down the regime, and the Johnny-come-lately political parties, including the communists and Muslim Brothers. Although the main role of this government was to return the country to an elective system, progressive elements tried to seize the moment to implement radical reforms. Much of the military's legislation was repealed; trade unions were legalized; women were enfranchised (against the old parties' opposition) and the voting age lowered; steps were taken to promote local control of foreign trade; and a commission was established to reform local government and do away with vestiges of Native Administration. Such measures, and attempts to institutionalize a political role for progressive forces through reservation of parliamentary seats, heightened the old parties' determination for early elections. In February 1965, they forced a reconstitution of the government, which, under their control, prepared for elections in April.

During their brief heyday in 1964–65, a particular focus of reformers was the structure of administration in rural areas, notably Darfur, a stronghold of "traditional" tribal authority. The structure established in 1960, with rubber-stamp provincial councils and Government Representatives, was scrapped. In December 1964, the judiciary's professional society in Khartoum called for separating judicial functions – the original basis of Indirect Rule – from tribal authorities.

But proposals[31] by the minister of cabinet affairs, the communist labor leader al-Shafiʿ Ahmad al-Shaykh, that would have transferred authority from tribal leaders to government appointees would hardly have resonated in Darfur, had they been heard there at all. The revolutionary moment was too brief for such a change and, after elections in April 1965, the restored political parties resumed control. Bizarrely, tribal chiefs formed their own "professionals" organization, which petitioned for specific improvements in their own terms and conditions; making the case for the status quo, *shaykhs* staged incidents, and even adopted tactics amounting to "working to rule" and "downing tools" to demonstrate their power.

NOTHING FORGOTTEN, NOTHING LEARNED: THE 1965–1969 PARLIAMENTARY REGIME

The Imam and His Nephew

The promise of the October Revolution of 1964 was not borne out in the elections of 1965. The electoral landscape was crowded, but the Umma and NUP dominated the horizon; several minor "parties" had as many candidates – two or three – as they did members. For the first time, northern regional parties, at least in name, appeared on the lists, purporting to represent marginalized peoples – the Beja Congress, the Nuba Mountains Federation – as did the communists and Muslim Brothers. In the territorial constituencies, the Umma won seventy-six seats, the NUP fifty-two, the communists three, and the PDP (despite a boycott) three, with the remainder going to the Beja Congress (ten) and independents. No polls were held in the south because of the fighting, but the Supreme Court later ruled that northern candidates there had met the conditions for election and were therefore seated, amid outrage and derision. A coalition took office in June, with Muhammad Ahmad Mahjub, an Umma politician, as prime minister, and the NUP warhorse, Ismaʿil al-Azhari, as president of a revived five-man Supreme Council.

Darfur had remained loyal to the party of the Mahdi family. The Umma (with 66.5 percent of the vote) won sixteen of Darfur's seats as against the NUP's six, with the Muslim Brothers, as the Islamic Charter Front (ICF), taking one seat and an independent one seat. Since the death of al-Siddiq al-Mahdi in October 1961, leadership of the Mahdist movement had been shared by his brother, al-Hadi, as imam, and al-Siddiq's young Oxford-educated son, al-Sadiq, as leader of the Umma. The two differed, and as al-Sadiq and his lieutenants tried to modernize and broaden the Umma, al-Hadi, in jealous pique, asserted the right to ultimate authority. Uneasy unity paid dividends in the Umma's 1965 victory at the polls. Further, because al-Sadiq had not yet reached the required age (thirty) for office, that unity was maintained when Muhammad Ahmad Mahjub became prime minister. But, from the day al-Sadiq won a by-election, the parliamentary party was split, as Mahjub looked to the imam's supporters to keep him in office and dissidents tried to oust him in favor of al-Sadiq. These differences were public, easily exploited by al-Azhari and others for their own purposes. Nonetheless, a showdown, which would be played out in Darfur and which above all else al-Sadiq wished to avoid, was postponed.[32]

The second parliamentary regime, like the first, was burdened from the beginning by deep rifts in an ostensibly powerful coalition. Analysis of the battle for leadership of the government has tended to blame al-Sadiq's impetuousness for the disastrous split of the Umma; we should also note al-Hadi's negativism and Mahjub's incompetence, while allowing that the country's economic and political condition – not least the continuing crisis in the south – required a degree of leadership to which no Sudanese politician could lay claim. In July 1966 Mahjub lost a confidence vote in the parliament, and al-Sadiq formed a new government. Less than a year later, in May 1967, Isma'il al-Azhari, warming to the role of kingmaker, combined with the imam's MPs to bring down al-Sadiq, and Mahjub returned as premier. Elections were scheduled for 1968.

The Umma and Darfur

Thus, whereas in 1965–69, as in 1956–58, the Umma looked to the western Sudan and, indeed, to Darfur for electoral strength, the issues that preoccupied it were not those of its constituents. Its internal politics, and the incessant machinations of al-Azhari, reduced the ability of the government to deal with the country's problems. Disastrously, the parliamentary regime was no more effective than its military predecessor in ending the war in the south. A view that the "north" was intent on enforcing the south's assimilation to Muslim-Arabic culture seemed borne out by events. Death and destruction in the south did not come cheaply, however, and the government had to devote precious resources to war. The degree to which foreign aid made this easier has yet to be fully examined.

As we have already seen in some respects, the economic performance of the second parliamentary regime was in any case poor, and blaming this on civil war hardly diverted attention from the regime's incompetence. Nominal GDP increased by 33 percent in the decade of the 1960s, a poor showing by any measure, including comparisons with neighboring states. Per capita income barely increased at all: population growth was outpacing the economy. The central government budget was in deficit throughout the period. Whereas revenue increased at a rate of 9.4 percent in the two decades after independence, expenditure increased at a rate of 11 percent. Increased expenditure did not result from investment: the ratio of development expenditure to recurrent expenditure, which stood at 54 percent in 1960–61, fell to 18 percent by 1970–71. The "productive schemes" promoted as sources of revenue had been badly planned and ineptly carried out, and they had fallen into deficit themselves. The balance of trade was nearly always negative because exports, still almost all agricultural, never kept pace with the volume and cost of imports. How many of Darfur's skins and hides must be exported – and how many inputs, in labor, water, and transport, must be accounted for – to finance one more deputy assistant commissioner's car? How much cotton produced by Darfur's migrant labor must be sold on the world market to pay for a shipload of Indian textiles? The resources of 90 percent of the country (and its people) were insufficient to support the unproductive 10 percent. The result was resort to external loans, not only for "big projects" and "development" but also to finance recurrent deficits.[33]

The political importance of Darfur to the Umma is evident in efforts made during the second parliamentary period to address related issues of water provision and land degradation. Soon after taking office, Mahjub's government embarked on a massive Anti-Thirst Campaign, which, however, emphasized politically expedient water provision at the expense of land-use planning. The Land Use and Rural Water Development Department was reorganized in 1966 as a corporation, with added functions, including notably its own geological section. Early phases of the program focused on the West, and drilling was conducted by both the corporation and (mainly foreign) private contractors. By the end of the period, almost all investment was devoted to borehole drilling rather than to *hafirs*: a community of interests had developed among local notables, MPs, the Umma leadership, government geologists, and foreign drillers, which overwhelmed the Cassandras who set the rules for distances between boreholes. That the drillers had won the day was clear in other ways, including the neglect and lack of maintenance of pumps and equipment at existing sites.[34]

It was against a background of economic decline, civil war, and partisan bickering that the election campaign of 1968 was fought. From his perch on the Supreme Commission – in effect, head of state – Isma'il al-Azhari ensured his role as fixer and spoiler by reuniting the "unionists" – his own NUP and breakaway PDP – into a Democratic Unionist Party (DUP). The Umma formally split in two, and when the votes were counted, the DUP won 41 percent (and 101 seats in parliament), al-Sadiq's Umma won 21 percent (36 seats), and al-Hadi's Umma 18 percent (30 seats). (Unafflliated Umma candidates won 2.5 percent of the vote and six seats.) The SCP, in a series of maneuvers worthy of the other parties, had been banned from the election. Northern regional parties won seats – clearly on the personal strength of local notables in a very crowded field: the Beja Congress won three seats and the Nuba Mountain Federation won two. A Western Sudan Union ran three candidates, who garnered 1,695 votes and no seats. Al-Sadiq al-Mahdi lost his own seat to a relative supporting his uncle.[35] The Umma split dissipated Darfur's potential strength in the new parliament. Fully 74 percent of the province's 207,000 votes had gone to Umma candidates, a higher proportion than in 1965. The DUP vote total was almost identical to that of the NUP in the previous election, at about 24 percent. Other parties and candidates, therefore, made almost no headway at all; the more things had changed, the more they had stayed the same. In effect, Darfur had voted its preference between the two Umma leaders, but that 86,000 opted for the "modernist" al-Sadiq as against 64,000 for the imam[36] might not mean much.

In May, a new coalition of the DUP and imam's Umma was formed, with Mahjub returning to warm the prime minister's chair and al-Azhari reelected president of the plural headship of state. As in all previous cases, the nominal array of forces inaccurately depicted the true state of Sudanese politics. Awakening to the ascendancy of the DUP, the two Umma leaders began a months-long confabulation to resolve their differences. Al-Azhari scoured the parliamentary pot for possible new coalition partners, even among southerners (ever-aspiring to be minister of animal resources) and leftists (under various law-evading rubrics). Prime Minister Mahjub, inured to the role of front man and ribbon-cutter, took pains to do nothing – to right the economy or resolve the civil war – that might cost him his job. When in April 1969 the Umma reconciliation was finalized, a grand new coalition loomed, and Mahjub was forced to resign. The army intervened and toppled them all.

The Wild West

We have noted that the Sudan's foreign affairs during the first parliamentary regime were dominated by the formalities required of newly independent states and by feckless indecision in the face of Egyptian bullying. Its military successor early showed a more muscular approach, not least in dealings with the Sudan's neighbor to the west, Chad, which achieved independence from France in August 1960. There, as in other former colonies, French financial and military support remained essential props and embarrassing reminders of dependence. The Chadian government, under the long-serving President François Tombalbaye, was dominated by a tiny educated elite from the south and was distrusted in the Muslim north and east as successor to the Europeans. After the French withdrew from the far north, at Tombalbaye's request, in the early 1960s and were replaced by Chadians, the local nomadic population rose in revolt. In 1964, this spread to central Chad and Wadai and across the borders of the Sudan.

Sudanese involvement in Chad was inevitable, but the role assumed by successive Khartoum governments involved choices. The international border was artificial and porous; ancient relations of conflict and cooperation had not ended with the fall of Wadai and the death of Ali Dinar; during colonial times, the large-scale movement of people was routine and, to an extent, regulated, whether pilgrims from afar on the *hajj* routes or locals with their herds. Now Chadian rebels sought sanctuary in Darfur, where they obtained arms and recruits, and it was at Nyala in 1966 that the Chad National Liberation Front, later called FROLINAT (Front de Liberation Nationale du Tchad)[37] was founded under Ibrahim Abatcha. Another group of Wadaians, the

Chad Liberation Front, stood apart; its leader, Ahmad Musa, was at one point jailed at El Geneina for political activities.

FROLINAT became an Arab Muslim cause and enjoyed the support not only of the Sudanese government but also of the Egyptian, Algerian, and other regimes with Cold War interests to pursue. Along the turbulent border and elsewhere, in bases and camps, the Sudanese authorities supported the Chadian rebels. That support increased after the October Revolution of 1964 and the return of parliamentary government, for the Umma, dominant in Darfur, could hardly turn its back on co-religionists in its backyard. Although the extent of Sudanese official involvement was probably unknown to Tombalbaye's government, its existence was obvious. But the Chadian regime was very weak: the only practical weapon it had was to turn the table and give succor to the southern Sudanese, whose pleas for help Tombalbaye had resisted.

Chad's dilemma mirrored the Sudan's. In Chad a repressive, inept government of African non-Muslims confronted a rebellion by Muslims and Arabs; in the Sudan, Arab Muslims ruled and non-Muslims in the south rebelled. An official rapprochement in 1967, after talks mediated by Niger in El Fasher, allowed the Sudanese and Chadian governments to step back from the brink but had no appreciable effect on the ground. El Geneina, the capital of Dar Masalit, which had been cut in two by the French and British colonial empires, was a hotbed of Chadian rebel activity. The Sudanese government came close to bestowing official recognition on FROLINAT, not only countenancing its offices and recruitment but also continuing material support. In 1968, Tombalbaye therefore turned to France, which agreed to intervene militarily in exchange for reforms. By 1969, when the governments of both the Sudan and Libya were overthrown, what had begun as an insurrection in Chad was on the verge of becoming a regional war.

9

DARFUR AND "THE MAY REGIME," 1969–1985

THE POLITICS OF MAY (1969–1976)

The Ascent of Colonel Nimayri

By May 1969 there was widespread agreement that parliamentary rule had not just failed to grapple with the country's problems but was also prominent among them.[1] Popular reaction to its overthrow occupied a narrow spectrum between apathy and resignation. The failure of the previous military regime in 1964 had at least been unattended by the bitter disappointment that seemed an inevitable consequence of the parties' rule; if soldiers could do little better, they certainly could do no worse – or so it seemed – and the rhetorical flourishes of a new regime provided some relief from the torpid inconsequentiality of the politicians. But in this belief Sudanese were wrong: no matter how bad things are, they can always get worse.

The Free Officers Movement that overthrew the parliamentary regime in May 1969 resembled only superficially the military regime of 1958–64. Within days of its coming to power, it depicted itself in the Nasserite mold as successor to the "popular forces" that had overthrown that earlier military regime and been thwarted by the politicians in 1965. Thus, although the usual steps were taken immediately – suspension of the (still provisional) constitution and suppression of its institutions, banning of the parties and arrest of their leaders, imposition of censorship – these were followed by more radical departures, some symbolic, others unmistakably indicating a change of direction. The country was renamed (as the Democratic Republic of the Sudan) and a Revolutionary Command Council (RCC) of ten, under the coup leader, Colonel Jaafar Muhammad Nimayri, age thirty-nine, was named to run the country. Four of the RCC's members were leftists of various stripes, as were at least eight members of the cabinet, including avowed communists.

During its first year in power, the regime burnished its claims to progressivism. It purged the civil service and security forces and nationalized banks, foreign assets, and large private agricultural holdings. It backed up Arab nationalist rhetoric with steps toward alignment with Egypt and Libya: the Economic Integration Agreement with Egypt in September 1969; the Tripoli Charter (December 1969) by which Egypt, the Sudan, and Libya would coordinate defense and foreign affairs; and the Tripartite Economic Agreement (April 1970), bringing Libya into the Sudan-Egypt integration pact. Closer ties were forged with socialist states, with immediate results in large development loans (including from Yugoslavia, which financed what came to be called "Tito's wells" in Darfur). There was crowd-pleasing populism, too: the Gezira tenants' debt was canceled and reduction of house rents decreed. Huge increases in the intakes of intermediate and secondary schools were announced. Through these and other steps, the regime won the acquiescence of progressive elements, including the more ideologically committed wing of the National Unionist Party (NUP).[2]

Early opposition came from the religious right. After attempts to conciliate al-Sadiq al-Mahdi failed, he was arrested in June 1971. His uncle, the Imam al-Hadi, withdrew to Aba Island. The regime's early policies seemed deliberately provocative and included, in addition to those mentioned already, abolition of Native Administration in Khartoum and Northern provinces and parts of Blue Nile province; the intention was announced of phasing it out elsewhere, including the Mahdist stronghold of Darfur. After Mahdists rioted in Omdurman in March 1970, Nimayri sent in the army. An air bombardment of Aba was followed by an assault by ground forces, and thousands of Mahdists died in the fighting that ensued. Al-Hadi was killed while trying to flee the country. His family's vast holdings were confiscated. Al-Sadiq al-Mahdi went into exile.

Misjudging his strength vis-á-vis the leftists, Nimayri turned on them to consolidate his hold on power. He purged the RCC and officer corps, dissolved progressive unions, and arrested leading communists. Overconfidence almost cost him his life; his opponents' did cost them

Figure 15. Col. Jaafar Muhammad Nimayri (seated, center) and members of the Revolutionary Command Council, 1969. After overthrowing the elected government of the Sudan, Nimayri remained in power until 1985, a period of increasing economic and political turmoil in Darfur. (Durham University Library, SAD 787/5.)

theirs. In July 1971, left-wing officers staged a coup. Nimayri was detained, an "industrial and agricultural revolution" was announced under a new RCC, and communist rallies were staged in the capital. Neighboring states intervened, Libya by holding coup leaders en route to Khartoum and Egypt by ordering troops stationed at the irrigation works south of the capital to resist. Nimayri escaped, and forces loyal to him regained control. The coup leaders were summarily executed, as were leading communist civilians. A purge ensued, extending from the cabinet to the civil service. The "May Regime" had survived, but at what cost? Having alienated, then smashed, both the organized right and left, Nimayri emerged without any obviously reliable constituency. The next decade and a half witnessed successive attempts to create one.

To consolidate his personal position, Nimayri reconstituted the RCC and promulgated a provisional constitution, under which a referendum, in September 1971, elected him president (with 99 percent of the vote).

Steps were taken to institutionalize a new "party," the Sudanese Socialist Union (SSU).[3] The most important result of Nimayri's policy, however, was settlement of the civil war. This had reached a stalemate. Yet,
although the regime had announced determination to reach a settlement
and had taken a few steps to do so, the time was not ripe for a deal
until mid-1971. Then Nimayri stood alone – unarguably atop if not tri-
umphantly astride – national politics, while the various southern rebels
had coalesced behind Colonel Joseph Lagu in a Southern Sudan Liberation Movement (SSLM). In July, having survived the coup, Nimayri
initiated secret talks with the rebels, and these culminated in the Addis
Ababa Agreement of February 1972.

The agreement, hailed as a triumph of African diplomacy, was generous in spirit but vague in detail, and implementation depended on
submission of personal and sectional interests to a common good. Duly
enshrined in the Regional Self-Government Act of March 1972 and the
constitution of 1973, it created power-sharing arrangements between
Khartoum and a unitary Southern Region with its capital at Juba and
its own elected assembly and council of ministers. Side agreements
dealt with cease-fire arrangements and integration into the national
army of rebel soldiers. Abel Alier was named provisional head of the
southern government, with elections to the regional assembly slated for
November 1973.

Nimayri emerged from this process an unlikely statesman, a pragma-
tist hailed as a visionary, who had done what the politicians had failed
to do: end the war while holding the country together. He used the
prestige thus accrued further to institutionalize his control. A rubber-
stamp Constituent Assembly was convened after sham elections in the
autumn of 1972, and a book-length constitution was promulgated in
1973, establishing a powerful presidency, a weak legislature, a subordinate judiciary, and the SSU as the sole party in a state "guided by Islam."
As a vehicle for state control, the SSU developed a vast apparatus of
patronage and bureaucracy at all levels, alongside the government. Not
least because of the system conceded to the south, a semblance of representative government was needed in the rest of the country, and this
was provided by managed elections to the People's (national) Assembly in May 1974. Half of its 250 members were elected in territorial
constituencies from among approved candidates and half from various
approved organizations. The irony of Nimayri's partial dependence for

support on the ex-rebels of the south was not lost on either his domestic enemies or bipolar world opinion.

This turn of the political kaleidoscope explains the regime's attempts at rapprochement with al-Sadiq al-Mahdi, who alone of the old party leaders had the pedigree to compete. Oft-rumored negotiations foundered, however, and he remained the exiled leader of the National Front of dissidents. Based at Oxford, and with Libyan support of Mahdist exiles, al-Sadiq launched a coup attempt in 1976 that was put down after bloody street fighting in the capital. Trials and mass executions followed; the Muslim Brothers were implicated, and al-Sadiq and a co-conspirator, Sharif Hussayn al-Hindi, were tried in absentia and sentenced to death. This test of strength ironically paved the way to a deal and, after secret mediation, Nimayri and al-Sadiq met at Port Sudan in July 1977 and made peace. The results of this National Reconciliation were al-Sadiq's return from exile and agreement to work within the constitutional apparatus; Nimayri's reciprocal commitment to a greater role for Islam; a general amnesty; and the rending of the National Front, whose rump fumed and squabbled in continued exile.[4]

Enter Gaddafi

Since his overthrow of the Libyan monarchy in September 1969, Colonel Muammar Gaddafi had chafed at a junior role in regional politics, which Egypt would always dominate, and his gaze turned southward, to the Sudan, Chad, and beyond. The parting of the ways with the Nimayri regime appears to have begun with the Addis Ababa Agreement in 1972, which with its promises of autonomy and self-rule for Africans offended Gaddafi's pan-Arab sensibilities. Having stood by in 1970 when Nimayri crushed the Mahdists, Gaddafi now allowed them to regroup in Libyan exile, and it was from Kufra, via the so-called Sarra Triangle, the barren southeast corner of Libya, that al-Sadiq al-Mahdi's insurgents launched their 1976 coup in Khartoum. Attempts to stir up trouble were much more successful in Chad.

Soon after taking power, Gaddafi had involved himself in the Chadian civil war. His regime denounced the Tombalbaye government, began a fitful courtship of FROLINAT, and financed and supplied rebels inside Chad. Subsequent thaws in relations between Chad and Libya were purely tactical, reflecting shifting circumstances. Most ominously,

Libya reopened a long-dormant territorial issue, sovereignty in the so-called Aouzou Strip, which had passed to Italy in a 1935 convention that France had never ratified. Libya and Chad inherited that dispute, but the territory had been considered worthless until Gaddafi made an issue of it. Following the assassination of Tombalbaye in April 1975 and the succession of General Felix Malloum, Libya formally annexed the Aouzou. That, and subsequent increased Libyan pressure on Chad, coincided with French disengagement, leaving the Malloum regime to confront a revivified FROLINAT on its own. Through his reckless support of al-Sadiq al-Mahdi's coup attempt in 1976, however, Gaddafi made his friends the enemies of Nimayri, the great survivor: Khartoum's support for FROLINAT ceased, and Nimayri sought to repair relations with Chad.

HARD TIMES IN DARFUR

Nimayri's domestic and international games of musical chairs were largely orchestrated in the capital. They echoed in the provinces and faded with distance, but in Darfur we may discern their impact not only in relation to Chad but also in administrative reforms, the evolution of local opposition, and the not unrelated deterioration of the provincial economy, in which long-term environmental and demographic changes also played a part.

The President and the Professor

The May Regime in its early phases benefited from enthusiastic support of young secularist professionals disgusted with the feckless politicians of the old regime. Imbued with socialist theory and eager to prove Sudanese ability to accomplish what others in the Arab world could not, they sought to rationalize a ramshackle system and so transform the country. Within weeks of assuming power in 1969, however, the regime was already prey to profound division – as the New Forces had been in 1964–65 – between the communists and radicals and what might be called (despite a high degree of ideological commitment and nationalist fervor) the realists. The communists' problem was a familiar one: they had played a leading role in bringing down the old regime, but their constituency was limited to themselves. Each announcement of radical plans cost the regime the acquiescence of another interest group. In this light, the leftist coup of July 1971 was a last throw of the dice by a movement already marginalized. In its aftermath of executions and purges, the initiative passed to pragmatists.

One of their principal aims was to destroy the vestiges of tribalism. Parliamentary regimes had paid lip service to "liquidating" Native Administration, but none took meaningful steps to do so. Although Nimayri and his army cohorts characteristically looked askance at any authority – traditional or modern – that rivaled their own, abolition of tribal dynastic rule had many proponents for its own sake. The most important was the theoretician of the May Regime, Jaafar Muhammad Ali Bakheit (1932–76), a young Cambridge Ph.D. and lecturer who in 1970 became minister of local government. Although like contemporaries elsewhere the May Regime would produce enormous amounts of ephemeral propaganda on this and other subjects, Bakheit's analysis was acute, and his prescriptions both idealistic and grounded in experience.[5] These shared the flaws of all top-down reforms, however, not the least of which was the whiff of elitism.

Under terms of the People's Local Government Act of 1971, a pyramidal structure of councils at the village, "rural" or town (and even neighborhood), district, and province levels was established. Boundaries were drawn deliberately to cut across rather than incorporate tribal *dars*. Procedures for selecting representatives, including election, were prescribed: reservation of seats for women (which failed), departments of government, and organizations; and proscription of tribal leaders and notorious politicians. Elections above the village level were indirect. When all was said and done, 86 warranted councils of the old system gave way to 500 in the new (and to some 4,000 village councils, 737 neighborhood councils, and even 281 nomadic-encampment councils). In Darfur, El Fasher Rural Council was superseded by the Eastern Darfur District Council, comprising four town or rural councils; Southern Darfur and Western Darfur Rural Councils were succeeded by Southwest Darfur District Council, with seven rural councils and one town council (Nyala); and Eastern Darfur, Northern Darfur, and Dar Masalit Rural Councils gave way to one (enormous) Northwest Darfur District Council, with nine rural councils and one town council at El Geneina. The executive at El Fasher would be styled provincial commissioner, his deputy as executive director.[6] All councils were advisory only. The province council could devolve powers to the districts but in fact never did so. Crucially, revenue previously accruing to local councils went, under the new system, to the Darfur Province Council, which also intermediated between the central ministries and their provincial representatives.

In theory, this system devolved and dispersed authority, but in practice, it tightened the center's grip at the expense of local control. Khartoum controlled the province through finance and patronage. At the provincial level, the multiplicity of councils was designed to devolve authority among ever-smaller units, but in practice, the power of the commissioner tended to increase because an enhanced role bestowed by Khartoum (especially over police) coincided with subordinate councils' chronic shortage of funds. In other words, Khartoum's ability to appoint or dismiss the province executive – and to confer or withhold funds – made him (if he was not already) a creature of the regime, especially in Darfur, where dependence on central government to pay the bills was by that time chronic. "Devolution" in Darfur never resulted in a local person's appointment to the top job; both the system and its chief officers were outsiders. In any case, the proliferation of political units was unmatched by the authority – or money – to do anything. At the center stood Nimayri, president of the republic, chairman of the SSU, paymaster in chief, and even, after 1971, occasionally self-proclaimed *imam.*

Pyramids are expensive. Easy to draw on paper, they require a high degree of organization to build. In the Sudanese case, impetus was meant to come from the SSU, mock paeans to whose proselytizing cadres echoed long into the night at Khartoum drinking parties but whose organization needed a pyramid of its own and whose zeal would not survive unmet payrolls. By 1974, when Darfur was divided into two "provinces," Northern (headquartered at El Fasher) and Southern (Nyala), the SSU reportedly had 2.25 million enrolled members, 6,381 "basic [or 'base'] units," 1,892 "branches," 325 divisions, 34 "areas," a congress for each province, a central committee, political bureau, general secretariat, and national congress, all encompassing 7,545 rural development committees and 78 unions. By 1980, there were 7,000 branches and 100,000 base units. The SSU's nomenclature would make Orwell blush – "assistant secretary general for ideology," secretary of the Committee on "SSU Thought and Doctrine" – but Sudanese only laughed. The central government was concomitantly bloated: by 1970 its bureaucracy had increased ten-fold since independence to 120,000, and the number of local government and public corporation employees had doubled in a decade, to 157,000 and 132,000, respectively. British District Commissioners would have envied the leave provisions: by 1978, the Sudan had forty-three annual public holidays, and officials were entitled to between four and ten weeks of vacation; a visitor in 1975 found offices closed for a holiday marking the arrival of the president of Yemen. It was famously said to take 136 separate steps to get a telephone line installed.[7]

The diffidence with which even defenders assessed the new system of provincial administration is striking: to work, it would need more money than it would ever have; and for all the contempt in which the old *shaykhs* and *nazirs* were held, there could not be "at present [1973], any large scale devolution of power to local communities."[8] The rationale for attacking tribal authority – that it was undemocratic, corrupt, and stood in the way of development – soon became a fig leaf for politicization of administration, first by loyalists and then by mere cronies.[9] The jargon of revolutionary change and democratic empowerment was used to taint the concept of professionalism. Remarkably, by law,[10] the new provincial commissioner was an agent of the revolution and served as secretary-general of the provincial SSU. With even the semblance of objective merit disdained, the way was open for wholesale corruption of Darfur's already flimsy administrative structure. Admittedly, such ideological concerns as occupied debate in Khartoum translated into farce in faraway Darfur, where the circadian rhythms of rains, harvests, and vendettas had more currency.

The practical limits of the new structure gradually became evident in several ways. Appointment of SSU factotums fostered popular circumvention of the council system. Important functions, which had already deteriorated since independence, did not improve through transfer to smaller units lacking management experience, personnel, and money; maintenance and operation of water yards, for example, were transferred to local governments. At the national level, too, the limits of policy became obvious – in Darfur's case more than any other province's outside the south – in the return of familiar names (and even faces) to the People's Assembly. That the assembly had no power mitigated in only a negative way the regime's claim to radicalism. And although much has been made in the early twenty-first century about underrepresentation of western Sudanese at high levels of the Sudanese state, neither education nor tribal affiliation – but cronyism – was the basis for appointment.[11]

From May to December: The Darfur Economy

In 1969 the new regime's commitment to development had been real. Overthrow of the economic system pursued since independence had been a principal motive of the Free Officers and their allies on the left. The flurry of activity that attended their accession to power in 1969 constituted an attempt not only to win support but also to burn bridges. Nationalizations, some uncompensated, were not limited to foreign companies symbolic of the colonial past but also included trading groups owned by the richest Sudanese. New labor laws, drafted by a committee chaired by the veteran union leader Shafiʿ Ahmad al-Shaykh, were enacted. But with the suppression of the communists after the failed coup of July 1971 – Shafiʿ Ahmad al-Shaykh was hanged – the regime's economic orientation shifted.

The new policy emphasized development through partnership between the government and private sector. In this scheme of things, the government would revert primarily to a role of developing infrastructure and attracting and channeling foreign capital. This emphasis would complement the burgeoning surpluses of Arab oil-producing countries: the Sudan had agricultural land in abundance and needed foreign investment to develop it; the oil producers had capital in abundance and needed food; the Sudan would become the "bread basket of the Middle East." A Five-Year Plan adopted in 1970 was revised in an expanded Interim Program for 1973/4–76/7 and followed by a Six-Year Plan for 1977/8–82/3. Laws were enacted to protect and encourage private investment. In the wake of nationalizations and in light of uncertain prospects, investment continued to prove elusive, and the government retained the major share in financing its development program. This required turning to foreign sources and, from 1972, the Sudan negotiated successive stabilization programs with the International Monetary Fund to obtain loans and satisfy foreign investors and international agencies. As usual, emphasis on infrastructure favored big projects in the east, especially in food production, and led to huge and costly irrigated works and processing plants, with disastrous results. By the end of the Six-Year Plan, the manufacturing sector was smaller in percentage terms than it had been in 1968.

The Six-Year Plan failed. Education, which would have required massive resources only to keep pace with population growth, may serve as an example. By 1982, the Sudan's literacy rate stood at 15 percent. Fewer than half of the seven-year-olds were in school. Technical education had expanded to reach 11 percent of secondary students instead of the 35 percent the plan had called for. In 1981, 32,000 students who qualified for secondary school could not enroll owing to lack of places; 55,000 secondary-school graduates could not find jobs. The much-publicized "brain drain" of teachers to other countries was unstoppable, even when the government denied exit visas. Many still found ways to escape, including reportedly trekking by camel across Darfur. Of those who stayed, many took jobs in the private sector. Secondary and university students routinely demonstrated and rioted; the government responded by closing the schools. Frequent budget cuts, failure to allocate budgeted amounts, shortages of teachers, the continuing bias of university students toward the arts and humanities, lack of books, power failures, even food shortages were among the problems the system faced by 1982, when a plan was completed to establish "Darfur University."[12]

During the Nimayri years, an increasing number of "development" schemes were designed merely to recover from the neglect and mismanagement of previous schemes. As one example of many that may be cited, a development plan for Southern Darfur (recommended in a study begun in 1972 and completed in 1974) that was launched in 1978 had its cost reduced from $97 million to $27 million in 1980 and its budget approved in 1982. By then, grand initial objectives had been modified to include inoculating cattle against rinderpest (because the vaccination program had been all but abandoned) and clearing water yards (two-thirds were dysfunctional). Future plans included vast mechanization of agriculture, which environmentalists had long viewed as disastrous. As usual, problems of staff and transport doomed the Southern Darfur Rural Development Program as they did the Western Savannah Development Corp.[13]

What might be called "short-termism" was the ironic bane of a dictatorial regime trying to appear responsive while its politics played out behind the scenes. For Darfur, this is unfortunately nowhere clearer than in the planning for and provision of water. As part of its early emphasis on development, the May Regime established a Ministry of Cooperation and Rural Development in 1969, which in 1973 merged with three other ministries into a Ministry of Agriculture, Food, Natural Resources, and Irrigation, incorporating the Rural Water Development Corporation (RWDC) but separating "water" from "rural development," with the former retaining corporate status and the latter becoming a department within the ministry. Subsequent reorganizations within the ministry were so frequently mooted that the extent to which they took place is unclear, but rural water planning effectively ended. This disconnection was made formal in 1983 when the RWDC was shunted to the Ministry of Energy and Mineral Resources, apparently to bring all issues of drinking water under one minister. By then, the whole system of the Soil Conservation, Land Use, and Rural Water Programming Administration had collapsed. The collection and collation of data had lapsed, records ceased, and business was conducted orally.

Instances abound of the negative effects in Darfur of these rearrangements, of the turf wars and careerism – and technical issues – behind them, and the partly consequent alliances that bureaucrats, politicians, and experts formed with Sudanese and foreign businesses and aid agencies. In effect, this amounted to the "politics of water," the history of which has yet to be written but which is doubtless as dirty as – if less glamorous than – that of Southern California. (A good example is of the Suq al-Naʿam project in northern Darfur, championed by Mam'un Muhammady in his home province when he was director general of the Rural Water Development Corporation.) Local bigwigs had an obvious stake in providing boreholes or *hafirs*; foreign companies drilled the former and sold machinery for the latter, which local companies built. Central government officials had political and personal incentives to accept any foreign-financed project they could get, so planning was skewed by the relative likelihood of aid, and prioritizing degenerated under the pressure to support conclusions with data. The result was not only haphazard, neglectful of long-term consequences, and biased against the neediest areas of Darfur and sections of its population, but it was also environmentally reckless. Poor situating of boreholes and lack of enforcement and controls led to rapid soil exhaustion around them.[14] In effect, provision of water created desert.

Although a global assessment of the costs and returns of development policy in Darfur since independence would be difficult, its relative insignificance is beyond doubt, and the uneven distribution of benefits clear. Development policy seemed to benefit most the developers; investment tended to be of the "enclave" type, by which tiny areas were selected without regard to social and economic context. Marketing of resulting products, if any, whether agricultural for export or manufactured for domestic sale, would fall to contractors who benefited from loans and subsidies, price fixing, and, even when the businesses failed, employment, patronage, and theft. In Zalingei, for example, a branch of the Agricultural Bank had opened in 1968 to make loans for local tobacco growing. As late as 1982, the area under tobacco – overseen by a Tobacco Bureau employing three university graduates, four technicians, and eleven extension workers – was less than 100 acres; the product was too poor for export, and fuel shortages and transport problems made it too expensive for sale on the open market: the National Tobacco Corporation bought it at a loss. One reason for the failure of Suq al-Na'am was dependence on diesel-powered pumps, in an area where fuel delivery was expensive and unreliable. The Sudan Textile Industries Company built a weaving mill at Nyala, first sited on the wrong side of the *wadi* and, once operational, soon shuttered after failing to get regular supplies of yarn (by rail from Sinnar) and fuel (from Port Sudan). Technicians for such schemes had to be brought in from the East, keeping them was always a problem, and there were numerous cases of project failure for lack of staff.[15] These problems had all been predicted.

A recurrent theme, as in the 1920s and 1930s, was the difficulty and cost of transport. By the end of the Nimayri era, Darfur was still unconnected to the East by good all-weather roads. A plan for a new road from Zalingei to Nyala (and thus to railhead), financed mainly by Saudi Arabia and West Germany, was adopted in 1976, but construction did not begin until 1980. By then, the railways, a financial black hole but still the main bulk carrier, were in a state of collapse; investment in plant and equipment had failed, and without spare parts the system resorted to cannibalism. Schedules were meaningless, by a factor of days and weeks. Strike-plagued, corrupt, and riddled with nepotism, absenteeism, low wages, and poor working conditions, the system almost ground to a halt. For Darfur, there was a chicken-and-egg aspect to the problem: rail rates were much lower from Nyala to Khartoum than vice versa because the province imported much more than it produced for export. Even so, tough independent truckers provided better service, and yet another government scheme, inevitably financed mainly through foreign aid, produced the South Darfur Transport Company.[16]

The 1973 Famine in Darfur and Its Effects

Even worse than the drought of 1973 were its implications. Not only has annual average rainfall in Darfur declined since records began in 1916 (at El Fasher by 2.1 mm per annum; at Nyala, since 1920, by 3 mm per annum; and at El Geneina, since the late 1920s, by 3.7 mm per annum), but the rainy season has also shortened and the patterns of rainfall have changed. This has been the primary cause of desertification in the western Sudan and across the whole savanna region, exacerbated by deforestation, the exhaustion of soil through overfarming, and overgrazing. The relative importance of these factors remains debatable but the long-term and worsening drought does not. The northernmost regions of Darfur, where human existence had already been most precarious, suffered first and most but ironically may thereby have been inoculated against the disastrous drought of 1983. Most Zaghawa migrated and did not return; those who remained abandoned villages where the wells dried up, clustered in larger settlements, and gradually shifted their animal husbandry from cattle to camels. Elsewhere in the province, the effects of the 1973 drought were discernible in infant mortality rates and increased grain prices. But Darfur still had the wherewithal to support more people even as drought ravaged the western and central Sahel, and in fact food shortages and higher prices in Darfur were in part a result of mass migration of Chadian refugees *into* the Sudan.[17]

Far more serious were the results of internal migration. In the wake of the 1973 drought this increased and, most significantly, did not reverse. As elsewhere, growth of both the human and animal populations and increasing aridity caused and correlated with further degradation of soil, decline in average agricultural yields, destruction of trees and scrub, and disappearance of perennial grasses. People moved south to escape the drought and began to settle in large numbers on land to which Fur and Birgid farmers held customary title since the days of the *hakura*

system. Those rights had been largely communal: very little land outside towns was registered at all, and the system had accommodated
transient populations and emergencies with what amounted to rent, or
even to symbolic recognition of the right to collect it; individuals or
small groups could be and were accommodated. This led to a process
of assimilation that extended even to linguistic and ethnic identity and
occurred in both directions, with, for example, Fur farmers acquiring
cattle and "becoming" Baqqara just as Baqqara settled and "became"
Fur.[18] Annual or occasional arrival of larger tribal groups for dry-
season grazing, although inherently problematic, never involved rights
to the land, let alone the carving out of tribal *dars*, and modus vivendi
evolved.

With the long-term drought and especially after 1973, however,
migration was massive and permanent. Migrants, although needy, were
under no pressure to assimilate and were conscious of their power
of numbers and access to government. Their very success – like that
of immigrants anywhere – could cause problems as, for example, in
Nyala, where local shop owners resented industrious Zaghawa: in local
elections in 1977, immigrants turned out in record numbers and won
almost all the seats, and slum dwellers ousted local worthies from the
town council.[19] Much more seriously, Khartoum had in 1970 asserted
ownership to all unregistered land, technically nullifying the traditional
basis on which most land in Darfur was claimed, a system that had
survived even the effective reservation to individuals or clans of land
planted with fruit trees and thus subject to continuous long-term care
and investment.

At the same time that new landless – we might say *dar*-less – tribal
groups were entering territory already fully claimed, changes in local
practice put new restrictions on it. Although market gardening long
predated the colonial era, development plans of the postwar era built
on earlier, ad hoc experiments to encourage horticultural diversity.
This required considerable investment, which was one factor in the
tendency to assign heritable rights to the land in question: who plants
and tends apple trees for passersby? The influx of drought-driven settlers
into southern Darfur resulted in overgrazing and thus in pressure on
water supplies and degradation of the land; mechanization has perhaps
been exaggerated as a factor in the extent of land degradation because
it applied to a relatively small area. Another related factor was the

increasing practice of enclosure,[20] by which lands were fenced off to protect cultivations or pasture from the depredations of others' (and, indeed, one's own) animals. Similarly, in the *wadi* beds, where much cultivation took place, farmers restricted access to herdsmen whose cattle, going down to water, would eat and trample the plants.

The upshot was ever-increasing scope for conflict between haves and have-nots, between sedentary and migrant populations, and between natives and – whether from elsewhere in the Sudan or from Chad – foreigners. That the international border did not correspond to ethnic boundaries explained seasonal migration but was not the salient feature in settlement: the continuing upheavals in Chad drove people out and kept them from returning; Gura'an, Bidayyat, and other pastoralists, whose homelands straddled the border in any case, came in large numbers. These therefore shared with internal migrants and others in Darfur age-old exclusion from rights to – and increasingly from use of – the land, rights that, long-standing and reified in the Native Administrations of the colonial regime and its successor, conferred political status. They had arrived too late to carve out *dars* – or had they? Tribal fighting in the 1980s took on elements of "ethnic cleansing" not because of a sweeping new ideology of Arabism but because the only way to establish a right to land was literally to occupy it. This in turn meant driving off the current inhabitants and, by destroying everything of value – villages, property, orchards – making it pointless for them to return.

Thus, the confrontation between pastoralists with their herds and farmers with their crops and orchards was not wholly unlike "range wars" in the nineteenth-century American West or conflicts between farmers and pastoralists elsewhere since time immemorial. But there were important differences, and these grew more pronounced with time, as each side sought to justify its actions and increase its appeal both locally and externally.

Darfur and the Libyan War in Chad

After the failure of the Libyan-backed Mahdist coup in July 1976, Nimayri decided to make the enemy of his enemy his friend and so to repair relations with Chad under its new president, Felix Malloum.[21] In September 1977, Nimayri presided over a conference in Khartoum at which Malloum made peace with his chief rival, Hissene Habre, in a new coalition government that would take on the FROLINAT rebels and their Libyan sponsor. But that government, its successors, and Chad continued to be rent by the conflicting ambitions of these and other would-be strongmen. Low-grade warfare, punctuated by spectacular desert battles, continued in the north between French-backed Chadian government loyalists and Libyan and Libyan-sponsored rebels. In 1980 Libya signed a treaty of amity with the hard-pressed Chadian president, Oueddi Goukouni, which permitted Libyan intervention as needed. This was duly followed by a full-scale invasion of Chad, to eliminate Hissene Habre, who fled, and the proclamation in January 1981 of an improbable union of the two countries.

The advent of Libya on the long western border of Darfur understandably alarmed the Sudanese regime. While a march to the Nile from faraway Darfur was hardly more likely than it had been in the days of Ali Dinar, Colonel Gaddafi had other ways of causing trouble. At the end of 1980, thousands of Hissene Habre's Northern Army Force (FAN), along with thousands of civilian refugees, had settled across the border in Darfur, where they were rearmed by Egypt, thus making even trumped-up incidents plausible. Evidence was adduced of Libya's arming the Zaghawa on the Chad side of the border and of welcoming Sudanese into the so-called Islamic Legion. The leading role in opposition to Libya had passed from France to the United States, which coordinated its efforts with Egypt and Chad's African neighbors, who were united against Libya's maladroit attempts to subvert them. Egypt offered unconditional support for Nimayri's regime. By 1981 it therefore appeared likely that the next front in Libya's confrontation with the world would be in Darfur.

That began when Habre's rebels began cross-border raids deep into Chad. The Libyans sent in reinforcements and, in September 1981, began aerial assaults along and across the border. The assassination in October of Anwar Sadat, the Egyptian president, although never linked to Libya, was followed by a crackdown in Egypt and the Sudan on Libyan agents and activities and support for a new anti-Gaddafi political movement in exile. Under international pressure and with promises of Western support, President Goukouni publicly ordered the withdrawal of Libyan forces from central Chad to the Aozou border. To fill the vacuum, the Organization of African Unity (OAU), with the support of France and the United States, sent a peacekeeping force to

Ndjamena, where it protected Goukouni's government against Habre's forces moving westward from Wadai. In June 1982, Goukouni fled the country, FAN troops occupied Ndjamena, and the OAU peacekeepers evacuated Chad. The new Chadian government, under Habre as president, was dominated by northern Muslims. But the Libyan regime, in the face of open hostility from much of Africa, continued to interfere in Chad by supporting exiles opposed to him.[22]

Notable among these was *Shaykh* Ibn Umar Sa'id, a protégé of Goukouni and leader of the so-called Burkan ("Volcano") Brigade of bedouin fighters and its political arm, the Democratic Revolutionary Council. Ibn Umar set up camp at Anjikuti near the Sudanese border town of Foro Baranga, where thousands of Chadian Arab refugees were already eking out a miserable existence, and soon made his presence felt by dispossessing Fur villagers. Driven out by Chadian forces in cross-border raids, Ibn Umar established a new base near Kutum, in alliance with the Libyan Islamic Legion, until driven from there too. His subsequent on-again, off-again relations with Libya were more than a marriage of convenience, however, for Ibn Umar was receptive to, if indeed he had not already espoused, a racist, pan-Arab ideology that accommodated Gaddafi's imperial ambitions and would prove disastrous later in Darfur.[23]

The congenital weakness of the Chadian state, not Libya's imperialism, remained the central problem. Both the new Chadian government and its opponents continued to seek support from across the border in Darfur. Sudanese of various political stripes and tribal loyalties enrolled into one or another of the Libyan special forces or Goukouni's ragtag army, which was trying to turn the tables on Habre in Ndjamena, while Habre's own loyalists recruited from among the Zaghawa on both sides of the border. In February 1983, a Libyan-backed coup attempt against Nimayri, easily foiled, provided the pretext for increased U.S. military support to the Khartoum regime and to Habre in Chad. Another such plot, this time to occupy and detach Darfur, was purportedly uncovered in November, possibly in aid of Nimayri's relations with the United States. A bizarre incident in March 1984, when a single Libyan plane bombed Omdurman, was enough to confirm Gaddafi's mania and the United States' knee-jerk support for Nimayri. But in Chad, stalemate was unofficially recognized by the so-called Red Line that left Libyan and Libyan-backed rebels in control to the north, while Habre's government solidified its hold on the south. In late 1983, the context of the struggle changed with the onset of drought and famine.

NIMAYRI CONTRA MUNDUM

"National Reconciliation"

Having survived the 1976 coup and engineered National Reconciliation – the expansive term for a deal with al-Sadiq al-Mahdi – in 1977, Nimayri seemed again to control the Sudanese political scene. Al-Sadiq was soon reduced to ineffectual philosophizing, as his erstwhile cohorts in exile denounced him and the regime at academic conferences. The Addis Ababa Agreement had ended the civil war in the south, and through deft maneuvers, often with the connivance of southern politicians, Nimayri manipulated the fledgling regional government for his own ends. The mountain of debt that a failed development policy and massive corruption would create for the Sudan was still on the horizon. The Cold War continued to make the Sudan worth courting, and Gaddafi's schemes, generally ineffective in achieving his own ends, were godsends to neighboring regimes in search of U.S. support; Nimayri took whatever aid he could get, and for a receptive American audience, any evidence of domestic dissent was blamed on Libyan agitation. Educated Sudanese declared that things were "worse than ever"; many left for the Gulf states and elsewhere, but many joined what they could not beat: when asked why he had accepted a ministerial position, a longtime opponent of the regime said: "my wife needed a refrigerator."[24]

It was lonely at the top. Nimayri's incentive in National Reconciliation had been to domesticate the religious opposition that had come close to toppling him, and in doing so he set in motion the forces that would eventually combine to bring him down. For the coup of 1976 made it obvious that no Khartoum regime could depend on a strategic alliance with deracinated northern secularists and politicians of the Southern Region: not only was this an inadequate basis for rule, it was also a cause for dissent. Nimayri knew that turning against the south would be popular in the north: trading one regional or interest group for another was a tactic; the strategy was to buy time.

Thus, the price for Reconciliation was reorientation of the regime's policy to reflect (or mimic) the expressed views of the religious right, where the celebrity of al-Sadiq al-Mahdi tended to overshadow a formidable rival, Hasan al-Turabi. A constitutional lawyer and lecturer, he had taken a leading role in the demise of the Abboud regime in 1964; as leader of the local Muslim Brotherhood (*al-ikhwan al-muslimun*), he organized the Islamic Charter Front (ICF) of the non-Umma religious right, and in the 1965 parliamentary elections he won one of the ICF's surprisingly high total of eleven seats, presumably with the support of Khatmiyya voters whose party (the PDP) boycotted the election. In parliament, al-Turabi espoused many of the goals of the Umma, including an Islamic constitution, and used that common ground to engineer proscription of the Communist Party. In the wake of the May 1969 Revolution, with its leftist orientation, the Muslim Brothers were suppressed, only to reemerge, in the mid-1970s, in tactical, mutually wary alliance with Nimayri.[25]

That this alliance lasted as long as it did and succeeded in keeping the reins of government in Nimayri's hands was partly the result of its disastrous economic policies, which by the last days of the regime had degenerated to kleptocracy and bankrupted the country. These had kept the army loyal, through lavish perquisites and increasingly formal involvement in state economic enterprises (largely via a Military Economic Board and the subsidiary corporations and private companies that had been nationalized).[26] Statistics from the period are copious and unreliable in every sphere, but trends are clear enough. Apologists touted a statistical decrease in reliance on agriculture; they seldom mentioned the reason, huge growth of an unproductive "service" sector, accounted for by the payrolls of the government, SSU, various quasi-government corporations and by such shadow entities as new "universities" (each with an office in the capital and a vice-chancellor, but no campus, faculty, or students), advisory councils, research institutes, and the like. Far from becoming the breadbasket of the Middle East, the Sudan witnessed a decline in agricultural production. For all the rhetoric about productive development, the major agricultural and agro-industrial schemes of the period had by the early 1980s all either failed or fallen short of projected returns.

This led to a perfect storm in national finance. Agricultural exports, always at the mercy of external demand, fell almost continuously: cotton, which in the 1970s still accounted for about half the value of the Sudan's exports, made up only 17.5 percent in 1981–82 but 50 percent again two years later. Mismanagement, poor maintenance, shortages of spare parts, fuel costs, bottlenecks because of railway and port problems, corruption, and finally drought cut production and increased wastage. As foreign earnings fell, all of these problems grew worse because of a lack of money to deal with them. Demand for imports remained high, however, because the country manufactured almost nothing that the elite modern sector wished to buy and little even of the inputs essential to keep agro-business functioning; remittances from abroad kept relatives solvent. Official foreign debt skyrocketed, and with it the government's room to maneuver contracted; because corruption kept it in power, prescriptions of the international agencies and foreign governments were especially unpalatable. The currency was repeatedly devalued, and foreign debt repeatedly restructured. Arrival in the capital of motor fuel was newsworthy; office workers – admittedly with nothing else to do – left work early to scour the shops for bread; the black market was an urban safety valve, a well-oiled regulator of the real economy, supplying everything from hard currency to hard liquor.

Declining national circumstances affected several areas of Darfur's agriculture, little of which admittedly was destined for export. The groundnut (peanut) industry in the southeast was a case in point. In the 1970s, an increasing price of fuel and hence of trucking, railway problems exacerbated by labor unrest, and rising costs of credit contributed to making the local crop less profitable at the same time that local grain prices were rising and cheap imported cooking oil competed in the local market. The export of gum declined in part because the cost of getting it to market made collection unworthwhile. Transport was also responsible for sharp increases in the prices of imports to the province, not only of food when need arose but of everything else as well. The case is persuasive, however, that global statistics obscure rather than illustrate the real effects in Darfur of the national economic decline because market mechanisms worked as they always had in shifting production from one crop to another and labor from one place to another.[27]

"Reconciliation" was not "national" but northern Islamist and was achieved by sacrificing the hard-won peace in the south. Nimayri had often invoked Islam when it suited him, but beginning in 1977 he had to give the Islamists something to show for their support. He appointed Muslim Brothers to positions in the government and SSU; Hasan al-Turabi became attorney-general, and a committee was set up to bring the country's laws into conformity with the *Shari'a*. Islamic banks were chartered. In 1980 a book published under Nimayri's name, *Al-Nahjj al-islami limatha? (The Islamic Way: Why?)*,[28] argued the need for Islamizing Sudanese society. (Both it and its sequel, *The Islamic Way: How?*, were best-sellers.) That these and other steps were vapid and temporizing was obvious, but the Muslim Brothers used the time thus bought – at a cost of others' disgust – to infiltrate further the army and civil service.

It was only in September 1983 that Nimayri, on the ropes, finally decreed application of the *Shari'a* in the Sudan. Citing rising crime statistics, he presided over a "festival of the destruction of alcohol" (the date of which would thereafter be yet another national holiday) and paradoxically declared an amnesty for 13,000 prison inmates.[29] By then, the beginnings of the second civil war were already evident in the south, in reaction to his abrogation of the 1972 agreement that had set up an autonomous regime there. This he had accomplished through a variety of means – not least the ineptitude and venality of southern politicians – but of most concern in the present context was the so-called policy of decentralization, by which the south was "redivided."

Darfur Becomes a "Region"

In 1980, the constitution was amended to allow reorganization of the northern Sudan into five "regions": North, East, Central, Kordofan, and Darfur. Khartoum would have its own administration; disputes over border areas between north and south were all resolved in favor of the north. An earlier plan, by which Darfur would have been amalgamated with Kordofan as the "region" of western Sudan – with its capital at Babanusa – was shelved after an almost unprecedented refusal of Darfur delegates to the SSU to go along with it.[30]

Under the consequent Regional Government Act, the case of Darfur is easy to consider because it involved no amalgamation or distribution of territory or people. In effect, the old province became the new region, with corresponding changes in titles of personnel; there was neither a theoretical alteration of sovereignty, as a nominally federal system would involve, nor a reshuffling of powers that had accrued to the provinces under the old system. A Darfur Regional Assembly, some of whose members would be elected directly, some indirectly through "popular organizations," had legislative powers, all of which could be overridden by the executive, now restyled governor. He (unlike the southern regional leader) would in turn be appointed by the president from among three nominees of a joint meeting of the Regional Assembly and Regional Conference of the SSU. He could be removed at any time by the president, who also appointed the regional council of ministers. When all was said and done, the new Regional Government of Darfur was a gussied-up version of the Anglo-Egyptian provincial system of 1944, replete with a governor and advisory council. Thus, "regional-ization" was recentralization with, as always, a proliferation of offices and explosion of expense.

Worse, the new system required amendment – yet again – of local government. This was nominally achieved in 1981, when Darfur's Exec-utive Council was replaced by elected area councils little different from those under the colonial-era Local Government Ordinance. The new councils had a wide variety of responsibilities, impressive on paper but meaningless without money; Darfur Region would continue to rely on Khartoum for grants-in-aid of its budget, which in turn would dole out money to local authorities. The new budget process, however, included no statutory criteria for deciding the level of subsidy for regional bud-gets, which – whether or not this was intended – resulted in protracted negotiation between Darfur and Khartoum and in greater scope for ad hoc decision making, favoritism, and corruption. Nor did approval of a regional budget, and its level of subsidy, necessarily result in allocation of funds; severe underfunding was congenital.

Nimayri's well-known wit may account for his declaration, in 1982, of 1 July as the first annual Decentralization Day. More sobering was a plan to replace various taxes with the Islamic *zakat*, supposedly to increase revenue, which, by law, must be spent in the region where it was collected. This was a grim prospect for impoverished Darfur, but because much of the government's current revenue was from regressive indirect taxation, the poor might have benefited. In any case, the result, as government finances lurched from crisis to crisis and the currency collapsed, was chaotic only when viewed by management consultants; at the local level, the ever-changing theoretical basis for community relations counted for little.

"Regionalization" had unintended consequences in Darfur. Nimayri's lip service to local empowerment was revealed by his appointment in November 1980, as governor of the region, of a Kordofani, al-Tayyib al-Mardi. The tiny educated elite of Darfur rebelled, demanding that devolution involve an actual transfer of power to natives of Darfur. In El Fasher and other centers, demonstrations occurred, in which the Muslim Brothers played a prominent role; the police were called in, and as many as twenty people were killed in rioting. In Khartoum, the Darfur Students Association petitioned Nimayri. The results of what came to be called the *intifada*, a term loaded by association with the Palestinian effort to "shake off" Israeli rule, were far-reaching. These included most notably the election as governor of Ahmad Ibrahim Diraige, the first Fur since Ali Dinar to preside in Darfur. But his accession and the appointment of other locals to the regional government that followed presented problems similar to those encountered by the government of the Southern Region: relations with the center were strained, or collapsed altogether, and intraregional tensions accentuated.

Whether because of such tensions or simply as a result of the abdication of responsibility that attended "regionalization," coordination between Khartoum and Darfur continued to deteriorate. The central-government establishment concentrated its interest on the capital region, whose volatile mix of relatives, Islamists, capitalists, foreigners, students, the educated and political class, and growing hordes of penniless slum dwellers required constant attention. Functions obviously requiring coordination, in fact those most important to the poor marginalized areas, theoretically "devolved" to – in effect were dumped on – the "regions." Thus, in water-resource planning and construction, Khartoum retained a huge and idle bureaucracy and responsibility for "national projects" and acted as middleman for supplying staff and equipment – a recipe for buck-passing and corruption. At the regional level, endemic shortages – of money, personnel, and equipment – partly obscured the process for prioritizing, providing, and maintaining water points, which, although no doubt always partly political, was wholly now so.[31]

Diraige, a Fur, and his deputy, Mahmud Bashir Jamma, a Zaghawa, ironically epitomized the dangers inherent in nominal home rule. Party politics in Darfur had been exceedingly weak and ideologically vacuous; the Umma's hold on the region was sectarian and did not depend on its policies. With the dissolution of parties under the May Regime, entry into government depended on membership of the SSU, which, however, was never known to deny it. Although everyone in the new regional government belonged to the SSU, most were at least loosely identified with the Umma. Although supporters of the *intifada*, styled "upheavalists," derided opponents, whatever their motives, as *kilab al-layl* ("dogs of the night"), the real divide, once a government was formed, was ethnic: the Fur were on one side and the Zaghawa and Arab tribes on the other. Government policy and its implementation, not unnaturally, were judged by who benefited, with the result that the Fur sense of entitlement that had bred (and been enhanced by) the revolt came to be seen or depicted as a restoration. The scope for manipulation of old tensions in the prevailing circumstances of economic decline and administrative confusion was immense, even without Chadian complications, drought, and famine.

Nimayri Declares War on the South

With "regionalization" of the north complete, Nimayri turned his attention to "redivision" of the south. In carrying this out, he had the cynical support of northern Islamists, Arab nationalists, jealous office seekers, and an indeterminate but substantial number of opponents of "special treatment" for southerners; crucially, he also had the support of southerners, mainly Equatorians, whose heterogeneity had made them subject to the majority rule of the much larger Nilotic peoples, especially the populous Dinka. In thus destroying the regime created by the Addis Ababa Agreement, Nimayri was not only appealing to the Islamist gallery, he was also re-insuring Khartoum's control of the south's newfound oil reserves. Nimayri played so well on intraregional ethnic tensions that even widespread recognition by southerners of what he was doing, and why, could not bring them to settle their own differences. In June 1983 he duly decreed division of the south into three "regions" corresponding to the old provinces of Bahr al-Ghazal, Equatoria, and Upper Nile, each now having the same status as the five northern regions, whose experience was adduced as a reason for such further "decentralization."

The year 1983 was a watershed. An army mutiny at Bor in the Upper Nile in May produced the nucleus of what would become the Sudan

People's Liberation Movement and Army; within months, open war broke out. The redivision decree abrogated the Addis Ababa Agreement and the constitutional and statutory elements that had ensued from it; where central control continued in the south, it was wholly discredited. And by what would thereafter be called the "September Laws," Nimayri decreed the *Shari'a*, or particular parts of it, to be the law of the land, completing the alienation of the south and his alliance with the Islamists. The effects of this were felt mainly in the capital region, where in 1984 a virtual reign of terror was imposed to cow an urban population on the brink of revolt over prices, shortages, and devaluations.

In April 1984 Nimayri therefore declared a State of Emergency, citing the recent one-plane Libyan air raid on Omdurman, strikes, enemies of *shari'a*, alcohol smugglers, old political parties, black marketeers, and others. He set up special "courts of decisive justice," with Islamist adepts presiding, to dispense instant judgments that included floggings and amputations. At an international conference marking the anniversary of his *shar'ia* declaration, which attracted the leader of the Afghan *mujahidin* and Muhammad Ali, the American boxer, Nimayri equated his state of emergency with the Prophet Muhammad's triumphal return from Medinan exile to Mecca. A show trial of Mahmud Muhammad Taha, the aged leader of the tiny pacifist Republican Brothers, on charges of heresy ended in his public execution. The usual suspects were rounded up, including al-Sadiq al-Mahdi and, finally, in early 1985, even the leaders of the Muslim Brothers. These and other outrages – some with an "Islamic" veneer, others in the name of security – were all obvious tactics in the regime's strategy of simply holding on. But by the time the capital reached the boiling point – and finally brought down Nimayri in April 1985 – it was too late for Darfur.[32]

THE DROUGHT AND FAMINE OF 1984–1985

Darfur's disaster was a local chapter in a trans-African catastrophe. For a long time, the drought in the eastern Sudan, and indeed in other countries, received much more attention than Darfur did, for several reasons. Certainly the effects of drought and crop failure were serious in the east: in 1985, the number affected in the Sudan as a whole was estimated at about 8.5 million, about a third of whom were in Darfur;

the absolute number for Kordofan, for what it is worth, was actually higher, at 2.87 million people.[33] But the most important reason for the suffering, and its neglect, was the Nimayri regime's denial of any crisis at all: to admit one would be to agree with the all-but-universal verdict that the regime was incompetent and corrupt. When huge camps sprang up around the capital, the government tried to depict the denizens as vagabonds. Eventually, the infamous *kasha* – a campaign to demolish the camps and force out the squatters – was instituted.[34] Foreign food aid was sneered at as patronizing, an excuse for interference, and a veil for conspiracies to bring down the regime.

Even what has been called "disaster tourism"[35] – the touching down at, photographing in front of, then disappearing from camps of destitute Africans – ironically played into the regime's hands by increasing the price in foreign aid of Sudanese political compliance and providing a basis for touting yet more "development plans"; Nimayri's facilitating the evacuation to Israel of the "Falashas" (Ethiopian Jews) was not coincidental. As the camps filled up with migrants, so Khartoum and accessible camps with desert scenery filled up with disaster tourists – the U.S. vice president and an enormous entourage among them – and with "aid officials," who had a perverse effect on the local economy and skewed priorities. A visitor to the capital, upon admiring a foreign hostess's heavy silver bracelets, was told that the best place to buy them cheaply was outside Omdurman, where women sold their jewelry for food; the black market was supplied in part from foreigners' commissaries.

The process by which the world awoke to the crisis in Darfur is itself fascinating, almost a case study in the relation of modern mass media and democratic governments' responsiveness to events. Khartoum did not officially admit the disaster until much of Darfur was in extremis, and its conduct then and thereafter has in retrospect been seen as heralding events in Darfur since 2000.

We have already noted the recognition of the related problems of aridity, deforestation, overgrazing, soil exhaustion, and desertification. Even had the prescriptions made in the 1940s been followed, the objective decline in average annual rainfall would have worsened Darfur's plight. But they were not. And the Nimayri regime, totalitarian but feckless, had neither interest in the region and its problems nor the discipline required to deal with these. Its focus was not on a province that fed itself but on those to the east, Kordofan included, that were meant to feed the Arab world. Desertification was well recognized but there was no political imperative to deal with it. Laws were not enforced, regulations were ignored, money was squandered or stolen. So many plans and programs, conferences and committees owed their well-funded existence to the problem that we suspect these were an end in themselves: the bureaucratization of desertification, a fitting adjunct to disaster tourism and one that ultimately must be followed by depopulation.

By 1983, when a census estimated Darfur's population at 3.25 million, the process of environmental degradation had thus been long under way. The demand for potable water had increased as its apparent supply declined and as herd sizes also continued to grow. The result was a cycle of overgrazing, deforestation, and soil exhaustion. As early as 1977 a visiting expert noted serious degradation in the Wadi Azum basin owing to overgrazing (largely by herds of migrants from the desiccated north) and consequent erosion and deterioration even in Jabal Marra. In the thorn lands and savanna, the annual grass fires that had characterized the region diminished because overgrazing and drought had killed the grass.[36] During Ahmad Diraige's governorship (1981–83), a reaction finally set in, and the Fur demanded wholesale removal of these "displaced aliens." In this they failed, but by raising the ante they pushed the Zaghawa into alliance with the local Arabs. The regional government, by resorting to collective punishment and exemplary justice, confirmed its opponents' suspicion of its own bias.[37]

The Sahelian famine of 1973 had only a minimal impact in Darfur.[38] But the impression was left, in Khartoum as much as in the outside world, that the rains had failed with equally devastating effect right across Africa, from the Atlantic to Ethiopia. That impression reinforced the notion in 1984–85 that drought and desertification were not only a long-term problem but were mostly or even entirely the result of human activity – not of heavy industrial progenitors of global warming but rather primitive and shortsighted overfarming of poor soil, overgrazing, deforestation for fuel or agriculture, ignorant expansion of herds, and spiraling human population growth.[39] Data referred to earlier indicate a long-term decline in average annual rainfall, beginning long before any of these factors can have made a difference and from a base point when Darfur had been severely depopulated (1916). Lack of rain, then, was the cause of the disaster. But not for the first time, a government would seem to have brought down the wrath of God in the form of drought: the great drought and famine of 1913–14, the disaster most comparable in severity to that of 1984–85, preceded the fall of Ali Dinar; admittedly within a downward trend line, rainfall statistics show a nadir in 1969 and a spike in 1985, coinciding exactly with the tenure of the Nimayri regime.

The historian of the Darfur famine of 1984–85 has produced a wealth of statistics, perhaps the most salient of which for our purposes is an estimate of "excess deaths," or deaths attributable to the famine: 108,000. This was terrible, but Western estimates of the number at risk of starvation had been in the millions.[40] The drought was worst in the northern part of the province: in 1983–84 northern Darfur met only 18 percent of its need for grain locally, whereas in 1983 southern Darfur met 90 percent and in 1984 less than 60 percent. What made 1985 so bad was failure of the harvest two years in a row and failure of the national grain supply at the same time: Darfur's farmers normally stored a year's worth of grain against emergencies, but when the 1984 crop failed, there was little or no reserve, and only about 3.5 percent of farmers had any surplus. The Sudan as a whole, and its mechanized sector in particular, which was geared to the market rather than farmers' own use, witnessed huge declines, resulting in the disappearance of *dura* in the Nile towns and the need to resort to imported wheat. In El Fasher, on the other hand, the price of grain increased fivefold between 1983 and 1985. Because of the countrywide shortage and collapse of transport, little or no Sudanese grain reached market in Darfur.

The result was mass migration, mostly from north to south, from areas where the drought and resulting crop failures were greatest to those where they were less. There was also considerable migration south-southeastward, into the Bahr al-Ghazal, Kordofan, the Nuba Mountains, the Central Province, and even to the Nile. Lack of water to drink was in some cases as much a factor in the decision to move as lack of food. In the early phases of the disaster, meat was more affordable than usual because pastoralists were more willing to eat it themselves in the absence of grain or were more willing to sell animals that were going to die anyway while they could still get a price. As much as half the province's livestock died off during the famine, and another 20 percent was sold – sometimes, because of the shortage of cash, to middlemen for resale or even export. But the most important factor in human survival was the availability of wild food, which people began to store as soon as (or before) it became clear that the crops would fail. Grain became, in effect, seasoning for grass and wild rice, and when various fruits, seeds, leaves, and berries, especially *mukheit*, gave out, people resorted to roots and bark and insects. Arcane knowledge became valuable: the traveling hungry might pass up edible grasses, and there were cases of ignorance resulting in death from poisoning.

The drought and famine had an important effect on labor and income in Darfur. Because most land in Darfur remained unregistered, people could not sell it even if they had been willing to do so. And although there was always a market for draft animals, keeping them if at all possible was a high priority because a donkey increased one's earning power as a porter. Only as a last resort did people eat grain seed because even at the nadir of the famine, all planned for the next planting; people even hid next year's seed before heading off to look for work or food elsewhere.[41]

As we have seen, migratory labor has long been a factor in Darfur's economy. In addition to much-publicized migration to the Nile of agricultural workers, only some of whom had also religious motives, whose stays there were measured in years (and whose remittances during the famine appear to have had only a small effect), there has been seasonal migration within Darfur for wage labor in clearing land, planting, weeding, harvesting, threshing, and the hard labor of digging wells. During the 1984–85 dry season, wages in some places fell to little more than half the cost of a meal, with utter destitution as a result. Many people were forced into any occupation, however lowly, that might keep them alive: gathering and selling firewood, carrying water, various crafts, odd jobs, and, finally, begging. In some areas, they competed with a large influx of Chadian refugees, which lowered even further the starvation wages; some Chadians passed right through to Kordofan and beyond. The poor were also at a disadvantage when it came to selling off their animals because they did so only as a last resort, at the height of the famine, when only middlemen had money.

Detailed study of the famine produced some surprising results. Contrary to collective wisdom, death rates during the famine did not correlate with income. Based on government data and case studies involving reasonable assumptions, the death rate for 1985 was perhaps three times normal. Mortality was higher among men than women and highest among children between ages one and four years, a group that accounted for more than half the excess deaths. The fact that the destitute tended to die at no greater overall rate than the better off has been attributed to location – rather perhaps as it might be during an epidemic: sanitary conditions, water supply, prevalence of childhood diseases, and availability of relief supplies and medical aid all mattered more than degree of destitution. And, of course, as in most famines, the direct cause of death was rarely starvation but rather disease – diarrhea, malaria, measles, and other illnesses, much of which was attributable to poor water, increased exposure owing to the migration and congregation of large numbers of people, and insufficient medical attention.

Only in major towns of Darfur had the notion of "government" reached the point where people expected food aid, meaning grain supplies at subsidized prices. The Darfur Regional Government began distributions in late 1983, but these did not keep pace with demand because of insufficient supplies, poor transport, and the lack of help from Khartoum; most of the food was sold in the towns. The Nimayri regime not only devoted inadequate resources to the crisis but, to hide it, also hampered investigations. When at one point the United Nations estimated that Darfur needed 39,000 tons of grain, the Sudanese government insisted on a much-reduced figure, then released even less. Diraige, the governor, a native of Zalingei and one of the few high-ranking members of the regime with any local credibility, denounced Nimayri in December and left the country. For his part, Nimayri blamed the regional government for not telling him about the famine![42]

International agencies eventually bypassed both central government and local officials. Between September 1984 and December 1985, some 97,000 tons of sorghum were delivered to Darfur by foreign and international agencies, most notably USAID (U.S. Agency for International Development). Distribution was uneven because of widely varying local conditions, and some areas, notably Dar Masalit, were inaccessible at times of greatest need. As always, the unreliability of transport from the east – and the corruption that resulted from officials' and companies' ability to blame that unreliability for everything that went wrong – was a major factor in delay. The German state of Lower Saxony went so far as to ship food overland from the Atlantic coast of Cameroon through Chad.[43]

The war in Chad made the famine in Dar Masalit arguably worse than anywhere else in Darfur. By 1985 there were perhaps 120,000 Chadian refugees in Dar Masalit alone (and many others across Darfur), and by May the population of El Geneina had quadrupled to 250,000. At that point, a European Union Airbridge began supplying El Fasher, El Geneina, and Nyala and eventually grew to a dozen aircraft, some of which made three return trips a day from Khartoum.[44] At the worst point of the famine, during the rains of 1985, the roads were as usual impassable, and food aid could be transported only by helicopter. In scenes reminiscent of a medieval siege, food stores in El Geneina had to be guarded against beggars, and corpses were collected every day from the market. A survey found more than 90 percent of refugee children and more than 50 percent of local children were malnourished. Because of the refugee population, there was little day labor even of the meanest kind.

The squatter camps familiar in Western media images were mainly near large towns and thus most easily accessible for food aid, but camp life itself was so bad that mortality rates were likely higher there than in areas receiving little or no such aid. There were large camps at Manawashi (outside El Fasher), Damaya (Nyala), Hujerat (Buram), and Assernei (El Geneina), as well as many smaller ones (Tendelti, Mellit, Malha, and elsewhere). These were not "relief camps" where people came for handouts once food aid began to arrive but rather slums to which they had already been drawn because of even worse conditions – lack of water, no work – in their homelands. Food aid may have had a bigger cumulative effect by bringing down the price of grain elsewhere, decreasing the rate of indebtedness, and possibly reducing the need to sell animals. The conclusion, then, is that the impact of food aid, which may have accounted for about 22 percent of a year's normal consumption in Darfur, was one of many factors in mitigating the effects of the drought and famine. More effective than food aid would have been strategies that kept people from migrating or, if these failed, improved sanitation and basic health care where they were forced to go.

Finally, it can hardly be doubted that the central government's inaction contributed to the severity and length of the famine.[45] When it was finally forced to act, moreover, it did so in an almost ludicrous parody of itself: Nimayri declared Darfur a disaster area and assumed personal responsibility for dealing with the problem within three weeks. A National High Council for Drought and Desertification (with three subcommittees) and a Relief Information and Coordination Support Unit were established. In Darfur, a High Technical Permanent Committee for Combating Drought, Desertification, and Disasters – the euphonious HTPCCDDD – was chaired by the director-general of the Department of Regional Affairs and Administration, with a spokesman from the People's Relief Committee, which coordinated with the Food Aid National Administration, the government's main intermediary with USAID. The Desert Encroachment and Rehabilitation Program (DECARP) of the Ministry of Agriculture and Irrigation duly began preparing sixteen long-term projects for funding by agencies of the United Nations. It must be said, too, that the downfall of Nimayri actually made things worse, at least temporarily, because of its chaotic circumstances and the uncertainty that followed.[46]

THIRD TIME UNLUCKY

Darfur and the Restoration of Parliamentary Rule

NIMAYRIISM WITHOUT NIMAYRI

The overthrow of Jaafar Muhammad Nimayri in April 1985 bore similarities to the fall of the military regime in 1964. Within a context of economic collapse, political torpor, and civil war, demonstrations and strikes threatened general insurrection. But Nimayri's end came only when the Sudanese army, alarmed that it might share his fate, stepped in and, in a word heard frequently at the time, "hijacked" the revolution. Nimayri was en route to the Sudan from Washington when General Abd al-Rahman Muhammad Siwar al-Dahab, the army chief, announced the army's deference to "the wishes of the people." Amid general rejoicing, Nimayri went into exile in Egypt, and a Transitional Military Council (TMC) was set up to run the country. The institutions of the May Regime were abolished or allowed to lapse: the "Permanent Constitution" of 1973 was suspended, the SSU dissolved. But the September Laws establishing Nimayri's *shari'a* remained on the books (although largely unenforced), an aspect of what the Sudan People's Liberation Movement and Army (SPLM/SPLA) radio called "Nimayriism without Nimayri."

What followed was a resumption, more smoothly than in 1965, of party politics. The very fact that every political group in the country, from the communists to the Muslim Brothers, had at one time or another collaborated with Nimayri made a general housecleaning impossible.[1] As in 1964–65, moreover, the vanguard of "new forces," intellectuals and professionals who had played a major role in bringing down the regime, were afterward outmaneuvered by the old-style politicians. Thus, the National Alliance for National Salvation called for a three-year transition to full civilian rule, while its reforms were enacted and a constituency developed; the old parties wanted immediate elections. A caretaker cabinet representing various strands of opinion, parties, professionals, southern politicians, and others was duly formed under the TMC to prepare for elections.

These, contested by dozens of "parties," were held in April 1986. The results indicated little change from the time of the last free elections, in 1968. Al-Sadiq al-Mahdi, leader of the Umma, which emerged as the largest party in parliament with 100 seats (of 301), formed a coalition with the DUP (63 seats) and several smaller parties; the only real surprise was the showing of the National Islamic Front (NIF), now the party name of the Muslim Brothers, which won 51 seats, largely through the revival (with 28 seats) of the so-called graduates' constituency, and became the official opposition in parliament. Ahmad Uthman al-Mirghani became president of the five-man Supreme Council of State; the Mahdi and Mirghani families again ruled the roost. Had they, and the other politicians, learned anything during eighteen years as pawns of Nimayri? The problems they faced reduced to four, all of which had grown worse since 1968: the parlous state of the Sudanese economy, which had deteriorated into famine and bankruptcy; the nature of the Sudanese state, which in practical terms meant the constitutional status of Islam; the resumption of civil war in the south, which arguably reflected the failure of successive regimes to deal with the economic and constitutional issues; and the deterioration of security in Darfur.

Al-Sadiq al-Mahdi's restricted room to maneuver was evident in all spheres, not least foreign affairs. Nimayri had ended as an embarrassing client of the United States, and the TMC had already begun to swing the pendulum, notably in relations with Libya. But Libyan aid, even had it been dependable, could not provide the vast sums the Sudan needed; the United States remained the country's largest donor by far (more than $250 million in 1985 alone) and had many ways of bringing its influence to bear. The Sudan's beggar status, to which the war in the south, disastrous in other ways, contributed, and reciprocal interference across its international borders rendered an independent foreign policy impossible. Nationalists were fobbed off with international conferences, state visits, incantations about Arab unity, and the like. In this regard, Nimayri was an easy act to follow, but the audience was restless: a visit

Figure 16. Sayyid al-Sadiq al-Siddiq Abd al-Rahman al-Mahdi, prime minister of the Sudan 1966–67, 1986–89. As a stronghold of Mahdism, Darfur has been an important source of support for the Umma party, the political vehicle of the Mahdi family. (Durham University Library, 747/6/2.)

by Gaddafi, who, as the first foreign leader to arrive after Nimayri's ouster, called for Libyan union with the Sudan, caused eye-rolling in Cairo and foot-dragging in Washington.

Southern Exposure

The Southern Regional Government established under terms of the 1972 Addis Ababa Agreement and consequent constitutional and statutory frameworks had been creaky from the start, even before the machinations of Nimayri and various southern politicians. Some elements of the old Anya Nya guerrillas never accepted the settlement and remained in largely ineffectual exile in Ethiopian camps, where, owing to Nimayri's aid for Eritrean rebels, the regime of the Dergue gave them fitful support, later supplemented from Libya. As Nimayri's intentions grew clearer, others joined or took to the bush in the south. Thus the rebellion of a southern army unit at Bor in May 1983 was a symptom, not a cause, of the breakdown in the regional system. "Redivision" and the notorious September Laws removed any doubt that Khartoum had, in effect, already declared war on the south. But the organization that soon gained control of the new rebellion, the SPLM/SPLA, had as its insistently announced goal not secession of the south but rather overthrow of the Old Regime in Khartoum, whose victims included all marginalized peoples of the country, not least the impoverished Muslim west.

This message resonated with progressive groups in Khartoum. (The spectacle of "Arab" northerners listening to SPLM radio's clandestine broadcasts, as they did the BBC and VOA, for news, showed how deep the rot had gone.) But it was characteristic of the nature of Sudanese politics that, after Nimayri, many northern intellectuals expected the southern rebellion simply to end. "What does Garang *want?*" became a cliché that did no credit either to those of the northern cultural elite who asked it or to the southern Sudanese whose interests it reduced to personalities. The SPLM played no role in the transitional government of 1985–86 and boycotted the 1986 elections, which were not held in parts of the south for security reasons. After forming a government, al-Sadiq al-Mahdi met Garang in Addis Ababa in July 1986, but the Umma leader refused to repeal the September Laws and the talks foundered. With the NIF and even the DUP ever-vigilant for Islamist advantage – the governing coalition broke up and was reconstituted repeatedly and eventually included the NIF – al-Sadiq reworded and clarified, defined and excepted, but never solved, because it was insoluble, the conflict between citizenship and *shariʿa*.

Al-Sadiq al-Mahdi occupied an uncomfortable middle in Sudanese politics. His dynastic credentials had never insulated him from attacks even from within the Mahdist movement, as the split with the *imam* had shown in the 1960s. Now he had to contend also with the NIF, who made *shariʿa* the sine qua non of Islamism, and whose influence, through the Islamic banks and especially in the army, was growing. There was no Sudanese Nation, only a State, and al-Sadiq, by dividing it, failed the test of leadership that history had offered with the mantle of the Mahdi. Southerners failed to sympathize with his dilemma: Khartoum always found ways to justify, or deny, exploitation of the south. The September Laws stayed on the books and the war continued, with Khartoum resorting to methods previously thought beyond the pale. Those included arming Muslim tribesmen in the southern parts of Kordofan and Darfur, who, while called *murahalin* (militias), were in effect privateers, licensed to raid and loot in the Bahr al-Ghazal on their own account. Their outrages culminated in April 1987 when, having been worsted by SPLA units there, Rizayqat *murahalin* massacred more than one thousand Dinka refugees at al-Daien in Southern Darfur.[2] By adopting this policy and defending what by 1989 were quite openly described as "popular defense forces," al-Sadiq not only admitted incapacity: the Rizayqat and Misiriyya tribesmen involved were mainly Mahdists and were seen as a potential sectarian rival to the Sudanese army.

Al-Sadiq al-Mahdi's dithering over *shari'a* was directly related to the government's deteriorating position in the south. "Concessions" – for this was how the issue was framed, notwithstanding a long secular tradition that retained important support – became even more difficult as the SPLA won victories in the field, notably in brief but highly publicized occupations of several "northern" towns in the regional borderlands. More important, by 1989 it controlled much of the land area of the south and several of its most important towns, and had solidified its position by absorbing rival groups and drawing increased support in Equatoria and the Bahr al-Ghazal.

Government by Default

The mutual antagonisms and jockeying for position that characterized the third parliamentary government were both a cause and a symptom of the country's intractable problems. In the economic sphere, Nimayri had left his successors no room for maneuver. The Sudanese pound had lost 90 percent of its value in the decade to 1986, when the country's foreign debt reached $11 billion: interest alone amounted to $800 million a year and, after repeated defaults, technical bankruptcy loomed. The TMC's 1985–86 budget called for expenditure five times greater than revenue, and early in 1986 the International Monetary Fund (IMF) ruled the Sudan ineligible for further loans. The conditions imposed for resumption, on which credits and loans from foreign governments and international agencies in part depended, were draconian. These included further devaluation (the money supply had increased by 40 percent in 1984 alone); extensive privatization (much of the modern sector had been nationalized under Nimayri's Military Economic Board); retrenchment and a freeze on salaries in the bloated public sector (the TMC had agreed to raise salaries by as much as 40 percent); and abolition of the subsidies on food, fuel, and other commodities that governments had relied on to keep the towns quiet. After the government negotiated such an austerity program with the IMF in September 1987, riots broke out around the country. Price controls were finally lifted in late 1988, again provoking a violent popular reaction and yet another government about-face. In 1984–85, 65 percent of the railway tonnage comprised foreign food aid.[3]

For Darfur, the period of the third parliamentary regime was one of recovery from the drought and famine of 1984–85, of reaction to the local repercussions of ineptitude at the center, and of increasing insecurity. The excellent rains of 1985 that extended the famine in Dar Masalit combined with ingenuity and self-discipline to produce record grain harvests in much of Darfur and consequent easing of economic conditions generally. The coincident overthrow of Nimayri elicited no local tears, nor is there discernible evidence of much local interest or involvement in the affairs of the TMC. In the accession of al-Sadiq al-Mahdi after a hiatus of twenty years, Darfur got what it had voted for. But the failure of the Umma-led coalitions of 1986–89 even to maintain law and order there, and its finally becoming but a leading contributor to and participant in its lawlessness, may well have been the surest proof of the Umma party's moral bankruptcy.

Upon assuming power in April 1985, the TMC had dissolved the regional assemblies, including Darfur's, and appointed transitional military governments in their place. Rather than a cabinet, the governor of Darfur had a "management committee" comprising regional directors of central government departments. This was echoed at lower levels, where each chief government officer chaired a committee drawn from the departmental hierarchy and the community. It is evident that these steps continued – they did not begin – "care and maintenance" at best. The disruptions of the Nimayri era had so weakened provincial government that in Darfur its skeletal remains did not support any real activity. A survey shortly after Nimayri was ousted showed that more than a third of senior and midlevel posts in Darfur were simply vacant; that senior posts were occupied by new graduates; and that experienced civil servants, including teachers, had quit and left. The whole country suffered a well-publicized "brain drain," notably to the Gulf states. Corruption, bureaucracy for its own sake, the failure of salaries to keep pace with inflation, and unwillingness of officials elsewhere to accept transfer to Darfur left the provincial government a shell.

Nonetheless, in May 1985 an unwieldy interdepartmental committee, notably excluding representatives of the regions themselves, was set up to study relations between the central and regional governments and between regional headquarters and the districts. Among its recommendations were tighter financial controls, frequent reporting, auditing and inspection by the Ministry of Finance, reassertion of central control over the civil service, and reinstatement of a Ministry of Local Government. These recommendations, reflecting temporary prominence of professionals during the transitional period, were largely uncontroversial and never implemented. Khartoum felt no urgency: when he took office, al-Sadiq al-Mahdi left the governorship vacant, with authority vested instead in an Administrative Council under a civil servant.[4]

The collapse of the sovereign coercive power created a vacuum. Although Darfur's underdevelopment could still be blamed in election campaigns on European colonialism, Khartoum did not provide even the overarching sense of security that the Condominium had achieved. In place of the implicit bargain to which Darfur had acquiesced in foreign rule, there seemed to be the poorer substitute of internal colonialism. The economy was undeveloped but dominated by riverain northern Sudanese and other "foreign" merchants. Neither through merit based on education nor through nepotism and corruption did people of Darfur carry much weight in their own affairs, let alone the Sudan's: a 1981 survey showed Darfur's percentage of senior posts in the civil and foreign services at zero,[5] whereas riverain Sudanese held the levers of economic power in Darfur. The drought of the Nimayri years, literally and figuratively, encapsulated and symbolized Darfur's plight. And, after all this, al-Sadiq al-Mahdi, whose base of support had always been Darfur, brought nothing but trouble.

In January 1986, the Khartoum elite's commitment to the regions was tested at a conference on decentralization. Amid platitudinous discussion of the relative merits of the old provincial system vis-à-vis Indian, Canadian, Australian, and other models, a discordant note was struck in a paper by Ahmad Ibrahim Diraige, the former governor of Darfur, who did not attend. In calling for a true federal system, he aligned himself with some southern Sudanese, whose public commitment to secession was hopefully dismissed as a bargaining ploy. His thoughts included elected state assemblies and governorships, judiciaries independent from Khartoum, reservation of local sources of revenue, and a constitutional amendment procedure ensuring change only with overwhelming state and popular support. This and similar plans advocated also by representatives of the Nuba Mountains and far eastern Sudan were rejected by the old-line politicians.[6] The eventual upshot, in 1988, was partial restoration, in Darfur and elsewhere, of Native Administration through legal recognition of tribal authority.

CIVIL WAR BEGETS CIVIL WAR

Chadian Migrations

Events in Darfur did not await conferences elsewhere. A symptom of the center's psychological remoteness and inability to maneuver were riots at Nyala in September 1986, when student protests got out of hand. The local commissioner was stoned, his house and other buildings burned down, two people were killed, and the army had to be called in to restore order. Bigger demonstrations occurred later in Khartoum and Omdurman.[7] Far worse were interethnic disturbances related to both the war in the south and continuing turmoil in Chad, which eventually made meaningless the international borders and unilateral efforts to restore security.

By the early 1980s, the Sudan's relations with Libya had degenerated into a personal feud between Nimayri and Gaddafi. After Nimayri was ousted in 1985, Khartoum and Tripoli immediately came to terms, which included cessation of Libyan support for the southern rebels and of Sudanese support for Hissene Habre's government in Chad. The Sudan's transitional government rearmed Chadian dissidents in Darfur and turned a blind eye to Libyan recruitment of footloose tribesmen and migrant workers into the "Islamic Legion." Al-Sadiq al-Mahdi's government was in no position to retreat from that policy. Libyan military activities in Darfur, in support of Chadian rebels and under cover of "relief" missions, increased, as did French and U.S. support for the beleaguered government in Ndjamena. Fearing the unpredictable Gaddafi but unable to do without Libyan military aid in continuing the war in the south, the Umma prime minister tried the role of mediator, to no avail. Libyan and Libyan-backed Chadian forces based in Darfur routinely attacked across the border.

The Chadian conflict entered a new phase in 1987. With French material support, the Habre government won a series of improbable victories in the Saharan borderlands of northeastern Chad and Darfur, forcing the Libyans out of Chadian territory altogether. Remnants of the Islamic Legion thereupon regrouped in Darfur, weakened in number but heavily armed by the Libyans. Emboldened by Khartoum's unwillingness or inability to rein them in, they and ill-assorted Chadian rebels continued raids into Chad that were indistinguishable from banditry, and Chadian government forces, in hot pursuit, penetrated far into Darfur.

First in self-defense, Zaghawa and Arab tribesmen newly and uneasily settled in central and southern Darfur since the onslaught of the drought, and others, notably the Bani Halba, armed themselves with automatic weapons easily obtained from the Libyans and their surrogates. Given the title of "tribal militias," these were no more – or less – than what the tribes had long relied on as a last resort in local disputes. What had changed were the political context and the level and availability of arms. Government in Darfur was arguably weaker than at any time since Ali Dinar; mechanisms for settling intertribal disputes were in disrepair and were unsupported by disinterested mediation. The tribes were armed not with Remingtons and blunderbusses but with AK-47s and grenade launchers mounted on Toyota pickups. Ethnic tension, already rising with the influx of migrants from the drought-stricken north and the chaos on the border, was stirred up by Libyan propaganda, which counted the ways in which the "rights" of "Arabs" had been trampled by the "African" regime in Chad and the "blacks" of Darfur.

The Fur Take Arms

The arming of the tribes was not limited to the Arabs. To the depredations of northern migrants into Fur farmlands had been added the wholly disruptive influx of Chadian Arab refugees, who came not only as individuals and as bands of rebel fighters but in what amounted to tribal migrations, and they were especially drawn to the haven of Jabal Marra. In general terms, this stretched the capacity of the region's productive land and water. At the local level, the result was a thousand pinpricks as the Chadians, with their animals, barged into the terraces and grain fields, orchards, and vegetable gardens of the Masalit and Fur. The Fur, disadvantaged by their generally sedentary way of life, began to organize their own militias (*milishiyyat*) to defend against what began ominously to be called *fursan* (cavalrymen; "knights" in the combatants' jargon) and *janjawid* (hordes). "Struggle units" of Fur tribesmen, organized in a tellingly (if grandiloquently) named Federal Army of Darfur, had by mid-1988 sprung up throughout the heartland, armed with the help of the Chadian government, from the black market, and across the porous international borders. Fighting between Fur and Arabs flared into what was called the War of the Tribes, but it had already taken on characteristics of a race war. Neither the regional government, at last dominated by the Fur, nor al-Sadiq al-Mahdi, in league with Libya, intervened effectively.

In the absence of state control, Darfur had been saved from anarchy by repeated resort to customary law and mediation. As we have seen, this regulator of tribal society had been recognized, encouraged, and indeed brokered by the British and had continued after independence when the "foreign" status of Sudanese administrators implied impartiality. Disputes over land or water, as well as theft, escalating to wounding and homicide, were settled by mediation and the payment of blood money (*diya*) or by compensation in kind and with agreement about future behavior.[8] With the accession of Diraige's Fur-dominated regional government in 1981, however, that sense of impartiality, already long dissipating, was lost. As the decades-long drought and Chadian troubles were making such disputes more likely, ideology was endowing them with a new ethnic and even racial element. While the massive influx of modern weapons was destabilizing relations and presenting an alternative – war – the power of government to broker and enforce settlements had waned.

A Battleground of "Isms"

Sahelian drought, "devolution," the accession of Diraige in 1981, Libyan intrigue, and increasing tribal conflict in a context of Chadian civil war were ill-assorted results of longer-term phenomena, manmade and natural, coming to a head at the same time. To this tinder were added half-baked "ideologies" – Africanism, Arabism, Islamism – that would spark and later even be used to justify the catastrophe at the turn of the twenty-first century. Nimayri's appointment of Diraige may not have been calculated to damn the Fur with what they had wished for, but "African" rule in Darfur, and how it was depicted, became part of the problem. Although pan-Arabism had not before the 1980s attracted much attention anywhere in the rural Sudan, let alone Darfur, it would now be invoked to defend brigandage and murder. And, as we shall see, one Sudanese brand of Islamism has long marched with the Arab identity of its agents, ample evidence of which was provided by Khartoum's decades-long project in the south. A hint of the elite's insouciant condescension may be found in Nimayri's appointment, in June 1984, of a National Committee for the Spread of the Arabic Language, one of the "target areas" of which was blithely stated to be Darfur.[9]

From the mid-1980s, both the regional government and national armed forces stationed in Darfur became, in effect if not always by intent, parties to ethnic conflict. Officials recruited ethnic Fur to the security forces, where they played a dual role of secret insurgents everywhere: police by day, thugs by night. Arab officers and soldiers followed suit. Outbreaks of violence were suppressed or ignored depending on who complained to whom. Although the Fur enlisted the support of other non-Arabs, they failed to win over the Zaghawa, in part because of the regional government's high-handedness. An embryonic, or perhaps resurgent, Fur national identity was ill-timed and misplaced. Limited at first to a small educated minority of the Fur, who were a minority themselves, this sense of pride, symbolized and embodied in triumphal control of the regional government, inevitably appeared to others, aggrieved for other reasons, as a threat. This increased the appeal of the propaganda peddled from Tripoli and Khartoum, while also disquieting other non-Arab elements in Darfur.[10]

The National Council for the Salvation of Darfur

It was in this context that the National Council for the Salvation of Darfur emerged. Responding to a racist appeal by an "Arab Alliance" (*tajamu al-arabi*) purporting to represent the Arab tribes, a group of Darfur intellectuals – "National" referred to Darfur, not the Sudan – organized a demonstration in Khartoum on 12 March 1988 against the government's complicity in the presence of Libyan and Chadian forces in Darfur. The response was spectacular – more than 40,000 turned out – but the situation in the west only deteriorated. In April, President Hissene Habre survived a coup by Zaghawa officials who resented the increasing preeminence of his fellow Gura'an. Led by Idris Deby, the surviving insurgents and some 2,000 others fled eastward into Darfur. There they were formally detained but in fact allowed to roam free, given political refugee status, and joined by other anti-Habre Chadians financed and rearmed from Libya. When Chadian forces raided Darfur to attack these miscreant Zaghawa, Sudanese regular army units were nowhere to be seen. In effect, Chad's interethnic warfare had merged with Darfur's.

Ethnic fighting reached a new level of intensity in the spring of 1989 and in so doing played a role in the overthrow of the Sudanese government. What were still dismissed officially as border problems and "frontier violence" had spread far into the interior of Darfur. Bani Halba and Salamat fighters had attacked Fur villages in Jabal Marra, killing many hundreds. Near Nyala, the government admitted what it called 3,000 "murders" in May alone. Fur refugees poured into the towns.

The governor, Tijani Sese, a Fur, took the initiative and, after much palaver and last-minute violence, convened at El Fasher on 29 May a peace conference of Fur and Arabs. Amid extravagant claims, several points stand out, not least each side's accusations of ethnic cleansing: the establishment of an "Arab Belt" or an "African Belt" across Darfur and the first official reference to *janjawid*. Negotiations were still under way when the government of the Sudan was overthrown on 30 June.

With redoubled incentive, the talks continued, however, and on 8 July, 110 Fur representatives, 110 Arabs, and 21 mediators signed a Reconciliation Agreement. Under government supervision, this called for liquidation and disarmament of all militias; reversion to the status quo ante bellum insofar as land and property were concerned; deportation of illegal aliens; specific rights of passage for tribal migration; and enforcement of existing laws. The Arab tribes agreed to pay some £S43 million in compensation, the Fur almost £S10.5 million, and the government a contribution of its own.[11]

The recent, galling role of the Sudanese army in Darfur, where Chadian rebels and local militias flouted its authority, was only its latest humiliation: senior officers were more concerned with defeat in the south. With the army publicly demanding changes, al-Sadiq al-Mahdi had reconstituted his governing coalition with the DUP, which, after months of haggling in foreign meetings, had reached a general agreement with the southern rebels. The stage had been set for a historic compromise between Khartoum and the south: al-Sadiq agreed to suspend implementation of the *shari'a*, to withdraw from defense agreements with Libya and Egypt, and to an immediate cease-fire in the south. A meeting in Addis Ababa between him and the rebel leaders was arranged and was widely expected to seal the deal. It was precisely to forestall this that on 30 June a group of officers staged the coup in Khartoum that overthrew the government.

THE STATE OF JIHAD

DARFUR AND THE NATIONAL ISLAMIC FRONT

Two decades after the military coup of 1989, the precise role in it of the National Islamic Front (NIF) and its leader, Hassan al-Turabi, remained uncertain. Within days of asserting themselves, however, General Omar Hasan al-Bashir and his fellow officers began to defer to the ideology, policies, and personalities of the NIF, so that the effect of if not the impetus for the coup was its rapid accession to power.[1] The timing of the coup, moreover, made it clear that the officers shared the NIF's rejection of any settlement with southern rebels that threatened the project of Arab-Islamic "Sudanization" that had long dominated Khartoum politics.

The new regime, therefore, took immediate steps not only to empower the NIF but also to scuttle the peace deal that al-Sadiq al-Mahdi and the Sudan People's Liberation Movement (SPLM) had all but signed. In addition to suspending the constitution, dissolving parliament, banning political parties, outlawing unions, and censoring the media, the Revolutionary Command Council (RCC) denounced the deal and, after a pro forma meeting with rebel leaders in Addis Ababa, withdrew from its predecessor's commitments. The regime produced proposals of its own, including a federal constitution under the *shari'a*, but no one was taken in, and the fighting resumed. Moreover, early steps were taken to expand the war, including adoption of ever more apocalyptic rhetoric. In short order, new legal instruments were enacted, reaffirming the *shari'a*; pliant *ulama* proceeded to legalize the killing of apostates and unbelievers, enhancing the atmosphere of terror in the capital and the jihadist character of the war against the south.

Islam, in its NIF exegesis, which responded flexibly and exempted official outrages, became the official basis for all policy. And although the Sudanese had never been much attached to "official" Islam, as decreed from Khartoum, circumstances favored the regime. These included the dismal record of the political parties, whose shameless leaders were handy foils; the discovery of oil in recoverable quantities and consequent reduction in foreign economic and political pressure and ease in obtaining military hardware; and inveterate northern disdain for southern pretensions to equality, which had been enflamed rather than diminished by the Sudan People's Liberation Army's (SPLA) successes in the field. There was, then, considerable scope for solidifying the NIF's hold on power, which a ruthless regime of opportunists was eager to grasp.

The NIF in Power

Although the totalitarian nature of the NIF regime was affirmed from the start, Khartoum's political discourse was so jaded that few took it at its word. The regime gained crucial breathing space. Purges of the army, civil service, and various agencies were nothing new, but in scale there was no precedent for what was taking place: thousands of public-sector employees were dismissed; the diplomatic corps was shorn of professionals and women; by 1993, some 2,500 officers had reportedly been cashiered; when judges protested politicization of the judiciary, scores were summarily discharged. Although formally the regime hewed to familiar lines, with the RCC[2] overseeing a mainly civilian cabinet and Bashir as prime minister, behind the scenes a committee system, dominated by NIF advisers, ensured ideological purity, and an unpublicized Committee of Forty, chaired by Turabi, set policy. As the dust cleared, moreover, true believers replaced the uninspired: a prominent early role was played by Dr. al-Tayyib Ibrahim Khayr, nicknamed al-Sikha ("the re-bar") who, as minister for presidential affairs, was Bashir's factotum, while Ali Uthman Muhammad Taha gradually emerged as strongman.

In determining to balance or even replace the army with a so-called Popular Defense Force, the NIF also gave an earnest of its radical intent. After initial purges, the regime went further, enlisting jihadists to fight in the south, subjecting civil servants and students to military training and ideological reeducation, initiating a draft, resorting to impressment, and, notoriously, regularizing and rearming tribal militias in southern Kordofan and southern Darfur against their neighbors to the south. Failed coup attempts ended with summary executions; senior officers went into exile, where some organized a cleverly named but largely ineffectual "Legitimate Command." Other organs of state security were similarly purged and politicized, replaced, or superseded by Orwellian cadres. The era of the "ghost house" ensued, during which individuals inimical to the regime disappeared or were imprisoned and tortured in unofficial jails.

A hard line was taken against other potential centers of disaffection, notably the old parties and their sectarian bases. Both al-Sadiq al-Mahdi and Muhammad Uthman al-Mirghani were imprisoned after the 1989 coup and, upon release, were subjected to harassment. Much of their enormous families' property was sequestrated, and both eventually went into exile, along with prominent members of their and other parties. The Khatmiyya order of sufis was banned. In October 1989, a National Democratic Alliance (NDA) of parties and unions announced its existence in opposition to the regime, but a campaign of civil unrest was harshly suppressed. The NDA was broad but shallow, riven by old divisions and shocked into depression by the ferocity of the regime. Its eventual alliance with the SPLM was likewise weakened by its evident opportunism and by splits among the southerners themselves.

Although never denying an intention to make the Sudan an Islamic state, the NIF regime faced the same problem Nimayri had encountered in abolishing parties and denouncing sects: the need for a vehicle to detect and control the popular will. This Turabi, who remained ostentatiously outside the regime as its eminence grise, sought to provide in a plethora of institutions rhetorically distinct from the Potemkin Sudanese Socialist Union (SSU) of the Nimayri regime but similar in totalitarian impulse. In 1990, a National Dialogue conference approved expansion of local committees into a hierarchy of district and regional bodies and a national Popular Assembly; elaborate procedures were later approved for (very) gradual implementation. In 1992, detecting signs of sectarian life in that process, the regime instead empanelled an advisory Transitional National Assembly to apply the well-worn rubber stamp. In 1993, the RCC appointed Bashir president, then formally disbanded itself.

Despite the occasional outburst by an independent or crank, however, neither the assembly nor Bashir had a defensible claim to

Figure 17. President Omar Hasan al-Bashir, long considered a figurehead, has proven adept at political survival. (Photo by Salah Malkawi/Newsmakers.)

legitimacy. Both were seen as creatures of the NIF. Rigged elections would not solve the problem and, if merely "guided," ran the risk of reemergent sectarianism. The proffered solution was the same as Nimayri's in the early 1970s, although arrayed in modest Islamist garb: a drawn-out process of base meetings, local gatherings, district selections, and regional conferences in 1992–95. When actual election was involved, people voted with their feet and stayed away; when the wrong candidates won, arrests followed. In 1996, one-party elections for the presidency and National Assembly were finally held, under controls so tight and abuses so flagrant as to vitiate the preordained results: Bashir was elected president, and Turabi became speaker of the assembly.[3]

Pages from an older book were taken in the NIF's provincial administration, but this time it was to the Condominium (or even

Turkiyya), rather than to the military juntas, that it looked. In 1991, recentralization was enacted, with Khartoum retaining the power of the purse, control of the judiciary, and the right to appoint governors and officials; General al-Tayyib Ibrahim remained governor of Darfur. The opportunity was taken to alter boundaries at the south's expense: the oil-producing Bentiu region was made part of Kordofan, and the copper mines of the western Bahr al-Ghazal were transferred to Darfur. In fulsome homage to devolution, this was followed in 1994 by division of each province into three separate states, and thus were reborn Northern, Western, and Southern Darfur, all of whose senior officials were appointed by the central government. Darfur's hand-to-mouth existence, which had long depended – sometimes literally – on *zakat*, was thus duplicated at three levels, nominally to eliminate officious middlemen but in effect increasing local dependence on an NIF satrap. By now, the careening vehicle of Khartoum's control had taken so many U-turns that administration itself was defamed; no one was surprised when, in 1994, the NIF reimposed Native Administration, with a council of tribal leaders advising the governor of each state.[4]

Meanwhile, the NIF's brand of Islam, like Nimayri's had been, was promulgated, institutionalized, and selectively enforced. A few hapless miscreants were flogged and even executed, to encourage the others. Stirrings in the army were mercilessly suppressed. The war in the south was reaffirmed as jihad; opposition was treason, and treason was apostasy. Breaking with medieval precedent, Christians were denied special status and instead were exempted from a few laws, but time-honored Sudanese heterodoxy was outlawed: singing and dancing were banned and women's relative freedom in public and the workplace was severely restricted. As usual, hard cases made bad law: medicine containing alcohol was prohibited; art classes were shut down. Sufi orders were harassed or suppressed, and a state-run umbrella organization sought to harness religious fervor for the regime's ends. In this, the familiar tools of divide and rule were used, both within the sectarian north and against the south.

Jihad in the South

Timed to forestall a peace agreement, the NIF coup had struck a blow to southern illusions about the good faith of the northern elite. But the new regime's determination to resume the war was unmatched by ability to fight it. With the regular army in the throes of massive purges, the cadres of NIF youth inexperienced and untrained, and (after the regime's inept support for the Iraqi invasion of Kuwait in 1990) its foreign sources of arms and material reduced, Khartoum was unable even to prevent further SPLA advances. The southern rebels occupied much of western Equatoria, turned the tables on the tribal militias of southern Darfur and Kordofan and reached tenuous truces, and opened up new sources of supply through East Africa. But important aspects of the SPLM's position were beyond its control. One was time or, rather, the susceptibility of all Sudanese movements to centrifugal forces over time; another was continuing reliance on the support of neighboring states, especially Ethiopia: when the Mengistu regime was overthrown in 1991, the SPLA lost bases, refugee centers, supply routes, and even its radio station. In the dislocation that followed, as in the very heterogeneity of the southern movement, Khartoum saw opportunity. While the NIF regime exploited the return from Ethiopia of southern refugees by interfering with international relief efforts, a movement was afoot within the SPLM to overthrow its leader, John Garang.

The split within the SPLM, redolent of the "tribalism" that had vitiated southern resistance in the 1960s, gave Khartoum time to regroup. Much territory was retaken while the SPLA engaged in combating "split-ists." But while the Sudanese army held the main towns, it and its "popular" adjuncts were never able to achieve decisive victory in the field. By the mid-1990s, the military position appeared to have reached stalemate, and the NIF, revolutionary fervor as usual shelved when necessary, entered into peace talks with the rebels. Negotiations were complicated by the continuing rift in the rebels' ranks. At international conferences, each faction was represented; they fell out ostensibly over the ultimate issue of the south's status. The "mainstream" SPLM maintained adherence to a unitary, secular Sudan, and the breakaway group demanded independence for the south, a difference that was eventually composed by agreement on the principle of self-determination. The obvious advantage Khartoum enjoyed in the protracted "peace process" brokered by the Intergovernmental Authority on Drought and Desertification (IGAD)[5] and other countries was largely frittered away by its support for various religiously tinged causes, often labeled by their opponents as terrorist, both in the region and further afield.

NIF policy of divide and rule achieved some success. In 1996, two minor southern rebel commanders signed a Peace Charter, which expanded thereafter into a United Democratic Salvation Front promising, among other things, a federal system for the Sudan with the option of southern independence in a referendum. In keeping with traditions of north-south relations, signatories got jobs. Whatever its ultimate intention in this arrangement, the government was able to exploit it to secure its hold on the all-important Bentiu oil fields. A proliferation of splinter groups, some merely names attached to soi-disant "leaders," also gave political advantage to Khartoum, beyond its obvious ability to pick them off, with jobs and titles, one at a time: foreign governments and organizations were more likely to throw up their hands and turn their backs on such disarray and the promise of endless war. But the "mainstream" SPLM soldiered on, and the practical value to Khartoum of side deals with leaders who had no followers was small.[6]

Some sort of "federal system," perhaps along the lines of the dishonored 1972 Addis Ababa Agreement, always seemed to most observers, local and foreign, an obvious and rational way forward for the multicultural Sudan. What stood in the way was not NIF fundamentalism but rather the nature of Sudanese nationalism, which had been conceived during the colonial era and brought to fruition at independence by the Khartoum elite. Although they saw Egypt and the Arab world as the font and origin of their culture, their Sudanese identity, by virtue of geography and history, was unique and, crucially, expansive. In the same sense that nineteenth-century Americans adopted "Manifest Destiny" in the New World, so Sudanese nationalists accepted a mission to spread their civilization to – or, put another way, foster its assimilation of – non-Muslims. In this view, colonial-era measures to support indigenous traditions in the south unfairly cut off backward peoples from a culture the British themselves admitted to be superior and were doomed to fail in the Darwinian struggle of history. Leaving aside the unacknowledged self-interest that undoubtedly informed this attitude, opponents of the Khartoum elite and defenders of the south dismissed it far too easily.

Since independence, the sense of mission had grown. The first generation of northern politicians had inherited a self-image as agents of civilization, saw the civil war as Africa's resistance to Modernity, and apprehended in the southern missionary-educated elite a colonial virus left behind to sap the nascent state. The conviction that history was on their side, moreover, made even the 1972 Addis Ababa Agreement palatable to northern nationalists because they never accepted the charge of cultural imperialism: Islam and Arabic would inevitably progress in the south, whatever political arrangements were enforced. During the last parliamentary regime, and with the accession of the NIF, this strain of Sudanese nationalist thinking was overwhelmed by the rhetoric of jihad and an ironic new defensiveness, as the Khartoum elite, always a minority, saw itself besieged. The populous south, restive Nuba Mountains, faraway Darfur (whose very name seemed separatist), the upper Blue Nile, Nubians who laughed at the idea of answering to Khartoum – centrifugal forces not only endangered political and economic control but also threatened their Sudanese national identity. What was Sudanese culture without the Sudan?

A minority had long held that the south was not worth keeping. Even the NIF considered the question: if Khartoum could keep the oil fields, why not jettison the rest?[7] The problem was that the south's independence might be the beginning, not the end, of disintegration. Better to keep the land and let the people go. High-handed redrawing of boundaries was a harbinger. Treatment of the Nuba of southern Kordofan was another. Always neglected, the heterogeneous Nuba had been inconvenient to categorize as northern or southern. Traditional political parties had done nothing for them and represented interests inimical to theirs; successive regional "parties" had won them a voice but little else. After the second civil war broke out, the Nuba were prey to Baqqara militias, and the SPLA began to win adherents there. Government repression worsened, and the Nuba Mountains became a war zone. In 1992, the NIF extended its declaration of jihad to include them, even though a majority of the Nuba were Muslims. Nuba farmers were herded off to camps and their land was sold to Arab developers. Mass murders of young men were widely reported, as was an actual *policy* of rape, and foreign food aid was withheld.[8] A similar fate befell people of the upper Blue Nile and some of the Beja of the eastern Sudan.[9] What in the early twenty-first century the world beheld in Darfur had all happened before.

The NIF versus the World

Assurances that the NIF must eventually recoil from the international opprobrium heaped on it over events in Darfur since 2003 fail to take account of the regime's willingness from its inception to court pariah status. Condemnation of its methods in prosecuting the war in the south; repressive internal policies; relations with Iran, Libya, and other disreputable regimes; and assistance to rebels in neighboring states and to terrorist organizations had little noticeable effect and were sometimes turned to its advantage in propaganda. The regime flouted international opinion by perfecting the "food weapon" – the ability of a sovereign state to control distribution of foreign food aid to civilians in the south, even during widespread famine – and indeed to exact concessions; in effect, Khartoum held its starving citizens hostage, forcing foreigners to pay for the privilege of feeding them. Khartoum usually held the upper hand, for example, in negotiations with the United Nations umbrella organization Operation Lifeline Sudan, founded in 1989, and was able to coordinate food aid with its own military priorities. The complexity of these operations, which involved agencies of donor governments as well as specialized UN agencies and were carried out through offices in Khartoum and East Africa far from routine media scrutiny, also played into the regime's hands. Although international condemnation became routine, it was as routinely parried as uninformed, one-sided, anti-Arab, and anti-Muslim. Lurid accounts of enslavement of southerners engendered campaigns in the United States and elsewhere to finance their purchase and manumission; the "Lost Boys," orphans who had walked hundreds of miles to Ethiopia to escape death, became famous around the world; death tolls in the millions were cited.[10] But the war went on.

If the world had been determined to intervene effectively for the southern Sudan during the 1990s, the parlous state of the Sudanese economy provided ample leverage. The external debt in 1989 was already $13 billion and, in the early 1990s, the country experienced hyperinflation, even as real gross domestic product (GDP) declined. In 1993, the World Bank ceased payment on the Sudan's loans, and the Arab Monetary Fund refused to step in with new ones. The International Monetary Fund repeatedly threatened expulsion and declared the Sudan "noncooperative" in 1990. Official foreign development aid fell from almost $2 billion in 1985 to only $127 million in 1993–94. Ironically, what had kept the country afloat were massive remittances from the hundreds of thousands of Sudanese – many highly educated, others with technical skills – who had fled to the Gulf and elsewhere and prospered. Although the most visible effects of this exodus and capital backflow were new housing extensions around the capital, much money flowed also through Islamic banks, the black market, and other conduits to productive investment.[11]

In its foreign relations, the NIF regime was not fastidious about Islamic credentials or consistent in its commitments: the enemies of enemies were its friends, among both unsavory regimes and shadowy terrorist organizations. The NIF embraced Shi'i Iran, supported Iraq's invasion of Kuwait, alienated Uganda over support of the rampaging Lord's Army, gave aid to rebels in Ethiopia and Eritrea, befriended Hamas and Hizballah, and strengthened ties with Libya. In the 1990s, Osama bin Ladin helped the regime negotiate an arms deal with Russia and was rewarded with land for agricultural schemes and training bases for Eritrean and Oromo rebels in the eastern Sudan. In 1991, at the time of the Gulf War, Hasan al-Turabi founded a Popular Islamic and Arab Conference to promote rebellion against Arab regimes that cooperated with the United States. In 1993, the United States in turn declared the Sudan a state sponsor of terrorism; in 1997, it imposed ineffectual economic sanctions; and in 1998, it bombed a pharmaceutical factory in Khartoum North that, it claimed – almost certainly wrongly – was a source of terrorist explosives. Relations with Egypt deteriorated throughout the period; in 1995, an unsuccessful attempt in Addis Ababa to assassinate President Hosni Mubarak led to UN sanctions against the Sudan.[12]

Khartoum's economic quandary and political ostracism were mitigated by the flow of oil that finally began in 1999. Talked up for so long that Sudanese had doubted its existence, oil had been detected in north-south border regions in the 1980s, but civil war and the generally low price of crude had delayed exploitation. Chevron, the major investor, departed in 1992, but U.S. sanctions did not prevent Austrian, Canadian, Chinese, Malaysian, Dutch, Qatari, Russian, Swedish, and other companies from moving in. The government's ability to secure the oil fields, and its entry as a minor – but not negligible – player in the international market, helped to finance the war and reduce foreign criticism of its policies. When momentum grew in the United States to boycott the Sudan and disinvest in oil companies doing business there, little effect was felt in Sudan's relations with Europe or East Asia. Arab states, although wary of the NIF, publicly belittled its serial outrages as internal matters. Most European Union governments continued normal diplomatic and commercial relations, even including bilateral aid arrangements, and winked while condemning human rights abuses. Pope John Paul II received Hasan al-Turabi.[13]

More important than international opinion in bringing Khartoum a settlement in the south were strains within the regime. By remaining outside the structure of government, Hasan al-Turabi reserved independence of action, and his forays into domestic and international affairs left open the question of where real power lay. At this President Bashir obviously chafed, but even occasional public refutations of Turabi's expressed views were widely discounted. By the late 1990s, however, a breach had clearly opened between the two. Adoption of an Islamic Constitution in 1998 paved the way for partial resumption of party politics under terms of what was in all but name another National Reconciliation, and after 2000 Turabi contented himself, publicly, with leadership of a National Congress party. Other dissidents – including even ex-President Nimayri – returned from exile, thus weakening the National Democratic Alliance. While Turabi was blamed for the regime's past excesses, relations with Egypt and other states were repaired.[14]

By 2000, the balance of forces in the south had not fundamentally changed. Arrayed against the government in Khartoum and its militias were the SPLM and its allies. Other groups and individual attention-seekers lent confusion, but the overall picture was much the same as it had been a decade earlier. That fact alone may have been the most important in leading the regime to consider terms: it came to the realization, through difficult experience, that a military solution was probably impossible. More importunate were cracks in the façade of Islamist unity in Khartoum, where, Nimayri-like, the regime of President Bashir saw in peace the opportunity to gain advantage over northern opposition. It remained uncertain whether the keystone of the peace deal – an eventual referendum that would allow southerners the choice of independence – would be kept. Doubts are fed by terror in other parts of the Sudan, especially Darfur.

JIHAD IN DARFUR

The Chadian Connection

The NIF regime forged close relations with Libya from the start.[15] Al-Sadiq al-Mahdi had been an embarrassed client of Tripoli; the NIF sought partnership. A bilateral ministerial committee was set up, and an Integration Charter would be ratified in 1990. Darfur's amalgamation with the Libyan province of Kufra was envisioned as a step in reviving Muammar Gaddafi's moribund notion of empire, but in practical terms the charter endorsed familiar formulas of closer cooperation: the NIF regime got military aid and Libya got a free hand to use Darfur as a staging area. The first NIF governor – titled political supervisor – of Darfur was General al-Tijani al-Tahir, a Fur from Kutum with close ties to the Libyan regime. In 1989–90, he led several delegations to Libya and visited Ndjamena to assure Hissene Habre's government of Khartoum's good intentions. In a series of agreements in Algiers in August 1989, Chad and Libya ostensibly resolved their differences, and the Sudanese government thereupon promised to curtail the activities of Chadian dissidents in Darfur. These developments, following the intertribal agreement at El Fasher in July, gave hope that peace might be restored to Darfur.

Hope dissipated quickly. In October 1989, Chadian government forces pursued into Darfur a new wave of Zaghawa and other refugees, who returned the favor with renewed cross-border raids. In retaliation, Habre's army launched a major offensive, advancing more than a hundred miles into Darfur. Its success against the rebels was indecisive, however, and within months their leader, Idris Deby, a Zaghawi himself, had reconstituted his forces with renewed aid from Libya and the Sudan. In March 1990, from bases north of El Geneina, he invaded Chad. After initial successes and heavy losses on both sides, the Chadian army repulsed the invaders and chased them back into Darfur. Amid ineffectual protests from Khartoum, the Chadians rampaged north of Jabal Marra, destroying villages and putting the Fur and Zaghawa inhabitants to flight. They withdrew in May, only to invade again in September. But Habre's inability to finish off his enemies proved fatal. Rearmed yet again by an implacable Gaddafi, and with the NIF's continued support, Deby was soon able to renew his own offensive. In

December 1990, having swept across Chad, he entered Ndjamena and overthrew the Habre regime.

Although the NIF's eagerness to establish closer ties with Libya was understandable as a practical matter, support of Chadian rebels against Habre illustrated its jihadist ideology. Whether rapprochement with Ndjamena in August 1989 was purely tactical or a turning point came later because of cross-border raids, by early 1990 the NIF was already dealing with Darfur as if that corner of Dar al-Islam were an appendage of pagan Africa. In Sudanese-Libyan rhetoric, the Arab world's border was moving to the south, and in Darfur the ideology of Sudanese nationalism, and what has been called "becoming Sudanese," encountered its severest test – and failed: not religion, nor language, and certainly not citizenship, but Arab identity through imputed Arab blood became the decisive factor in excluding the Other. The demonstrable invalidity of this distinction, as indeed the rejection of old traditions of coexistence and the bonds of Islam, would be discounted in what increasingly became a struggle for land, a struggle in which the whole notion of ethnic or tribal *dars* could be trumped by claims of race.

NIF Rule in Darfur

As the longtime stronghold of the Umma party, Darfur posed a particular challenge to the NIF. That successive regimes had proven unworthy of Darfur's support was a basis on which Sudanese intellectuals and ideological parties criticized the territorial system of elective government: no matter how badly Khartoum treated Darfur, its people still voted for the Umma. Under various rubrics, the Muslim Brothers had been no exception: in the last parliamentary elections in 1986, the NIF had won almost half the votes of the educated elite of Darfur, who voted in the special "graduates" constituency, but only 15.5 percent in the territorial constituencies.[16] The NIF denounced sectarianism in favor of those it had marginalized, allied with minorities against a problematic majority, denounced the evident corruption of the old parties, and used intertribal and even intratribal relations for its own purposes. In this way, the NIF had appealed to educated Sudanese, in Darfur as elsewhere.

Once the NIF took power, contradictions between theory and practice soon appeared. The riverain Arab elite dominated the NIF as it had every other major party; non-Arabs had to defer to the party, not the party to them. This bias had been reinforced by the percolation north-ward, into Darfur, of the southern civil war. The SPLM had failed to attract many northerners with its secular-nationalist call for a "New Sudan": the success it had (aside from a few disgruntled politicians' thumbing their noses at ex-colleagues) was largely among non-Arabs, notably in the Nuba Mountains. Attempts to open a front in Darfur had been forestalled by the *murahalin*, but appeal to the Fur and other non-Arabs caused concern in Khartoum. Both the SPLM and Fur rebels opened offices in Ndjamena in the late 1980s and tried to take advan-tage of the African-Arab aspect of the Chadian civil war. In December 1991, an SPLA force of Dinka under the joint command of Daud Yahya Bulad, a Fur who was a disaffected Muslim Brother, and Abd al-Aziz Adam al-Hilu, a Masalati, invaded from the Bahr al-Ghazal. They were easily defeated by the Bani Halba militia before they could even attempt to raise revolt. The Bani Halba followed up by looting and burning Fur villages allegedly suspected of collaboration with Bulad.[17]

Despite the ease with which the SPLA invasion was put down, the notion that Darfur was ripe for revolt was not far-fetched. The first two years of NIF rule had been disastrous; in a context of renewed drought and famine, the regime had isolated itself internationally, worsened an already dismal economic situation, suffered repeated defeats in the south, and seen its westernmost province traversed by the forces of foreign governments and rebels.

NIF policies hit particularly hard in Darfur. In the economic sphere, its notion of national self-reliance translated into privatization, a pro-cess by which NIF politicians and cronies took ownership of public property. Making a virtue of necessity, self-reliance also meant doing without foreign aid: the NIF would not abide international agencies' and donor countries' prescriptions for austerity. One result was hyper-inflation; another, when drought struck again in 1989–90, was famine. Like Nimayri before it, the NIF denied a crisis its policies had helped to create: grain had been exported for foreign exchange, experts' advice had been rejected as alarmist, price rises were blamed on profiteers, and a ham-fisted foreign policy had led to panic hoarding in the expectation that food aid would end. Those who ate invoked national pride at the cost of those in want: "We will never accept any food aid, even if famine is declared" was the declaration, in October 1990, of the government's

Economic Affairs Committee. Rationing was its final solution, carried out by – and for – loyalists and focused on securing the capital region and main towns. In a showdown with the Americans, the NIF finally backed off, exempting foreign food aid from its attempts to control interregional shipments. The government's failure to allow systematic study of the disaster and to produce reliable statistics has left experts to speculate on the effects in Darfur and elsewhere.[18]

The *Janjawid*

In the aftermath of famine, cross-border depredations in the closing months of the Habre regime in Chad, and Daud Bulad's abortive foray into Darfur, the NIF governor, al-Tayyib Ibrahim, was aware of the danger of driving the non-Arab population into the arms of the SPLM. But his masters in Khartoum had other ideas. A turning point occurred in 1994 with the division of Darfur into three "states." On its face this seemed innocuous enough, another pendulum swing engineered to increase Khartoum's control by diminishing the size and power of provincial administrative units. But in Darfur's case, much more was in play. Boundaries were gerrymandered to make the Fur a minority in each of the states. New Native Administration posts were doled out to NIF loyalists, mostly Arabs, who assumed territorially based jurisdictions even in non-Arab areas. The Nimayri-era land registration law was invoked to dismiss hereditary but unregistered rights to land.

Dar Masalit may serve as an example of what ensued, and one with clear implications for the future. As we have seen, although latecomers to princely status, the Masalit sultans had been successful in maintaining their position and the identity of their people, even as Dar Masalit became a crossroads in the Chadian wars. Large numbers of Chadian Arabs had settled there, as had Zaghawa and others driven by incessant drought in northern Darfur and Kordofan. This influx taxed the Masalit regime, but accommodation was made through the sultan's recognition of tribal *shaykhs*' authority and their continuing to exercise it while answering to him. In was only in the mid-1990s, with or because of open support from the NIF, that outsiders began to claim *rights* based on their occupation of land.

In March 1995, the governor of Western Darfur, the state incorporating Dar Masalit, decreed division of the *dar* into thirteen "emirates," of which five were assigned to the Masalit and eight to Arab tribal new-comers. Because the new Native Administration arrangements called for the "emirs" to elect the sultan, the future of Dar Masalit – as a *dar* for the Masalit – was suddenly rendered untenable. These political changes were followed by ever-increasing Arab raids on Masalit herds. In one notorious raid alone, 40,000 head of cattle were taken and twenty-three people killed. Open attacks on Masalit villages began. When in June 1996 Arab raiders burned seven villages in one day, the government did nothing. By late that year, all of Dar Masalit was involved. At a peace conference in El Fasher in November, representatives of the Arab tribes openly disputed Masalit rights to unregistered land. The media-tors produced only an ambiguous recommendation: the new emirates should be retained, without prejudice for the ownership of land.[19]

Within days, the fighting resumed. Abandoning even the appearance of neutrality, the government in effect legalized the war on the Masalit. As it (and its parliamentary predecessor) had done before, the NIF began to arm tribal militias – in this case, Arabs under the command of their new emirs – and in Khartoum the hereditary rights of the Masalit were dismissed. During the governorship of General Hasan Sulayman, forces entered Masalit villages, confiscated weapons, arrested leaders, and carried off young men for military service in the south. Raids by Arab militias followed: they burned the houses, shot fleeing occupants, and destroyed the crops to make return difficult. Tens of thousands of Masalit fled into Chad. In December 1997, Khartoum declared a state of emergency in Darfur, the practical effects of which were difficult to discern.

General Muhammad Ahmad al-Dabi was sent to the region in Febru-ary 1999, ostensibly to restore order but in fact to put down Masalit resistance, which was now publicly referred to as treasonous complicity with the SPLA. His personal militia, moved from Kordofan to south-ern Darfur, trained local Arabs for the government's "popular defense forces" in the west. Since non-Arabs were not allowed to enlist, these became in effect another local militia, which the Masalit called *janjawid*, a term that eventually merged all the Arab militias, whether local or of Chadian, Libyan, or other origins, under one malevolent rubric. Thou-sands of Masalit were killed and tens of thousands put to flight.[20]

Another example of local war that presaged the slaughter of the early twenty-first century was the conflict between the Baqqara Rizayqat and

Zaghawa in Southern Darfur. As we have seen, the Rizayqat have long been a turbulent presence; when al-Sadiq al-Mahdi enlisted their militias to fight across the Bahr al-Arab against the SPLA, he set a precedent. By the 1990s, they did not depend on Khartoum for arms nor on the spoils of war because there was an open market in the cheap weapons that had flooded neighboring Chad. In Rizayqat country, like Dar Masalit, there was a conflict between traditional inherited rights and the revolutionary concept of equal access to unregistered land. In an already tense situation around al-Daien, where Zaghawa fleeing the parched north had settled in large numbers, ready access to abundant modern weapons and NIF animosity toward the non-Arabs made open warfare difficult to avoid. Local requests for government intervention were ignored. In September 1996, Rizayqat horsemen attacked the villages of Zaghawa and other tribes, and non-Rizayqat residents in al-Daien were set upon and their shops and houses looted and burned. At a peace conference six months later, the Rizayqat demanded wholesale eviction of the Zaghawa, but mediation arranged for the payment of blood money by both sides.

Similar cases occurred elsewhere in Darfur, fed by the cheap automatic weapons that had poured into the region during the Libyan campaigns against Chad and precipitated by conflicting "rights" to land. The Baqqara Rizayqat came to blows with all their neighbors – not least the Dinka to the south – over tribal boundaries and rights of way. Their cousins, the northern camel-herding Rizayqat, found the position reversed when they sought rights to land in Dar Zaghawa, a dispute that likewise erupted into bloody warfare in 1995. A survey of tribal peace conferences during this period refers to violent outbreaks between the Rizayqat and Birgid, Rizayqat and Habbaniyya, northern Rizayqat and Zaghawa, Zaghawa and Mima and Birgid, and the Meidob and Kababish. In 1997, a peace conference of all the tribes of Darfur was called at Nyala.

The "Arab Alliance"

Thus, there were disturbing new elements in Darfur's tribal warfare during the 1990s: cheap and plentiful modern weapons, a growing tendency to endow with constitutional significance differences over land rights, and the government's abandonment of neutrality in favor of the

Arabs. That support was not merely tactical but also reflected the racist ideology of the so-called Arab Alliance, many of whose members were not even Sudanese but had come from Chad. The remoter origins of this grouping are uncertain, but the hand of Libya has been detected in its organization. To what extent Libya's Islamic Legion and missionary *Da'wa* were inspired by a racist ideology is less important than the effect, which was to make sense of the Sahelian chaos of the 1970s and 1980s by reducing it to "Arabs" versus "Africans."

In this scheme of things, the Sudan's Arab Muslim movements – the northern political parties – had struggled for decades against the Christians and animists of the south, whose resistance was fueled by neighboring African states and the shadowy involvement of Europeans and Israelis. In Darfur, the Fur, Masalit, and other "Africans" had lorded it over Arab tribes and allied themselves with Christians and pagans against the Arabs of Chad. Even farther west, had not Africans succeeded the French colonialists and oppressed Arab Muslims in Mali and Mauretania? Whether any of this withstood scrutiny mattered less than the facility with which it could be said to make sense and to legitimize as "resistance" what was otherwise murder and rapine.

The ideology stemming from this premise had found fertile ground in Darfur because of the progressive atrophy of the Sudanese state since independence, a process hardly masked by the Nimayri regime's totalitarian façade in the 1970s and 1980s. Even such landmarks as the Land Registration Act of 1970 may be seen as a tactic by which a weak government divided to rule. With the election of Diraige in 1980, Fur ethnic pride triumphed even as Arab tribes seemed to suffer disproportionately from drought and famine. Incidents had long occurred of armed bandits selectively robbing and beating Africans while letting Arabs go. Tellingly, reference began to be made to Fur, Masalit, and other "Africans" as *zurqa* (blacks), much as northern Sudanese in general still referred (privately) to southerners as *abid* (slaves). That "Arabs" were often as dark as "blacks" mattered as little as that former "masters" were as dark as "slaves": "Africa begins at Calais," someone once said, and defining economic and political opponents in racial terms was not nearly as strained as foreigners assumed.

In any case, as we have seen, in 1987 a group of Arab tribal leaders from Darfur, using the rubric Arab Alliance, addressed an open letter to al-Sadiq al-Mahdi, then prime minister, complaining of underrepresentation in regional government. If their demands for administrative changes and half the government posts went unmet, they purported to fear the consequences. There is doubt about the provenance of this letter and no evidence that it was taken seriously at the time. On the contrary, even amid the continuing Fur–Arab "war," al-Sadiq appointed a Fur, Tijani Sese, as regional governor. A subsequent "manifesto" and political-military program of the Arab Alliance, together called "Quraysh 1,"[21] advocated destruction of the regional government and the murder of black tribal leaders. This marked an escalation of the Fur–Arab war that the 1989 tribal peace conference at El Fasher could hardly paper over.

During that war, Musa Hilal of the Mahamid section of northern Rizayqat first came to prominence. His father, Hilal Muhammad Abdallah, had during a long *shaykh*-ship sought increased influence by welcoming from Chad other Rizayqat tribesmen, a policy pursued also by his rival for tribal leadership, *Shaykh* Adud Hassaballah of the Mahariya. In this both were successful, but neither could contend with the effects of drought. Increasingly impoverished as their pastures dried up, Rizayqat were forced to settle on land no one else wanted or to work as day laborers in the towns. Libya offered a third alternative: many went there to work or to train in desert camps of the Islamic Legion. With the collapse of the Nimayri regime in 1985 and the accession of al-Sadiq al-Mahdi, the borders with Libya opened wide. Darfur became the transit route for war materiel passing to the fronts and rebels in Chad, and many Rizayqat returned to their homeland, armed to the teeth and ready for battle in the Fur–Arab war of 1987–89. By then, leadership of the Mahamid had fallen to Musa Hilal, in alliance with Libya. Musa was stripped of the tribal *shaykh*-ship in 1988 by the Fur governor, Tijani Sese, who was, however, seen off in the aftermath of the NIF coup.[22]

With the advent of the NIF, Musa Hilal came into his own. Aggrieved by the desertification of their lands, armed with Kalashnikovs and a racist ideology that justified their indiscriminate use, his militia ranged against the Zaghawa and into Dar Masalit, where they became involved in the 1996–99 fighting noted earlier. Disputes of the usual kind between tribes, which in the past would have been settled with palavers and payments, Musa Hilal now preferred to deal with through ambush and raid. In league with politicians in Khartoum, he became the spearhead of ethnic cleansing that would spread throughout Darfur. A plan of action, anonymous, amateurish, but no less fiendish for that, appeared in 1998–99 as "Quraysh 2," claiming that the Sudan – from the Nile to Lake Chad – had been usurped from its rightful owners, Arab descendants of the Prophet Muhammad. To retrieve it, they should not scruple to cooperate with the NIF and even southern Sudanese, but should rely on their Arab brothers in Libya and beyond. We cannot know to what degree disparate elements that have come together in the ethnic cleansing of Darfur subscribe to such views, but the implications beyond Darfur, for Chad and the Central African Republic, are clear.[23]

The Roots of Rebellion

During the course of the Arab war of the mid-1980s, self-defense forces sprang up among the Fur, armed partly through alliance with the Habre regime in Chad and partly through gunrunning from the Central African Republic. There is evidence, too, of contacts with the SPLM, whose enemy, the Khartoum regime, was increasingly seen as the enemy of the Fur. Resistance to Arab depredations – whether these were Chadian- or Libyan-inspired and whether carried out with the connivance or in defiance of the government – had at first no ideological content: there is little evidence of real attachment to the idea of an "African Belt." Darfur had produced nothing comparable even to the regional "parties" of the Nuba Mountains and the eastern Sudan, let alone political-military organizations comparable to those of the south during the first civil war and the SPLM. The Darfur Development Front of 1965 (like many "parties" of that era) had been a few educated youths with a fancy name. The mobilization of Fur opposition to appointment of a non-Fur governor in 1981 and the electoral inroads of the NIF are evidence of the relative lateness and multipolarity of Fur political consciousness.

That late mobilization of Darfur's "Africans" testifies to the salience of "becoming Sudanese," a paradigm only lately discredited. Educated non-Arabs were all Muslims, all spoke Arabic, all had adopted some cultural norms of the *jallaba* in their midst. Far from resenting Arab superiority, Fur especially were widely seen as condescendingly lordly heirs to an ancient culture. That view was reinforced by the election of Diraige, son of a Fur *shartay*, as governor in 1981, and by the patronage that ensued. Organization of *jakab* units under local *akadas* in the later 1980s was defensive and practical, not driven by a sense of Fur nationalism. It was emergence of the Arab Alliance that stimulated further response: when government inaction gave way to downright collusion with Bani Halba and Rizayqat marauders in 1996, self-defense units sprang up among the Masalit. In one episode, farmers under Khamis Abbakir attacked and defeated a government force at Jabal Endia. Thus, by the time of the all-tribal peace conference at Nyala in 1997, interest in a regional structure similar to that of the southern Sudan after 1972, including an ex officio vice presidency of the republic, and in proportional distribution of resources and jobs was hardly evidence of revolutionary nationalism, let alone, as Khartoum incessantly claimed without irony, of "separatism" and "racism." Diraige's Sudan Federal Party was little more than a name.

Also relatively late were attempts – or, at any rate, sustained attempts – to link Fur self-defense units in a common front. In 1996–97, efforts began in Darfur, Khartoum, and among Fur living abroad to raise money for arms and to coordinate resistance within the region. The local effort focused on Jabal Marra, the historic redoubt of the Fur and terrain ideal for guerilla resistance. Veterans and deserters came in from the Sudanese army to train recruits there. Under the leadership of Abd al-Wahid Muhammad al-Nur, a lawyer who would become first chairman of the Sudan Liberation Army, cells were also set up in Zalingei and in the Wadi Salih. Ahmad Abd al-Shafiʿ, the SLA's future coordinator, organized the large Fur community in the Khartoum region. There, and in other eastern towns with Fur migrant communities, social activities took on a political dimension and money was raised for the cause. But it was apparently not until 2000 that military camps were established in Darfur[24] and even later that what may be called offensive military activity began.

The critical impetus for creation of a common cause among the victims of the "Arab Alliance" came from the NIF regime itself. Each of the several major groups that would eventually form the nucleus of revolt – the Fur, Zaghawa, and Masalit – was the focus of ever-increasing violence from Arab militias, and pleas for government protection fell on deaf ears or were even punished. A pioneering researcher's interviews at the time tell the same story – of sympathetic officials unable to act because of orders from Khartoum and of ordinary members of the community having leadership thrust upon them by the government's discrimination and mistreatment.[25]

There was little in the record of the Zaghawa, prominent victims of the decades of drought and notable participants in the Chadian wars, to suggest common cause with the Fur against the Arab Alliance or NIF. But in several incidents in the late 1980s, Arab militiamen attacked and killed some 200 Zaghawa migrating south from drought, then failed to honor terms of the peace. In both the Alliance's rhetoric and its depredations against the Fur and Masalit, the Zaghawa saw their future. As early as 1991, tribal leaders petitioned the NIF government, explicitly charging it with fomenting unrest within and between the non-Arab tribes and with seeking "apartheid" in Darfur. By the late 1990s, as *janjawid* outrages increased, Zaghawa activists began to organize and strike back, at first on a small scale. In part because some local officials were paid collaborators of the regime, the local community was split, however, and it was not until 2001 that widespread civil disobedience began. In a notorious episode, *janjawid* killed 125 people at Abu Gamra, including two head teachers and 36 people meeting to discuss reopening local schools. This finally led to organized resistance; contact was made with Abd al-Wahid Muhammad in Khartoum. In July, he accompanied Da'ud Tahir Hariga to Kornoi in northern Darfur, and in a meeting of the Zaghawa camp leaders, agreement was reached to make common cause against the NIF and *janjawid*.

THE DESTRUCTION
OF DARFUR

THE REVOLT

The NIF Split

From its first days in 1989, the true balance of power within the
National Islamic Front (NIF) regime was unclear. Was General Bashir
a stalking horse for the NIF, its public face, or its clever exploiter? Was
Hasan al-Turabi the party ideologue, self-proclaimed "Guide," power
behind the throne, or imam-in-waiting? Or did both just strut and crow
while a military strongman, Ali Uthman Muhammad Taha, ruled the
roost? Whenever it seemed that the fog was clearing, something happened to stir confusion, at least in the public mind. Through it all,
however, the determination of the generals to rule and the ability of
Turabi to make trouble were constant themes. By the late 1990s, with
multiple crises confronting the regime, it seemed that a shaking out was
at hand.

While musings about personal precedence occupied Khartoum's
chattering classes, the rest of the world said it wanted peace and stability in the Sudan. The disastrous war in the south, with its massive
refugee crises, famines, and atrocities, and its spillover into neighboring states, had finally begun, unconscionably late, to attract sustained
attention outside the region. The Sudan's official economy continued to
teeter on the verge of collapse, awaiting the oil production that would
save it and lubricate the regime's political relations with the international community. Thus, the recurring public displays of ferment, or
petulance, within the NIF hierarchy exasperated the Sudan's neighbors
and erstwhile partners, who would be happy with a military dictator of

the traditional type but were repeatedly embarrassed by the mercurial Turabi. Crucially, too, the apparently limitless flexibility of Turabi's Islam had cost him credibility within his own movement.

In late 1999, the split between Turabi and Bashir reached crescendo. Having first made a "reconciliation" agreement with al-Sadiq al-Mahdi, on 12 December Bashir declared a state of emergency and dissolved parliament, moves Turabi publicly denounced as a coup. Neighboring states rushed to congratulate the regime and assure it of support, glad to be rid – or so they thought – of Turabi. Mutual recriminations continued, however, and the fact that Turabi seemed untouchable revived his mystique. In June 2000, he was removed from his position in the NIF (since 1998 styled National Congress Party) and announced formation of a new political vehicle, the Popular Patriotic Congress (PPC). Thus, while the regime held on with support of the regular army and pragmatists of the old school, Turabi turned to the less sophisticated provincial bases of his personal support, not least in Darfur. The fact that Bashir had already shut down the NIF's provincial offices may in part have reflected wariness of Turabi's surviving power base. But after PPC delegates signed a bizarre "Memorandum of Understanding" with the Sudan People's Liberation Movement (SPLM) in February 2001, committing Turabi to alliance with the southerners in peaceful opposition to the NIF regime, he was finally jailed in a train of events highly reminiscent of 1985, when his arrest after years of collaboration had endowed him with "opposition" status just before the regime was overthrown.[1]

Darfur and the Southern Peace Process

By jettisoning Hasan al-Turabi and moving to repair relations with the Umma (and thus divide the opposition), the government signaled an intention to act pragmatically to stay in power. The same motive lay behind its willingness to negotiate with the SPLM. This did not mean that it would give up its Islamist credentials. Over several years, in a series of negotiations punctuated by long gaps and continued fighting, the two sides moved closer together or, rather, with outside mediation, so narrowed their ostensible differences as to make a truce seem feasible. We emphasize "ostensible" differences, however, because the peace deal finally achieved in 2005 would depend, as the admittedly more deeply flawed and ultimately failed 1972 Addis Ababa Agreement had depended, on Khartoum's willingness to see it through.

Credit for achieving peace is due mainly to the SPLM and NIF themselves, without whose willingness, however Machiavellian or even feigned it proves to be, no deal could have been concluded. Nonetheless, many other interests converged to bring this about. Not least, the U.S. government, after the terrorist attacks of 11 September 2001, rearranged its foreign relations in a bleak parody of the Cold War, in which all sovereign states (and their usurpers) were either "for" or "against" the "War on Terror." The Sudanese government reportedly increased its level of cooperation – the beginnings and extent of which are difficult at this remove to assess – with the CIA.[2] The U.S. government's consequent softer line toward Khartoum – and more direct involvement in the "peace process" – went some way toward blunting the force of condemnation emanating from American religious and humanitarian groups. Not for the first time, a host of mediators pursued settlement far more urgently than the parties. In a series of agreements over several years (2002–04), the chief components of a comprehensive deal were agreed to piecemeal. But the suspicion arose that Khartoum used the international myopia induced by this "peace process" to buy freedom of action in Darfur.

Since its founding in 1983, the SPLM had consistently called for creation of a "new Sudan," secular and egalitarian, in which marginalized regions, including Darfur, would come into their own. This message had never attracted much support outside the south. SPLA forays into Darfur had been notably unsuccessful. Far from raising the Fur and Masalit against Khartoum, the SPLA faced offensives from militarized Baqqara Arabs. Now, in the incremental "peace process," even rhetorical bases for such interregional alliance – and thus implicitly for the "new Sudan" – were whittled away. It is safe to generalize that the vast majority of Sudanese, northern and southern, as well as most interested outsiders, had treated SPLM rhetoric as just that: a way to throw off the "separatist" tag anathematized in Africa and reduced by foreigners to "tribalism." Somewhere between a unitary Sudan under the heel of an Islamist government and the secular paradise of a New Sudan was where realists, whose number grew to include most European governments as well as the United States, the Sudan's neighbors, and the disestablished northern political parties, saw the future. The issues reduced ultimately to one: self-determination for the south. Defining the options available through "self-determination" and the mechanism through which it would be exercised, and indeed defining "the south" (to the ultimate exclusion of the Nuba Mountains and other border regions) took three long years.[3]

While foreign governments, conflict-resolution experts, and, fitfully, international media focused on the southern Sudan, where the consequences of the long war were unarguably horrendous, the deterioration in Darfur received scant attention. There were several reasons for this, all relevant to an understanding of how events unfolded during and after the period. The length and complexity of the southern crisis had engendered what amounted to a local subsidiary of the global "disaster relief industry": departments of foreign ministries, branches of aid organizations, special southern Sudan–centered overseas charities, parliamentary committees, missionary organizations and slave rescuers, oil drillers and oil services companies, American university endowment managers, peace institutes, unemployed Sudanese expatriates, adoption facilitators, all-terrain-vehicle dealers, conference organizers, media watchdogs, nutrition assessment teams, Sudanese politicians, arms dealers, disaster tourists, East African aircraft-leasing companies, stringers, grant writers, and others had stakes in the duration of the war and the terms of its settlement. Nothing like this had yet evolved around Darfur. Second – and for various reasons – the world reduced the war to Arab Muslim northerners against African "Christian or animist" southerners, with an almost Manichean precision that made it seem easy to understand, not least after September 2001, when it could be seen as a local battle in the worldwide "conflict of civilizations." In this scheme of things, Darfur "belonged" to "the north," and its problems must be of an exasperatingly "tribal," not global, nature: were Darfur dissidents using Khartoum's preoccupation in the south for their own advantage or even petulantly demanding attention while southerners died? Finally, the very ability, against all odds and despite important defections, of the SPLM to hold together and the increasing sophistication, as the war went on, of its propaganda, had given "the south" an identifiable human face on the international scene, long before Darfur's rebels had coalesced or even named themselves, let alone attracted foreign media attention.

In January 2005, a Comprehensive Peace Agreement (CPA) signed in Nairobi finally ended the war between Khartoum and the SPLM. Under its terms, the south had the right to exercise self-determination by referendum six years later. John Garang, the SPLM leader, would become first vice president of the Sudan. When he died in a plane crash in July 2005, the position went to his successor as chairman of the SPLM, Salva Kiir. Islamic law would not be applied in the south. Revenue from the borderland oil fields would be evenly divided between the central government and the Southern Region. The national army would evacuate the south, and joint units with the SPLA would be formed in the Khartoum area.

By the time of its signing, the CPA had already been endangered by events in Darfur. Among both Sudanese and foreign participants in the "peace process," the perception was widespread that Khartoum had agreed to terms seemingly favorable to the south because of a new preoccupation with the west, which all Islamists saw as integral to the Sudanese homeland. Besides, six years was a long time in Sudanese politics, and once the west was brought to heel, the NIF, or its successor in Khartoum, could trump up excuses for renouncing the deal with the south: it had happened before, and now (mid-2009) there is much reason to suppose it will happen again. This scenario embarrassed foreign interlocutors, who bristled at the notion of buying peace in the south at the cost of genocide in the west. In any case, the descent of the west had begun long before the southern negotiations neared completion, and the westerners were fighting for survival, not a referendum.

But the war in the south affected the rebellion in Darfur in several ways, and although it would be an exaggeration to see the latter as a continuation elsewhere of the former, there were indeed common elements in the behavior of the serial antagonist, the NIF regime. The degree to which SPLM propaganda influenced thinking within the Fur, Masalit, and other communities in Darfur and the diaspora cannot be measured, but the fact of such influence is clear enough in statements by rebel leaders – notably including the founding manifesto of the Sudan Liberation Army (SLA) – and in Khartoum's own propaganda. Realization that "Africans" of Darfur had been marginalized in much the same way as southerners (and others) was crucial, for it cleared the way for an ideology of protest against economic deprivation and racial discrimination rather than of "tribal warfare" or supine exploitation by coreligionists.

Despite NIF charges that self-defense forces in Darfur were treasonous adjuncts of the SPLM, contacts with the southern leadership, secretly within the country and more casually in friendly capitals abroad, bore little fruit: the quixotic "invasion" of Da'ud Bulad in 1991 was a unique and wholly abortive event that seemed only to emphasize the futility of SPLM claims to speak for the disenfranchised west. Attempts by the SPLM since 2005 to mediate or to facilitate negotiations between the NIF regime and Darfur's rebels have failed, not least because of the SPLM's ambiguous junior partnership in Khartoum's "government of national unity" (GONU).

The Justice and Equality Movement and the *Black Book*

As the southern "peace process" unfolded and fighting continued in the south, Darfur descended into undeclared but disastrous civil war. In the midst of this there appeared in May 2000 the *Black Book* (*al-kitab al-aswad*), a polemic purporting to reveal decades of Darfur's neglect and underdevelopment by successive Khartoum regimes dominated by a few riverain Arab tribes. This was the work of dissident members of the NIF and others who, since 1993, had met secretly to discuss the need for change. They established a committee in 1997 to gather information. The plan was to inform, not inflame, the masses. By the time the *Black Book* was published, its authors had already concluded that more than public education would be needed to bring about the degree of change the Sudan required.

Several aspects of the *Black Book* are important. First, its apparent joint authorship was anonymous:[4] the book itself credits "Seekers of Truth and Justice," but there was strong suspicion that disillusioned Muslim Brothers, or even Hasan al-Turabi, was behind it. That so many possible authors were mooted spoke volumes against the government. Second, widespread shock at revelations in the book, almost all of which were drawn from public documents and government publications, testified to the immaturity of Darfur's – and the country's – politics: any few educated Sudanese could have produced the damning statistics about underrepresentation of the peripheral regions in the Sudan's parliaments, cabinets, councils, and provincial governorships since independence. Similar statistics had long illustrated southerners' case against Khartoum, and progressive northerners had for decades railed against the disparities in economic development the book condemns. The innovation of the *Black Book* was a further breakdown of the beneficiaries' ethnicity *by tribe*, which showed continuing dominance of the Shayqiyya, Ja'aliyyin, and Danaqla Arabs. Third, the regime's Nixonian instinct upon publication was not to respond but to find the "leakers": only an insider, it was thought, could have obtained the book's data – an inaccurate charge that revealed the ignorance of the bureaucracy.

Reaction to the *Black Book* was therefore surprising mostly because it contained so little that was new. The analogy may be made to the emperor's new clothes, because all educated Sudanese, and especially those interested in politics – the two sets of people are nearly identical – knew the makeup of successive regimes and relative enrichment of a few tribes. But whereas some observers would have quietly ascribed this to merit or even luck – location, access to colonial-era educational opportunities, age-old commercial ties – for others, notably Westerners, the *Black Book* brought the subject into the open. Disparities were not, the *Black Book* seemed to tell them, the result simply of Darfur's remoteness and climate but of *policies* pursued by the Khartoum elite to keep them poor; domination of government institutions by riverain Arabs was not the result simply of their higher education but also of their nepotism and indeed organization of the government to serve their own interests. In other words, the *Black Book* made a coherent case for the conscious underdevelopment of Darfur, a case, moreover, into which the depredations of the *janjawid* could be rationally fitted: ethnic cleansing was political and economic discrimination carried to an extreme.

In any event, the *Black Book* helped to unite disparate elements of Darfur's resistance. Within a few days of publication, it had been widely distributed within the Sudan and abroad. The government's almost hysterical reaction coincided with growing fear of the mischief Hasan al-Turabi was capable of unleashing against the regime in Darfur and with increased support for Arab militias there. Thus, the *Black Book* ironically served a purpose for its targets, who intensified activities to counter the threat to the Arabs they purported to see in its "racism" and "separatism." Prominent in this effort were several northern Rizayqat: General Abdallah Safi al-Nur, both before and especially after he was made governor of Northern Darfur in January 2000; Jibril Abdallah, the provincial minister of education; and General Husayn Abdallah Jibril, a powerful member of the Khartoum parliament. During Abdallah Safi al-Nur's governorship, heavier weapons were handed over to the Arab militias, new recruits were brought in, and efforts increased to disarm non-Arabs. At the same time, Baqqara Rizayqat were prominent in ratcheting up the violence in Southern Darfur. These included Abdalla Ali Masar, Hasabu Abd al-Rahman, and Abd al-Hamid Musa Kasha, a minister in the central government; General Adam Hamid Musa, of the Zayyidiyya, later governor of Southern Darfur, also played a role in obtaining arms for Musa Hilal and his *janjawid*. In May 2001, summary courts of justice were introduced in the region, and amputations, cross-amputations, and stonings were reported.[5]

Efforts to organize the Arabs against the Fur, Masalit, and Zaghawa were not limited to Darfur or even to the Sudan. Both Abdallah Safi al-Nur and Musa Hillal recruited thousands of Arabs in Chad, who, depending on their tribal affiliations, were sent to one of several camps in Darfur – Mistiriha for Rizayqat; Jabal Adula for Baqqara Rizayqat and Ma'alia; Gardud for Sa'ada and Bani Halba; and Jabal Karju for Tarjam, Ta'aisha, and Salamat – where they were trained and outfitted by the NIF government.[6] It was only to an outside world wholly ignorant of events in Darfur that this – had it been acknowledged at all – could be described as defensive activity. On the contrary, the government was combining and escalating aspects of an old policy: alliance with and use of local, aggrieved (or greedy) surrogates to achieve its ends. Although Khartoum may have been correct in labeling the steps taken to organize resistance among the non-Arabs as a "rebellion," it was so only in a formal sense.

Meanwhile, the activists behind the *Black Book*, perhaps impressed by the force of their own case, had taken steps to transform their quiescent cellular groups into a political and military organization. This, the Justice and Equality Movement (JEM), was publicly announced in August 2001. Its program logically followed from the revelations of the *Black Book*. It dismissed separatism and called for radical constitutional reform, regional empowerment, and social democracy but not secularism: Muslims should have the right to apply the *shari'a* to themselves. JEM's founding chairman was Khalil Ibrahim, a medical doctor hailing from the Zaghawa Kobe, who dominated the movement. In an attempt to broaden its appeal, Nur al-Din Dafa'allah of the Misiriyya was made deputy chairman, and members of other tribes were appointed to various posts of uncertain weight.[7] JEM thus had the makings of a regional political party, bringing together Islamists disillusioned with the NIF – and with Hasan al-Turabi – and Darfur intellectuals with no place else to go.

ORGANIZING THE REVOLT

The Darfur Liberation Front

In July 2001 Fur and Zaghawa resistance leaders met at Abu Gamra to forge an alliance against the *janjawid*-NIF program in Darfur. These included Abd al-Wahid Muhammad al-Nur and Abduh Abdallah Isma'il for the Fur and, for the Zaghawa, Khatir Tur al-Khalla, Abdallah Abbakir, and Juma'a Muhammad Hagar, veterans of Idris Deby's campaign against Hissene Habre in Chad and all soon to be military commanders in Darfur. The bloc was expanded in November when, at Zalingei, Masalit resistance fighters joined. Military training began in Jabal Marra and in February 2002 the first offensive operation of what would be called the Darfur Liberation Front (DLF) took place when a government post near Nyala was attacked and destroyed. Had the raid been against a *janjawid* camp, the regime might have shrugged it off as a surprising turn in "tribal warfare," but an overt act against the government was something new. Khartoum predictably denounced the DLF as a fifth column for southern rebels but feared a connection between them and the military forces of the northern Sudanese opposition-in-exile in Eritrea. Over the wisdom of armed resistance in Darfur there was still debate, and the DLF apparently received no such support. The two leading Fur figures in the exile community, Ahmad Ibrahim Diraige and Sharif Harir, having issued in July 2002 a joint declaration urging Darfur unity in opposition, still disagreed on strategy.[8]

In Khartoum, Fur members of the torpid parliament sent a highly publicized account of *janjawid* raids to the president, with dates, times, locations, and casualty figures, and with evidence of Arab settlement where Fur villagers had been dispossessed: this was ethnic cleansing in all but name. Raids were sometimes simultaneous and thus coordinated; cattle were not just rustled but simply killed; not only houses but also even trees were destroyed, to render targeted locations uninhabitable; nearby police and soldiers took no action, or they arrested complainants. Villages were being renamed in Arabic. Faced with a public demand for action, in May 2002 Bashir appointed a Committee for Restoration of State Authority and Security in Darfur under Ibrahim Muhammad Sulayman, a retired general and governor of Northern Darfur and a Berti. A professional soldier, he concluded that rebel demands could be met in negotiations. He arrested leaders of both sides, including Abd al-Wahid Muhammad al-Nur and the *janjawid* captain himself, Musa Hillal, who was shipped off to Port Sudan. But "moderating influences" were not what the government or, at any rate, its military intelligence, which was pulling the strings in Darfur, wanted.[9]

When rebel raids continued, the government decided to hold a Fur Leadership Conference, which, with some 129 delegates, began on 16 August at Nyertete under the chairmanship of Husayn Ayub, a son of Ali Dinar and recognized head of the former royal family. Moderates saw this as a traditionally sanctioned last chance for peace; hard-liners welcomed its publicity and potential for buying time and saving face, even as the sluggish southern "peace process," at Machacos in Kenya, had reached yet another critical phase. It is notable that Abd al-Wahid Muhammad al-Nur and other Fur militants were not released from jail to participate. Rather than endorsing government bromides, however, the conference sent a delegation to a DLF camp in Jabal Marra to hear its side. The ensuing consensus statement of the conference, while rejecting the notion that one group or party spoke for all the Fur, condemned both the *janjawid* and the government, whose forces had fomented and joined in the rapine. The conference demanded what the government could hardly refuse: that it carry out its central responsibility for maintaining security.[10]

That the government had no intention of doing so was already clear. There was no reason to think that Fur unanimity, however surprising, would bring about a change in Khartoum's policy. Its purpose in holding the Nyertete conference was to improve its public face; even as the conference was under way, the government was making plans to expand assistance to the *janjawid*. At a second conference, held in September at Kas by the governor of Southern Darfur, Salah Ali al-Ghali, another former general and a known sympathizer with the "Arab Alliance," all the region's problems were blamed squarely on the Fur self-defense forces and troublemaking followers of Hasan al-Turabi in the militias; the "conference" even demanded the return of Musa Hillal (who was living under "house arrest" in the capital). Jabal Marra was declared a closed district and surrounded by government troops.

It was in this context that, at Budke in October, the DLF elected its first officers: the Fur Abd al-Wahid Muhammad al-Nur as chairman and Abdallah Abbakir of the Zaghawa as chief of staff; the post of deputy chairman, unfilled until early 2005, was reserved for a Masalati. Perhaps more notably, leadership posts were soon thereafter given to several Arabs, including Ahmad Kubbar, a renegade Rizaygat veteran of the SPLA, and Idris Nawai of the Kordofan Hawazma. Both sides prepared for war: when Ali Uthman Muhammad Taha, the vice president and regime strongman, visited El Fasher in November with the finance minister, Zubayr Ahmad al-Hasan, they promoted development schemes on the one hand and, on the other, warned that what had happened to the south in *its* war was a preview of what was in store for Darfur.[11]

The Sudan Liberation Movement/Sudan Liberation Army (SLM/SLA)

That word of the founding of the DLF came first from the government indicated its stake in shaping the debate over Darfur. Where the very name originated is uncertain: the armed force came first, then its title, then its metamorphosis into a "movement." This last turn of events apparently resulted from contacts with the SPLM, during which the necessity of a political program, if only to deflect the inevitable charges of "tribalism" and "racism" from Khartoum, was urged: resistance without politics was banditry; politics without arms was wind. In the resulting manifesto, issued on 16 March 2003, the SPLM's influence was clear. The document called for a secular state and self-determination for Darfur, denounced the oppression of all the Sudan's marginalized peoples, and urged Darfur's Arabs to join the SLM/SLA in bringing about a New Sudan. Within days of publication, the southern rebel movement, at yet another crossroads in the "peace process," endorsed it. The upshot of this convergence was probably most significant in helping to bring Darfur to the attention of the outside world, where the Western media were preoccupied with Iraq.[12]

Relations between the SLM/SLA and the southern rebel leadership, although useful to both, introduced a discordant element to the fragile alliance of the Darfur resistance. Holding together fiercely independent tribesmen with long histories of intrasectional and even intraclan rivalry was difficult enough without taunts from Khartoum of subservience to southern infidels and slaves. Relations between the Fur and Zaghawa had not recovered from the troubles of the 1980s. Sections of the Zaghawa had gone separate ways in the Chadian wars. The SLM/SLA's leadership was inexperienced and, as Darfur began to attract Western attention, drawn to the glamour of external affairs. And between JEM's Islamists and the SLA's insistent secularism was a gap that enemies could easily widen. There was even generational tension between the older, educated, and more politically experienced and the younger cadres.[13] As against a ramshackle resistance Khartoum had decades of experience in dividing and ruling, it had an army with heavy weapons, it had local agents in the *janjawid*, and it was fighting on its enemies' land, amid their homes and families.

DARFUR'S SORROW: 2003–2004

Early Rebel Successes

Ali Uthman Muhammad Taha's threat, purposefully delivered in El Fasher in November 2002, soon proved to have been serious. But faced with rebellion in the west as it tried to settle in the south, Khartoum opted for the same apparently ambiguous approach that had failed in that war. In doing so, there is considerable evidence not only of ineptness and indecision but also of gross underestimation of the willingness or ability of the rebels to resist. On 26 February 2003, an SLA force of 300 well-armed men in thirty "technicals" (pickup trucks)[14] attacked the garrison town of Golu and killed 200 soldiers. The government reaction was confused in the extreme: when a low-level mission was sent to "negotiate" with the rebels, officials in Khartoum and at the southern peace talks dismissed them as bandits, belittled the raid, and then demanded surrender, failing which the army could "solve the situation in twenty-four hours."[15] But Ibrahim Muhammad Sulayman, governor of Northern Darfur, was nonetheless sent to London to meet Dr. Khalil Ibrahim of the JEM, predictably to no avail; the choice of talking to the disaffected Islamist in exile was telling. After the rebels took the border town of Tinay and its garrison's supply of arms and ammunition in March, President Bashir, visiting El Fasher, promised that the army would be "unleashed."[16] On 25 April, SLA and JEM forces attacked both El Fasher and Nyala. At El Fasher, they surprised the sleeping garrison at the airport, destroying planes and helicopters, capturing vehicles and weapons, killing or capturing scores of soldiers, and carrying off the base commander, General Bushra Isma'il.[17] In a battle near Kutum in May, the SLA killed 500 soldiers and took 300 prisoners. In July, a second assault on Tinay left some 250 government soldiers dead. On 1 August, the SLA actually occupied Kutum, killing much of the garrison in the process.

Its threats and boasts ringing ever more hollow, the government realized that a stationary (and increasingly demoralized) army was no match for the inspired and highly mobile rebels and their lightning-like guerrilla tactics. Khartoum's response was therefore two-pronged. On the political front, a campaign of repression began. A state of emergency was declared and hundreds of alleged rebel sympathizers were arrested. The governors of Northern and Western Darfur were dismissed. President Bashir appointed a "special task force" of loyalists and old Darfur hands, including the ministers of the interior and defense, state security officials, and al-Tayyib Muhammad Khayr and Abdallah Safi al-Nur, both former governors of Darfur. In a move first viewed as conciliatory but in retrospect ominous of the reign of terror about to be unleashed, Bashir also dissolved the special courts of summary justice in the region.

Even as the rebels' string of victories continued, the government held back, preparing a devastating response. Desultory negotiations, which had included an approach by two prominent Umma faction-alists, ended.[18] Advice from moderates such as Ibrahim Muhammad Sulayman was rejected. The special task force planned coordination of the army with the *janjawid*. Recruitment drives began among the Arab tribes, and the support or at least acquiescence of tribal *shaykhs* was bought with cash and the usual promises of future consideration – pump schemes, schools, vaccination campaigns, and the like. Thousands of young tribesmen came in to be armed; non-Arabs answering the call were turned away. Everyone else – convicts, fugitives, desperadoes – was welcomed, the shadier the better. The government appointed military advisers to the *janjawid* and began to supply communications equipment and artillery.

Most ominously of all, the notorious Musa Hilal, like some noxious germ, was released from house arrest in the capital, reportedly with a specific appointment as a *janjawid* captain of all the captains. Under his orders, thousands of militiamen moved from southern Darfur to the north, where he established a new base at Jabal Sirru. By one account, there were by this time at least six brigades of *janjawid* in league with the regular army, with martial names and a piratical esprit de corps. The leader of one such, the Victory Brigade, Abd al-Rahim Ahmad Muhammad "al-Shurkatalla," boasted that he was Izrael, the Angel of Death.[19] Such men as these had little interest in taking on the rebels. As JEM and SLA strategy had consisted of surprise attacks on army posts, so the *janjawid* would make surprise attacks on civilians in their towns and villages. In this strategy, the army's role would be largely to provide air support: bombing, strafing, and transporting, while also sometimes mopping up after the *janjawid* were finished with a place.

The NIF-*Janjawid* Alliance in Action

This strategy was implemented well before the end of 2003 and, within a year, had effectively turned much of Darfur into a killing field. Around the middle of 2003, the SLA noticed a shift in the government's and *janjawid*'s focus from rebel camps to civilians. The division of labor was remarkably efficient against a largely unarmed and sedentary population. Several methods were perfected. In one, old transport planes with open rear ramps flew low over targeted villages and rolled out barrels filled with explosives and shrapnel. Helicopter gunships or jet fighters would follow, destroying buildings with rockets or heavy machine-gun fire. Ground forces – *janjawid* on horseback or camels or in "technicals," or soldiers in trucks, or a combined force – would then surround the settlement and move in.

What happened next varied from place to place only in detail. Women and girls were raped, anything portable of value was taken, animals were rustled or killed, and houses still standing were torched; stragglers were shot or stabbed and children sometimes tossed into burning houses. Wells were polluted with dead bodies. Survivors reported frequent verbal abuse: racial epithets, the words *zurqa* ("black") and *abid* ("slaves") perhaps most often, and shouted claims to Arab ownership of the land. In some cases, women and girls, after rape, were branded to make permanently visible their humiliation; in others they were abducted, ravished over time, then released or killed depending on the whim of their tormenters. For similar effect, villagers were mutilated and their bodies left exposed; torture, decapitation, schoolchildren chained together and burned alive – there seemed to be no limit. On some occasions, men and boys were lined up and executed, in others they were led off, never to be seen again. Some towns and villages were attacked several times before they were finally burned down. Everything was destroyed, even the mosques. However horrific the details, the ultimate object was always the same: destruction of settlements and property, depopulation of the land through the death of the men, death or spoliation of the women, and the flight in terror of survivors.[20]

Early in the cycle of violence, local police and other government officials decamped, leaving whole districts to fend for themselves. This in turn allowed the "security forces" to claim that those areas were under rebel control, thus justifying the attacks that followed. In this way, the government and *janjawid* not only "ethnically cleansed" an area but also created the very recruits to the rebel cause it claimed to suppress. Young men whose villages and cultivations had been destroyed and who, with surviving relatives, were in refugee camps in Darfur or were charity cases in Chad had all the more incentive to join the rebellion. Groups of refugees were indeed hunted down, whether in flight that was slowed by the old and young or, once gathered in or on the outskirts of towns, as if for easier targeting by the *janjawid*. In some cases, this was systematic: troops and *janjawid* would conduct hut-to-hut searches of refugee areas, ascertain the home village of the young men, then take them away to be executed. Men of rank were special targets. The disappearance of all legal authority created a vacuum filled by *janjawid* brigands: unofficial roadblocks were set up to shake down anyone brave enough to travel; protection money was extorted from villages not yet marked for destruction; people likely to earn a ransom were kidnapped. Encountering aid workers, refugees declined food, lest they be attacked later by *janjawid* wanting to steal it.[21]

According to the U.S. State Department, by August 2004 at least 400 villages in Darfur had been destroyed – other estimates are much higher – 200,000 refugees had crossed into eastern Chad, and some

1.2 million "internally displaced persons" (IDPs in the inimitable jargon of this field) remained in the western Sudan. Most of these had fled to the main towns, notably Kabkabiyya, Kutum, El Fasher, El Geneina, and Zalingei, where they were relegated to camps on the outskirts. There, often destitute and frequently without male relatives, women and girls foraging or collecting firewood were picked off and raped or murdered by roaming *janjawid*. Altogether, the UN estimated that about one-third of Darfur's population – 2.2 million of 6 million – had by then been affected by the violence. But the *janjawid* and Sudanese army had by then limited their areas of operation almost entirely to Northern and, especially, Western Darfur; Southern Darfur had been relatively unscathed. And the numbers – of villages destroyed, people killed and put to flight – were increasing all the time.[22]

Death Watch

As evidence of ethnic cleansing continued to pour out of Darfur, Khartoum's response was commensurately cynical. Any such policy was denied: the accusations were all false, the result of misinformation, rebel propaganda, Western media bias against Arabs and Islam, Zionist machinations, troublemaking neighboring regimes, the inevitable occasional excess in war, and political dissidents – everyone from superannuated communists to Hasan al-Turabi – trying to scuttle the southern "peace process." When the UN's departing Humanitarian Coordinator for Sudan denounced as war crimes what was happening in Darfur and stated undiplomatically that everyone knew who was behind it, Khartoum branded him a liar and lodged an official protest.[23] Undeniable insecurity in Darfur was blamed on rebel activity, itself only the latest, albeit a serious, example of age-old "tribal conflicts" on a wild frontier. This was the government's line, even as it continued to act in concert with the *janjawid*. In effect, Khartoum had handed to the baser elements of the local population a license to kill; "impunity," as one expert account has put it, "was an integral, official part of the new order." Not only were local officials told not to interfere, they were ordered to supply the *janjawid* with what they needed to get the job done.[24]

After the world began to pay attention, the government added cynical frills to its cover story: handovers of militia weapons were faked for the media, and hapless convicts were taken from their cells and executed as *janjawid*. It hardly seems necessary to report the details of specific documents, tape-recorded conversations, and bald admissions because the evidence for Khartoum's instigation and complicity is overwhelming. Ultimately, the government fell back on the most disarming excuse of all: it was doing its best but the situation was out of control; it would do better. Much time and attention have been spent since 2003, to Khartoum's advantage, on the dubious task of defining the unfolding carnage: was it a race war, ethnic cleansing, or genocide?

Whatever the rest of the world called the mayhem, relief policy made even clearer which side the government was on. As miserable as the refugee camps in Darfur were, people in them were still alive. Rape and murder of stragglers outside the camps were an inefficient method of winnowing. The government therefore put to work its vast experience in the southern Sudan to starve the refugees. It promised full cooperation with and complete access for humanitarian agencies, but experts report a deliberate strategy employing multiple delaying tactics: "a farrago of bureaucratic entanglements" confronted relief workers – travel permits, fuel permits, safety tests for drugs, customs delays of vehicles, minute enforcement of detailed regulations. Food aid was confiscated, stolen, fed to animals, and, in at least one case, impounded as "genetically modified." In a UN investigation of the camp at Kaylak in April 2004, death rates were found to be 40 to 150 *times* higher (by age group) than those denoting "emergency." By the end of the year, a UN official estimated that 10,000 people per month were dying in the camps. Sometimes, when a foreign dignitary was due to visit a specific camp, he arrived to find it had been emptied the day before. But denunciation of Khartoum's lies and trickery seemed an end in itself, assuring the world that those lied to had not been fooled. There were no consequences.[25]

In July–August 2004, an Atrocities Documentation Team assembled by the U.S. State Department from among staff and delegates of independent professional organizations conducted private, semistructured interviews of 1,136 randomly selected Sudanese refugees in some nineteen places in Chad. Sixty-one percent reported that they had witnessed the killing of at least one relative, 16 percent reported having been raped or been told of a rape by the victim. Analysis of this and similar surveys notes that the results are likely underestimates of most atrocities. When all or almost all of a village's people were wiped out, there would be no one left to report the details. As elsewhere, even the most sensitive interviewing techniques could not induce all women to report rape. And most refugees in eastern Chad were from the westernmost parts of Darfur, not least because those from elsewhere had less chance to reach the international border alive. It also has to be borne in mind that people surveyed in such studies, in refugee camps and elsewhere, often simply did not know the fate of relatives and neighbors.[26]

International reaction to the burgeoning crisis in Darfur was for a long time negligible. The industrial democracies preferred official ignorance to embarrassing knowledge of anything that might stand in the way of a settlement in the south and the flow of oil from the Sudan, which by late 2003 already amounted to some 300,000 barrels per day and would likely soon double or triple. (Hopes for oil, the sale of prospecting rights, and recent rumors of strikes in Darfur itself have thus far only fed ever-wilder conspiracy theories.) Most African and Asian governments disdained interference. Aerial bombardment of civilians in Darfur, admitted as evidence that the violence had worsened, ironically only increased hopes that the government was likely to settle soon *in the south*. That the Americans especially wanted a deal in the south more than Khartoum did only emboldened the regime. Periodicals with supposed access to inside information did little reporting of the atrocities and the general news media almost none.[27] *Africa Confidential*, often the first to report rumors and gossip, admitted as late as mid-May 2004 to ignorance of events in the Fur heartland.[28]

This could not last. Despite all the restrictions, Sudanese and foreign aid workers got through, as did even the odd reporter (incognito), embassy officials, merchants, truck drivers, and others. Again calling on its reservoir of experience in the south, the government pursued a policy designed to suppress as much information as possible and to discredit the rest. Sudanese reporters were the first victims: the few newspapermen who dared to report even on *rebel* attacks were intimidated and arrested, and state censorship or lack of interest took care of the rest. By one account, the very word *janjawid* did not appear in the Khartoum press until September 2003. Journals that tried to evade restrictions were suppressed. Foreign reporters were denied visas or not permitted to travel westward; in Khartoum, or abroad, Sudanese who talked to reporters or to aid officials faced arrest at home and indefinite detention. Relief officials suspected of leaking information risked deportation. Print journalism always comes before television; when the Arabic station Al-Jazira beat the rest of the world to the story of atrocities in Darfur, its Sudan bureau was promptly shut down.[29]

Had the government been able to secure the border with Chad, the story of Darfur's sorrow would have been even later in emerging. But when tens of thousands of refugees crossed into Chad, Khartoum was unable to control access to them and, from there, to Darfur itself. It tried. Masalit on the Sudanese side were offered money to patrol the border, and when they refused, their villages were destroyed and soldiers posted to patrol the resulting wasteland.[30] But the Sudanese writ did not run to the Chadian camps, whose inhabitants had nothing to lose from telling their stories. And while the Sudanese army had become adept at slaughtering civilians in villages, it had never been a match for smugglers and nomads; foreign reporters and even television crews with SLA guides or entrepreneurial locals crossed over with increasing frequency and got the story out.

As always in impending human disasters, the warnings and revelations of experts tended to be ignored or discounted as special pleading until the mass media arrived. How and why this happens – and, indeed, why relatively minor tragedies are taken up with alacrity while other more serious cases are never taken up at all – is a study in itself. In the case of Darfur, Amnesty International and the International Crisis Group published accounts in July and December 2003, respectively. If revelations by Sudanese expatriates attracted any attention, they were not pursued; disclosures by the usual opponents of Khartoum – pro-south activists, old northern politicians in exile – were easy to shrug off and difficult to check. The very rare, brief newspaper reports in Europe and the United States seemed otiose and "for the record." The *New York Times* and *Le Monde* finally published harrowing accounts in January 2004.[31] This was already late in the day, but the snowball effect began and "Darfur" was certified a crisis.

Early mass media accounts were poorly drawn. Africa had long experience of foreign correspondents swooping in and buttonholing English-speakers in hotel bars. Many accounts bore datelines of Nairobi, Johannesburg, and other remote haunts of third-hand sources. "Balance" required potted denials from a Sudanese *charge d'affaires* or demurrals by out-of-touch academics about age-old tribal conflicts; the influence of Rider Haggard and the Foreign Legion was discernible in purple prose, while the testimony of relief experts seemed risky to publish unconfirmed. In tabloids and electronic headline news (and in some government circles), stereotypes persisted. In the serious media, these eventually gave way: seasoned correspondents were assigned and went to Khartoum, Chad, the camps, and into Darfur. In some cases, greater coverage did indeed provide "balance" as when, in analytical pieces in the quality press, attempts were made to move past al Qaeda–era fancies and explain Darfur's ethnic makeup. After an uncertain start, the *New York Times* provided characteristically sober reporting, and one of its regular op-ed writers, Nicholas Kristof, took up Darfur as a personal cause, publicly challenging President George W. Bush and the U.S. Congress to act. In Britain, the *Guardian* took the lead. Eventually, of course, "Darfur" found its presumably self-explanatory place in left-liberal litanies, as an issue about which something must be done.

THE WORLD'S RESPONSE

Attempts at Mediation

Contacts between the Darfur rebels and the Sudanese government in 2002–03, as Khartoum was preparing what some would call the "final solution," inevitably came to naught. Even abject surrender would have left the rebels at the mercy of the *janjawid*, which the government had no intention of trying to disarm. From the time the army–*janjawid* whirlwind struck in mid-2003, attempts to mediate failed.

Several of these were orchestrated by Idris Deby's government in Chad, which had an obvious interest in the outcome of the crisis, in which, moreover, it was increasingly and sometimes unwillingly involved. A series of meetings in September–November 2003 achieved a forty-five-day truce so that humanitarian assistance could reach refugees in Darfur, but this was not honored, and attempts to salvage it broke down amid mutual recriminations. Khartoum's only interest was in appearing reasonable, so agreement was easy when there was no intention to honor it. In this context, rebel demands – for international observers, investigation of war crimes, and SLA participation in the continuing north-south "peace process" – exhibited bravado bordering on the fantastic. The refugee crisis within Darfur was at this point growing by tens of thousands a month.[32]

Khartoum similarly used other foreign attempts at mediation to stall. After Ali Uthman Muhammad Taha, the vice president, met Ahmad Ibrahim Diraige, the Fur elder statesman, in Nairobi in January 2004, Diraige agreed to attend a conference in Geneva under the auspices of the Henri Dunant Foundation to open a dialogue. The Sudanese government then backed out, ostensibly because the Geneva meeting had been "politicized," and called instead for a "reconciliation conference" – in Khartoum. These antics might have provoked mirth; that they were designed to buy time was obvious. In February, Bashir declared the army in full control in Darfur and offered yet another poisoned olive branch: a peace conference, full amnesty, and complete access for humanitarian agencies.[33]

After the 2003–04 onslaught, President Deby tried again. Talks were held in Ndjamena in April 2004, this time with the participation of the African Union (AU), which appointed the former prime minister of Niger, Mahid Elgabid, as co-chair with the Chadian foreign minister. The NIF regime entered these talks with renewed vigor, having purportedly suppressed an attempted coup by Hasan al-Turabi at the end of March. The talks resulted in a detailed Humanitarian Cease-fire, which, among other things, established a monitoring commission, required the release of prisoners, and committed the Sudanese government to "neutralizing" the militias and providing unimpeded access to refugees.[34] For all that, the cease-fire was poorly drafted and was broken within days or even hours; sources conflict.

As the killing continued in Darfur, the talks were institutionalized. They dragged on chaotically in Ndjamena – where Deby's government itself barely survived a coup attempt in May – Addis Ababa, and Abuja, with frequent adjournments, walkouts, and delays. Neither the chairmen (Elgabid was replaced in September by Sam Ibok) nor the rebel delegates could match the skill – or the diplomatic resources – of Khartoum's representatives, whose object, after all, was merely to sound plausible in the face of intermittent international concern while the ethnic cleansing progressed. Plausibility was enough because the concern was verbal only – indeed, usually in writing – and rarely emanated from the highest levels of Western governments: such signals were not mistaken in Khartoum. In stalling; prevaricating; milking propaganda

Figure 18. The refugee camp at Kalma, Southern Darfur. By the end of 2006, some 2.5 million people of Darfur had been made refugees in the fighting. (Photo by Khamis Ramad-han/Panapress/Getty Images.)

value; setting one would-be mediator against another; raising legal technicalities; requiring time for consideration, research, and consultations; drafting counterproposals; protesting crowded calendars; and employing all the mumbo-jumbo of diplomacy when one side holds the advantage, the Sudanese government – with almost half a century of institutional memory gained from the "Southern Problem" – was a past master.

"The World's Worst Humanitarian Disaster"

The international community from the start treated the Darfur disaster as a "humanitarian" rather than a political issue. Media reporting understandably (if stereotypically) focused first on the refugees in Chad, then on those in Darfur itself; occasional forays into charred villages and rare footage of *janjawid* in action only later made the question of responsibility unavoidable. The overriding interest of those foreign governments capable of influencing events was the success of the north-south peace talks. Both Khartoum ostensibly and the United States and other interested governments necessarily tried to separate the two conflicts, but the fact that the foreigners were keener on settling the southern war than Khartoum was played into the hands of the ethnic cleansers of the NIF regime. Thus, early international attention focused on relief for survivors of the slaughter rather than on ending it.

The first UN High Commissioner for Refugees (UNHCR) appeal for aid for Darfur was made in September 2003, when there were already 70,000 refugees in Chad and an estimated 400,000 in Darfur. But the first food aid even for the camps in Chad did not arrive until February 2004, at which point there were still no effective mechanisms for providing food for the much larger number of displaced people in Darfur itself. Despite Khartoum's repeated promises of "unimpeded access," few international aid workers were allowed in. As late as May 2004, Britain's Disaster Relief Committee was unable to make an appeal because aid officials had not yet reached the displaced. Local food prices shot up. Thousands braved the walk across Darfur and Kordofan to Khartoum, where new shantytowns appeared. By February 2004, as many as 2.5 million people, the vast majority in squalid "camps" in Darfur, without clean water or adequate sanitation, surrounded by *janjawid* and Sudanese soldiers, were expected soon to require food aid. By one estimate, some 120,000 tons of food were needed for the next rainy season, but only 52,000 tons would be available: "genocide by attrition" was the likely result.[35] Countless other displaced remained in rebel-held territory, cut off. It was in this context, in March 2004, that Mukesh Kapila called Darfur "the world's worst humanitarian crisis," a phrase that has stuck but of course avoided blame.

The attention of the media, international organizations, charities, and foreign governments combined to raise massive amounts of money for relief. But this would never be enough without political intervention. Early in 2004, the UNHCR appealed for $21 million, an amount raised by June to $56 million. The UN's Office for the Coordination of Humanitarian Affairs (OCHA) asked for $54 million in March but raised the figure to $166 million in September. The World Food Program needed $100 million. A donor conference in Geneva in June had a target of $236 million. The UN asked for $722 million for 2004–05. With the prospect at long last of finalizing a north-south peace agreement, the UN estimated the total amount needed for Sudan relief in 2005 at $1.5 billion.[36] Much was pledged, less of course given. Even as massive amounts were spent, however, it was becoming clear that a policy of emergency feeding of people trapped in what amounted to insecure concentration camps was not sustainable. Who guards the guards?

Darfur in the Balance, 2004–2005

Whether Khartoum's goal was genocide (killing most of the non-Arabs) or ethnic cleansing (driving out those who survived), it has since 2004 involved fine-tuning in the light of the international community's fickle attention. Only because of pressure from nongovernmental organizations; domestic groups; interested legislators; and individuals in the media, academe, and elsewhere has governments' interest been sustained. There has been an almost palpable sense that the developed world would gladly wash its hands of Darfur if that pressure subsided. On the other hand the internationalization of the crisis has called into question the motives of some activist groups and individuals and, thus, of the very nature of the movement to "save Darfur."

Impetus to solve the crisis was perhaps greatest from the United States but has been fitful in the extreme and responsive only to pressure. Darfur has at times dominated headlines, then disappeared when some other issue (Iraq, Iran, Lebanon, global financial crises) or "humanitarian disaster" (the Indian Ocean tsunami, Hurricane Katrina) grabbed the headlines. Even granted such preoccupations and the fact, much rehearsed, that Washington reacts only when constituents demand that it do so, the Darfur crisis presented unpalatable policy choices that the Bush administration (2001–09) chose not to face and the Obama administration (2009–) made no flashy early attempt to address. This was most obvious in the Anglo-American role in bringing about the north-south peace agreement, which was finally signed on 9 January 2005: that the NIF government of the Sudan was murdering its own people admittedly made the work of foreign mediators much more difficult, but by the time the deal was signed, London's and Washington's far greater interest in the south than in Darfur was starkly clear. In May 2004, the Sudan was removed from the U.S. government's list of states uncooperative in its "War on Terror," even as the Sudan was accused of genocide in Darfur; a month later, members of the U.S. House of Representatives sent a list of known *janjawid* and their NIF sponsors to President Bush; the Senate compiled its own. Religious groups, university divestment campaigns, and rights organizations kept the issue alive, even when cataclysms elsewhere allowed the administration to look away.

This in turn resulted from the fact that in the "War on Terror," the Sudanese government might, despite itself, have a role to play. Cooperation in intelligence matters has often been cited, usually on anonymous authority, as a particular point of U.S. interest; the Sudan's strategic location, as neighboring states collapse or fall to Islamists, remains undeniable. Americans' demand for cheap oil touches on an emerging competition with China for influence in Africa. Because there is little international interest in breaking up the Sudan, the unpalatable alternative has been to moderate the NIF's behavior until its overthrow by something better. The looming crisis of the 2011 Southern referendum now occupies as much attention as did the long negotiation of the 2005 CPA; Darfur is threatened with relegation from emergency status to the chronic care unit of global crises.

The European response has been similar, if more deftly excused by the inertia institutionalized in the European Union's external-affairs apparatus. While justifiably calling on the UN to act, the Europeans – who, after all, with Russia hold three of the Security Council's five permanent seats – failed to take any steps that would constitute action; the UN, lest its critics forget, is little more than the corporate existence of its members. Thus, aid – still in insufficient amounts – has continued to pour in to relief operations, but the absence of will to act politically has, especially most recently, allowed the crisis to worsen. It could hardly do otherwise, because Khartoum's assessment of foreign opinion in part determines its own maneuvers: where it sees – and, indeed, is told – that it can act with impunity, or nearly so, it will.

Whether the crisis met a definition of "genocide" has occupied much attention. Under international law, "genocide" and "crimes against humanity" might require action, including steps to stop them and punishment of those responsible; "ethnic cleansing" is undefined, as are "reign of terror," "another Rwanda," and "scorched-earth policy." In November 2003, the BBC used the term "ethnic cleansing" in reference to Darfur, and in March 2004, a USAID administrator, in testimony before Congress, referred to "ethnic cleansing" and "population clearing." After the UN's undersecretary for humanitarian affairs referred in April 2004 to "ethnic cleansing" in Darfur and its high commissioner for human rights, Bertrand Ramcharan, told the Security Council in May of the Sudanese government's "repeated crimes against humanity," nothing happened. In June, the secretary-general was unwilling even to apply the term "ethnic cleansing" and, upon signing a statement with the Sudanese government in July, by which it promised to disarm the *janjawid*, he publicly admitted (with suitable diplomatic code language) that the UN member-states that mattered were unwilling to intervene militarily. Temporizing, too, is undefined in international law.[37] In defense of the International Criminal Court's much-criticized indictment, in 2009, of President al-Bashir for crimes against humanity, this context of inaction may be cited.

The U.S. government made clear its own unwillingness to consider military intervention. Barring that, the range of options mooted in Europe and the United States was pathetically limited: such mild "sanctions" as were mentioned would take months or years to have any effect; limits on foreign travel by Sudanese officials and *janjawid* commanders and freezing their foreign assets were threats so ludicrous as to mock the murderous violence. Although some observers argued that the threat of eventual trials for war crimes might mitigate the violence, the evidence on the ground has not supported this. Declaration of a "no-fly zone" was mooted from time to time and had the advantages of military intervention without troops. Discussion of an international "peacekeeping" force in 2004 was not only desultory but also deranged: there was no peace to keep. For this reason, among others, much attention was paid to the willingness and ability of the African Union (AU) to take the leading role, one its proponents saw as a test of its (and Africa's) capacity, and a solution that would allow the Americans and Europeans to wash their hands of the crisis. In late July 2004, the AU took up the task of creating an African monitoring force and received early support from Nigeria and other member-states.

It was not until 9 September 2004 that General Colin Powell, in testimony before the Senate Foreign Relations Committee, described the events in Darfur as "genocide," even then taking many by surprise. A few days later, the European parliament chose the phrase "tantamount to genocide." The Sudanese were not stupid, and weasel words translate well into Arabic. But the 1948 International Convention on the Prevention and Punishment of Crimes of Genocide defines "genocide" as inflicting on a group "conditions of life calculated to bring about its physical destruction in whole or in part," and by this definition, to which signatories of the convention are ipso facto committed, Powell's use of the term was accurate, most especially in regard to the Masalit and Zaghawa. Under terms of the convention, moreover, official discernment of deliberate activity defined as genocide requires reference to the UN, which is why politicians were so skittish about the word. The UN's subsequent Commission of Inquiry on Darfur reported (in January 2005) likely "genocidal intentions" *by individuals* but insufficient evidence of the Sudanese government's intent, and recommended prosecution in the International Criminal Court of some fifty-one perpetrators of war crimes (named in a secret annex appended to Security Council Resolution 1593 in April 2005). These included twenty-seven government officials. A pruned list was leaked in February 2006. "Genocide" had become a threshold.[38] Incessant argument, tending either toward the legalistic or the utopian, about the wisdom and likely impact of indictments of Sudanese officials, has revealed or precipitated rifts in the huge international activist "community" and within and between governments.

The Sudanese government itself continued to act with impunity in part because of its much-trumpeted willingness to negotiate. We have seen how this began, with cease-fire agreements in the autumn of 2003 and in April 2004, both of which it broke before the ink was dry. A series of such elaborate agreements, in a pattern long familiar in the north-south war, between the Sudanese government and the rebels ensued, and continues. Negotiations have had many sponsors. Those brokered by the AU implicitly endorsed the international division of labor in the way both Africa and interested foreign governments wanted: Africa took responsibility, the rest of the world paid. This in itself reduced the pressure on Khartoum by endorsing the notion that Darfur was an "African problem" like any other, while the agreements Khartoum entered into could be described as "progress."

At the end of May 2004, at Addis Ababa, the two sides agreed to terms of reference for a cease-fire commission and the deployment of international observers to Darfur. The cease-fire failed, but in July the AU, without assigning blame, arranged to send 132 observers, protected by 300 soldiers. "Observing" genocide made no sense and risked making the AU complicit, but it bought time for all concerned except the people of Darfur. For the AU, like the UN, was no more than its members: a split between its Arabs and Africans would wreck the enterprise and, in any case, the AU's resources were very modest.

Seen in this light, the tiny monitoring team was heroic: in November 2004, it actually reported a Sudanese government plan to resume the offensive.

In June 2004, the UN Security Council adopted Resolution 1556, giving the Sudan thirty days to disarm the *janjawid*, arrest their leaders, and allow relief agencies full access to the displaced in Darfur. This called Khartoum's bluff over repeated claims of ability to assert control, but no knowledgeable observer believed that the *janjawid* could be disarmed in a month – if at all. Khartoum submitted a plan, which was rejected out of hand, and after the deadline passed asked for an extension. The UN's Special Representative, Jan Pronk, agreed, even as the UN itself reported continuing air attacks in Darfur. But by the end of the extended period, the government had fulfilled none of its commitments. Meanwhile, after Khartoum rejected a proposal by the AU to establish a committee of inquiry into human rights abuses in Darfur, the Security Council, in Resolution 1564, established its own, the International Commission of Inquiry mentioned earlier.[39]

The negotiating track continued to parallel the ethnic cleansing. Talks had moved from Addis Ababa to Abuja, the Nigerian capital, in August. On 9 November 2004, the two sides signed the "Abuja Protocol" on the "enhancement of the security situation in Darfur." In one of the most cynical documents of the age the Sudanese government, after expressing "utmost concern over the repeated violations of the relevant provisions of the Humanitarian Ceasefire Agreement" and "condemning all acts of violence against civilians and violations of human rights and international humanitarian law," agreed again to disarm the *janjawid*. (Progress toward that end had already been achieved in a formal, but brazen, sense: some *janjawid* were incorporated into the army and police, often simply by donning a uniform.) A separate "protocol" on "improvement of the humanitarian situation in Darfur," signed the same day, committed Khartoum to "guarantee unimpeded and unrestricted access for humanitarian workers and assistance"; "removal of all restrictions and procedures which may hinder free movement and access by land and air, without escort"; authorization of "cross-border humanitarian activities," at the UN's discretion; freedom for relief organizations "to travel along routes proposed by the UN, without restrictions or escorts, in order to deliver assistance to areas controlled by any Party"; and much more. In mid-November, this was followed by – we might better conclude that it preempted – Security Council Resolution 1574, demanding "an immediate end to violence" in Darfur.⁴⁰

The Abuja Peace Process

A Comprehensive Peace Agreement (CPA) between the Sudanese government and the Sudan People's Liberation Movement was finally signed on 9 January 2005. The delicacy of that southern "peace process" had long been cited by involved Western governments and others as a reason for going slowly, holding back, and generally avoiding pressure on Khartoum to stop the slaughter in Darfur. Freed from that preoccupation, would they now finally exert the pressure needed to save Darfur?

Several factors militated against this. In the Security Council, only Britain and the United States were interested in an aggressive UN stance: Russia had arms contracts with the NIF regime; China, the Sudan's largest oil customer, as usual breezily invoked long-standing commitment to noninterference in the internal affairs of sovereign states; France, Darfur's old colonial neighbor, saw the Sudan through a Chadian lens and recoiled from action that might further destabilize the tottering regime of Idris Deby. In early 2005, President Bush had just been reelected to a second term, but the United States – and, more important, American public attention – was fully occupied by the worsening, long-term crisis of Iraq, increasing tensions with Iran, and the hydra-headed "War on Terrorism"; in this agenda, Darfur was "other business," seldom reached. And Britain, the fifth permanent member of the Security Council (and former colonial master), had settled into the role of junior partner in U.S. overseas enterprises and of consultant for the Sudan's post-CPA security arrangements.⁴¹

Unwillingness to get involved was explained in many ways. The fragility of the CPA was cited, just as its negotiation had been: nothing must be done to risk it. The death on 30 July 2005 of John Garang, founder of the SPLM and an architect of the CPA, made permanent the need to nurture the southern peace that, admittedly, few objective observers expected to last. Further, even when governments had acted over Darfur, as in making Security Council resolutions, they had done so at least in part to be *seen* to be acting, responding to pressure from domestic constituencies and international relief organizations; when the pressure subsided and attention was diverted, past platitudes and incomplete processes were invoked to postpone confrontation. The conclusion is inescapable that wishful thinking dominated policy toward Darfur: the hope that the problem would disappear – ideally, to be sure, through a just solution but, in any case, without the need for intervention. In practice, this meant continued resort to a "peace process" brokered by the AU, alone or in concert with other organizations, and, more recently, by the governments of Libya and Qatar.

That process played into the hands of the Khartoum regime. Bureaucratic, formal, replete with adjournments for consultations and the preparation of proposals and responses, it (like the eponymous Arab-Israeli "peace process") took on a life of its own that was hardly related to events on the ground, fostering an illusion of progress, or even the potential for progress, "as long as the parties are talking." An undeniable improvement in the mortality statistics from Darfur has ironically made progress less urgent and contributed to the impression of a long-term or "intractable" problem there, again institutionalized on the Arab-Israeli model.

In stage-managing the "peace process," Khartoum was predictably helped by the ineptness of the rebels. The SLM/SLA's lack of political experience, seen as proof that it took up arms reluctantly and in self-defense, did not serve it well as a movement or in international conferences. The JEM's leadership has had the opposite problem, if anything too concerned with politicking. Originating in disaffection from the corrupt Islamism and Arab supremacism of the NIF, JEM, under Khalil Ibrahim, remained in only tactical – and at times not even tactical – alliance with the secularist SLM/SLA. Splits between the groups, and within them, over strategy – let alone an ultimate political program – were inevitable. In a pattern much copied since, in the summer of 2004 defectors from JEM, under Jibril Abd al-Karim Bari, set themselves up as a National Movement for Reform and Development (NMRD), raided in Dar Rizayqat, then demanded their own place at the Abuja conference table; fearing further splits and consequent chaos, the AU rejected the demand. JEM denounced the defectors as a front for Khartoum, and the SLA refused to deal with them. In November, the JEM-SLM rift erupted into violence. Emergence of other groups, such as *al-Shahana* in western Kordofan, and the continuing existence of tribal militias, notably in Southern Darfur, complicated the situation and lent credence to exasperation over "tribal warfare."[42]

Suspicions about the origins and intent of the NMRD were strengthened by events in Southern Darfur. Despite enormous pressure from Khartoum and its local agents, the major tribes there had not unleashed their militias – the *murahalin* that, in the north-south war, had served as a prototype for the *janjawid* – against their non-Arab neighbors. When in July 2004 the SLA dissidents raided Dar Rizayqat, they were routed; still, the Rizayqat were not drawn into the war. Credit for keeping the peace, then and since, went to the *nazir*, Sa'id Mahmud Ibrahim Musa Madibbu, whose family we have encountered in every era. Peaceful relations with the neighboring tribes, Arab and non-Arab alike, were reaffirmed. Arguably by then the leading native figure in Darfur, the *nazir* (along with other tribal notables) made representations in the Abuja talks and, extraordinarily, in October 2004, accepted an invitation to take part in a peace conference in Libya. The so-called Darfur Tribes Initiative showed promise in a number of ways, not least in building on traditional institutions to find local settlement to tribal disputes.

The government apprehended in this initiative a loss of control over events in Darfur and took steps to undermine it. Exit visas were denied to most of the tribal leaders wishing to attend a second conference in January 2005. Worse, like regimes before it, the government took steps to upset the balance of power in Southern Darfur. In an effort to devalue Sa'id's status, it promoted other notables to the rank of *nazir*, including the *shaykh* of the neighboring Ma'alia, long subsidiary to the Rizayqat, with whom Sa'id had recently taken pains to remove tribal irritants. Clearly, the ability of the Southern Darfur tribes to hold firm against the cyclone to the north and, indeed, to withstand exploitation is only partly within their own control: Libya's interest in "mediating" extended to supplying food aid and vehicles to a faction of the SLA. The greatest danger in Southern Darfur was Khartoum's power to wreck but inability to govern,[43] a paradox that revealed inherent weakness in its entire policy in the western Sudan. In any case, Colonel Gaddafi's new role as regional statesman was enhanced in the so-called Tripoli Agreement of February 2006, by which the Sudan and Chad agreed to disarm each other's cross-border insurgents.

The longer the fighting – and the negotiating – went on, the more the SLM/SLA was prey to internal divisions. Still a very young movement, in more ways than one, the SLM/SLA was perforce decentralized militarily and always susceptible to splits over the differing interests of its components and a political agenda inchoate to the vanishing point. A formal split occurred during the glacial negotiations at Abuja when the SLM chairman, Abd al-Wahid al-Nur, refused to defer to SLA military commanders who appeared from time to time and asked for a place at the table. His chief rival, Minni Arkoy Minawi, and his partisans would not be reconciled. Outsiders' attempts to unite the factions failed, and both were recognized at the Abuja talks. Because the split had little or no ideological component, it seemed manageable at first; differences over tactics could be composed in private and a common stand in the talks still be maintained. Early in 2006, however, the fears of foreign facilitators were realized when "SLM/SLA (Abd al-Wahid)" itself split, and defectors predictably demanded AU recognition, which was refused.

As the rebels fell out, "world opinion," unaccompanied by credible threats of intervention, held little fear for the NIF regime and none for the *janjawid*. After the UN's "special representative for the prevention of genocide" – whose very title implied routinization of the ultimate crime – visited Darfur and denounced a "culture of impunity," *janjawid* supported by Sudanese aircraft killed hundreds in new attacks and raided into Chad in September 2005. After the UN General Assembly committed the organization to responsibility for protecting all people from genocide, war crimes, and ethnic cleansing, Khartoum denounced both the UN and the AU and banned Sudanese newspapers from reporting on Darfur. Adding insult to injury, the government demanded AIDS tests for soldiers deployed to protect the AU monitoring mission. In September, the NIF formed a new Government of National Unity (GONU), incorporating many of its old southern enemies, notably including, as foreign minister and international face of the regime, the articulate sometime-SPLM commander, Lam Akol Ajawin.[44]

The NIF's immediate goal of keeping the Americans and Europeans out of Darfur was one they shared – conspiracy theorists notwithstanding. Thus, while adamantly rejecting the fulminations of the world body, it paid attention to the AU and upheld its role in "monitoring" (and later "peacekeeping"), even as atrocities continued. By the middle of

2005, however, that role was universally admitted to be insufficient; Khartoum had failed to stop the violence and, more to the point, had failed to stop the reporting of the violence. The humanitarian situation in Darfur had continued to deteriorate for the reasons we have seen: utter insecurity, for residents and foreign relief workers alike; continuing – albeit intermittent – outrages by *janjawid*; and, as a result, increasing hardship in and around the miserable, unsanitary, insufficiently provisioned camps in which more than 2 million people were immured.

In January 2006 the AU, limited by its mission's terms of reference and hamstrung by too few troops and a lack of financial and logistical support, publicly called for the UN to take over its role in Darfur. If – whether because events overcame their reluctance or popular demand made holding back politically impossible – the Europeans and Americans, as NATO or a "coalition of the willing," agreed to place forces in Darfur, Khartoum knew that the game would be up. Eyewitness reporting from their own commanders, the technical support these would need, deployments required to protect the forces, the rebels' ability to influence events – these would mean Khartoum would lose control and never regain it. Even worse: Khartoum had been interfering again in Chad's political chaos, supporting a faction in opposition to President Deby just as the Chadian leader made deals with his fellow Zaghawa in the SLA.[45] Once in place in Darfur, a strong UN force might become a permanent fixture. The stage was set for more temporizing agreements.

In March 2006, the AU's Peace and Security Council extended the mandate of its force in Darfur, which was expiring, for another six months, after which it might hand over responsibility to the UN, a position the Security Council unanimously endorsed. This posture suited all parties except those in Darfur who would die or be maimed or raped in the interval. Meanwhile, the NIF welcomed silence from the wider Muslim world and was fully supported by the Arab League in a Khartoum summit meeting at the end of March. A subsequent coup attempt in Chad, after which, in mid-April, Chad broke diplomatic relations with the Sudan, further displayed Khartoum's potential for destabilizing the region; as of old, the border between Darfur and its western neighbors was breaking down, with each central government supporting rebellion in the other's territory and locals playing one side against the other. The introduction of a strong foreign force there – UN troops with a clear mandate, adequate logistics, and the interest of their home governments and media – might stabilize the border in the Chadian government's favor.[46] Thus, even the potential for collapse in Chad was an ironic impetus to a deal over Darfur between the rebels and Khartoum.

The Darfur Peace Agreement (DPA),[47] signed by the Sudanese government and the SLM/SLA (Minawi) in Abuja on 5 May 2006, was the result of extensive preparation, long discussion, and the application of enormous effort concerted by phalanxes of government representatives and international experts. Even after the two sides had agreed in June 2005 to a Declaration of Principles on which to base a settlement, the negotiations and the violence had continued for another year. Although formally an arrangement between a sovereign state and rebels, the DPA was no mere cease-fire. It established a framework for peace, security, rehabilitation, and administration unlike anything Darfur had enjoyed since its incorporation in the Sudan. Clearly inspired by the experience of the agreement that ended the north-south war in January 2005, the document entered into areas of constitutional law and national administration and, if implemented, would have heralded transformational changes for the Sudan as a whole. But in this as in any such agreement, implementation – and thus the good faith of the parties – was the ultimate test and one that even the most skeptically redundant language could not avoid.

The negotiations dragged on for many months. The chief mediator was Salim Ahmad Salim, the veteran Tanzanian diplomat. Much of the negotiating for the rebels was done by the SLM/SLA factional leaders, Minni Minawi and Abd al-Wahid al-Nur, and by their security experts, Ali Tirayu, Muhammad Adam, and Taj al-Din Nyam. The government's chief negotiator was Dr. Majdhub al-Khalifa, whose security experts were led by General Ismat al-Zayn; toward the end of the talks, Ali Uthman Muhammad Taha, the Sudanese vice president, spent two weeks in Abuja. But the comprehensive nature of the DPA – much of it reads like a constitution – required expertise in several fields. On the rebel side, this was provided by (among others) Abd al-Jabbar Dusa for the SLM/SLA (Minawi); Ibrahim Madibbu, Abd al-Rahman Musa, and Abu'l-Bashar Abbakar for the SLM/SLA (Abd al-Wahid); and Jibril Khalil and Ahmad Tugud Lissan for JEM. Many others attended from time to time. The Sudanese government benefited from participation by veterans of the SPLM, now members of the reconstituted Khartoum regime; Lual Deng, an old hand, played a big role in talks over compensation and development. At one time or another, the governments of Canada, Egypt, Eritrea, France, Libya, the Netherlands, Nigeria, Norway, the United Kingdom, and the United States were involved, as were various multilateral organizations. At a critical late stage, the U.S. deputy secretary of state, Robert Zoellick, and the British Minister for International Development, Hilary Benn, intervened. There were, in other words, too many cooks or, we might say, chefs, much of whose urgency was unconnected with the negotiations at hand. The result was haste to sign an agreement rather than care to reach a settlement.

Although the prospects for implementation of the DPA were slim, its comprehensive nature rendered it a likely reference in all subsequent attempts at settlement and as a marker in national political debate for a long time to come.

The DPA's security arrangements included highly detailed plans for cease-fire arrangements, partial disarmament, and disposition of rebel fighters. These were never carried out, mainly because Khartoum was unwilling (and probably unable) to impose terms on the *janjawid*; Darfur's Arabs were not formally represented at Abuja at all, but the general assumption that they were mere agents of the NIF regime was unfounded. The agreement also included arrangements for later accession to its terms. These involve further negotiation, roles for the Cease-fire Commission and the AU, and reliance on a "Darfur-Darfur Dialogue and Consultation [*sic*]" (an organ conceived in the 2005 Declaration of Principles), which would create a Peace and Reconciliation Council. At the time of signing, ad hoc arrangements were made for "declarations of commitment" by members of nonsignatory groups.

The "Peace Process" Since Abuja (2006–2009)

As the lengthy negotiation of the DPA neared an end in April 2006, important elements of the SLM/SLA denounced the draft as insufficiently protective of Darfur's interests and lacking mechanisms for enforcement. The SLM/SLA faction of Abd al-Wahid al-Nur refused to sign, as did Khalil Ibrahim of JEM. All efforts to win them over failed. Immediately after the ceremonies on 5 May, members of Abd al-Wahid's SLM/SLA, including its chief negotiator, Abd al-Rahman Musa, asked to sign in their own right. "Letters of Commitment" were duly registered from Abd al-Rahman Musa, Ibrahim Madibbu, and Adam Salih Abbaker of Abd al-Wahid's SLM/SLA, and from Abd al-Rahim Adam Abu Risha, JEM's general secretary in Southern Darfur. Others followed; this fractionalization was ominous, but according to plan Minni Minawi was installed in Khartoum as senior assistant to the President of the Sudan on 5 August. Subsequent events soon clarified his error, if they did not exculpate dissidents for theirs.

Khartoum's willingness to negotiate the DPA and the timing of its doing so were probably predicated on keeping the UN out of Darfur; in late April, just before the Abuja talks concluded, President Bashir rejected even *planning* for such a contingency, which, in May, the Security Council authorized anyway. The mandate of the AU Mission was set to expire at the end of September, and without the AU or a successor, the cease-fire and security arrangements of the DPA could not be implemented even if Khartoum and the rebels wanted them to be.

As the tug-of-war continued between the Sudanese government (which was not without allies) and those countries arguing for a UN takeover of the AU Mission's role, the relevant Security Council resolutions remained in effect. These involved an embargo on arms shipments and the threat of sanctions on individuals. They also held out the prospect of trials for genocide and other crimes against humanity. If the permanent members of the Security Council backed up its threats with action, the Sudanese government would be left with few options. After further brinkmanship, in which the people of Darfur were in effect hostages, the AU's Peace and Security Council, meeting in New York on 20 September, voted to extend the life of its force until the end of 2006.

In any case, the security situation in Darfur was deteriorating even as the DPA was signed. Violations of the previous cease-fire agreements, still in force, were frequent. These included *janjawid* attacks on villages and murders of civilians, hijacking of vehicles, and violent outbreaks between SLA factions. Factional infighting had increased throughout March and April. Local commanders were declaring their own "no fly zones." The number of incidents ironically increased after the DPA was signed: partisans of the nonsignatory factions, united in a National Redemption Front, took a hand in fomenting violent disturbances in the refugee camps; AU Mission convoys were attacked and personnel killed. This upsurge was exacerbated by continuing deterioration of relations

Figure 19. The Sudan Liberation Army (SLA). Established as a self-defense force, the SLA has been prey to factional strife. One faction signed the Darfur Peace Agreement in Abuja in May 2006, while others continue the struggle. Here, five fighters are shown with their vehicle. (Jehad Nga/Corbis.)

between the Sudan and Chad even after the Tripoli Agreement of 8 February 2007: in mid-April, the Chadian government withdrew from its role in mediation, and Khartoum responded by demanding removal of Chadian military observers from Darfur. At any time, the volatile situation in Chad, on access to whose eastern regions the Darfur relief effort depended, could reshuffle the deck of which the humanitarian efforts in Darfur and Chad, and the whole DPA, were built.

Subsequent diplomatic activity orchestrated by international organizations and foreign governments therefore involved attention to the evident flaws in the DPA; patching up differences among the fissiparous rebel groups, at least to present a common negotiating position; and defending the interests of the internally displaced persons (IDPs) in the camps, which were rapidly evolving into permanent settlements or de facto extensions of nearby towns. Although progress was made in each of these areas, there has been no real breakthrough.

A so far insurmountable problem has been an atomization of the Darfur rebel groups, a phenomenon not unlike that which long afflicted successive Southern political-military opposition to the Sudanese government. In August 2007, for example, a meeting at Arusha of factional leaders under auspices of the AU and UN agreed to put forward a united front at a new round of peace talks, but even that confabulation excluded important stakeholders, and the rebels remained divided among themselves. Poorly articulated – or unidentifiable – differences betrayed factional or personal interests that lent an unmistakable sense of mere banditry to some rebels' activities.

On the international level, the AU and UN continued, through their high-powered special envoys, Salim Ahmed Salim and Jan Eliasson, to win the cooperation of relevant neighboring states. In Tripoli in July 2007 Libya, Eritrea, and Chad agreed to cooperate, and a new round of peace talks among the factional leaders was scheduled for the Libyan port of Sirte at the end of October. The so-called Sirte Process soon petered out because it failed to include important stakeholders and proliferating rebel factions; media reports revealed "conferences" for their own sake, five-star respites for weary guerillas, in contrast to which Khartoum's otherwise transparent posturing and stalling seemed almost statesmanlike.

After JEM staged an insurrection in Khartoum in May 2008 it entered into negotiations that likewise seemed by mid-2009 to have reached a dead end. These talks, sponsored by the government of Qatar, involved more international brokers than rebel factions; other rebel groups boycotted, and agreement in January 2009 to implement so-called confidence-building measures could not make up in jargon what it lacked in substance. JEM's own fitful participation seemed premised on reviving a dormant public profile. These and other international attempts at mediation achieved little beyond formal structures by which interested parties – notably but not only the Sudanese government, whose willingness to talk increased in inverse proportion to the likelihood of results – could deflect criticism. In defense of major international actors it may be said that the amorphous Darfur rebel movements, their poor leadership and lack of political experience, and the ease with which they could be manipulated in high-sounding but lowdown deals with external and Sudanese interests for immediate gain, argued for "benign neglect" while quiet efforts were made to identify, create, or await and encourage a unifying force.

These efforts were in any case complicated by developments within Khartoum's "Government of National Unity" that had culminated, on

11 October 2007, with the SPLM's "suspension" of participation in the coalition in the face of insufficient progress over issues outstanding since the CPA had been signed in January 2005. Even if the Darfur rebels had somehow devised a united front, the Sudanese government now lacked one. Ironically it was thus the SPLM, which had conducted formal talks with Darfur rebel leaders in 2006 and 2007 and maintained frequent unrecorded contacts, that temporarily comprised the missing link.

By the end of 2007 the differences between the NIF and SPLM had been papered over, and the Southern party resumed its place in the government. But the breakdown in relations had represented more than normal coalition brinkmanship. As various deadlines and desiderata of the CPA loomed, lack of progress in one or another area called into question the whole North-South settlement. These included completion of a national census, the festering sore of the Abyei issue and other North-South boundaries, the elections scheduled for 2009 (since rescheduled for February and then April 2010) and, ultimately, the referendum on independence due in 2011. Jockeying for electoral advantage – which would involve the traditional Northern sectarian parties as well as the NIF and SPLM – could not help but complicate (and be complicated by) developments in Darfur and the prospects for a negotiated settlement there. Darfur's rebels seemed seldom to realize that their quarrels might be of diminishing concern in Khartoum and Juba – and indeed in Washington and Beijing.

In terms of Darfur's internal security, there has likewise been a series of developments that, moreover, and taken together, indicate stasis rather than progress. In November 2006 intensive negotiations led to international agreement at Addis Ababa to establish a "hybrid" peacekeeping force under the auspices of both the UN and African Union. After further negotiation the Sudanese government finally agreed in June 2007, and UN Security Council Resolution 1769 formally established UNAMID in July. That force, ultimately to consist of some 20,000 (mostly African) troops, did not succeed AMIS until the end of the year, and its mandate was extended. Its activities have been hampered by constricted terms of reference (which included limits to its armaments), continuing insecurity, and lack of cooperation from the parties whose "peace" it is nominally meant to keep. Nevertheless the trend in murderous violence has diminished to the point of "low-intensity conflict"; although of small comfort to victims, a graph would show a strikingly downward trend with occasional spikes.

Khartoum's reluctance to accept a formal UN presence in Darfur had always stemmed from a sustained fear of direct Western intervention and the "regime change" assumed to be the ultimate goal of its many foreign and domestic enemies. That view was sustained by developments in Chad, where the Deby regime's survival of its own civil war seemed dependent on continuing chaos in Darfur. Efforts to deal with the Chadian imbroglio, including internationally brokered talks in Qatar between the Sudanese and Chadian governments, have lately gained more credibility; without a real settlement – rather than another hollow truce – the prospects for progress in Darfur remain poor.

Evidence of the Khartoum regime's overriding fear of external intervention – and of its ability to turn that fear to its advantage – was spectacularly illustrated in early 2009 when, after months of tension and rumor, the International Criminal Court in The Hague handed down indictments of President Beshir for crimes against humanity (but not genocide). While some Darfur activists in the West celebrated, the regime rallied African and Arab governments and turned out demonstrations in the Sudan in support of the President, who immediately traveled abroad to show his defiance of the court's writ. Practical observers worried about the fate of Darfur's IDPs, dependent as they are on Western aid, while experts within and outside the Sudan argued about the effect of the indictment on the prospects for a settlement. Speculation aside, it is clear that the indictment complicated efforts by the new Obama administration, and others, to exert influence in Khartoum, and by mid-2009 the indictment was effectively a dead letter.

Several other developments since the stillbirth of the DPA are notable. These include shifting alliances and sociopolitical changes within Darfur, actual or presumed changes in policy of the major foreign powers toward the crisis, evolution of nongovernmental actors' role in efforts toward settlement, and events on the national political scene in light of the global recession and the imminence of the elections of 2010 and referendum of 2011.

Popular attention to the *janjawid* during and after 2003–05 tarred with one brush the Arab population of Darfur, many of whom had little or no involvement in the worst atrocities. Without direct representation at Abuja, their interests were neglected. In the horse-trading that is essential in Sudanese politics, and through intervention in intratribal affairs, Khartoum has generally been able to maintain the upper hand. But important elements of southern Darfur's (and neighboring southern Kordofan's) Arab population had always held back from involvement. A major (though short-lived) falling-out between the government and Abbala Arab militia in 2007, during which tactical alliances were explored with the SLA, showed even more clearly that Darfur's Arabs were not simply dumb creatures of the riverain politicians, and that bribery had its limits. The triumphal racist propaganda of a few years ago has given way to practical economic and electoral concerns. While the inchoate politics of "Arab Darfur" are unpredictable, resurgent activities of the traditional political parties, especially of the Mahdist Umma Party, might combine at any time with local self-interest. Readers have only to look to the history of the Turkiyya, the Mahdiyya, and the Anglo-Egyptian colonial era for prototypes.

A similar evolution involves the politics of the camps. Conditions there have changed over time, and by 2006, when casualty rates in actual fighting in Darfur had dropped markedly, the lifelines established by humanitarian organizations – tenuous, insecure, but increasing in number and regularity – had resulted in a modus vivendi. The camps developed aspects of permanence, running the gamut from civil-society organizations and schools to gang warfare and organized crime. Their greatest vulnerability became the Sudanese government's ability at any time to sacrifice them in its dealings with the Europeans and Americans; foreign humanitarians were as much hostages as the people they were trying to protect. This was most clearly revealed when, the day after President Beshir's indictment by the ICC, Khartoum ordered immediate cessation of some of the most important aid organizations' activities in Darfur, and deportation of their personnel.

This drastic step underlined the difference between foreign humanitarian organizations in Darfur and the international movement to "save Darfur." A unique aspect of the crisis has indeed been the degree of organization of that movement and the range of activities it has produced. While on the one hand "the world's worst humanitarian disaster" should appear only to the most jaded observer as a normal African event, the degree to which international, nongovernmental interest has been focused, and sustained, has been remarkable. It has included creation of numerous organizations and coalitions of organizations, mobilization of university students and even schoolchildren, divestment campaigns, coordinated pressure on corporations, boycotts, and the whole range of tactics unseen perhaps since the anti-apartheid movement. A new element has been the availability and use of the Internet. This has allowed degrees of instantaneity and rumor, of organization and propaganda, of mobilization and misinformation previously unknown, as every real or would-be stakeholder – from the United Nations Security Council to secondary-school penny drives, and from the Sudanese government to Darfur factions existing in name only – has gone public.

This phenomenon itself has been controversial. The Sudanese government has alternately condemned and ridiculed the international activist movement by reference to the usual litany of authoritarian regimes' bugaboos, and not without a receptive audience. That audience has grown along with the ill-assorted organizations and individuals with whom the movement to "save Darfur" has been associated. Rhetorical questions of interest – why has Darfur elicited such attention, when arguably far worse humanitarian disasters (notably in the Congo) have received so little? why do opponents of military intervention elsewhere call for it in Darfur? why do pacifists advocate war? which Western governments would benefit from "regime change" in Khartoum? – go largely unanswered or have degenerated into academic nit-picking. Incident is the oxygen of activism, so stasis in the Sudan, even if only apparent, imbued these and similar questions with increasing interest, and thus contributed to an impression of faddishness and naivety.

That impression had gained currency from the failure of Western governments to take any crowd-pleasing public steps to resolve the Darfur crisis. The Bush administration's invocation of "genocide" (increasingly controversial as the domestic political background of that decision has come to light), was not followed by steps consonant with the obligations thus incurred. The U.S. general election campaign of 2008 paid occasional lip service to Darfur, but the early Obama administration has treated the issue as susceptible to diplomacy. Like other Western governments and many Sudanese, this administration apprehended the looming 2010 elections in the Sudan and the 2011 referendum on the status of the South as inseparable from (if not more important than) a resolution in Darfur. President Obama's special envoy, General Scott Gration, has been active both in high-profile negotiations (including notably talks in Doha between the Sudanese government and the JEM) and, with more promise of results, behind the scenes. The replacement in June 2009 of Khartoum's chief negotiator for Darfur, Nafie Ali Nafie, by Ghazi Salah al-Din, was widely seen as a sign of changing attitudes. Only time will tell.

By mid-2009 it seemed certain that important developments in the interrelated Sudanese social, economic, and political crises were imminent. As well as precipitating events, the principal actors, local, national, and international, have been awaiting a turn of the kaleidoscope to rearrange forces and recalibrate relations among them. Whether national elections are held as scheduled, whether Darfur can vote in them, and what government emerges from them; whether the 2011 referendum in the South is held, whether the South will peacefully win its independence or descend yet again into civil war, and whether independence, if achieved, will itself be only a prelude to new disasters; developments in Chad – and indeed in Eritrea and Egypt; Khartoum's ability, under its present or a future government, to forge a new political dispensation; whether Darfur is doomed to a generation of infighting or can revive or build anew a political system capable of accommodation, even as objective economic and environmental circumstances counsel pessimism; how the Western powers complicate or help to resolve the cascading problems of Darfur, the Sudan, and indeed the northeast-African and Sahelian regions: these are some of the questions to which the very near future should provide some answers, and to which history is a weary guide.

Counting the Dead

The Sudanese government's wars on its own people have, in general, been poorly documented. Regarding the north-south war of 1983–2005, international agencies and foreign media reported for years a toll of 1 million dead, a consensus number that then leapt to 2 million, thereafter to be modified with quotation marks and hedging adjectives. No one knows the actual toll. Similarly in Darfur's case, media and relief organizations early reported 100,000 dead, a number that then doubled and for many months generally held steady at "200,000," "some 200,000," "at least 200,000," and so forth, some of these accounts citing, or based on other accounts citing, UN surveys.[48] There are several reasons for uncertainty. Village populations before the *janjawid* whirl-wind are uncertain, and those inhabitants who survived were dispersed. The *janjawid* and Sudanese army are known to have destroyed bodies: thrown them down wells, burned them, buried them in mass graves, and, of course, left them as carrion. Some internal refugees remained inaccessible: as many as 500,000 in October 2004, when early estimates were made. In the camps, whether in Chad or Darfur, assigning causes of death has been problematic, as it is in times of famine: are malnour-ished children dying from dysentery in squalid camps surrounded by *janjawid* to be counted as victims of genocide? In those circumstances, comparing crude mortality rates with those of normal times has allowed conclusions to be drawn about the effects of the disaster if not about specific causes of death.

In April–June 2004, Doctors without Borders conducted a survey of several refugee camps in Darfur that then held 215,000 people. Extrap-olation based on that survey (and conservatively discounting other par-tial studies, which produced higher numbers) tentatively concluded that about 150,000 people had died by June 2004, and as many as 180,000 by September. When account is taken of an extrapolation from figures in the U.S. State Department report on refugees in Chad mentioned earlier, the total number of victims would have reached 210,000 by Septem-ber 2004. Using later UN figures to supplement these, the same analyst reached a total number of casualties of 280,000–310,000 by the begin-ning of 2005. Any estimate must take account of the fact that people continued to be killed in raids and in and around the camps in Darfur, and a range of 350,000–400,000 was supported by the best scientific analyses.[49] General media reports tended to accept 200,000–300,000, while some foreign activists put the number as high as 500,000.

In any case, it is now unarguable that the level of murderous violence greatly subsided after 2005. Like other aspects of the Darfur crisis, this has provoked an unedifying controversy among governments, NGOs, activists, and academics, much of it partisan and fruitless. The fact remained, however, that insecurity has since then always threatened and periodically caused spikes in violence and mortality, and a trend toward an arguably "acceptable" level of murder and rapine does not preclude a return to episodic or general depredation; Darfur and neighboring territories are awash with arms, and the promise of the 2010 national elections and 2011 Southern referendum is more than balanced by the perils their conduct and aftermath may bring.

By mid-2009, the number of people in Darfur in need of humanitarian assistance, mostly IDPs in the camps, was in most sources placed at about 2.5 million. Thus far, no serious outbreak of epidemic disease, a constant threat, had occurred, but this might change at any time, not least because conditions fluctuate. The warnings of increased insecurity and mortality, issued after the ICC indicted President Beshir and after Khartoum, in retaliation, told humanitarian organizations to leave, have not yet been fully realized; some received early permission to return. The likelihood is that UNAMID, inadequate as it is to keep the (nonexistent) peace, will be left to fill the humanitarian void, and that the future of the IDPs will in large measure depend on the national political developments that await.

GLOSSARY

abd (pl. *abid*):   slave

Amir (pl. *umara*):   emir, commander

ansar: helpers (The term described followers of the Prophet Muhammad at Medina and was revived by the Sudanese Mahdi for his followers.)

bamia: okra (*Hibiscus esculentus* Linn.)

Baqqara: cattle; Baqqara Arabs: cattle-keeping tribes

bilad al-Sudan: "land of the blacks"

dadingawi: from *abo dadinga*, Fur title revived under the Condominium

damur: coarse cotton cloth, homespun

dar: abode, land, territory

Darb al-arba'in: "the Forty-Days Road"; caravan route between Darfur and Egypt

dimangawi: from *aba dimang*, "master of the Dima," Fur title revived under the Condominium

dimlij: district chief, Darfur tribal *shaykh*

diya: blood money

dura:	a variety of sorghum (*Sorghum vulgare* Pers.)
effendi:	during the Turkiyya, honorific for an educated man; later derisive
faqih (pl. *fuqara*):	holy man; in Sudanese Arabic (fiki), takes the same plural as *faqir* (mendicant)
fasbir:	camp; sultan's courtyard; El-Fasher: capital of Darfur
fitr:	a tax
fula:	a large pool of water, lake, pond
fursan (sing. *faris*):	horsemen
hafir:	a pit, man-made pond
hajj:	the pilgrimage to Mecca
hakura:	land; landed estate
hashab:	the gum-producing *Acacia senegal* Willd
hukumdar:	commissioner; during the Turkiyya, governor-general
imam:	prayer leader
jallaba:	peddler, merchant
janjawid:	comb, *jinn* (spirit), *jawad* (horse); ghost-riders
jihad:	war for the faith
jizzu (Ar. *jaz*):	desert area of northern Darfur
jurenga:	soldiers
khalifa:	successor, regent; in English, Caliph
khalwa:	Qur'anic school
kuttab:	elementary school

majlis:	council
malik:	king
ma'mur:	during the Condominium, district assistant to *mufattish*
mandub (pl. *manadib*):	agent
maqdum:	viceroy
miralai:	colonel
muawin:	in Darfur during the Condominium, official between the *mufattish* and tribal leaders
mudir:	governor
mufattish:	inspector; district commissioner
mufti:	head of the *ulama*
muhajarin:	"emigrants"; those who followed the Prophet from Mecca to Medina; in the Sudan, those who left home to join the Mahdi
mukheit:	a shrub or small tree, *Boscia senegalensis* (Pers., Lam.) with edible fruit
murahalin:	travelers; in Sudan, tribal militiamen
nazir:	paramount chief
qadi:	judge of Islamic law
quz (*qoz, goz*):	sand; sandy area
sayyid:	master; honorific: Mr.; descendant of the Prophet
shari'a:	the Law of Islam
shartay:	Darfur chief
shaykh:	chief, especially tribal or religious chief

sirdar:	commander; title of the commander-in-chief of the Egyptian army
sufi:	Muslim mystic
takkiyya:	strip of cloth, used as medium of exchange
ulama (sing. *alim*):	learned men of Islam
umda:	sedentary chief, mayor
ushur (sing. *ushr*):	the Muslim tithe; in Sudan, a land tax
wadi:	seasonal river, riverbed
zakat:	Muslim alms-tax
zariba:	an enclosure, as for animals; a camp
zurqa (col. pl. Ar. of *azraq*):	blue; in western Sudan, blacks

ABBREVIATIONS IN THE BIBLIOGRAPHY AND NOTES

BD	Richard Hill, *A biographical dictionary of the Sudan*, London 2nd ed., 1967
BSOAS	*Bulletin of the School of Oriental and African Studies*
DI	Director of Intelligence
DPMD	Darfur Province Monthly Diary
£E	Egyptian pounds
FO	Foreign Office; classification in the National Archives, United Kingdom
RFACS	*Reports on the finances, administration, and conditions of the Sudan*
RHL	Rhodes House Library, Oxford
£S	Sudanese pounds
SAD	Sudan Archive, University of Durham Library
SGA	Sudan Government Archives, *Dar al-Watha'iq*, Khartoum (classified as CIVSEC, DARFUR, INTEL, KORDOFAN, NORTHERN, PALACE, and SECURITY)
SIR	*Sudan intelligence report*

SNR	*Sudan notes and records*
SOAS	School of Oriental and African Studies
SPIS	Sudan Political Intelligence Summary
SSIR	Sudan Secret Intelligence Report
USNA	U.S. National Archives, Washington, DC

NOTES

CHAPTER ONE. THE "ABODE OF THE BLACKS"

1. For the geography of Darfur, see J. D. Tothill, ed., *Agriculture in the Sudan*, London 1948; G. M. Craig, *The agriculture of the Sudan*, Oxford 1991; and K. M. Barbour, *The republic of the Sudan*, London 1961. See also A. J. Whiteman, *The geology of the Sudan republic*, Oxford 1971.

2. Marie-Jose Tubiana and Joseph Tubiana, *The Zaghawa from an ecological perspective*, Rotterdam 1977, 5, 49–50, 81.

3. R. S. O'Fahey and J. L. Spaulding, *Kingdoms of the Sudan*, London 1974, 160–61.

4. Tubiana and Tubiana, *The Zaghawa*, 5.

5. Captain Count Gleichen, *Handbook of the Sudan*, London 1898, 67; *SIR*, January 1922; R. T. Paterson, "Darfur Province," in Tothill, *Agriculture*, 851; *RFACS* for 1906, Cmd. 3394; *RFACS* for 1948, Cmd. 8181; *Report of the Sudan Medical Services for the year 1940*, Khartoum nd; *Report of the Medical Services . . . 1949*, Khartoum nd; *Report of the Medical Services . . . 1956/57*, np, nd [Sudan Agency, Cairo c. 1950], SAD 695/9; Republic of Sudan, Ministry for Social Affairs, *First population census of Sudan 1955/56. Last (9th) interim report*, Khartoum 1958; R. S. O'Fahey, *State and society in Dar Fur*, New York 1980, 1; B. Yongo-Bure, "The first decade of development in the southern Sudan," in Mom K. N. Arou and B. Yongo-Bure, eds., *North-South relations in the Sudan since the Addis Ababa Agreement*, Khartoum 1988, 373, citing Bank of Sudan, *Annual report*, 1983, 9; Republic of the Sudan, *Sudan almanac 1961*, Khartoum 1961, 111, and *1963*, Khartoum 1963, 79; Mohamed El Awad Galal-el-Din, "Population and labour force in the Sudan," in Ali Mohamed El-Hassan, ed., *An introduction to the Sudan economy*, Khartoum 1976, 31; Alexander de Waal, *Famine that kills*, Oxford 1989, 36. For the problem generally, see Peter F. M. McLoughlin, "A note on the reliability of the earliest Sudan Republic population estimates," *Population Review* 7, 3, 1963. Historical estimates (and revisionist theories) are in G. Ayoub Balamoan, *Peoples and economics in the Sudan 1884–1956*, Cambridge, Mass., 2nd ed., 1981. For politicized British colonial estimates, see M. W. Daly, *Empire on the Nile*, Cambridge 1986, 18–23.

6. O'Fahey, *State and society*, 3–4.

7. *Ibid.*, 30–31.
8. *Ibid.*, 6–7.
9. For the tribes, see H. A. MacMichael, *A history of the Arabs in the Sudan and some account of the people who preceded them and of the tribes inhabiting Darfur*, 1922 ed. reprinted London 1967.
10. Yusuf Fadl Hasan, *The Arabs and the Sudan, from the seventh to the early sixteenth century*, Edinburgh 1967, 163.
11. O'Fahey, *State and society*, 6.
12. *First population census*, 23–24.
13. O'Fahey, *State and society*, 9.
14. P. F. M. McLoughlin, *Language-switching as an index of socialization in the Republic of the Sudan*, Berkeley 1964; R. E. W. Thelwall, "A linguistic survey in El Fasher secondary school," *SNR* LII, 1971, 46–55.
15. O'Fahey, *State and society*, 8.
16. See Paul Doornbos, "On becoming Sudanese. Aspects of ideological transformation in rural Sudan," paper presented to a conference on state, capital and transformation in Sudan, University of East Anglia, July 1984.

CHAPTER TWO. LORDS OF MOUNTAIN AND SAVANNA:
THE ORIGINS AND HISTORY OF THE FUR STATE TO 1874

1. Especially important is the work of R. S. O'Fahey and his students at the University of Bergen.
2. See especially the work of Jay Spaulding on the Sudanese Nile valley, including *The heroic age in Sinnar*, East Lansing 1985.
3. Gustav Nachtigal, *Sahara and Sudan*, IV, *Wadai and Darfur*, trans. Allan G. B. Fisher, Humphrey J. Fisher, Berkeley and Los Angeles 1971, 272ff., provides a remarkable account of early Darfur history, based on traditions he collected there in 1873.
4. O'Fahey and Spaulding, *Kingdoms*, 110–16; *cf.* MacMichael, *A history*, I, 66–76. For ancient sites, see H. G. Balfour-Paul, *History and antiquities of Darfur*, Khartoum 1955; A. J. Arkell, "Darfur antiquities II, Tora palaces in Turra at the north end of Jebel Marra," *SNR* XX; and G. E. Wickens, "A brief note on the early history of Jebel Marra and the recently discovered Tora city of Kebeleh," *SNR* LI, 1970.
5. O'Fahey and Spaulding, *Kingdoms*, 116. *Cf.* MacMichael, *A history*, 91ff.
6. O'Fahey, *State and society*, 72–74.
7. *Ibid.*, 74–78.
8. O'Fahey and Spaulding, *Kingdoms*, 121, 205–14.
9. *Ibid.*, 120.
10. Ibid., 121–22, citing *Wansleben in Paulus*, 1792–98, III, 45–46; G. D'Albano, *Historia delta missione Francescana in Alt-Egitto-Fungi-Etiopia*, ed. G. Giamberardini, Cairo 1961, 47; Krump, *Hoher und Fruchtbarer Palm-Baum des Heiligen Evangelj*, Augsburg 1710, 285; and *Kitab al-tabaqat*, ed. Yusuf Fadl Hasan, Khartoum 1971, 137–38; O'Fahey, comp., *Arabic literature of Africa, volume 1. The writings of Eastern Sudanic Africa to c. 1900*, Leiden 1994, 41.
11. In Sudanese Arabic, both *faqih* (holy man) and *faqir* (poor man, beggar) take the plural of the latter, *fuqara*, in a perhaps significant conflation.

12. "There is no god but God, and Muhammad is the messenger of God."
13. O'Fahey and Spaulding, *Kingdoms*, 122–23.
14. *Ibid.*, 126–28.
15. O'Fahey and Spaulding date Ahmad Bukr's death to c. 1730 (*ibid.*, 129) but O'Fahey gives 1720 elsewhere, e.g., *State and society*, 11. The dates of Umar Lel's invasion of Wadai in *Kingdoms*, 132, is a misprint. Richard Hill, *BD* 255, dates Muhammad Dawra's death to 1732.
16. Nachtigal, *Sahara*, 355.
17. O'Fahey and Spaulding, *Kingdoms*, 129–34.
18. *Ibid.*, 133–37.
19. *Ibid.*, 137–40.
20. W. G. Browne (1768–1813), *Travels in Africa, Egypt, and Syria, from the year 1792 to 1798*, London 1799, and Muhammad Umar Sulayman (al-Tunisi) (1789–1857), *Tashhidh al-adhan bi-sirat bilad al-Arab wa'l-Sudan*, ed. Khalil Mahmud Asakir and Mustafa Muhammad Musad, Cairo 1965. Translations by A. Perron of al-Tunisi are *Voyage au Darfour*, Paris 1845, and *Voyage au Ouaday*, Paris 1851. Bayle St. John, *Travels of an Arab merchant in Soudan*, London 1854, is a summary. Al-Tunisi is not Muhammad b. Ali Zayn al-Abidin al-Tunisi, the authenticity of whose account of about the same time has been questioned (O'Fahey, *Arabic literature*, 66–67). A memoir of Muhammad Zayn al-Abdin (Hill, *BD* 388) has apparently been lost; a German translation of a Turkish translation is G. Rosen, *Das Buch des Sudan*, Leipzig 1847. A biography of Charles Cuny, who died in Darfur in 1858, is H. Roy, *La vie heroique et romantique du Docteur Charles Cuny*, Paris 1930.
21. Nachtigal, *Sahara*, 324–45 *passim*; O'Fahey, *State and society*, 14–25.
22. Nachtigal, *Sahara*, 260–62; O'Fahey, *State and society*, 23–28, 98.
23. R. S. O'Fahey and M. I. Abu Salim, *Land in Dar Fur. Charters and related documents from the Dar Fur sultanate*, Cambridge 1983, 22–25. The last sultan, Ali Dinar, is thought (*ibid.*, 22) to have dictated in Fur to scribes simultaneously translating into Arabic.
24. Nachtigal, *Sahara*, 326, 329, 365; O'Fahey and Spaulding, *Kingdoms*, 149–51; O'Fahey, *State and society*, 33–35.
25. See Nachtigal, *Sahara*, 324–45; O'Fahey, *State and society*, 29–30, 37; O'Fahey and Spaulding, *Kingdoms*, 151–54.
26. Nachtigal, *Sahara*, 325–45; O'Fahey, *State and society*, 34, 149–53; O'Fahey and Spaulding, *Kingdoms*, 152–53. Nachtigal (412) lists more than twenty "maliks." MacMichael, *A history*, 105, reports that in 1916 the *orrengdulung*'s "privileges and powers were nil."
27. Nachtigal, *Sahara*, 328–29, 332–33, 337–38; O'Fahey, *State and society*, 40–43. In Egyptian usage, *mamluks* were "white" slaves; African slaves were *abid*.
28. Nachtigal, *Sahara*, 324–25; O'Fahey, *State and society*, 69–71.
29. Nachtigal, *Sahara*, 326; O'Fahey, *State and society*, 88–90.
30. O'Fahey, *State and society*, 49–68.
31. *Ibid.*, 83–87.
32. *Ibid.*, 92–95; Nachtigal, *Sahara*, 254.
33. O'Fahey, *State and society*, 95.

34. *Ibid.*, 96–100.

35. *Ibid.*, 139.

36. Terence Walz, *Trade between Egypt and bilad al-Sudan 1700–1820*, Cairo 1978, 30–50; O'Fahey, *State and society*, 135–39. See also Dennis D. Cordell, *Dar al-Kuti and the last years of the trans-Saharan slave trade*, Madison 1985. Cf. William Y. Adams, *Nubia, corridor to Africa*, London 1977, 612, who found it incredible that items Browne listed as imports over the Forty-Days Road in 1793 could be "destined for . . . the semi-wilderness of Kordofan and Darfur."

37. Walz, *Trade*, 3–9; O'Fahey, *State and society*, 139–44. A late account of Kobbei is Nachtigal, *Sahara*, 252–56. A. J. Arkell, *A history of the Sudan to 1821*, London 1961, 2nd ed., 43–45, postulates that at least part of the Forty-Days Road dates to the third millennium B.C., but Egypt's trade with the Nilotic Sudan is older still: see Mutwakil A. Amin, "Ancient trade and trade routes between Egypt and the Sudan, 4000 to 700 B.C.," *SNR* LI, 1970, 23–30.

38. Yusuf Fadl Hasan, "The Fur sultanate and the long-distance caravan trade 1650–1850," in *idem* and Paul Doornbos, *The central bilad al-Sudan. Tradition and adaptation*, Khartoum nd, 204–10; Umar al-Naqar, *The pilgrimage tradition in West Africa*, Khartoum 1972; John Lewis Burckhardt, *Travels in Nubia*, 1819, repr. London 1987, 406–10; Walz, *Trade*, 22–25. For trade with the Nile valley, see Anders Bjorkelo, *Prelude to the Mahdiyya*, Cambridge 1989.

39. O'Fahey, *State and society*, 101–04; Nachtigal, *Sahara*, 358–59; Yusuf Fadl Hasan, "The Fur sultanate," 204. Cloth was a medium of exchange even at Kobbei as late as 1873 (Nachtigal, *Sahara*, 234, 247, 253–54).

40. Nachtigal, *Sahara*, 331; O'Fahey, *State and society*, 104–09.

41. *Ibid.*, 366–68. These included cat worship, evidence that human sacrifice had been only recently discontinued, and rites of various holy rocks and trees.

42. MacMichael, *A history*, 100–03.

43. See n. 10.

44. O'Fahey, *State and society*, 116. See also P. M. Holt, "Holy families and Islam in the Sudan," *idem, Studies in the history of the Near East*, London 1973, 121–34; and Nachtigal, *Sahara*, 245–46.

45. Fur traditions refer to a *kitab dali*, or "book of Dali," embodying customary law, and both Nachtigal (*Sahara*, 273, 368–70) and Na'um Shuqayr (*Ta'rikh al-Sudan al-qadim wa'l-hadith wa jughrafiyatuhu*, Cairo 1903, vol. 2, 137–38) refer to it, the latter as the *Qanun Dali*, but none has been found (O'Fahey, *Arabic literature*, 50). O'Fahey (*State and society*, 109–10) opines that the "book" might be "a generic term for Fur legal custom."

46. O'Fahey, *State and society*, 109–14, 116; O'Fahey, *Arabic literature*, 287.

47. Examples exist of Fur sultans' correspondence with the rulers of Egypt, the Ottoman sultan, and even Napoleon (R. S. O'Fahey, "The affair of Ahmad Agha," *SNR* LIII, 1972, 202–03.)

48. Hill, *BD*, 276–77; O'Fahey and Spaulding, *Kingdoms*, 146–49 (including a schema of Muhammad al-Fadl's *fashir*). A description (1873) of Sultan Ibrahim's palaces is in Nachtigal, *Sahara*, 261–62, 265–67.

49. O'Fahey and Spaulding, *Kingdoms*, 162.
50. Richard Hill, *Egypt in the Sudan 1820–1881*, London 1959, 12; Hill, *BD*, 264.
51. O'Fahey and Spaulding, *Kingdoms*, 173.
52. O'Fahey, *State and society*, 99–100; Nachtigal, *Sahara*, 254.
53. Al-Zubayr's manuscript of some episodes in his Sudan career is "Sirat al-Zubayr Basha" (SAD 110/3), 1876. H. C. Jackson, *Black ivory, or the story of El Zubeir Pasha, slaver and sultan, as told by himself*, Khartoum 1913 (repr. New York 1970) is based on Shuqayr, *Ta'rikh*, "supplemented" from other documents. (See O'Fahey, *Arabic literature*, 72.) Photographs of al-Zubayr are in Shuqayr, *Ta'rikh*, vol. 2, opp. 60; M. W. Daly and Jane R. Hogan, *Images of empire*, Leiden 2005, 268, second from left; and M. W. Daly and L. E. Forbes, *The Sudan*, Reading 1994, 52.
54. Nachtigal, *Sahara*, 317–19; Jackson, *Black ivory*, 32, 55–56.
55. O'Fahey and Spaulding, *Kingdoms*, 179–83; Hill, *Egypt*, 136–38; O'Fahey, *State and society*, 100; Nachtigal, *Sahara*, 242–43, 246, 261, 319–23, 371–75; Jackson, *Black ivory*, 58–69; Hill, *BD*, 39.

CHAPTER THREE. THE ENDS OF THE TURKISH WORLD

1. For terminology and the nature of the Turkiyya, see Richard Hill, *Egypt*, 1–4; Bjorkelo, *Prelude*, 34–35; and P. M. Holt, *The Mahdist state in the Sudan*, Oxford, 2nd ed., 1970, 14.
2. For the Turkiyya generally, see Hill, *Egypt*. For the Nile campaign and rebellion, see Bjorkelo, *Prelude*. A contemporary account by an American officer accompanying Muhammad Ali's army is George Bethune English, *A narrative of the expedition to Dongola and Sennaar*, London 1822, Boston 1823.
3. Hill, *Egypt*, 108.
4. *Ibid.*, 49–65. An early account of "an expedition to collect live animals" is in Paul Santi and Richard Hill, *The Europeans in the Sudan*, Oxford 1980, 35–51. See also Richard Hill, ed., *The Sudan memoirs of Carl Christian Giegler Pasha*, London 1984, 97. For wild-animal dealers, see, e.g., Hill, "Lorenzo Casanova" (*BD*, 96), "Josef Natterer" (*BD*, 292–93), and "Leopoldo Ori" (*BD*, 298–99).
5. Both Muhammad Ali and Muhammad Sa'id visited the Sudan, the former with disappointment, the other with horror (Hill, *Egypt*, 67–68, 94–95; Santi and Hill, *The Europeans*, 52–73).
6. Sometimes rendered Abu Widan.
7. Hill, *BD*, 330.
8. See Hill, *Egypt*, 80–89.
9. Hill, *BD*, 41–42; Santi and Hill, *The Europeans*, 74–92, gives a contemporary view of his rule and death.
10. Treaties providing privileges for their respective states' citizens within the Ottoman Empire. See Santi and Hill, *The Europeans*, 1–34.
11. As late as 1878, the German Giegler, already postmaster, was apparently nominated for simultaneous appointment as British consul in Khartoum: *The Sudan memoirs of Carl Christian Giegler Pasha*, 127.

12. Santi and Hill, *The Europeans*, 123, provides a glossary of trade goods and the "only known account of the day-to-day life of an ivory buyer from within": the journal of J.-A. Vayssiere in 1853–54 (127–68).

13. See G. Douin, *Histoire de regne du Khedive Ismail, III, L'empire africain*, Cairo 1936, *passim*; Stefano Santandrea, *A tribal history of the western Bahr El Ghazal*, Bologna 1964, 26–32; and Hill, "Andrea Debono," *BD*, 110–11.

14. One loophole allowed traders to bring concubines and children north: it was easy, if challenged, to ascribe such status to any women and children, who were then nonetheless sold.

15. Pierre Crabites, *Americans in the Egyptian Army*, London 1938, 14–16, counts five generals, twenty colonels, and, in all, fifty American officers in the Egyptian army.

16. For Gordon's appointment, see Shuqayr, *Ta'rikh*, ii, 92–104; for Muhammad Ra'uf's, *ibid.*, 105–08.

17. *Ibid.*, iii, 82–84.

18. Travelers' accounts include those of Pellegrino Matteucci (Hill, *BD*, 235), who with A. M. Massari (*ibid.*, 234) traversed Darfur in 1880; C. T. Wilson (*ibid.*, 379) and R. W. Felkin (*ibid.*, 125–26), in 1879; and Panayotis Potagos, 1876–77 (*ibid.*, 308).

19. For Erastus Sparrow Purdy and Henry Prout, see Hill, *BD*, 309–10, 311; Crabites, *Americans, passim*; and *The Sudan memoirs of Carl Christian Giegler Pasha*, 83–84. Crabites, 88, was unable to locate Purdy's report or Prout's note, but extracts were published, as was *Carte du nord de Dar-For*, made by Mahmud Sabry (Hill, *BD*, 226). Another member of the mission, J. G. Pfund, died at El Fasher (*ibid.*, 306).

20. R. S. Schuyler: Hill, *BD*, 209.

21. Rudolf C. Slatin, *Fire and sword in the Sudan*, London 1896, 55–56. Hill styles him Muhammad Harun al-Rashid Sayf al-Din (*BD*, 256). *Cf.* Shuqayr, *Ta'rikh*, v. ii, 93; O'Fahey, *State and society*, 16; and Lidwien Kapteijns, *Mahdist faith and Sudanic tradition*, London 1985, 77.

22. Richard Hill, *Slatin Pasha*, London 1965, 11; Slatin, *Fire and sword*, 73.

23. For the postal service, for example, see Paul Santi and Richard Hill, *The Europeans*, 213, 222, 225–26. For failure to extend the telegraph, see *The Sudan memoirs of Carl Christian Giegler Pasha*, 82–88.

24. Bjorkelo, *Prelude*, 117–18.

25. For factors in the diaspora, see Spaulding, *The heroic age*, 238–96, *passim*. Other terms applied to the peddlers included *bahhara* (river dwellers), *awlad al-bahr* (sons of the river), and *awlad al-balad* (townspeople); big traders by the 1860s preferred the term *tajir* (merchant).

26. Holt, *The Mahdist state*, 39; *Colonel Gordon in central Africa... from original letters and documents*, ed. George Birkbeck Hill, London 1881, *passim*.

27. Kapteijns, *Mahdist faith*, 64, 71.

28. *Colonel Gordon*, 360.

29. *Ibid.*, 369.

30. Slatin, *Fire and sword*, 56–57; Hill, *BD*, 18, 154–55, 256–57, 361, 389.

31. Kapteijns, *Mahdist faith*, 62–63; "Report on Dar Masalit," nd, SAD 730/10.

32. *Colonel Gordon*, 238–39, 240; Bernard M. Allen, *Gordon and the Sudan*, London 1931, 114–20; Slatin, *Fire and sword*, 57–58.

33. *Colonel Gordon*, 241–43.
34. *Ibid.*, 244–45.
35. *Ibid.*, 247.
36. *Ibid.*, 250; MacMichael, *A history*, I, 82–83, 268.
37. *Colonel Gordon*, 248, 267–68.
38. *Ibid.*, 269. For long-term effects of the slave trade, see Stephanie Beswick, *Sudan's blood memory: the legacy of war, ethnicity and slavery in south Sudan*, Rochester 2004, 157–63, 198ff.
39. *Colonel Gordon*, 270–85; Allen, *Gordon*, 120–23; Hill, *BD*, 350–51.
40. *Colonel Gordon*, 277–78.
41. Slatin, *Fire and sword*, 58, 73. According to Giegler, government expenditure in El Fasher and Dara alone in 1878 was 130,000 pounds (sterling), receipts only 17,000, and accrued debt already 100,000: *The Sudan memoirs of Carl Christian Giegler Pasha*, map 2 (after xxxii).
42. *Colonel Gordon*, 321.
43. *Ibid.*, 348.
44. *Ibid.*, 346.
45. *Ibid.*, 349–50.
46. *Ibid.*, 355.
47. Allen, *Gordon*, 145–52; Hill, *BD*, 350–51; Holt, *The Mahdist state*, 38–39; Santandrea, *A tribal history*, 25. Gordon had wished Sulayman hanged, lest he "be made much of" in Cairo, like his father: *Colonel Gordon*, 337.
48. Hill, *BD*, 119, 133–34, 136, 233–34, 237–38, 309–10, 318–19, 319–20, 333; Slatin, *Fire and sword*, 108–09; Holt, *The Mahdist state*, 38; *The Sudan memoirs of Carl Christian Giegler Pasha*, 139ff. Cf. Allen, *Gordon*, 141.
49. See Hill, *BD*, *passim*; Crabites, *Americans*, *passim*.
50. See Slatin, *Fire and sword*, 100.
51. *Ibid.*, 1–5, 59; Hill, *Slatin Pasha*, 10. See also *The Sudan memoirs of Carl Christian Giegler Pasha*, 131.
52. Slatin, *Fire and sword*, 73–85; Kapteijns, *Mahdist faith*, 63. *Colonel Gordon*, 335. Cf. Hill, "Muhammad Harun al-Rashid Saif al-Din," *BD*, 256–57. Hill, *BD*, 297, states that al-Nur Muhammad Anqara personally performed the decapitation.
53. For authorship of *Fire and sword*, see M. W. Daly, *The sirdar*, Philadelphia 1997, 71–72.
54. Slatin, *Fire and sword*, 96.
55. Hill, *BD*, 270.
56. Muhammad Ra'uf dismissed Gessi, too, and Giegler had Paolo Zucchinetti, another Italian, expelled on charges of sedition (Shuqayr, *Ta'rikh*, v. ii, 105–08); *Colonel Gordon*, 39–42, 310–13, 390; Holt, *The Mahdist state*, 40; Hill, *BD*, 136, 391; Allen, *Gordon*, 163. For Giegler on Gessi, "the Garibaldi of Africa" whom he depicts as a shameless reprobate, see *The Sudan memoirs of Carl Christian Giegler Pasha*, 27–28; and on Messedaglia, "a rascal and a knave" and "a crook to the end," *ibid.*, 149–50.
57. Slatin, *Fire and sword*, 102–03.
58. *Ibid.*, 103–12; *BD*, 314–15, 325. Cf. Hill, *Slatin Pasha*, 13–14.

CHAPTER FOUR. DARFUR AT THE END OF TIME:
THE MAHDIYYA, 1885–1898

1. The best brief introduction to the concept of the Mahdi remains Holt, *The Mahdist state* 1970.
2. *Ibid.*, 59–65.
3. Musa al-Mubarak, *Ta'rikh Dar Fur*, 47–57.
4. *Ibid.*, 50–57; Slatin, *Fire and sword*, 148–70, 181–94; F. R. Wingate, *Mahdiism and the Egyptian Sudan*, London 1891, 24–26.
5. *Fire and sword*, 204–05, 210–17. For a full discussion, see Richard Hill, *Slatin Pasha*, 15–18.
6. *Fire and sword*, 219–22.
7. *Ibid.*, 222–27.
8. *Ibid.*, 248.
9. Wingate, *Mahdiism*, 97–98; Holt, *The Mahdist state*, 75–76.
10. Holt, *The Mahdist state*, 69–72; Allen, *Gordon and the Sudan*, 186. See also M. W. Daly, ed., *The road to Shaykan*, Durham 1983.
11. Musa al-Mubarak, *Ta'rikh Dar Fur*, 69–73.
12. *Ibid.*, 64–68; Holt, *The Mahdist state*, 75–76; Slatin, *Fire and sword*, 256–75; Wingate, *Mahdiism*, 130–32; Hill, *BD* ("Sa'id Bey Juma'"), 325. Wingate (*Mahdiism*, 131) states that al-Sayyid Jum'a's decision to resist was precipitated by a *fiki*'s criticism of his smoking cigarettes.
13. Holt, *The Mahdist state*, 87–95.
14. *Ibid.*, 91–93; Slatin, *Fire and sword*, 274–75; Allen, *Gordon and the Sudan*, 260.
15. One of these, Muhammad al-Mahdi al-Sanusi of the Sanusiya sufi order, never responded to the Mahdi's letter of appointment (Holt, *The Mahdist state*, 112–13).
16. Holt, *The Mahdist state*, 138; Wingate, *Mahdiism*, 235, provides a version of the Khalifa's proclamation to the people of Darfur.
17. Wingate, *Mahdiism*, 133.
18. Kapteijns, *Mahdist faith*, 75.
19. Musa al-Mubarak Hasan, *Ta'rikh*, 73–75; Slatin, *Fire and sword*, 377; Hill, *BD*, 4.
20. Slatin, *Fire and sword*, 377–79.
21. This is another example of borrowing from the days of early Islam: the *ashraf* (sing. *sharif*) were the family of the Prophet Muhammad.
22. Musa al-Mubarak, *Ta'rikh Dar Fur*, 84–88. *Jihadia*: black infantrymen of slave origin, many of whom were veterans of al-Zubayr's and other private armies or of the Egyptian army. Hamdan himself was half-Mandala.
23. Musa al-Mubarak, *Ta'rikh Dar Fur*, 88–93; Holt, *The Mahdist state*, 143–46; Slatin, *Fire and sword*, 396.
24. Kapteijns, *Mahdist faith*, 76, 276 n. 6.
25. Musa al-Mubarak, *Ta'rikh Dar Fur*, 99–107; Holt, *The Mahdist state*, 153–54; Wingate, *Mahdiism*, 257–58. More details are in Slatin, *Fire and sword*, 412–15.
26. Musa al-Mubarak, *Ta'rikh Dar Fur*, 107–16, 123–30; Holt, *The Mahdist state*, 156–57; Hill, *BD*, 367; Slatin, *Fire and sword*, 427–29.

27. Kapteijns, *Mahdist faith*, 77–81, 88–94.

28. *Ibid.*, 88–92; Kapteijns and Spaulding, *After the millennium*, 205–06.

29. Musa al-Mubarak, *Ta'rikh Dar Fur*, 155–69; Kapteijns, *Mahdist faith*, 84–88; Holt, *The Mahdist state*, 157–59; Kapteijns and Spaulding, *After the millennium*, 330–34. Cf. A. B. Theobald, *The Mahdiya*, London 1951, 148.

30. Musa al-Mubarak, *Ta'rikh Dar Fur*, 170–73; Kapteijns and Spaulding, *After the millennium*, 106, 230–36; Kapteijns, *Mahdist faith*, 86, 95–96; Holt, *The Mahdist state*, 259.

31. The series titled *Intelligence Report, Egypt*, produced by F. R. Wingate as the Egyptian army's director of military intelligence, contains numerous examples of unfounded rumors from Darfur, including invasions by Rabih Zubayr (4 July 1892; 7 October 1892; 8 November 1892; 18 September 1893; 21 December 1893; 29 August 1894; 33 December 1894).

32. Kapteijns, *Mahdist faith*, 84, 86–88, 94–96, 279 n. 33; Holt, *The Mahdist state*, 158; Wingate, *Mahdiism*, 374–79. See also Kapteijns and Spaulding, *After the millennium*, 293. Wingate's explanation of how the "wild reports" of Abu Jummayza gained currency in the eastern Sudan is an invention justifying his earlier incorrect intelligence reports.

33. Kapteijns and Spaulding, *After the millennium*, 118, 318.

34. Musa al-Mubarak, *Ta'rikh Dar Fur*, 75ff.

35. *Ibid.*, 139–48; Holt, *The Mahdist state*, 160–64, 197; Hill, *BD*, 134–35.

36. Musa al-Mubarak, *Ta'rikh Dar Fur*, 177–81; Holt, *The Mahdist state*, 165.

37. Among the notable Ta'aisha commanders were Mahmud Ahmad, Hamdan Abu Anja, Uthman Adam, Arabi Dafallah, al-Khatim wad Musa, Zaki Tamal, Muhammad wad Bushara, the brothers Yunus and Uthman al-Dikaim, Yusuf Anqara, Bashir Abdallah Muhammad Andarqi, Abd al-Baqi Abd al-Wakil, Abd al-Qadir wad umm Maryum, Ibrahim Malik, Zaki Uthman, Ahmad wad Ali wad Ahmad and his brother Hamid, Khatir Himaydan, Isa wad al-Zayn, Umar Salih, Muhammad Zayn Hasan, Sa'd Allah Sa'dan, Bishari Muhammad Raida, Fadl al-Hassana, Ahmad Fadil Muhammad, Ahmad wad Hilu, and Ya'qub and Harun Muhammad Turshayn, the Khalifa's brothers.

38. Holt, *The Mahdist state*, 244–47.

39. *Ibid.*, 128–32. Exceptions to the suspensions were made for cases of trust, debt, orphans' property, and manumission.

40. Holt, *The Mahdist state*, 261–64. Cf. Kapteijns, *Mahdist faith*, 107–08; and Hill, *BD* (Abd Allahi Ahmad abu Jalaha wad Ibrahim), 3.

41. de Waal, *Famine*, 59.

42. Musa al-Mubarak, *Ta'rikh Dar Fur*, 181–88; Kapteijns, *Mahdist faith*, 51–52, 97–99. The nicknames echo a Sudanese proverb: "*Yaum 'asal yaum basal*" ("Honey today, onions tomorrow"): S. Hillelson, *Sudan Arabic texts*, Cambridge 1935, 3–4.

43. Musa al-Mubarak, *Ta'rikh Dar Fur*, 191–96; Kapteijns and Spaulding, *After the millennium*, 335–49; A. B. Theobald, *Ali Dinar, last sultan of Darfur 1898–1916*, London 1965, 25, 27–30; Kapteijns, *Mahdist faith*, 101–03; Hill, *BD*, 45, 386; Holt, *The Mahdist state*, 159. Ali Dinar's own version, stating that he was forced by Abu'l-Khayrat's murderers to accept the title or be killed himself, is in the Arkell papers, SOAS 3/13.

44. Hill, *BD*, 224; Kapteijns, *Mahdist faith*, 117–18.

45. See Kapteijns and Spaulding, *After the millennium*, 406–15, 428–32.
46. Kapteijns, *Mahdist faith*, 99–103; Musa al-Mubarak, *Ta'rikh Dar Fur*, 199ff.; Kapteijns and Spaulding, *After the millennium*, 224, 248, 261, 380.
47. Kapteijns, *Mahdist faith*, 103–07, 131. See also Kaptiejns and Spaulding, *After the millennium*, 284–87, 288–93.
48. Kapteijns and Spaulding, *After the millennium*, 121, 251, 296. Sanin Husayn's precise ancestry is debated.
49. Kapteijns, *Mahdist faith*, 104–13.
50. *Ibid.*, 108.
51. *Ibid.*, 110, 113–15. See also Kapteijns and Spaulding, *After the millennium*, 143–53.
52. Kapteijns, *Mahdist faith*, 113–22.
53. De Waal, *Famine that kills*, 62. "White Bone" refers to animal skeletons (*ibid.*, 76).
54. Ahmed Bayoumi, *The history of the Sudan health services*, Nairobi 1979, 45–53, 55–65; De Waal, *Famine that kills*, 63–64.

CHAPTER FIVE. BETWEEN AN ANVIL AND A HAMMER:
THE REIGN OF ALI DINAR, 1898–1916

1. For an overview, see John Marlowe, *Anglo-Egyptian relations 1800–1953*, London 1954.
2. Salisbury to Cromer, 3 February 1899, FO 633/7/185; Cromer to Salisbury, 10 February 1899, FO 633/6/309.
3. See M. W. Daly, *Empire on the Nile*, Cambridge 1986, 11–18. See also A. A. El-Erian, *Condominium and related situations in international law*, Cairo 1952.
4. *SIR* 60; Theobald, *Ali Dinar*, 30–33; Kapteijns and Spaulding, *After the millennium*, 416–22; MacMichael, "The Darfur Who's Who."
5. Theobald, *Ali Dinar*, 35–43; Daly, *Empire*, 172; Wingate to Cromer, 2 June 1901 and 7 June 1901, SAD 271/6. The relevant correspondence is at FO 78/5087. For British fears of Ali Dinar's aggression, see, e.g., Owen to Wingate, 24 July 1907, SAD 281/1, and H. D. Palmer, "Note on Army Budget Proposals for 1911," 2 October 1910, encl. in Palmer to Wingate, 2 October 1910, SAD 298/1. Annual tribute was paid in kind and, along with gifts the sultan sent, sold for cash (Theobald, *Ali Dinar*, 77–78).
6. Quoted in Theobald, *Ali Dinar*, 70. For titles and reports, see Daly, *Empire*, 172.
7. *RFACS* for 1901, *Egypt No. 1* (1902); Theobald, *Ali Dinar*, 33–34, 54; Hill *BD*, 58.
8. Samuel Bey Atiya, "Senin and Ali Dinar," *SNR* VII, 2, 1924, 63–69.
9. Theobald, *Ali Dinar*, 54, 77. For the sultan's campaigns against the tribes: *Ibid.*, 44ff.
10. *Ibid.*, 63–64, 67–69.
11. Kapteijns, *Mahdist faith*, 171–76.
12. Wingate to Cromer, 24 August 1910, FO 633/14/89.
13. Kapteijns, *Mahdist faith*, 180–97; Hill, *BD*, 16.

14. For the literary relations of Wingate and Slatin, see Daly, *The sirdar*, 70–79, and, e.g., Slatin to Wingate, 12 November 1912, SAD 183/2, one of Slatin's many letters on Darfur bearing Wingate's authorship.
15. The Foreign Office knew Slatin had nothing to do: Vansittart to Herman, 19 October 1911, FO 371/1114.
16. For Ali Dinar's "terms of appointment": Kitchener to Grey, 29 May 1913, FO 371/1637. The other relevant correspondence, with illuminating FO minutes, is in the same file.
17. Theobald, *Ali Dinar*, 123–37.
18. *Ibid.*, 136–37.
19. O'Fahey, *State and society*, 119, quoting Ali Dinar.
20. *Ibid.*, 17, 71. Ali Dinar awarded his father the rank of sultan posthumously (*ibid.*, 127), a conceit appealed to fitfully even by the sultan of Wadai (Kapteijns and Spaulding, *After the millennium*, 11).
21. O'Fahey, *State and society*, 116–17, 121, 123, 127; L. B. Jureidini, "The miracles of Ali Dinar," *The Muslim world*, VI, 1917, 409–14. For Abu Kauda, Hussayn Ibrahim Qarad, and leaders of the *Mahmal* caravan, see MacMichael, "The Darfur Who's Who."
22. In "The Darfur Who's Who," *passim*, not written for publication, MacMichael identified court officials by ancient title, then dismissed them, accurately or not, as "of no importance" or having "no power or influence." As a nephew of Lord Curzon, the jealous bearer of many titles, he may have enjoyed referring, e.g., to one "Gurut" as "warden of blunderbusses" (*ibid.*, 18).
23. Hill, *BD*, 25–26, 193. *Cf.* O'Fahey, *State and society*, 126; and MacMichael, "The Dar Fur Who's Who," 18.
24. For example, Karamallah Muhammad Kurqusawi, executed in 1903 (Hill, *BD*, 196–97), and Tahir Nurayn, "said to have spent a year at the bottom of a well" at Ali Dinar's command (*ibid.*, 353).
25. G. D. Lampen, "History of Darfur," *SNR* XXXI, 2, 1950, 203–04.
26. O'Fahey, *State and society*, 127–29; MacMichael, "The Darfur Who's Who." For relations with the Sanusiyya, see Jay Spaulding and Lidwien Kapteijns, *An Islamic alliance: Ali Dinar and the Sanusiyya, 1906–1916*, Evanston 1994, 1–49.
27. MacMichael, "The Darfur Who's Who."
28. Theobald, *Ali Dinar*, 209–11; O'Fahey, *State and society*, 54, 89–91.
29. O'Fahey, *State and society*, 110–14; Hill, *BD*, 26, 359; R. S. O'Fahey, "The office of *qadi* in Dar Fur: a preliminary enquiry," *BSOAS* XL, 1, 1977, 110–24; MacMichael, "The Darfur Who's Who," 39. MacMichael (*ibid.*, 35) wrote that Ramadan Ali had "little more to do with military operations than the Duke of Cornwall [the Prince of Wales, as colonel-in-chief] has to do with Light Infantry," that is, nothing. *Cf.* Lampen, "History of Darfur," 204–05.
30. O'Fahey, *State and society*, 101, 105; de Waal, *Famine that kills*, 64. *Cf.* Lampen, "History of Darfur," 205, whose conclusions about corruption of the system appear to be based on no sources.
31. Theobald, *Ali Dinar*, 214–15; MacMichael, "The Darfur Who's Who."
32. Except where otherwise cited, the narrative that follows is based on Daly, *Empire*, 171–91.

33. See Daly, *Empire*, 152–71. Maqbula was a daughter of Nurayn, who, like Zakariyya, Ali Dinar's father, was a son of Sultan Ibrahim Qarad.
34. Adjutant-general to DAAG, 26 June 1915, SAD 127/2; Wingate to Savile, 26 July 1915, SAD 127/3.
35. Wingate to Savile, 26 July 1915, SAD 127/3.
36. Wingate to Savile, 1 August 1915, SAD 127/3.
37. de Waal, *Famine that kills*, 65–66; Kapteijns, *Mahdist faith*, 51–52, 192–93.
38. E. E. Evans-Pritchard (*The Sanusi of Cyrenaica*, Oxford 1949, 128) dismissed the notion.
39. Spaulding and Kapteijns, *An Islamic alliance*, 45–48, 176–77.
40. Ali Dinar was said to have been outraged at having a baby named after him. For Wingate as propagandist, see Daly, *The sirdar*, 39–62 *passim*.
41. Wingate to Kelly, 21 June 1916, SAD 200/7; Wingate to C. E. Wilson, 16 June 1916, SAD 200/7; Wingate to Sharif Hussayn of Mecca, 24 June 1916, SAD 137/7; Wingate to Stack, 5 July 1916, SAD 201/2.
42. McCowan to Wingate, 12 November 1916, SAD 130/7.
43. MacMichael to ADI, 27 May 1916, SAD 128/5. MacMichael added characteristically: "Officers and officials stationed at Fasher in future should be extremely well housed."

CHAPTER SIX. "CLOSED DISTRICT": ANGLO-EGYPTIAN
COLONIAL RULE IN DARFUR, 1916–1939

1. The issue of financing the conquest was solved in the usual way: Egypt paid (Daly, *Empire*, 186–87).
2. This section is based on Daly, *Empire*, 188–91. The quotations are from MacMichael, "Memorandum. Concerning the future status of Darfur," nd, SAD 127/3, and "Memorandum concerning the administrative policy to be followed in Darfur in the immediate future," 6 March 1916, SAD 127/7 (emphasis added).
3. MacMichael studied Sudanese tribal history, produced several books and many articles, and founded *SNR*.
4. H. A. MacMichael, "Report on Dar Masalit," Lampen papers, SAD 730/10; Daly, *Empire*, 187–88. The convention called for a boundary commission; a protocol delimiting the border was signed in January 1924.
5. See Kapteijns, *Mahdist faith*, 210–12; MacMichael, "Report on Dar Masalit."
6. Kapteijns, *Mahdist faith*, 212.
7. The Second Coming of Jesus is in some traditions associated with (but in others is independent from) manifestation of the Mahdi.
8. A. J. Arkell, "Mahdism in the Western Sudan," 1926, SGA, CIVSEC 56/2/18.
9. See, e.g., A. J. Arkell, Act. Resident, Dar Masalit, to Governor, Darfur, 21 August 1925 and 13 September 1925, SGA, INTEL 9/2/26.
10. Daly, *Empire*, 282–84; Kapteijns, *Mahdist faith*, 212–14. For the comment about worldwide unrest: *SIR* November 1921; for the rumor about houses and dogs: Kapteijns, *Mahdist faith*, 212; on intercourse with infidels: Savile to DI, 28 February 1922, INTEL 2/50/425. Regarding McNeil's culpability, see, e.g., Maffey to MacMichael, 25 November 1928, SAD G/s469.

11. A. J. Arkell, "Mahdism in the Western Sudan," 1926, SGA, CIVSEC 56/2/18.

12. Sir Angus Gillan, interview with the author, 24 May 1976. Gillan spent almost the entire period 1910–32 in Kordofan and Darfur and was civil secretary from 1934 to 1939.

13. Daly, *Empire*, 285; G. M. Hancock, "Mahdism and native administration in the Western Sudan," 6 May 1931, SGA, CIVSEC 56/2/18; Arkell, "Mahdism in the Western Sudan."

14. For the quotation on Dar Masalit: A. J. Arkell, "Note on Mahdism in Western Sudan," SGA, CIVSEC 56/2/18. For remarks of the director of intelligence: Willis to civil secretary, 13 May 1923, SGA, INTEL 9/2/26. The other agents were Muhammad Ali Abdallah (Kutum), Abd al-Mun'im Muhammad (Nyala), and Maqbul Abu Harun (Dar Rizayqat): "List of agents of Sayed Abdel Rahman El Mahdi," encl. in Balfour to governors, 1 December 1921, SGA, PALACE 4/8/42. For SAR's disclaimers, see, e.g., his letter to the governor-general, 6 December 1925, SGA, SECURITY 6/8/47.

15. Grigg, resident Dar Masalit, to governor, Darfur, 8 February 1927; civil secretary to governor, El Fasher, 20 February 1927; acting governor, Darfur, to civil secretary, 10 April 1927; Associate Resident, Dar Masalit, to Governor, Darfur, 29 September 1928, SGA, CIVSEC 5/1/9. Other details of the "Mahdi" are in the same file. See also SSIR 14, 26 May 1927, FO 371/12375. See also Lethem to Palmer, 19 June 1925, and to Tomlinson, 10 August 1925, RHL 11/1. G. J. Lethem visited from Northern Nigeria in 1925.

16. "Migration from Kordofan and Darfur to White Nile Province. Note of a meeting...on June 12th, 1926," SGA, SECURITY 6/8/47; George Bredin, interview with the author, 10 June 1976; Lethem to Palmer, 13 September 1925, and Palmer to Lethem, 6 September 1925, RHL 11/1. For Mahdists in the army, see SSIR 9, 30 November 1926, FO 371/11614, and Davies to Kaid el 'Amm, 25 May 1926, SGA, KORDOFAN 1/16/79; *cf.* H. J. Huddleston, "Notes on the possibility of a Mahdist rising in the Sudan necessitating the employment of external reinforcements," 9 August 1926, FO 141/573/17246.

17. Clarke to Governor, Blue Nile, 24 April 1918, CIVSEC 60/1/1. For one fanciful Fallata "odyssey" (and conversion to Mahdism), see SSIR 18, 6 November 1927, FO 371/12375.

18. Public Security Intelligence, "Mahdism and El Sayed Abdel Rahman El Mahdi, K. B. E., C. V. O.," 28 April 1935, FO 371/19096; SPIS 48 (March–April 1945), 49 (May 1945), 55 (December 1945), Perham Papers, RHL 576/1; Robertson to Mayall, 19 July 1944, SAD 521/1.

19. SPIS 62 (December 1946), Perham Papers, RHL 576/2.

20. K. D. D. Henderson, letter home, 14 December 1926, SAD 537/10.

21. Kapteijns, *Mahdist faith*, 312 n. 18, criticizes the present author for belittling Davies's role in noting that he had "left for Dar Masalit with the major works on indirect rule in his luggage." She misses the point: Davies (*The camel's back*, London 1957, 145) claimed to have gone there "*in 1920* [emphasis added], armed with Lord Lugard's, *The dual mandate in British tropical Africa*, which was not published *until* 1922. For Lugard, see I. F. Nicolson, *The administration of Nigeria 1900 to 1960*, Oxford 1969.

22. Kapteijns, *Mahdist faith*, 215. The comment about a "Lugardian emirate" is from G. N. Sanderson's introduction to *The memoirs of Babikr Bedri*, v. 2, London 1980, 47.

23. Kapteijns, *Mahdist faith*, 216–24. The diary of Davies's 1920 visit to Dar Masalit is in the University of Edinburgh Library, GEN 1899. For the recommendation of a spy, see Arkell to Governor, Darfur, 22 September 1926, SGA, DARFUR 1/24/134.

24. B. A. Lewis, *Handing over notes, Dar Masalit*, 1952, SAD 600/3; Perham diary, 17 February 1938, RHL 50/7; *RFACS* for 1927, Cmd. 3284.

25. Acting Resident, Western Darfur, to Governor, Darfur, 20 January 1932, SGA, CIVSEC 1/22/65.

26. Boustead, Annual Report for Western Darfur–Zalingei District, 1938, RHL 547/2. Sese Muhammad Atim was a member of the hereditary *dimangawi*'s family. Relevant correspondence is at SGA, CIVSEC 1/20/61. For Boustead's own account, see *The wind of morning*, London 1974, 110–25.

27. Dupuis to civil secretary, 28 March 1929, SGA, CIVSEC 1/21/62.

28. *RFACS* for 1929, Cmd. 3697; for 1930, Cmd. 3935; for 1933, Cmd. 4668; for 1934, Cmd. 5019; Hill, *BD*, 327.

29. Dupuis, "Proposals for devolution in Dar Rizeigat," 22 April 1928, SGA, CIVSEC 1/20/61; Dupuis to civil secretary, 30 December 1929, SGA, CIVSEC 1/21/63.

30. Governor of Darfur to civil secretary, 4 June 1932, SGA, CIVSEC 1/22/65; E. A. Balfour, covering note to letters, nd, SAD 606/6. *RFACS* for 1934, Cmd. 5019; for 1936, Cmd. 5895; for 1937, Cmd. 6139; for 1938, Cmd. 6139; Boustead, *The wind*, 121.

31. Lampen, *Handing over notes*, 23 March 1949, SAD G/s 886.

32. Dupuis to civil secretary, 30 December 1928, SGA, CIVSEC 1/20/61.

33. Dupuis to civil secretary, 2 March 1929, SGA, CIVSEC 1/21/62.

34. E. A. Balfour, covering note to letters, nd, SAD 606/6.

35. Lampen, "Native Administration in Southern Darfur," 10/31, encl. in Lampen to governor, Darfur, 21 November 1931, SGA, CIVSEC 1/22/65.

36. Daly, *Empire*, 372–73. On the Baqqara joint court: Dupuis to civil secretary, 25 February 1929, SGA, CIVSEC 1/21/62; *cf.* Lampen, "Native Administration in Southern Darfur," 10/31, encl. in Lampen to governor, Darfur, 21 November 1931, SGA, CIVSEC 1/22/65. On the Nyala Missiriyya and Humr: Dupuis to civil secretary, 3 July 1929, SGA, CIVSEC 1/21/62. The quotation about avoiding division is from P. Ingleson, "Proposals in regard to Native Administration in Western and Southern Darfur Districts," 26 June 1938, RHL 546/1.

37. Dupuis to civil secretary, 11 April 1929, SGA, CIVSEC 1/21/62.

38. Sudan Government, *Report of Lord De La Warr's Educational Commission*, np, 1937.

39. "Minutes of the Province Education Officers' Meeting, March 21st–24th 1939," SAD 662/10.

40. "Report on the Gordon Memorial College, Khartoum," in Maffey to Lloyd, 2 March 1929, SAD G//s; *RFACS* for 1936, Cmd. 5575; Mohamed Omer Beshir, *Educational development in the Sudan 1898–1956*, Oxford 1969, 200.

41. P. Ingleson, "Education in Darfur," 21 February 1938, RHL 546/7.
42. Creed to governor, Darfur, 10 June 1926, SGA, DARFUR 1/24/134. Emphasis added.
43. W. F. Crawford, "Note on education in Southern Darfur District with reference to my conversation with the Governor at Id el Ghanam," 16 February 1933, encl. in Crawford to governor, Darfur, 16 February 1933, SGA, DARFUR 1/5/30.
44. On Khartoum Province: R. K. Winter to Dupuis, 5 February 1933, SGA, DARFUR 1/5/30. Ingleson, "Education in Darfur," 21 February 1938, RHL 546/7.
45. Acting resident, Western Darfur, to governor, Darfur, 20 January 1932, SGA, CIVSEC 1/22/65.
46. Crawford, "Note on education in Southern Darfur." Emphasis added.
47. Winter to financial secretary, 17 April 1935, SGA, CIVSEC 17/6/33. See also Matthews to civil secretary, 18 June 1930, SGA, CIVSEC 1/11/37. At a conference in 1982, tensions between former administrators and teachers were obvious: Deborah Lavin, ed., *The Condominium remembered. Proceedings of the Durham Sudan historical records conference 1982*, Durham, 2 vols., 1993 [*sic*].
48. *RFACS* for 1938, Cmd. 6139.
49. *RFACS* for 1939–41, Cmd. 8097.
50. *RFACS* for 1930, Cmd. 3935; for 1931, Cmd. 4159; for 1935, Cmd. 5281; S. C. J. Bennett, E. R. John, and J. W Hewison, "Animal husbandry," in Tothill, ed., *Agriculture*, 664–65.
51. *RFACS* for 1928, Cmd. 3403; for 1932, Cmd. 4387; for 1934, Cmd. 5019.
52. For the epidemic, see Bayoumi, *The history*, 222–29; for Bence-Pembroke's comment: Governor, Darfur, to Director of Intelligence, 23 November 1926, SGA, DARFUR 1/24/134.
53. Bayoumi, *The history*, 194–97.
54. *RFACS* for 1926, Cmd. 2991; for 1928, Cmd. 3403; for 1929, Cmd. 3697; for 1930, Cmd. 3935; for 1931, Cmd. 4159; for 1932, Cmd. 4387; for 1935, Cmd. 5281; for 1936, Cmd. 5575; for 1938, Cmd. 6139. Bayoumi, *The history*, 211–12, 222–29; R. C. Maxwell-Darling, "Locusts in the Sudan," in Tothill, ed., *Agriculture*, 404–05. Published reports, though circumlocutory, seem to contradict de Waal's conclusion, based on oral sources, that the 1930–31 famine did not kill people (*Famine that kills*, 68).
55. *RFACS* for 1928, Cmd. 3403; for 1929, Cmd. 3697; for 1932, Cmd. 4387; for 1933, Cmd. 4668; for 1936, Cmd. 5575.
56. *RFACS* for 1938, Cmd. 6139. For example, airstrip work paid 1.5 piastres per day (100 piastres = £E 1).
57. *Ibid.*
58. *RFACS* for 1929, Cmd. 3697; for 1930, Cmd. 3935.
59. *RFACS* for 1932, Cmd. 4387.
60. *Report on medical & health work in the Sudan for the year 1934*, Khartoum, nd; *RFACS* for 1938, Cmd. 6139; *Report of the Sudan Medical Service for the year 1940*, Khartoum, nd; *Report of the Medical Services, Ministry of Health, Sudan Government for the year 1949*, Khartoum, nd.

61. *RFACS* for 1931, Cmd. 4159.

62. *RFACS* for 1932, Cmd. 4387.

63. *Ibid.*; *RFACS* for 1933, Cmd. 4668.

64. *Annual Report of the Department of Economics and Trade, 1934*, Khartoum 1935; *1935*, Khartoum 1936; *1936*, Khartoum 1937; *1945*, Khartoum 1945 [*sic*].

CHAPTER SEVEN. UNEQUAL STRUGGLES, 1939–1955

1. SAD 527/1.

2. For a summary of the war, see M. W. Daly, *Imperial Sudan: The Anglo-Egyptian Condominium, 1934–56*, Cambridge 1991, 127–37.

3. K. D. D. Henderson, *The making of the modern Sudan. The life and letters of Sir Douglas Newbold...*, London 1953, 124, 156–58, 160.

4. E. A. Balfour, covering note to letters, nd, SAD 606/7.

5. Henderson, *The making*, 169, 212, 231, 236.

6. *Ibid.*, 231.

7. *RFACS* for 1942–44, Cmd. 8098. The quotation is from Newbold to Mayall, 14 August 1942, in Henderson, *The making*, 266.

8. *RFACS* for 1945, Cmd. 7316; B. A. Lewis, *Handing over notes*, Dar Masalit, 1952, SAD 600/3; E. A. Balfour, covering note to letters, nd, SAD 606/7. See, e.g., Henderson, *The making*, 266–67.

9. *RFACS* for 1942–44, Cmd. 8098; for 1945, Cmd. 7316.

10. *RFACS* for 1945, Cmd. 7316; G. F. March, "Transport in the Sudan," in Tothill, ed., *Agriculture*, 181–83.

11. *RFACS* for 1939–41, Cmd. 8097; for 1945, Cmd. 7316.

12. Sudan Government, *Report of the Soil Conservation Committee*, Khartoum 1944; U. C. W. Rath, "The climate of the Sudan," 1953 conference on Food and Society in the Sudan, Khartoum 1954, 1–3.

13. *Report of the Soil Conservation Committee*; Advisory Council for the Northern Sudan, *Proceedings of the first session (1944)*, Khartoum 1945, 21–26.

14. Muhammad Hashim 'Awad, *Al-istiqlal wa fasad al-hukm fil-Sudan*, np, nd, 117–18.

15. DPMD, January 1945; *RFACS* for 1945, Cmd. 7316. For Boustead's second tour, see *The wind*, 175–81.

16. *RFACS* for 1945, Cmd. 7316; Hill, *BD*, 160. For the views of the informed passerby: Ina Beasley, *Before the wind changed*, Oxford 1992, 150–54.

17. DPMD, January 1945; *RFACS* for 1939–41, Cmd. 8097; for 1942–44, Cmd. 8098.

18. Advisory Council for the Northern Sudan, *Proceedings of the first session*.

19. Daly, *Imperial Sudan*, 193–201. A survey is G. H. Bacon, "Education," in Tothill, *Agriculture*, 222–47.

20. For the figure for the Ahlia school: DPMD for January 1945. For the quotation about cowherds: DPMD, September 1944. The rest of the paragraph: *RFACS* for 1939–41, Cmd. 8097; for 1942–44, Cmd. 8098; for 1945, Cmd. 7316.

21. DPMD, January 1945; RFACS for 1942–44, Cmd. 8098; for 1945, Cmd. 7316. Interesting anecdotes are in Beasley, *Before the wind*, 125–70.

22. DPMD, October 1945.
23. Robertson to Mayall, 6 March 1948, SAD 521/10. This section relies on Daly, *Imperial Sudan*, 262–80.
24. *RFACS* for 1948, Cmd. 8181; Tim Niblock, *Class and power in Sudan*, London 1987, 64–65.
25. Robertson to Mayall, 10 March 1951, SAD 522/14. This section derives from Daly, *Imperial Sudan*, 280–301.
26. See, e.g., K. D. D. Henderson, *Set under authority*; Somerset 1987, 189.
27. *RFACS* for 1948, Cmd. 8181.
28. *Ibid.*; *RFACS* for 1949, Cmd. 8434; for 1950–51, Cmd. 9798. For abuses, see, e.g., DPMDs for 1946.
29. Even in 1948, Robertson, the civil secretary, had written – and he later published – his conclusion that "the administration of the District is in a backward state.... Without a court-house, a decent dispensary, a lock-up and offices it is difficult to see how the institutions of local government, which we seek to found, can be built up" (*Transition in Africa: from direct rule to independence*, London 1974, 139). For the offices of Eastern District, which Robertson described as "the real Sudan": *ibid.*, 156–57.
30. Lampen to Robertson, 12 March 1947, SAD 527/5; B. A. Lewis, *Handing over notes*, Dar Masalit, 1952, SAD 600/3.
31. *RFACS* for 1948, Cmd. 8181; for 1949, Cmd. 8434; for 1950–51, Cmd. 9798; for 1951–52, Cmd. 9841; Henderson, *Set*, 184–85.
32. *RFACS*, for 1948, Cmd. 8181; for 1949, Cmd. 8434; for 1950–51, Cmd. 9798.
33. *RFACS* for 1951–52, Cmd. 9841.
34. K. D. D. Henderson, Darfur Province annual report for 1949, 7 February 1950, SAD (uncatalogued); *RFACS* for 1949, Cmd. 8434; DPMD, July 1949; Robertson to Mayall, 12 December 1949, SAD 522/7.
35. Henderson to Robertson, 29 October 1949, SAD 528/5.
36. "Financial Secretary, Sudan Government. Post-War Development" (with attachments), March 1946, SAD 635/14.
37. Information herein is from the Five-Year Plan for Post-War Development, SAD, except where otherwise noted.
38. See G. N. Sanderson, "The ghost of Adam Smith: ideology, bureaucracy, and the frustration of economic development in the Sudan, 1934–1940," in M. W. Daly, ed. *Modernization in the Sudan*, New York 1985, 101–20.
39. C. Wilkens, "Transport in the Sudan," in Ali Mohamed El-Hassan, ed., *An introduction to the Sudan economy*, Khartoum 1976, 104.
40. Lampen to Robertson, 23 February 1946, SAD 527/1, 17; April 1947, SAD 527/5.
41. Lampen to Robertson, 16 November 1945, SAD 526/15.
42. Lampen to Robertson, 29 March 1949, SAD 528/1.
43. The information here, unless otherwise noted, is from Development Branch, Finance Department, "The Sudan development programme 1951/56," 1953, SAD 662/11.
44. John Stone, *The Sudan economy: introductory notes*, Khartoum 1953, 29.
45. *Ibid.* Stone's magisterial "Sudan economic development, 1899–1913" was shelved because by crediting the huge Egyptian contribution to Sudan

development and insufficient reference to British "good government," it might be useful to Egyptian propagandists (G. W. Bell, Permanent Under-Secretary, Ministry of the Interior, to J. Carmichael, Ministry of Finance, 9 May 1954, SAD 696/11).

46. C. W. Williams, "Note by the Director of Education on the government plan for educational development in the Northern Sudan for the next ten years," 16 February 1946, SAD 658/6; Ministry of Education, Revised Ten-Year Plan 1949–1956, SAD G//s701; DPMD, January 1949; *RFACS* for 1950–51, Cmd. 9798; for 1951–52, Cmd. 9841.

47. Hammed Tewfik Hammed, "Main features of development possibilities and their relation to budget surpluses" ("Top Secret"), 30 October 1955, SAD.

48. Andrew Shepherd, Malcolm Norris, and John Watson, *Water planning in arid Sudan*, London 1987, 57–62.

49. *RFACS* for 1949, Cmd. 8434; for 1950–51, Cmd. 9798; for 1951–52, Cmd. 9841; Henderson, *Set*, 184; Shepherd, Norris, and Watson, *Water planning*, 50–51.

50. Lampen to Robertson, 17 April 1947, SAD 527/5; *RFACS* for 1948, Cmd. 8181; for 1949, Cmd. 8434; for 1950–51, Cmd. 9798.

51. *RFACS* for 1949, Cmd. 8434; for 1950–51, Cmd. 9798.

52. Development Branch, Finance Department, "The Sudan development programme 1951/56," SAD 662/11.

53. DPMD, March, April 1949, March, April, May 1950; *RFACS* for 1950–51, Cmd. 9798; Lampen to Robertson, 23 February 1946, SAD 527/1, 17 April 1947, SAD 527/5; *Annual Report of the Ministry of Agriculture 1953–1954*, Khartoum 1955. Cf. Beasley, *Before the wind*, 155.

54. *RFACS* for 1951–52, Cmd. 9841; Robertson to Lampen, 13 March 1946, SAD 527/1; Lampen to Robertson, 7 December 1946, SAD 527/4.

55. *Report of the Medical Services, Ministry of Health, Sudan Government for the year 1949*, Khartoum, nd; and for 1956/7, np, nd; *RFACS* for 1950–51, Cmd. 9798; for 1951–52, Cmd. 9841; B. A. Lewis, *Handing over notes*, Dar Masalit, March 1952, SAD 600/3; C. A. Willis, *Report on slavery and the pilgrimage*, 1926, SAD 212/2.

56. *RFACS* for 1951–52, Cmd. 9841.

57. SPIS 51, July 1945.

58. See, e.g., SPIS 62, December 1946.

59. DPMD, March, April 1949; DPMD March, April, May 1950; DPMD January 1952; *RFACS* for 1950–51, Cmd. 9798.

60. See Al-Fatih Abdullahi Abdel Salam, "Intra-party conflicts: the case of the Umma party," in Mahasin Abdel Gadir Hag Al-Safi, ed., *The Nationalist movement in the Sudan*, Khartoum 1989, 139–70.

61. Ibrahim Bedri, "The Socialist Republican Party" (and attached untitled note), nd, SAD 534/11; al-Fatih Abdullahi Abdel Salam, "Intra-party conflicts," 142–43.

62. G. W. Bell, untitled note, 29 May 1952, SAD 696/2.

63. R. C. Mayall, Sudan Agent, London, to Robertson, 22 March 1949, SAD 522/4. Henderson's real forte, Mayall wrote, was journalism. Robertson agreed (Robertson to Mayall, 30 March 1949, SAD 522/4).

64. DPMDs, 1952–53. Ibrahim Bedri reportedly charged that al-Malik Rahmatalla Mahmud had been "bought, one way or another" (G. W. Bell, untitled note, 29 May 1952, SAD 696/2).

65. See Daly, *Imperial Sudan*, 352–60. Bell's quotations are from *Shadows on the sand: the memoirs of Sir Gawain Bell*, London 1983, 201–02. For the Robertson quotation (italics in the original): *Transition*, n. 151. See also Awad al-Sid al-Karsani, "Muhammad al-Hafiz al-Tigani and the Sudan," in Mahasin Abdel Gadir Hag Al-Safi, ed., *The nationalist movement*, 202–18.

66. Most information on the MPs is from "House of Representatives: biographies of members elected in November, 1953," 2nd ed., March 1954, and "The Senate: Brief biographies of members elected and nominated in December, 1953," 2nd ed., March 1954. A copy of the former is enclosed in Joseph Sweeney, U.S. liaison officer, Khartoum, to Department of State, 19 January 1954, USNA 745W.521/3–2054.

67. Director of establishments to public relations officer, 21 December 1952, SAD 696/8.

CHAPTER EIGHT. COLONIAL LEGACIES AND SUDANESE
RULE, 1956–1969

1. See G. N. Sanderson, "Sudanese nationalism and the independence of the Sudan," in Michael Brett, ed., *Northern Africa: Islam and modernization*, London 1973, 97–109.

2. Republic of Sudan, Ministry of Social Affairs, Population Census Office, *First Population Census of Sudan 1955/56, Last (9th) interim report*, Khartoum 1958, 4, 5, 7, 10.

3. *Ibid.*, 23–24.

4. *Ibid.*, 19.

5. *Ibid.*, 38–40, 54–55.

6. *Second interim report*, 18–19, 20–21; *Fifth interim report*, 18–19, 20–21, 40, 41, 46.

7. Hammed Tewfik Hammed, Ministry of Finance, to Secretary-General, Council of Ministers, 30 October 1955, "Top Secret," SAD. See P. M. Holt and M. W. Daly, *A history of the Sudan*, London 2001, 146–48.

8. Government of the Sudan, *Memorandum on the budget estimates of the Republic of the Sudan for 1958–1959*, np. May 1958.

9. Peter Bechtold, *Politics in the Sudan*, New York 1976, 166–71, 188–96.

10. Niblock, *Class*, 217–19.

11. *Ibid.*, 220–22.

12. Sudan Government List, March 1956; Republic of the Sudan, Government List, October 1959; Republic of the Sudan, Staff List, 1963; Mohamed Abdel Rahman Ali, "Public finance in the Sudan," in Ali Mohamed El-Hassan, ed., *An introduction to the Sudan economy*, 138–39.

13. Abdel Rahman Abdel Wahab, "Development planning in the Sudan: policy and organization," in Ali Mohamed El-Hassan, ed., *An introduction*, 219.

14. Ali Ahmed Suliman, *Issues in the economic development of Sudan*, Khartoum 1975, 133–35; Mohamed Mirghani Abdel Salam, "Agriculture in the Sudan," in Ali Mohamed El-Hassan, ed., *An introduction to the Sudan economy*, 42;

Bodour Osman Abu Affan, *Industrial policies and industrialization in the Sudan*, Khartoum 1985, 12–20, 77.

15. Abdel Rahman Abdel Wahab, "Development planning in the Sudan: policy and organization," in Ali Mohamed El-Hassan, ed., *An introduction*, 219–20; Abdel Rahim Mirghani, *Development planning in the Sudan in the sixties*, Khartoum 1983, 10.

16. Bodour Osman Abu Affan, *Industrial policies*, 25–36; Mohamed Omer Beshir, ed., *Sudan: aid and external relations*, Khartoum 1984, *passim*; A. B. Zahlan, ed., *The agricultural sector of Sudan*, London 1986, 383–89.

17. Republic of the Sudan, *Ten-Year Plan of economic and social development 1961/62–1970/71, Explanatory memorandum on 1965/66 development budgets*, Khartoum 1965.

18. Republic of the Sudan, *Ten-Year Plan, explanatory memorandum*; Ahmed Safi el Din, "A survey of the Sudanese economy," in Mohamed Hashim Awad, ed., *Socio-economic change in the Sudan*, Khartoum 1983, 11–38; Abdel Rahim Mirghani, *Development planning in the Sudan in the sixties*, Khartoum 1983, 72–75; *Sudan almanac 1963*, 271.

19. Ali Mohamed El Hassan, "Structure of the Sudan economy," in *idem*, ed., *An introduction*, 1–23; Mohamed El Awad Galal-el-Din, "Population and labour force in the Sudan," in *ibid.*, 28.

20. Ali Mohamed El Hassan, "Structure," 9–11; Mohamed Mirghani Abdel Salam, "Agriculture in the Sudan," in Ali Mohamed El Hassan, *An introduction*, 60–63; Syed M. Nimeiri, "Industry in the Sudan," in *ibid.*, 99; Abdel Ghaffer M. Ahmed, "Planning and the neglect of pastoral nomads in the Sudan," in Gunnar Haarland, ed., *Problems of savannah development*, Bergen 1982, 40; Bodour Osman Abu Affan, *Industrial policies*, 50–54, 84; Tubiana and Tubiana, *The Zaghawa*, 83–93.

21. E. N. Dafalla, "The veterinary officer," in Philosophical Society of the Sudan, *The health of the Sudan*, Khartoum 1963, 152; M. M. Baasher, "Livestock development in the central rainland of the Sudan – potential and problems," in Philosophical Society of the Sudan, D. J. Shaw, ed., *Agricultural development in the Sudan*, v. 2, Khartoum 1966, 389–90; Tubiana and Tubiana, *The Zaghawa*, 93–94.

22. Awad Abdalla El-Awad Radaf, *Sudan gum*, Bergen thesis 1983, 47–50, 53, 73, 116.

23. Republic of the Sudan, *Ten-Year Plan, explanatory memorandum*.

24. Republic of the Sudan, *Sudan almanac, 1963*.

25. Republic of the Sudan, *Sudan almanac, 1961*, 157–58.

26. Shepherd, Norris, and Watson, *Water planning*, 72–82.

27. Bayoumi, *The history*, 106.

28. A. O. Abu Shamma, "International aspects of public health," in Philosophical Society of the Sudan, *The health*, 101; Khalafalla Babiker El Bedri, "Health education of the public," in *ibid.*, 130; Ahmed Ali Zaki, "A survey of the future health requirements in maintaining and improving the health of the Sudan," in *ibid.*, 175; *Sudan almanac, 1963*, 284; Bayoumi, *The history*, 148, 261–62, 274–79, 281–91; *The Merck manual*, 17th ed., 1999, 1250–51.

29. See, in this regard, Gaafar Mohamed Ali Bakheit, "The politics of Native Administration, 1964–69," in John Howell, ed., *Local government and politics in the Sudan*, Khartoum 1974, 45–64.
30. Sharif Harir, "'Arab Belt' versus 'African Belt': ethno-political conflict in Dar Fur and the regional cultural factors," in *idem* and Terje Tvedt, ed., *Short-cut to decay*, Uppsala 1994, 154–57.
31. Gaafar Mohamed Ali Bakheit, "The politics of Native Administration, 1964–69," in Howell, *Local government*, 48–50.
32. Al-Fatih Abdullahi Abdel Salam, "Intra-party conflicts," 146–59.
33. Ali Mohamed El Hassan, "Structure," 1–23.
34. Shepherd, Norris, and Watson, *Water planning*, 87–98.
35. Bechtold, *Politics*, 246–50.
36. *Ibid.*, 250–54.
37. This section is based on J. Millard Burr and Robert O. Collins, *Africa's thirty years' war*, Boulder 1999.

CHAPTER NINE. DARFUR AND "THE MAY REGIME," 1969–1985

1. This section relies on Bechtold, *Politics*, 259–81; Niblock, *Class*, 233–86; and Holt and Daly, *A history*, 166–79.
2. For the origins of the Free Officers Movement, see Niblock, *Class*, 234–41.
3. Sometimes also called the National Socialist Union.
4. The politburo was a who's who of Sudanese public life. The assembly had nine members from Southern Darfur, seven from the north, two from each province's council, and others from "popular organizations" or nominated by Nimayri.
5. See, e.g., his "British administration and Sudanese nationalism, 1919–1939," Cambridge Ph.D. 1965, and two chapters in Howell, ed., *Local government*, 25–32, 45–64. See also Mansour Khalid, *Nimeiri and the revolution of dis-May*, London 1985, 36–37, 46–48, 146, *passim*.
6. Appendix II, Howell, ed., *Local government*, 128; Niblock, *Class*, 259.
7. P. R. Woodward, "Government and infrastructure," in Craig, ed., *The agriculture*, 141; *Sudanow*, December 1977, January 1980; personal knowledge. See also the National Socialist Union, secretariat-general, *Document of the National Founding Congress, Draft of the basic rules*, and *idem*, *Draft of the Charter for National Action*, 1972.
8. John Howell, "The reform of local government, 1971," in *idem*, ed., *Local government*, 71.
9. See Mutasim el-Beshir, "The political role of the local government officer," in Howell, ed., *Local government*, 83–84.
10. Extracts from the People's Local Government Act 1971 are printed as an appendix to Howell, *Local government*, 117–23; *Sudanow*, December 1977.
11. *Al-kitab al-aswad*, np nd; Shepherd, Norris, and Watson, *Water planning*, 94.
12. *Sudanow*, May 1978, January 1983.

13. de Waal, *Famine*, 69–71; *Sudanow*, January 1981, December 1982, June 1983.
14. Shepherd, Norris, and Watson, *Water planning*, 95–100, 108–15.
15. *Ibid.*, 18–22. *Sudanow*, April 1978, August 1982, December 1982, August 1983.
16. *Sudanow*, February 1980, June 1980, August 1983.
17. de Waal, *Famine*, 71, 81–85, 91–97.
18. Gunnar Haaland, "Economic determinants in ethnic processes," in F. Barth, ed., *Ethnic groups and boundaries*, 1969, 53–73.
19. *Sudanow*, January 1978.
20. *Zaraib al-hawa*, or "closing off the air."
21. Except where otherwise stated, this section is based on Burr and Collins, *Africa's thirty years' war*.
22. *Sudanow*, July 1983.
23. Julie Flint and Alex de Waal, *Darfur: a short history of a long war*, London 2005, 51, 54–55; Burr and Collins, *Africa's thirty-years' war*, 180–83, 199–200.
24. Private information.
25. Gabriel Warburg, *Islam, sectarianism and politics in Sudan since the Mahdiyya*, London 2003, 178–84.
26. *Sudanow*, October 1984.
27. de Waal, *Famine*, 104–11.
28. Abdel Salam Sidahmed, *Politics and Islam in contemporary Sudan*, Richmond, Surrey 1997, 120.
29. *Sudanow*, October 1983.
30. Mansour Khalid, *Nimeiri*, 210–11; *Sudanow*, January 1980, May 1980.
31. Shepherd, Norris, and Watson, *Water planning*, 30–38.
32. *Sudanow*, October 1984; octogenarian reminiscence: personal information.
33. M. A. Mohamed Salih, "Ecological stress, political coercion and the limits of government intervention," in Anders Hjort af Ornas and M. A. Mohamed Salih, eds., *Ecology and politics*, Uppsala 1989, 115.
34. *Ibid.*, 110–11.
35. See de Waal, *Famine, passim*.
36. G. E. Wickens, "Natural vegetation," in Craig, ed., *The agriculture*, 56–57, 58, 60, 61–62.
37. Sharif Harir, "'Arab belt,'" 174–75.
38. This section, unless otherwise noted, is based on de Waal, *Famine*.
39. See, e.g., *Sudanow*, January 1985.
40. *Sudanow*, July 1985.
41. *Sudanow*, October 1985.
42. Mansour Khalid, *Nimeiri*, 206–07. See also P. R. Woodward, "Government and infrastructure," in Craig, ed., *The agriculture*, 142–43; *Sudanow*, August 1984.
43. *Sudanow*, March, July 1985.
44. *Sudanow*, November 1984, January 1986.
45. A government mouthpiece, *Sudanow*, reported in May 1984 the Sudan's having won something called the "Africa Environment Award," recognizing Nimayri's "special attention to environmental problems."
46. *Sudanow*, August 1984, July 1985, December 1985.

CHAPTER TEN. THIRD TIME UNLUCKY: DARFUR AND THE RESTORATION OF PARLIAMENTARY RULE

1. Bona Malwal, in an interview with *Sudanow* in which, as editor, he had published fulsome encomia of the dictator, recalled in May 1985 writing "articles very critical of the government I was a member of."
2. Ushari Mahmud and Sulayman Baldo, *El Diein massacre and slavery in the Sudan*, Khartoum 1987.
3. *Sudanow*, October 1984, December 1985, June 1986.
4. Al-Agab Ahmed Al-Teraifi, "Regionalisation in the Sudan. Characteristics, problems and prospects," in Peter Woodward, ed., *Sudan after Nimeiri*, London 1991, 106–10; *Sudanow*, June 1986.
5. Sharif Harir, "'Arab belt,'" 154–56.
6. Al-Agab Ahmed al-Teraifi, "Regionalisation," 109–16.
7. *Sudanow*, October 1986.
8. For examples, see Sharif Harir, "'Arab belt,'" 169. See also Mohamed Suliman, "The rationality and irrationality of violence in sub-Saharan Africa," in *idem*, ed., *Ecology, politics & violent conflict*, London 1999, 25–44.
9. *Sudanow*, September 1984.
10. Sharif Harir, "'Arab belt,'" 174–76.
11. *Ibid.*, 166, 170–74; Flint and de Waal, *Darfur*, 56.

CHAPTER ELEVEN. THE STATE OF JIHAD

1. For theories of the coup, see Gabriel Warburg, *Islam*, London 2003, 205–08; *Africa confidential* 41, 20, 13 October 2000.
2. *Africa confidential* 34, 21, 22 October 1993. A list of RCC members, including two from Darfur, Col. Muhammad al-Amin Khalifa and Tijani Adam Tahir, is in Ann Mosley Lesch, *The Sudan – contested national identities*, Oxford and Bloomington 1998, 226–27; for the first two cabinets, see 227–30.
3. *Africa confidential* 34, 21, 22 October 1993; Lesch, *The Sudan*, 117–25.
4. Lesch, *The Sudan*, 125–27.
5. The name changed in 1997 to Intergovernmental Authority on Development (IGAD).
6. *Africa confidential* 39, 10, 15 May 1998; Douglas H. Johnson, *The root causes of Sudan's civil wars*, 2nd ed., Oxford 2004, 91–110 *et passim*.
7. *Africa confidential* 39, 10, 15 May 1998; 39, 14, 10 July 1998. Cf. Abdelwahab El-Affendi, *Turabi's revolution*, London 1991, 148.
8. Johnson, *The root causes*, 130–35; *Africa confidential* 34, 21, 22 October 1993.
9. Johnson, *The root causes*, 135–39.
10. *Ibid.*, 143 n. 1.
11. Karl Wohlmuth, "Alternative economic strategies for the Sudan," in Harir and Tvedt, eds., *Short-cut*, 204–47; Johnson, *The root causes*, 159.
12. Warburg, *Islam*, 212–13; *Africa confidential* 41, 13, 23 June 2000; Johnson, *The root causes*, 102–03, 137. Cf. Abdelwahab El-Affendi, *Turabi's revolution*, 146.

13. *Africa confidential* 34, 21, 22 October 1993; 39, 14, 10 July 1998; 41, 10, 12 May 2000; 41, 13, 23 June 2000; Johnson, *The root causes*, 162–65.
14. *Africa confidential* 39, 10, 15 May 1998; 40, 24, 3 December 1999; 41, 1, 7 January 2000; Warburg, *Islam*, 215–16.
15. This section is based on Burr and Collins, *Africa's thirty years' war*.
16. Abdelwahab El-Affendi, *Turabi's revolution*, 141–42.
17. Flint and de Waal, *Darfur*, 20–21, 25–26, 57; Gerard Prunier, *Darfur: The ambiguous genocide*, London 2005, 73–74.
18. Wohlmuth, "Alternative economic strategies," 217–23; Alex de Waal, *Famine crimes: Politics and the disaster relief industry in Africa*, London 1997, 98–105; Prunier, *Darfur*, 71. See also Abdel-Galil Elmekki, "Food crises: their roots in a country's political and developmental crises," in Mohamed Suliman, ed., *Ecology*, 228–56. The chairman's quotation is from African Rights, *Food and power in Sudan: A critique of humanitarianism*, London 1997, 132. See also de Waal, *Famine crimes, passim*.
19. Atta el-Battahani, "Tribal peace conferences in Sudan: The role of the joudiyya institution in Darfur, Western Sudan," in Gunther Baechler, Kurt R. Spillman, and Mohamed Suliman, eds., *Transformation of resource conflicts: Approach and instruments*, Bern 2002, 423–28; Flint and de Waal, *Darfur*, 68–69.
20. Flint and de Waal, *Darfur*, 57–61, 72–73; Prunier, *Darfur*, 74–75.
21. The author is unknown. "Quraysh" is the Meccan tribe of the Prophet Muhammad.
22. Flint and de Waal, *Darfur*, 33–36, 41–49, 55–56.
23. *Ibid.*, 53–54, 61.
24. *Ibid.*, 66–72.
25. *Ibid.*, 67–69, 71–76.

CHAPTER TWELVE. THE DESTRUCTION OF DARFUR

1. *Africa confidential* 40, 24, 3 December 1999; 41, 1, 7 January 2000; 41, 13, 23 June 2000; 41, 20, 13 October 2000; 42, 2, 26 January 2001; 43, 4, 22 February 2002.
2. *Africa confidential* 42, 20, 12 October 2001; 43, 4, 22 February 2002.
3. *Africa confidential* 42, 16, 10 August 2001; 42, 20, 12 October 2001.
4. *Cf.* Prunier, *Darfur*, 93.
5. Flint and de Waal, *Darfur*, 17–20, 63–64; *Africa confidential* 43, 23, 22 November 2002.
6. Flint and de Waal, *Darfur*, 64.
7. *Ibid.*, 88–96.
8. *Ibid.*, 76–77, 81–82; *Africa confidential* 43, 23, 22 November 2002. Sharif Harir was a former lecturer in anthropology in Norway.
9. Flint and de Waal, *Darfur*, 77–80, 97–98; *Africa confidential* 43, 23, 22 November 2002.
10. Flint and de Waal, *Darfur*, 79–80.
11. *Ibid.*, 80–81, 98; Prunier, *Darfur*, 91–92.
12. Flint and de Waal, *Darfur*, 81–83.
13. Prunier, *Darfur*, 94.

14. Usually Toyota Land Cruisers with the roofs removed and with mounted automatic guns. See Prunier, *Darfur*, 178 n. 57.
15. *Al-Khartum*, 4 March 2003, quoted in Prunier, *Darfur*, 93.
16. Flint and de Waal, *Darfur*, 99.
17. Details of the raid are disputed. *Cf.* Prunier, *Darfur*, 99–100, and Flint and de Waal, *Darfur*, 95–96.
18. Prunier, *Darfur*, 95.
19. *Africa confidential* 45, 10, 14 May 2004; Flint and de Waal, *Darfur*, 102–03; Prunier, *Darfur*, 98.
20. Bureau of Democracy, Human Rights, and Labor and Bureau of Intelligence and Research, U.S. Department of State, "Documenting atrocities in Darfur," September 2004; *Africa confidential* 45, 10, 14 May 2004; Prunier, *Darfur*, 100–01; Flint and de Waal, *Darfur*, 104ff.
21. Flint and de Waal, *Darfur*, 108–10, 114–15; Prunier, *Darfur*, 113.
22. "Documenting atrocities in Darfur"; Flint and de Waal, *Darfur*, 112.
23. Prunier, *Darfur*, 114.
24. Flint and de Waal, *Darfur*, 106, 110–11.
25. *Ibid.*, 112–13; Prunier, *Darfur*, 108, 130–34; *Africa confidential* 45, 10, 14 May 2004.
26. "Documenting atrocities in Darfur."
27. *Africa confidential*, 44, 8, 14 April 2003; 44, 13, 27 June 2003; 44, 21, 24 October 2003; 44, 24, 5 December 2003; *Cf.* Prunier, *Darfur*, 115–16, 125.
28. *Africa confidential*, 45, 10, 14 May 2004.
29. Flint and de Waal, *Darfur*, 115–17; Prunier, *Darfur*, 113, 125, 130.
30. Flint and de Waal, *Darfur*, 115–17.
31. Prunier, *Darfur*, 124–27.
32. *Ibid.*, 108–09.
33. *Ibid.*, 112–13.
34. A text is appended in Abdel Ghaffar M. Ahmed and Leif Manger, eds., *Understanding the crisis in Darfur*, Bergen 2006, 87–90.
35. Prunier, *Darfur*, 112, 117; *Africa confidential* 45, 10, 14 May 2004. Estimates of the number of internally displaced at this stage disagreed widely.
36. Prunier, *Darfur*, 134–38.
37. *African confidential* 45, 13, 25 June 2004; Prunier, *Darfur*, 152–57.
38. See Prunier, *Darfur*, 157 (citing Christopher Ayad, "Querelle semantique autour du 'genocide' du Darfour," *Liberation*, 15 September 2004); Flint and de Waal, *Darfur*, 129–32. For likely defendants, see *Africa confidential* 46, 4, 18 February 2005, and 47, 5, 3 March 2006.
39. *Africa confidential* 45, 18, 10 September 2004; Flint and de Waal, *Darfur*, 127–28; Abdel Ghaffar and Manger, eds., *Understanding*, 105–07.
40. Abdel Ghaffar and Manger, eds., *Understanding*, 95–104.
41. See, e.g., *Africa confidential* 46, 3, 4 February 2005.
42. *Africa confidential* 45, 23, 19 November 2004; 46, 4, 18 February 2005; Leif Manger, "A background paper to the meeting...," in Abdel Ghaffar M. Ahmed and Leif Manger, eds., *Understanding*, 81–82.
43. Flint and de Waal, *Darfur*, 122–26; *Africa confidential* 46, 25, 16 December 2005; 47, 7, 31 March 2006.
44. *Africa confidential* 46, 20, 7 October 2005; Prunier, *Darfur*, 121.

45. *Africa confidential* 47, 7, 31 March 2006; 47, 9, 28 April 2006.
46. See *Africa confidential* 47, 9, 28 April 2006.
47. This section, except where otherwise noted, is based on the text of the DPA, public documents of the African Union, news accounts, and private information.
48. See Prunier, *Darfur*, 151.
49. John Hagan and Alberto Palloni, "Death in Darfur," *Science*, 15 September 2006, 1578–79; Prunier, *Darfur*, 148–52, 192 n. 67.

BIBLIOGRAPHY

Archival sources for this book include unpublished government correspondence and reports from provincial and central government files in the National Records Office, Khartoum; the British National Archives (formerly the Public Record Office), mainly in the series FO 78 (Cairo consular records), FO 371 (political correspondence), and FO 633 (Cromer papers); the National Archives, Washington, D.C.; the Sudan Archive of the University of Durham Library; and Rhodes House Library, Oxford. Details and references to documents from other sources are listed in the notes. Official publications and unpublished articles are included with secondary sources that follow.

Abdel-Galil Elmekki, "Food crises: Their roots in a country's political and developmental crises," in Mohamed Suliman, ed., *Ecology, op. cit.*

Abdel Ghaffer M. Ahmed, "Planning and the neglect of pastoral nomads in the Sudan," in Gunnar Haarland, ed., *Problems of savannah development*, Bergen 1982.

_____, and Manger, Leif, eds., *Understanding the crisis in Darfur*, Bergen 2006.

Abdel Rahim Mirghani, *Development planning in the Sudan in the sixties*, Khartoum 1983.

Abdel Rahman Abdel Wahab, "Development planning in the Sudan: Policy and organization," in Ali Mohamed El-Hassan, ed., *An introduction, op. cit.*

Abdel Salam Sidahmed, *Politics and Islam in contemporary Sudan*, Richmond, Surrey 1997.

Abdelwahab El-Affendi, *Turabi's revolution*, London 1991.

Abu Shamma, A. O., "International aspects of public health," in Philosophical Society of the Sudan, *The health, op. cit.*

Adams, William Y., *Nubia, corridor to Africa*, London 1977.

Advisory Council for the Northern Sudan, *Proceedings of the first session (1944)*, Khartoum 1945.

African Rights, *Food and power in Sudan: A critique of humanitarianism*, London 1997.

Ahmed Ali Zaki, "A survey of the future health requirements in maintaining and improving the health of the Sudan," in Philosophical Society of the Sudan, *The health, op. cit.*

347

Ahmed Safi el Din, "A survey of the Sudanese economy," in Mohamed Hashim Awad, ed., *Socio-economic change, op. cit.*

Al-Agab Ahmed al-Teraifi, "Regionalisation in the Sudan: Characteristics, problems and prospects," in Peter Woodward, ed., *Sudan after Nimeiri*, London 1991.

Al-Fatih Abdullahi Abdel Salam, "Intra-party conflicts: The case of the Umma party," in Mahasin Abdel Gadir Hag Al-Safi, ed., *The nationalist movement, op. cit.*

Ali Ahmed Suliman, *Issues in the economic development of Sudan*, Khartoum 1975.

Ali Mohamed El-Hassan, ed., *An introduction to the Sudan economy*, Khartoum 1976.

———, "Structure of the Sudan economy," in *idem*, ed., *An introduction, op. cit.*

Allen, Bernard M., *Gordon and the Sudan*, London 1931.

Anonymous, *al-kitab al-aswad*, np nd.

Arkell, A. J., "Darfur antiquities II, Tora palaces in Turra at the north end of Jebel Marra," *SNR* XX 1937.

———, *A history of the Sudan to 1821*, London 2nd ed., 1961.

Atiya, Samuel Bey, "Senin and Ali Dinar," *SNR* VII, 2, 1924.

Atta el-Battahani, "Tribal peace conferences in Sudan: The role of the joudiyya institution in Darfur, Western Sudan," in Gunther Baechler, Kurt R. Spillman, and Mohamed Suliman, eds., *Transformation of resource conflicts: Approach and instruments*, Bern 2002.

Awad Abdalla El-Awad Radaf, *Sudan gum*, Bergen thesis 1983.

Awad al-Sid al-Karsani, "Muhammad al-Hafiz al-Tigani and the Sudan," in Mahasin Abd al-Gadir Hag Al-Safi, ed., *The nationalist movement, op. cit.*

Baasher, M. M., "Livestock development in the central rainland of the Sudan – potential and problems," in Shaw, ed., *op. cit.*

Bacon, G. H., "Education," in Tothill, *Agriculture, op. cit.*

Balamoan, G. Ayoub, *Peoples and economics in the Sudan 1884–1956*, Cambridge, Mass., 2nd ed., 1981.

Balfour-Paul, H. G., *History and antiquities of Darfur*, Khartoum 1955.

Barbour, K. M., *The republic of the Sudan*, London 1961.

Bayoumi, Ahmed, *The history of the Sudan health services*, Nairobi 1979.

Beasley, Ina, *Before the wind changed*, Oxford 1992.

Bechtold, Peter, *Politics in the Sudan*, New York 1976.

Beers, Mark H., and Berkow, Robert, *The Merck manual*, 17th ed., Whitehouse Station, N.J., 1999.

Bell, Gawain, *Shadows on the sand*, London 1983.

Bennett, S. J. C, John, E. R., and Hewison, J. W., "Animal husbandry," in Tothill, *op. cit.*

Bjorkelo, Anders, *Prelude to the Mahdiyya*, Cambridge 1989.

Bodour Osman Abu Affan, *Industrial policies and industrialization in the Sudan*, Khartoum 1985.

Boustead, Hugh, *The wind of morning*, London 1974.

Browne, W. G., *Travels in Africa, Egypt, and Syria, from the year 1792 to 1798*, London 1799.

Burckhardt, John Lewis, *Travels in Nubia*, repr. London 1987.

Burr, J. Millard, and Collins, Robert O., *Africa's thirty years' war*, Boulder, Colo. 1999.

Cordell, Dennis D., *Dar al-Kuti and the last years of the trans-Saharan slave trade*, Madison 1985.

Crabites, Pierre, *Americans in the Egyptian Army*, London 1938.

Craig, G. M., *The agriculture of the Sudan*, Oxford 1991.

Dafalla, E. N., "The veterinary officer," in Philosophical Society of the Sudan, *The health, op. cit.*

Daly, M. W., *Empire on the Nile: The Anglo-Egyptian Sudan, 1898–1934*, Cambridge 1986.

———, *Imperial Sudan: The Anglo-Egyptian Condominium, 1934–56*, Cambridge 1991.

———, ed., *Modernization in the Sudan*, New York 1985.

———, ed., *The road to Shaykan*, Durham 1983.

———, *The Sirdar*, Philadelphia 1997.

———, and Forbes, L. E., *The Sudan*, Reading 1994.

———, and Hogan, Jane R., *Images of empire*, Leiden 2005.

Davis, Reginald, *The camel's back*, London 1957.

Doornbos, Paul, "On becoming Sudanese: Aspects of ideological transformation in rural Sudan," paper presented to a conference on state, capital and transformation in Sudan, University of East Anglia, July 1984.

Douin, G., *Histoire de regne du Khedive Ismail, III, L 'empire africain*, Cairo 1936.

Egyptian Army, *Intelligence Reports, Egypt*.

El-Erian, A. A., *Condominium and related situations in international law*, Cairo 1952.

English, George Bethune, *A narrative of the expedition to Dongola and Sennaar*, London 1822, Boston 1823.

Evans-Pritchard, E. E., *The Sanusi of Cyrenaica*, Oxford 1949.

Flint, Julie, and de Waal, Alex, *Darfur: A short history of a long war*, London 2005. (2nd ed. as *Darfur: A new history of a long war*, London and New York 2008).

Gaafar Mohamed Ali Bakheit, "British administration and Sudanese nationalism, 1919–1939," Cambridge Ph.D. 1965.

———, "The politics of Native Administration, 1964–69," in Howell, ed., *op. cit.*

Giegler, C. C., *The Sudan memoirs of Carl Christian Giegler Pasha*, ed. Richard Hill, London 1984.

Gleichen, Captain Count, *Handbook of the Sudan*, London 1898.

Haaland, Gunnar, "Economic determinants in ethnic processes," in F. Barth, ed., *Ethnic groups and boundaries*, 1969.

Hagan, John, and Palloni, Alberto, "Death in Darfur," *Science*, 15 September 2006, 1578–79.

Hartwig, Gerald W., and Patterson, K. David, *Schistosomiasis in twentieth century Africa: Historical studies on West Africa and Sudan*, Los Angeles 1984.

Henderson, K. D. D., The making of the modern Sudan. *The life and letters of Sir Douglas Newbold...*, London 1953.

———, *Set under authority*, Somerset 1987.

Hill, George Birkbeck, ed., *Colonel Gordon in central Africa...from original letters and documents*, London 1881.

Hill, Richard, *A biographical dictionary of the Sudan*, London 2nd ed., 1967.

———, *Egypt in the Sudan 1820–1881*, London 1959.

Hillelson, S., *Sudan Arabic texts*, Cambridge 1935.

Holt, P. M., "Holy families and Islam in the Sudan," *idem, Studies in the history of the Near East*, London 1973.

———, *The Mahdist state in the Sudan*, Oxford 2nd ed., 1970.

———, and Daly, M. W., *A history of the Sudan*, London 5th ed., 2001.

Howell, John, ed., *Local government and politics in the Sudan*, Khartoum 1974.

———, "The reform of local government, 1971," in *idem*, ed., *Local government, op. cit.*

Jackson, H. C., *Black ivory, or the story of El Zubeir Pasha, slaver and sultan, as told by himself*, Khartoum 1913, repr. New York 1970.

Johnson, Douglas H., *The root causes of Sudan's civil wars*, Oxford 2nd ed., 2004.

Jureidini, L. B., "The miracles of Ali Dinar," *The Muslim world*, I, 1917.

Kapteijns, Lidwien, *Mahdist faith and Sudanic tradition: The history of the Masalit sultanate, 1870–1930*, London 1985.

———, and Spaulding, Jay, *After the millennium: Diplomatic correspondence from Wadai and Dar Fur on the eve of colonial conquest, 1885–1916*, East Lansing 1988.

Khalafalla Babiker El Bedri, "Health education of the public," in Philosophical Society of the Sudan, *The health, op. cit.*

Lampen, G. D., "History of Darfur," *SNR* XXXI, 2, 1950.

Lavin, Deborah, ed., *The Condominium remembered: Proceedings of the Durham Sudan historical records conference 1982*, Durham 2 vols., 1993 [*sic*].

Lesch, Ann Mosley, *The Sudan – contested national identities*, Oxford and Bloomington 1998.

MacMichael, H. A., *A history of the Arabs in the Sudan and some account of the people who preceded them and of the tribes inhabiting Darfur*, 1922 ed., repr. London 1967.

Mamdani, Mahmood, *Saviors and survivors: Darfur, politics, and the War on Terror*, New York 2009.

Mansour Khalid, *Nimeiri and the revolution of dis-May*, London 1985.

March, G. F., "Transport in the Sudan," in Tothill, *Agriculture, op. cit.*

Marlowe, John, *Anglo-Egyptian relations 1800–1953*, London 1954.

Maxwell-Darling, R. C., "Locusts in the Sudan," in Tothill, *Agriculture, op. cit.*

McLoughlin, Peter F. M., "A note on the reliability of the earliest Sudan Republic population estimates," *Population Review* 7, 3, 1963.

———, *Language-switching as an index of socialization in the Republic of the Sudan*, Berkeley, Calif. 1964.

Mohamed Abdel Rahman Ali, "Public finance in the Sudan," in Ali Mohamed El-Hassan, ed., *An introduction, op. cit.*

Mohamed El Awad Galal-el-Din, "Population and labour force in the Sudan," in Ali Mohamed El-Hassan, ed., *An introduction, op. cit.*

Mohamed Mirghani Abdel Salam, "Agriculture in the Sudan," in Ali Mohamed El Hassan, *An introduction, op. cit.*

Mohamed Omer Beshir, *Educational development in the Sudan 1898–1956*, Oxford 1969.

———, ed., *Sudan: Aid and external relations*, Khartoum 1984.

Mohamed Salih, M. A., "Ecological stress, political coercion and the limits of government intervention," in Anders Hjort af Ornas and *idem*, eds., *Ecology and politics*, Uppsala 1989.

Mohamed Suliman, ed., *Ecology, politics & violent conflict*, London 1999.

———, "The rationality and irrationality of violence in sub-Saharan Africa," in *idem*, ed., *Ecology, op. cit.*

Muhammad Hashim 'Awad, *Al-istiqlal wa fasad al-hukm fil-Sudan*, np nd.

———, ed., *Socio-economic change in the Sudan*, Khartoum 1983.

Muhammad Umar Sulayman al-Tunisi, *Tashhidh al-adhan bi-sirat al-Arab wa'l-Sudan*, ed. Khalil Mahmud Asakir and Mustafa Muhammad Musad, Cairo 1965.

Musa Mubarak al-Hasan, *Ta'rikh Dar Fur al-siyasi, 1882–1895*, Khartoum 1970.

Mutasim el-Beshir, "The political role of the local government officer," in Howell, ed., *op. cit.*

Mutawakil A. Amin, "Ancient trade and trade routes between Egypt and the Sudan, 4000 to 700 B.C.," *SNR* LII, 1970.

Nachtigal, Gustav, *Sahara and Sudan, IV, Wadai and Darfur*, trans. Allan G. B. Fisher and Humphrey J. Fisher, Berkeley and Los Angeles 1971.

National Socialist Union, *Document of the national founding congress, draft of basic rules*, np 1972.

———, *Draft of the charter for national action*, np 1972.

Na'um Shuqayr, *Ta'rikh al-Sudan al-qadim wa'l-hadith wa jughrafiyatuhu*, Cairo 1903.

Niblock, Tim, *Class and power in Sudan*, London 1987.

Nicolson, I. F., *The administration of Nigeria 1900 to 1960*, Oxford 1969.

O'Fahey, R. S., "The affair of Ahmad Agha," *SNR* LIII, 1972.

———, comp., *Arabic literature of Africa, volume 1. The writings of eastern Sudanic Africa to c. 1900*, Leiden 1994.

———, "The office of *qadi* in Dar Fur: A preliminary enquiry," *BSOAS* XL, 1, 1977.

———, *State and society in Dar Fur*, New York 1980.

———, and Abu Salim, M. I., *Land in Dar Fur. Charters and related documents from the Dar Fur sultanate*, Cambridge 1983.

O'Fahey, R. S., and Spaulding, J. L., *Kingdoms of the Sudan*, London 1974.

Paterson, R. T., "Darfur Province," in Tothill, *Agriculture, op. cit.*

Perron, A., trans., *Voyage au Darfur*, Paris 1845.

———, trans., *Voyage au Ouaday*, Paris 1951.

Philosophical Society of the Sudan, *The health of the Sudan*, Khartoum 1963.

Prunier, Gerard, *Darfur: The ambiguous genocide*, London 2005.

Rath, U. C. W., "The climate of the Sudan," *1953 Conference on food and society in the Sudan*, Khartoum 1954.

Republic of the Sudan, *Sudan Almanac 1961*, Khartoum 1961.

———, *Sudan Almanac 1963*, Khartoum 1963.

———, Ministry of Social Affairs, *First population census of Sudan 1955/56*, Khartoum 1958.

————, *Ten-Year Plan of economic and social development 1961/62–1970/71*, Khartoum 1965.

Robertson, James, *Transition in Africa: From direct rule to independence*, London 1974.

Rosen, G., trans., *Das Buch des Sudan*, Leipzig 1847.

Roy, H., *La vie heroique et romantique du Docteur Charles Cuny*, Paris 1930.

St. John, Bayle, *Travels of an Arab merchant in Soudan*, London 1845.

Sanderson, G. N., "The ghost of Adam Smith: Ideology, bureaucracy, and the frustration of economic development in the Sudan, 1934–1940," in M. W. Daly, *Modernization, op. cit.*

————, Introduction, *The memoirs of Babikr Bedri*, v. 2, London 1980.

————, "Sudanese nationalism and the independence of the Sudan," in Michael Brett, ed., *Northern Africa: Islam and modernization*, London 1973.

Santandrea, Stefano, *A tribal history of the western Bahr El Ghazal*, Bologna 1964.

Santi, Paul, and Hill, Richard, *The Europeans in the Sudan*, Oxford 1980.

Sharif Harir, "'Arab Belt' versus 'African Belt': Ethno-political conflict in Dar Fur and the regional cultural factors," in *idem* and Tvedt, *op. cit.*

Shaw, D. J., ed., *Agricultural development in the Sudan*, Khartoum 1966.

Shepherd, Andrew, Malcolm Norris, and John Watson, *Water planning in arid Sudan*, London 1987.

Slatin, Rudolf C., *Fire and sword in the Sudan*, London 1896.

Spaulding, Jay, *The heroic age in Sinnar*, East Lansing 1985.

————, "Pastoralism, slavery, commerce, culture and the fate of the Nubians of northern and central Kordofan under Dar Fur rule, C.1750–C.1850," in *International Journal of African Historical Studies* 39, 2.

————, and Kapteijns, Lidwien, *An Islamic alliance: Ali Dinar and the Sanusiyya, 1906–1916*, Evanston 1994.

Stone, John, *The Sudan economy. Introductory notes*, Khartoum 1953.

Sudan, Republic of, *Government List*, 1959.

————, *Staff List*, 1963.

Sudan Government, *Annual report of the department of economics and trade, 1934*, Khartoum 1935; *1935*, Khartoum 1936; *1936*, Khartoum 1937; *1945*, Khartoum 1945 [*sic*].

————, *Annual report of the Ministry of Agriculture 1953–1954*, Khartoum 1955.

————, *Memorandum on the budget estimates...*, np May 1958.

————, *Report of Lord De La Warr's Educational Commission*, 1937.

————, *Report on medical and health work in the Sudan for the year 1934*, Khartoum nd.

————, *Report of the Medical Services, 1949*, Khartoum nd.

————, *Report of the Medical Services... 1956/57*, np nd.

————, *Report of the Soil Conservation Committee*, Khartoum 1944.

————, *Report of the Sudan Medical Service for the year 1940*, Khartoum, nd.

Sudan Government list, np March 1956.

Sudanow, Khartoum.

Syed M. Nimieri, "Industry in the Sudan," in Ali Mohamed El Hassan, *An introduction, op. cit.*

Thelwell, R. E. W., "A linguistic survey in El Fasher secondary school," *SNR* LII, 1971.

Theobald, A. B., *Ali Dinar, last sultan of Darfur 1898–1916*, London 1965.

———, *The Mahdiya*, London 1951.

Tothill, J. D., ed., *Agriculture in the Sudan*, London 1948.

Tubiana, Marie-Jose, and Tubiana, Joseph, *The Zaghawa from an ecological perspective*, Rotterdam 1977.

Tvedt, Terje, and Sharif Harir, eds., *Short-cut to decay*, Uppsala 1994.

Umar al-Naqar, *The pilgrimage tradition in West Africa*, Khartoum 1972.

United States of America, Department of State, Bureau of Democracy, Human Rights, and Labor and Bureau of Intelligence and Research, *Documenting the atrocities in Darfur*, September 2004.

Ushari Mahmud, and Sulayman Baldo, *El Diein massacre and slavery in the Sudan*, Khartoum 1987.

de Waal, Alexander, *Famine that kills*, Oxford 1989.

———, *Famine crimes: Politics and the disaster relief industry in Africa*, London 1997.

Walz, Terrence, *Trade between Egypt and bilad al-Sudan 1700–1820*, Cairo 1978.

Warburg, Gabriel, *Islam, sectarianism and politics in Sudan since the Mahdiyya*, London 2003.

Whiteman, A. J., *The geology of the Sudan republic*, Oxford 1971.

Wickens, G. E., "A brief note on the early history of Jebel Marra and the recently discovered Tora city of Kebeleh," *SNR* LI, 1970.

———, "Natural vegetation," in G. M. Craig, ed., *The agriculture, op. cit.*

Wilkens, C., "Transport in the Sudan," in Ali Mohamed El-Hassan, ed., *An introduction to the Sudan economy*, Khartoum 1976.

Wingate, F. R., *Mahdiism and the Egyptian Sudan*, London 1891.

Wohlmuth, Karl, "Alternative economic strategies," in Harir and Tvedt, eds., *Short-cut, op. cit.*

Woodward, P. R., "Government and infrastructure," in G. M. Craig, ed., *The agriculture, op. cit.*

Yongo-Bure, B., and Arou, Mom K. N., eds., *North-South relations in the Sudan since the Addis Ababa Agreement*, Khartoum 1988.

Yusuf Fadl Hasan, *The Arabs and the Sudan*, Edinburgh 1967.

———, "The Fur sultanate and the long-distance caravan trade 1650–1850," in *idem* and Paul Doornbos, *The central bilad al-Sudan, op. cit.*

———, ed., *Kitab al-tabaqat*, Khartoum 1971.

———, and Doornbos, Paul, eds., *The central bilad al-Sudan: Tradition and adaptation*, Khartoum nd.

Zahlan, A. B., ed., *The agricultural sector of Sudan*, London 1986.

INDEX